ENTERPRISE DEVELOPMENT WITH VISUALAGE® FOR JAVA™, VERSION 3

ENTERPRISE DEVELOPMENT WITH VISUALAGE® FOR JAVA™, VERSION 3

DALE R. NILSSON
PETER M. JAKAB
BILL SARANTAKOS
RUSSELL A. STINEHOUR

WILEY COMPUTER PUBLISHING

John Wiley & Sons, Inc.
New York • Chichester • Weinheim • Brisbane • Singapore • Toronto

Publisher: Robert Ipsen
Editor: Theresa Hudson
Assistant Editor: Kathryn A. Malm
Managing Editor: Angela Murphy
Electronic Products, Associate Editor: Brian Snapp
Text Design & Composition: Benchmark Productions, Inc.

Designations used by companies to distinguish their products are often claimed as trade-marks. In all instances where John Wiley & Sons, Inc., is aware of a claim, the product names appear in initial capital or ALL CAPITAL LETTERS. Readers, however, should contact the appropriate companies for more complete information regarding trademarks and registration.

This book is printed on acid-free paper. ∞

Published by John Wiley & Sons, Inc.
Published simultaneously in Canada.

This publication is designed to provide accurate and authoritative information in regard to the subject matter covered. It is sold with the understanding that the publisher is not engaged in professional services. If professional advice or other expert assistance is required, the services of a competent professional person should be sought.

Library of Congress Cataloging-in-Publication Data:
Enterprise development with VisualAge for Java : version 3 / Dale R. Nilsson
   p.cm
  ISBN 0-471-38949-8 (pbk./CD-ROM : alk. paper)
   1. Java (Computer program language) 2. VisualAge. 3. Application
software--Development. I. Nilsson, Dale R.
  QA76.73.J38 E547 2000
  005.13'3--dc21
                                          00-036818

Printed in the United States of America.
10   9 8 7 6 5 4 3 2 1

CONTENTS

ACKNOWLEDGMENTS

A number of dedicated professionals helped us with this book. Our managers, Clyde Saletta, Oma Sewhdat, and Tom Kristek, provided their support, and most importantly the permission to write this book. To IBM who gave us permission to use the VisualAge logo and include the CD with the book. Our legal eagle, Terry McElroy, for his wisdom and contract approval. Thanks to Sheila Richardson who helped with the book agreement and the Write Now program.

We were very happy to add contributions from Greg Hester of CrossLogic Corporation. The in-depth technical review from Bryon Kataoka of Commercial Solutions helped improve the quality and accuracy of the book. It was great to have some "fresh eyes" to look over the book and ensure the instructions are complete.

Thanks to Kathryn Malm and Terri Hudson of John Wiley & Sons, who were great getting this book through the rigors of publishing, and Gerrie Cho for her help with the book production. Jim Ramaker was able to moonlight as our copy editor, and he was able to fix the typos that happen from writing in planes and hotels. Also thanks to the many people in the VisualAge for Java team who assisted us with information and support.

INTRODUCTION

The use of Java has exploded since the introduction of VisualAge for Java in July 1997 and the follow-on releases of VisualAge for Java have helped many developers create state-of-the-art Java applications. Java and VisualAge for Java have been accepted by many developers throughout the world to help them be productive. This book helps you learn how to use VisualAge for Java with step-by-step instructions, building a variety of sample Java applications. This book also has numerous screen captures of the actual VisualAge for Java product that give you visual feedback on the progress of your Java applications.

When this book was written, there were hundreds of Java books in publication, many of which are merely introductory books that include the JDK with some sample exercises with spinning gifs. Another fault of many Java programming books is the pages and pages of overly complicated code that also adds to the page count. This book avoids these shortfalls and provides the unique feature of stepping the developer through design decisions while building Java applications.

This edition of the book is totally updated and re-written including new sections that cover JFC Swing components, Servlets, Enterprise JavaBeans (EJBs), Java Server Pages (JSPs), data access beans with JDBC, Team Programming, and Tool API.

Overview of This Book

This book is adapted from a workshop to help introduce VisualAge for Java into the marketplace. The authors taught this course to customers and IBM developers to jump-start the introduction of VisualAge for Java. The attendees provided feedback each time the course was conducted, and this feedback was used to improve the course content. The course was taught to developers from all over the world, including the United States, Canada, Germany, England, Spain, China, Australia, Peru, Mexico, Argentina, India, and Japan.

We had many requests for the course materials from people who had heard about the workshop and wanted to learn VisualAge for Java. We decided to convert the workshop into a book that could be used in the course and by individuals for self-study. To make the book, we combined the course presentation materials, the lab scripts, lecture content, and experiences with customers. While writing the book, we improved the sample applications from the workshop. We improved their design, used better controls or widgets, and tried different variations in design.

With the rapidly evolving status of Java and supporting tools, there is always some late-breaking news. With this in mind, we try to describe and use the "stable" parts of Java. This book covers JavaBeans which are essential for visual development and very well-supported in VisualAge for Java. We also focus on enterprise development using server-side Java programming with the JSWDK and the WebSphere Test Environment.

This book is the result of a truly collaborative effort between the authors. The chapters show the collective knowledge and experience of all the authors and provide the reader with a comprehensive view of Enterprise Development using VisualAge for Java. The authors drew on their experience using VisualAge for Java with customers for the material in this book. The team working on this book was separated by many miles, but they were connected by email and a common language, Java. The result of this effort is an easy-to-follow comprehensive handbook for learning how to use VisualAge for Java in real world programming.

Certification

This book helps prepare you for IBM VisualAge for Java certification, which is part of the IBM Object Technology certification. You can get more information at www.ibm.com/software/ad/certify. Following is a short description of what each level entails. For full information please consult the certification Web site.

IBM Certified Specialist VisualAge for Java. The Specialist works with others to give technical sales support regarding application development services related to design, implementation, and deployment of Java-based solutions. These Java-based solutions include applications, applets, and servlets and typically make use of the JavaBeans component model and Java Database Connectivity (JDBC) technology. The Specialist is expected to possess high level knowledge of object-oriented design methodologies, VisualAge for Java, and the use of the Java language.

IBM Certified Solution Developer VisualAge for Java. The Solution Developer provides application development services related to design, implementation, and deployment of Java-based solutions. These Java-based solutions include applications, applets, and servlets and typically make use of the JavaBeans component model and Java Database Connectivity (JDBC) technology. The Solution Developer is expected to apply object-oriented design methodologies, make proper use of VisualAge for Java, and exhibit proficiency in the use of the Java language itself.

IBM Certified Solutions Expert. IBM WebSphere Studio, V3 designs and creates the front-end portion of the Internet/Intranet application. This individual creates Web elements, assembles the elements, and tests, publishes, and maintains the application.

IBM Certified Specialist. IBM WebSphere Application Server, Standard Edition, V3 works with site designers and Webmasters giving technical sales support on building a Web site using the IBM WebSphere Application Server, Standard Edition, V3. This includes knowledge of: Application Server concepts and programming model, implementation of distinct layers for Presentation, Controller and Model, thread safe server-side programming, development, testing, debugging and deployment of:

- Java Servlets and JavaBeans
- Java Server Pages (version 1.0)

Installation and configuration of the WebSphere Application Server. Utilization of WebSphere facilities and APIs.

IBM Certified Solution Developer. IBM WebSphere Application Server, Standard Edition, V3 works with the Web site designer and Webmaster to provide and build the components needed for an Internet/Intranet site. This Certified Solution Developer creates and maintains Web applications from a set of defined specifications, and provides technical assistance for IBM WebSphere Application Server components.

The IBM Certified Enterprise Developer. IBM WebSphere Application Server, Advanced Edition, V3 works with business analysts, application architects, and application assemblers to create enterprise software components (Enterprise JavaBeans, EJBs) which model an organization's practices, processes, and concepts. This developer mentors application assemblers on the usage of EJBs as well as specific enterprise software components within the business domain. This developer also works with system administrators and deployers to configure and deploy components and applications.

How This Book Is Organized

Each chapter in this book starts with a brief description of what is covered and ends with a summary. The book has a number of small applications to illustrate a broad range of application development topics. This book starts out slowly with quite a bit of detail. As you progress in the book, the instructions become briefer and the amount of function in the applications increases.

Chapter 1: Breaking Open the Box

Chapter 1 gets you started on the right foot. It covers installation considerations, the help system, and starting VisualAge for Java. This chapter introduces you to the integrated development environment (IDE) and the various views, and you can try some IDE customization. This chapter describes the repository and the workspace and shows you how to make bookmarks in the IDE. Finally, you learn how to import Java classes into the IDE and how to run an applet.

Chapter 2: Building the Hello World Applet

Chapter 2 shows you how to build the Java Hello World applet. To do this, you create a project and a package; then you use the Applet SmartGuide and generate a simple Applet. You learn visual builder basics, including using categories, using a label, setting properties, and testing an applet. You improve the applet by using invisible beans and visual connections. You then run the completed applet.

Chapter 3: Making an Adding Machine

Chapter 3 covers JavaBeans basics including GUI beans, invisible, and composite beans. You learn about Layout Managers and develop an applet using a GridBagLayout with TextFields, Labels, and a Button.

Chapter 4: Making Logic Beans

Chapter 4 has more information on JavaBeans, covering properties, events, and methods. This chapter shows you how to create your own invisible JavaBeans using the SmartGuide in VisualAge for Java. You learn how to edit the generated methods and how to use invisible beans in the Visual Composition Editor.

Chapter 5: Debugging Beans

Chapter 5 covers debugging Java programs using the VisualAge for Java integrated Debugger. You learn how to debug a Java program by stepping through the code, inspecting objects, and changing code. You also learn how to use the Scrapbook and the Console windows in VisualAge for Java. You learn how to set breakpoints and conditional breakpoints in your Java code.

Chapter 6: Building the Advanced Calculator GUI

Chapter 6 has information on more advanced user interface beans in AWT, including a good overview of the different types of JavaBeans. You learn how to use the ominous GridBagLayout Manager and GridBag Constraints. You also learn additional functions in the IDE, such as copying beans, setting tabs stops, editing bean properties, and morphing beans.

Chapter 7: Building the Advanced Calculator Logic

Chapter 7 shows you how to extend invisible beans with additional behavior, how to incorporate exception handling for error detection and correction into your Java programs. You learn how to import classes and Java files into the IDE. As you finish the Advanced Calculator applet, you use a message box and add numeric-only TextFields to the applet. You also learn how to modify the beans palette in the Visual Composition Editor.

Chapter 8: Deploying Java

Chapter 8 covers the important task of creating the runtime files. You learn how to export and package Java files, class files, and Jar files. You learn the basic HTML tags needed to test a simple applet. Finally, you test Java applets and applications outside the VisualAge for Java IDE.

Chapter 9: Building the Internet Address Applet

Chapter 9 has a comprehensive sample Java program that uses a CardLayout manager. You also learn how to define constructors in VisualAge for Java and how to use them in the Visual Composition Editor. You master layering in Java and how to use Variables and Factory Objects in the Visual Composition Editor.

Chapter 10: Working with JFC

Chapter 10 introduces you to the Java Swing classes. You learn how to create user-generated Events and add them to your Java programs. This chapter includes a very good lab that has a Swing graphical interface and utilizes user-defined Java events. It includes JButtons, JLabels, and JPanels.

Chapter 11: The Reminder Application

Chapter 11 shows you how to use a number of more complex user interface beans using Swing components. You develop a Reminder List program and use Menus and Submenus. You create Checkbox Groups with Radio buttons. You also use Event-to-Code connections and add a File dialog to your Java program. Finally, this chapter covers a very important aspect of programming overlooked by many developers: It shows you how to develop user Help for a Java program and use a Web Browser to display HTML Help.

Chapter 12: The Database Editor Application

Chapter 12 covers JDBC and the data access beans in VisualAge for Java. You learn how to connect to a relational database and construct an SQL query for the database. You build a Java Swing program to display the query using the JTable bean in a notebook using a JTabbedPane.

Chapter 13: Team Development

Chapter 13 shows you how to use the Team Development features in VisualAge for Java. You learn about the different kinds of Editions and Users. You see how to employ best practices for your development process and you learn about the SCM interface to external flat file versioning systems.

Chapter 14: Servlets

Chapter 14 covers server-side Java development with Servlets using the JavaServer Web Development Kit (JSWDK) and Http Servlets. It also includes labs detailing how HTML and Servlets can interact using the WebSphere Test Environment. This chapter introduces Java Server Pages and the JSP Monitor in VisualAge for Java.

Chapter 15: Using Enterprise JavaBeans

Chapter 15 builds on what you learned in chapter 14 with more advance server-side Java development. You learn about the EJB architecture including entity beans and session beans. You learn how to create EJB groups and EJBs in VisualAge for Java. You use the Persistence Builder to map an EJB to an existing database and learn how to configure and run the EJB servers in VisualAge for Java. You develop a complex EJB application that uses EJBs controlled by a servlet to access a database that sends a response as a JSP.

Chapter 16: Integrating External Tools

Chapter covers the tools API that lets you add your own functions and features to VisualAge for Java. This chapter shows you the different places and context that you can add your tool and provides an exercise with a sample tool as an example.

Chapter 17: Advanced Enterprise Development Topics

Chapter 17 has information on many of the other Enterprise tools in VisualAge for Java. Finally, this chapter has a section that covers Visual Design Patterns for help on using the Visual Composition Editor

Conventions in This Book

This book contains many instructions for completing the sample Java applications. These instructions are lists and use a number of conventions to make instructions, tool text, and Java programming information as clear as possible.

The screen captures displayed in the pages of this book are from the Windows version of the VisualAge for Java product. The OS/2 and AIX screens are virtually identical with only minor system specific exceptions like the file dialog and the frame window icons.

The field names in the VisualAge for Java user interface and the information to be entered in those fields are in bold to differentiate them from instructions. For example, an instruction in the book may read: Enter **John Smith** in the **Name** text field.

The book also uses bolding to improve readability of VisualAge for Java terms and Java language terms. For example, you will use the **GridBagLayout** that is part of Java AWT.

The instructions to build the samples frequently tell you to press a button on a VisualAge for Java tool. We refer to these buttons by their names, but most of the buttons appear with only a graphic image. To make it clearer, there will frequently be a graphic in the margin that gives you a visual cue to the referenced button. For example, you will see the instruction: press the **Run** button.....

When instructions are given in the book for entering information into VisualAge for Java, the words *enter* and *type* are used interchangeably.

A monospaced font is used to show code segments. Anything typed in this font should be taken literally and entered exactly as shown. This font is also used for code listings, because it preserves spacing in the code. When entering code or code segments, be aware that many of the lines of code in the book had to be split into two or more lines. This is because of the line width available on the page. Every effort has been made to split the lines in a way that will cause no problems, even if you enter them as shown, in multiple lines. However in some case, for example when we had to split a literal string, you should join the lines in the page into a single line of code.

Terms Used in This Book

A number of terms in this book use Java language statements and AWT terms, and these are not necessarily Standard English words. For example, the JDK library provides the classes **JFrame** and **FlowLayout**. The first time this class name is used in the book, it is mentioned by its formal name. In later sections of the book, an informal term is used and is not bolded (for example, frame or flow layout).

In the VisualAge for Java product documentation, there are some terms that are not commonly used between developers. For example, some on-line books use the term *Visual Composition Browser*, and in other places *Visual Composition View*. The instructions in this book try to use the new VisualAge term *Visual Composition Editor*.

The Java language gives you the ability to create applets, applications, and servlets. Applets are usually integrated in a Web page, run in a browser like Netscape Navigator, and are subject to the Java security model. Applications run separately in a frame are not subject to the Java security model, so they can write to your disk drive. Servlets run on a Server and provide a response as HTML or JSP to the client Web browser. Because it is very awkward to constantly refer to *writing Java applets, applications,* and *servlets* this book frequently uses the phrase *writing Java programs* when referring to Java programming. Whenever we specifically mean applets, applications, or servlets we say so in the text.

Throughout this book, we refer to Java classes and JavaBeans interchangeably. The user interface of VisualAge for Java refers to both classes and beans, so the appropriate term is used when referring to the user interface.

Disclaimer

The authors wrote this book under an agreement with IBM. The agreement between the authors and IBM requires the following disclaimer:

> The opinions expressed herein are those of the authors and do not represent those of their employer.

Who Should Read This Book?

This book is targeted at the reader who is familiar with object-oriented programming and the Java programming language. A general understanding of graphical user interfaces and a familiarity with the Java AWT classes and their functions is very helpful. There are many sources for learning Java and the JDK classes, which include self-study books, interactive CD-ROMs, and formal education. Other books that can help you with these areas are listed in the Related Publications section.

This book will be a great help for anyone new to VisualAge for Java. You will learn how to use the development environment, starting from the very basics to building complete Java applets and applications, including their deployment. This book has many examples on proper object-oriented implementations using VisualAge-unique visual construction tools. Even people who are familiar with the other VisualAge products will get a lot of valuable information from this book's extensive coverage of the Java JDK classes, the JavaBeans event model, and server-side Java programming.

What's on the CD-ROM?

The CD-ROM contains the Professional edition of VisualAge for Java 3.0. With this version, you can complete all of the sample applications and applets in this book. Follow the instructions in Chapter 1 to install VisualAge for Java from the CD-ROM. For more up-to-date information on the installation of the components on the CD-ROM and other late-breaking news, please read the READ.ME file on the root directory of the CD-ROM.

In the CD-ROM you find the following:

- VisualAge for Java Version 3 Professional Edition
- DB2 UDB Personal Edition Version 5.2 60day trial
- Samples needed for the exercises
- All the completed projects in the book

If you already have VisualAge for Java installed, you need to install the samples on the CD-ROM for many of the excercises in the book.

Getting Support

Support for VisualAge for Java is provided through the Web site for the product at www.software.ibm.com/ad/vajava. This includes a section for frequently asked questions (FAQs), forums for posting questions, and samples. There are also a number of service and support, fee-based offerings from IBM. One way to get help on a project is by sending an e-mail note to tecteam@ca.ibm.com with your request.

Summary

VisualAge for Java is a very powerful high-end tool set that contains a very tightly integrated development environment (IDE) with lots of features and functions. Many enterprises have adopted VisualAge for Java for mission-critical Java development. Its feature-rich IDE can be a little intimidating if you are accustomed to editors, compilers, and debuggers that work on files as in the Java Development Toolkit (JDK). This book will help you master the VisualAge for Java IDE and be confident that you can use VisualAge for Java to write your own Java solutions. We hope you enjoy the book.

ABOUT THE AUTHORS

Dale Nilsson received a B.S. in Computer Science from California State University Long Beach. He has been programming since 1976 and has worked for the State of California, McDonnell Douglas Corporation, IBM, and as an independent consultant. Dale Nilsson has held various development, management, and planning positions in IBM and has worked with customers and vendors throughout the United States, Europe, Asia, and South America. Dale is currently on the VisualAge Services team consulting and mentoring customers developing VisualAge for Java and WebSphere projects worldwide. He is a Sun Certified Java Programmer, an IBM certified VisualAge for Java, VisualAge for C++, and WebSphere Instructor. Dale Nilsson has authored 4 books and many articles on Java, C++, and object-oriented development in various industry publications, and he works with the VisualAge for Java certification team as an assessor. Contact Dale at xnilsson@hotmail.com.

Peter M. Jakab is a Senior Software Consultant for IBM's Software Solutions Lab, where he provides consulting and education to customers that develop real-world Java applications. Peter has been with IBM Canada for 30 years, the last 10 in the IBM Toronto Lab. He has held a variety of leadership positions as a Manager and Development Project Leader. In his current position he is responsible for the technical aspects of the IBM Professional Certification Program for Object Oriented technology products and the WebSphere family of products. He is a Sun Certified Java Programmer, IBM WebSphere Developer, IBM Certified VisualAge for Java Developer, and IBM Certified VisualAge for C++ Developer. He is also one of the lead assessors for the VisualAge Certification Practicums. Peter has published four technical books in the areas of VisualAge programming using Java and C++.

 Dale Nilsson and Peter Jakab are part of the team that developed and deployed the VisualAge for Java and VisualAge for C++ Certification Program. Their experience from these projects, their engagements with customers on software development projects, and their background in object-oriented application development form the foundation for this book.

Bill Sarantakos received a BMath in Computer Science with Electrical Engineering from the University of Waterloo, Waterloo, Ontario, Canada. He has been programming for 18 years including almost 12 years with IBM at the IBM Toronto Lab. He has worked as the team leader of the C run-time team, as a member of the WorkFrame team and as a C++ front-end developer on the VisualAge C++ products and their predecessor products, on both OS/2 and Windows NT. For the last 3 years, Bill has been a founding member of the VisualAge for Java and C++ Services team (TecTeam) where he has provided object-oriented programming, consulting, and mentoring services to IBM customers. He is as a Sun Certified Java Programmer, an IBM Certified Developer VisualAge for Java, an IBM Certified Developer VisualAge for C++, an IBM Certified OS/2 Warp Developer, and an IBM Certified DB2 Application Developer. Bill also works as an assessor at the VisualAge certification sessions.

Russ Stinehour is the President and CEO of CrossLogic Corporation and has over twenty years of software development experience including sixteen years of project management, product planning, architecture and applications development with IBM. Russ holds a B.S. in Systems Science from Michigan State University and an MBA from the University of North Carolina at Chapel Hill. Russ has created and taught courses in Object-Oriented Analysis and Design, Client Server Technologies, Graphical User Interface Design, Smalltalk Programming, VisualAge for Java and IBM VisualAge for Java Certification. Russ is a Sun Certified Java Programmer, IBM Certified VisualAge for Java Developer and IBM Certified VisualAge for Smalltalk Developer. As a technical manager at CrossLogic, Russ contributes to the education and services side of the business, keeping CrossLogic a premier IBM Business Partner and leader in the industry.

Greg Hester is the founder of CrossLogic Corporation and is the Vice President of Technology. Greg holds a B.S. in Computer Science from North Carolina State University and has over 15 years of experience in systems programming, applications development, compiler technology, object technology and consulting. Greg has developed object technology applications for Fortune 500 clients and products in Java, Smalltalk, and C++

for CrossLogic. Greg has created and taught courses in Java Applications Development, Advanced Java Programming, VisualAge for Java and IBM VisualAge for Java Certification, and Smalltalk Programming. Greg is a Sun Certified Java Programmer, IBM Certified VisualAge for Java Developer, and IBM Certified VisualAge for Smalltalk Developer. As the senior technical person for CrossLogic, Greg contributes to the software, education, and services side of the business, helping CrossLogic to provide solutions for today's problems and tomorrow's needs. Greg Hester and Russ Stinehour can be reached at:

CrossLogic Corporation
206 East Chestnut Street, Suite 3
Ashville, NC 28801
(704) 232-1100

Bryon Kataoka provided the technical review of the book. Bryon Kataoka (CTO for Commerce Solutions Inc.—CSI) has a number of IBM certifications including VisualAge for Java, VisualAge for C++ and DB2, as well as a Sun Java programmer certification. Bryon's practices include Java Mentoring, project startup and management, and cooperative team development. CSI is a system integration, consulting, soluitons-based company that specializes in VisualAge for Java, WebSphere Application Server and DB2 UDB. Bryon can be contacted at:

Commerce Solutions Inc.
120 Montgomery St. Suite 1430
San Francisco, CA 94104
(707) 769-3009 fax (707) 769-3024
e-mail: bkataoka@CommerceSolutions.com.
Web site: http://www.CommerceSolutions.com.

What's in Chapter 1

The CD-ROM included with this book has a copy of the Windows version of VisualAge for Java, the completed applications covered in this book, and the data required for the exercises. This is a lot of software, and this chapter covers some of the considerations when installing these components. This chapter covers:

- Understanding installation hardware and software considerations
- Using the VisualAge for Java online help system
- Starting VisualAge for Java
- Adding classes in the workspace
- Running a Java applet
- Changing program properties
- Versioning Java code

Welcome to *Enterprise Development with VisualAge for Java, Version 3*! The instructions for installing the software on the CD-ROM included with this book are in "Installing the Necessary Software." Even though this chapter covers basic material on using VisualAge for Java, you need to complete it before you start building the sample applications. The sample applications in this book require VisualAge for Java Version 3 and some sample files on the CD-ROM. If you already have VisualAge for Java installed, you still need to install some of the sample files from the CD-ROM. You should review the *read.me* file on the CD-ROM for install information. The next sections cover specific information on computer environment issues that affect the VisualAge for Java development and run-time systems.

What Hardware and Software Do You Need?

When using application development tools, you need to consider the hardware and software requirements of both the development environment and the target run-time environment. This section describes the factors you should consider in the development environment. VisualAge for Java is a robust application development system, and you need sufficient hardware and the required software to be productive while using it. One of the essential considerations is that VisualAge for Java is repository-based and not file-based (see "How the IDE Stores Data," later in this chapter).

There are many other considerations for the systems that run your applications and applets. Throughout the book, there is information on these considerations as well as a wide number of options available when you build applications and applets. There are a number of changes in Version 3 that help you manage development time memory usage. You can usually assume that users of your applications probably have less powerful systems than the one you use when developing an application.

Tuning applications to increase performance is somewhat of an art, because most work to improve performance is usually done at the very end of the development cycle. It is fair to say that you should apply different optimization techniques for the special characteristics of each application. Using the iterative development process is a good way to ensure adequate application performance. Throughout this book, you will use iterative development, and you should continue to use it in all of your development work.

Hardware Requirements

VisualAge for Java is a comprehensive Java development toolset that requires enough computing power to satisfy a demanding programmer. This section covers the typical hardware needed to run VisualAge for Java.

Java Programming Requirements

The typical Java developer using the Java Development Kit (JDK) can use an average desktop computer to develop Java programs. The average desktop computer has more speed and memory all the time, so the term average is relative to when you bought your computer. You can use an average computer because file-based Java development requires only a text editor and the JDK. In a file-based environment, you use some basic libraries, a compiler, and a debugger. Most JDK developers rely on trace information and `system.out` to determine programming errors.

This is an adequate environment for dabbling in Java, but you really need a bigger and better development environment and more computing horsepower to have a truly productive development system. For Java Web development, you probably have a browser, a local area network connection, other development tools, and access to an HTTP server, all of which take precious computing power.

VisualAge for Java Programming Requirements

VisualAge for Java provides a complete integrated development environment (IDE) to develop applications and applets in the Java language. VisualAge for Java proves the old adage that software expands to fill the ever-expanding hardware capacity. There are two key features that cause VisualAge for Java to need a real beefy development system. First, it has a repository-based IDE instead of working on files like many other Java development systems. This consumes additional resources, but at the same time provides a much more responsive and coherent development environment. The second feature is the abundance of views, browsers, and tool windows in the VisualAge for Java IDE. Java development in this environment uses the standard Abstract Windowing Toolkit (AWT), Java Foundation Classes (JFCs), class libraries, other JDK classes, vendor-supplied class libraries, the class browser, the Debugger, online help, visual builders, and other tools. All of these tools and services make you more productive and enable you to construct applications with a lot of function. However, these tools and services consume many system resources when used at the same time.

This high-powered development system requires a robust computer consisting of a fast processor, plenty of disk space, and lots of memory. You can make VisualAge for Java Professional Edition work (or limp along) on a computer with a processor running at a clock speed of 233 MHz with 64MB of ram installed, but you will see faster performance with more memory or a faster processor. Strangely enough, adding memory seems to provide better performance improvements than increasing processor speed. The amount of free ram directly affects the amount of paging the operating system must perform to keep all of the applications running. You should have at least 128MB of RAM (many developers have 256MB or more) and at least a 300-MHz Pentium processor with 500MB of fixed disk space to hold the product and the additional virtual memory required at run time. The hardware requirements for the Enterprise Edition are a lot higher than those for the Professional Edition.

You also need sufficient disk space for virtual memory. In Windows NT, the standard size of 50MB of virtual memory is not enough for optimal performance; a minimum of 200MB or more is much better. Use the settings under by selecting **Control Panel => System => Performance** to increase it. These are pretty big numbers, but the maximum is required only if you install all components, samples, and online documentation. The best guideline is to install only the components that you will actually use.

VisualAge for Java requires a high-resolution display so it works in SVGA 800 × 600, but many windows and menus do not completely fit in this resolution. You should have a display that supports an SVGA 1024 × 768 or higher 1240 × 1024 resolution, especially when designing graphical user interfaces using the visual builder. You need a large monitor for very high resolutions to be usable, typically a 17-inch monitor is the minimum size for 1240 × 1024. When you are using multiple tools like the Visual Builder, a browser, a console window, and a Debugger window, you can use as much screen real estate as these higher resolution displays allow.

Software Requirements

At the time this book went to press, the VisualAge for Java product is available on the following operating environments:

- VisualAge for Java Version 3.0 for Windows runs on Windows NT Version 4.0 with Service Pack 3, Windows 95, or Windows 98. VisualAge for Java 3.02 supports Windows 2000.

- VisualAge for Java Version 3.0 runs on AIX, IBM's version of UNIX.

- VisualAge for Java Version 3.0 for OS/2 runs on OS/2 Warp Version 4.

The VisualAge for Java for Windows development environment is 32-bit, so it does not run on Windows 3.1, but there is not very much Windows 3.1 development anymore. One of Java's many key benefits is its write-once, run-anywhere capability. You can develop applications on any of the supported development systems and run them on Windows 3.1 or any other operating environment that has a supporting Java Virtual Machine (JVM). Chapter 8, "Deploying Java," covers deploying Java programs. You need to keep in mind that most end-user systems running Windows may have slower processors and less memory than your development system. You can get IBM-developed JVMs from the www.java.ibm.com Web site. This site also has information on JDKs and JVMs for other IBM operating systems like OS/400 and MVS.

The VisualAge for Java Professional Edition product is included on the CD-ROM with this book and usually costs $149. There are virtually no limitations on the Professional Edition. There is a no-charge edition called VisualAge for Java Entry Edition that provides all features and functions found in VisualAge for Java Professional with the following modifications or limitations:

- Repository is limited to 750 classes.

- Documentation can only be viewed through the support page on the Web.

- No documentation is shipped with the product.

- Product is licensed for non-commercial use.

- No support is provided.

To find out which edition and version of the product you are running, display the About VisualAge box from the Help menu. The About box should look like Figure 1.1. The labs in this book generate a lot of classes, and if you have VisualAge for Java Entry Edition, you may exceed the 500-class limit.

In order to run the exercises in this book, you need VisualAge for Java Version 3 and you should have at least the first fix level (Version 3.02) installed. If you already have your own copy of the product installed, you should install the VisualAge for Java 3.02 upgrade, which is a complete re-install of VisualAge for Java. Refer to the read.me file on the CD-ROM for information on installation.

Figure 1.1   About VisualAge.

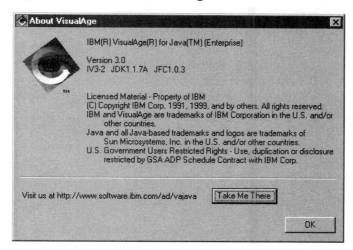

The exercises in this book have been created and tested using the products at the level found in the CD-ROM. It is very unlikely that a patch will introduce problems; in fact, each patch set usually fixes a number of problems and can even improve performance, and they are available at VisualAge Developer Domain at www.ibm.com/software/vadd.

> **NOTE**
>
> We have published books on VisualAge for Java since Version 1, and every time we update the hardware requirements, the numbers usually double. Fortunately, the hardware prices are fairly consistent and in many cases much cheaper. After two years, you can usually buy four times the hardware for 75 percent of the original price. Progress is amazing.

Development versus Run-Time Requirements

It is important to take into consideration both development and run-time environments when you develop an application. If you develop applications on a 500-MHz Pentium III with a 20-inch SVGA display and 512MB of RAM, they will not show the same performance running on a 166-MHz 486 system with a low-resolution 12-inch VGA display and 32MB of RAM. Throughout this book, there are suggestions and pointers that cover some of the many design and deployment decisions that need to be made for an application to run well in a given environment. They also cover the trade-offs required to build an application that is flexible enough to run in many environments. Not many books cover this mysterious part of application development.

Installing the Necessary Software

The CD-ROM included with this book includes VisualAge for Java Professional Edition for Windows. The Windows version runs on Windows 95, Windows 98, Windows NT, or Windows 2000. If you already have VisualAge for Java installed, you must still install the sample applications and solutions to the exercises provided on the CD-ROM in order to complete the exercises in this book. For you hard-core command-line programmers, install the contents of the CD-ROM as follows:

1. Place the CD-ROM in the CD-ROM drive.

2. Open a command prompt window.

3. Switch to the root directory of the CD-ROM and in the command prompt window, enter **install**.

For those of you who prefer GUIs, install the contents of the CD-ROM as follows:

1. Place the CD-ROM in the CD-ROM drive.

2. Open the **My Computer** icon.

3. Select the CD-ROM drive.

4. Double-click (open) the Install file.

Please read the information in the **Installation and last minute information** window of the installation program. This has detailed instructions on how to install the different components available in the CD-ROM and any other important information that did not make the deadline for this book. This same information is available for printing in the read.me file, which is also found in the root directory of the CD-ROM.

What's in the VisualAge for Java Folder?

 After installing VisualAge for Java on either Windows NT or Windows 95, an IBM VisualAge for Java for Windows category is added to the Programs folder of the Start menu. You can get to it with the following steps:

On the task bar, select Start, Programs, and then IBM VisualAge for Java.

If you installed the OS/2 version, you now have a folder on your desktop for VisualAge for Java for OS/2.

Open VisualAge for Java by double-clicking the mouse on this menu item. The items in the IBM VisualAge for Java folder are:

- IBM VisualAge for Java. The start icon for the Product.
- read.me. A text file that has some good installation tips and information on migrating from Version 2 to Version 3.
- Register VisualAge for Java.
- Release Notes. An .html file with tons of information on the many components in VisualAge for Java.
- Uninstall. For VisualAge for Java.

Using VisualAge for Java Documentation

In the Professional and Enterprise Editions of the product, the various help icons start the default Web browser, load the HTML-based help system, and start the HTML search engine.

This page contains reference information and user guides for the VisualAge for Java tools, the AWT class library, and the components currently installed.

Finding Information

From this page, you can browse or search for the information you need on VisualAge for Java, Java, and AWT. The Netscape version has the different types of documentation listed at the top, categories listed on the left, and specific contents in the center main section of the browser. This gives you a convenient way to quickly find the information you need. You can quickly and easily get to any item you choose from this browser.

The online documentation is preferred over the hard copy because the search function in the browser is very useful and it is always available. If you need some information, you can easily get to the search screen, enter the search argument, and get a list of all the occurrences containing what you are looking for. You can locate any of the items in the list by selecting it from the list.

You can use the search screen to easily locate a specific class or method you want to review. You can also enter more abstract concepts. For example, if you are interested in learning more about the Remote Method Invocation facility in Java, you can just search for *RMI*.

Sometimes it is better to narrow down the search by entering a more specific argument. For example: enter *RMI samples* instead of just *RMI*. If you don't qualify the search, it may take a long time and will probably yield a very long list of unrelated topics.

If you know what you are looking for, you can go directly to that area of the documentation. For example, if you need to look up the AWT **Frame** class in the Reference document:

1. Select the References page of the notebook.

2. Select **JDK 1.1** at the bottom of the list on the left.

3. Select **package java.awt** under the JDK 1.1 API list. The main panel displays the reference information for the java.awt package.

4. Scroll down to the Class Index and select **Frame**.

When you are finished with help, close all the open Web browser windows to conserve system resources. However, if you have a high-powered system, you may want to keep the browser open for quick access.

Finding the Tutorials

There are a number of good tutorials in .pdf files that were installed with VisualAge for Java. You should refer to these tutorials for additional help in learning the IDE and tools in VisualAge for Java. You can view the .pdf files from the menu bar by selecting Help => PDF Index. The .pdf files are located in the subdirectory x:\IBMVJava\doc\pdf. You will need the Adobe Acrobat Reader, available free on the web from Adobe at www.adobe.com/products/acrobat/ readstep.html. You can also get a plug-in for your Web browser to view the .pdf files. There is a lot of good information in these .pdf files that is specific to different functions in VisualAge for Java. There are additional .pdf files in the Enterprise Edition with information and tutorials for the additional tools and generators in the Enterprise Edition.

Starting VisualAge for Java

Because VisualAge for Java is not just a Java compiler but a fully integrated development environment, the IDE is used to launch all other related tools. You only need to start VisualAge for Java from its icon on the folder or the task bar. Be very careful the first time you start VisualAge for Java after installation. There is some initial configuration work before the IDE displays. Be patient and whatever you do, don't turn off your computer while this post-install process is running.

The majority of the exercises in this book are completed inside the IDE. Later in Chapter 8, we cover deploying Java programs and how to make your programs work outside the IDE.

There is a section later in Chapter 13, "Team Development," that covers using the team versioning support in VisualAge for Java Enterprise Edition. There are some basic set-up steps for installing the team versioning, and you can migrate from the Professional Edition to the Enterprise Edition at any time. Most of the set up and maintenance of the team repository is done by a team lead or a LAN administrator, so it is only necessary for you to understand the basics.

Figure 1.2   VisualAge for Java welcome screen.

Start the VisualAge for Java IDE by locating and double-clicking its icon.

Make sure that VisualAge for Java starts up correctly. The VisualAge for Java splash screen should display for a short period of time, then the Welcome dialog opens as shown in Figure 1.2.

After a few seconds, the VisualAge for Java Workbench appears on your screen, as shown in Figure 1.3.

The Integrated Development Environment

VisualAge for Java has a very tight IDE with a ton of function. This section introduces you to some of the basic features of the IDE. Additional specific features of the IDE are covered throughout this book.

IDE Windows

In this book, the terms *IDE* and *Workbench* are used interchangeably to refer to the main window of VisualAge for Java. The IDE actually has a number of other windows, which are selected from the Windows menu in the Workbench. These windows include:

Figure 1.3   Workbench.

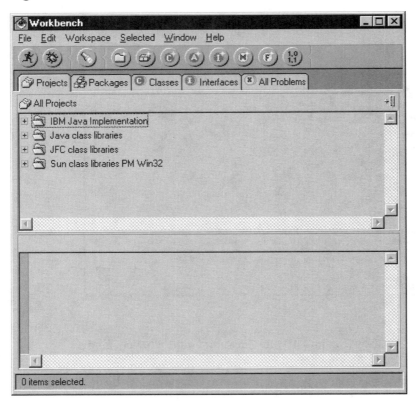

Clone. A useful function, which creates another Workbench window. Remember that another instance of the Workbench will take up a lot of resources and it may be difficult to work with two.

Scrapbook. A scratch pad where you can experiment or test Java code without creating a project, package, class, or method.

Repository Explorer. A read-only view of the classes available in the repository and the place for Repository maintenance.

Console. A window for viewing Standard In, Standard Out, and a list of threads needing input.

Log. A window for displaying development-time system-generated messages.

Debugger. A separate multi-paned window with the debugger functions.

Options. Your facility for customizing the Workspace, setting classpaths, and specifying your preferences.

Workbench. The main IDE window for working with Projects, Packages, and Classes. There are specific browsers for classes that you should use when working on an individual class.

Tip

If any of these windows is active, either open or minimized, VisualAge for Java is running. Often users will close the Workbench window and assume that VisualAge for Java has closed. It is best to select File => Exit VisualAge to completely close VisualAge for Java.

IDE Views

The Workbench is command central for the VisualAge for Java IDE. The IDE gives you access to the Java classes you are working with in the VisualAge for Java development environment. There are a number of views in the Workbench; they show the program elements loaded in the workspace.

The Projects view is the default view. It initially appears when you start the Workbench. It appears as an expandable tree view, because projects contain packages, which contain classes, which contain methods. There is a convenient option on the Workbench that lets you split the window vertically instead of horizontally by selecting Window => Flip Orientation. The screen pictures in this book show the default horizontal layout.

If you have previous knowledge of the Java language, you are probably familiar with the following terms:

- Package
- Interface
- Class
- Method

You are probably not familiar with the term *project*. This is because a project is not a Java program element. Projects are implemented in VisualAge for Java to help you organize packages, and they have no significance in the Java programming language. Use projects to group the packages that comprise an application or to group associated packages.

Switch through the pages of the Workbench to get familiar with the other views:

The Packages view lists all packages in the project, classes in the selected package, methods in the selected class, and source code for the selected method.

The Classes view lists all classes, methods in the selected class, and source code for the selected method.

The Interfaces view lists all interfaces, methods in the selected interface, and source code for the selected method.

The Managing view is available in the Enterprise Edition and provides ways to manage code ownership.

The EJB view is available in the Enterprise Edition and provides specific functions for working on Enterprise JavaBeans.

The Unresolved Problems view lists all problems detected in the classes that are loaded in the workspace.

How the IDE Stores Data

VisualAge for Java stores programming data in two files. The first file, called the repository, can be found in the x:\IBMVJava\Ide\Repository directory; the file name is ivj.dat. The second file, called the workspace, can be found in the x:\IBMVJava\Ide\Program directory and it is named ide.icx. You should back up these two files occasionally. In the unlikely case of a corrupted workspace or repository or a system failure, you can use the backup files to recover your work.

Repository

The repository is the central store for the different versions of all the classes that you use in VisualAge for Java. The repository retains information about all of the program elements ever loaded. When you delete items from the Workspace, the items are not deleted; rather they are retained for future use. This means it grows with time, consuming more and more disk space as new classes and versions of classes are created.

VisualAge for Java has a function in the Repository Explorer Window that permanently deletes any classes from the Repository. To use this function, select *Window*, then *Repository Explorer*. First you mark items to *Purge*, and then you *Compact* the Repository and the items marked for deletion are removed. Chapter 13 covers how to use the repository maintenance and some features that are available only in the Enterprise Edition.

Workspace

The workspace holds all classes that you are currently working with, including those that your classes refer to. The workspace is sometimes referred to as the *image*. The following projects must be loaded into the workspace for VisualAge for Java to work properly:

- IBM Java Implementation (special classes for the IDE)Java class libraries
- JFC class libraries (if you use Java Foundation Classes)

- Sun class libraries PM Win32

In the next section, you learn how to load classes into the workspace. Only packages and classes loaded in the workspace can be used to develop Java programs. Referring to packages or classes that are not loaded in the image results in reference errors. You can reference classes outside the IDE by listing them in the **Workspace classpath** setting found in Window => Options => Resources.

You should delete any projects, packages, or classes that you are no longer using. This improves the tool performance and speeds up the initial program load. Remember that deleted program elements are not really deleted, but moved from the workspace into the repository. A good way to explain this concept is to think of the workspace as essentially a subset of the contents of the repository. There are some minor exceptions to this, but for now this definition is adequate.

Adding Java Classes to the Workspace

You can load with Java packages and classes into the workspace by adding them from the repository or by creating them directly in the workspace. There are a few sample projects in the repository that you can load into the workspace to use as examples or to quickly verify that all is working fine. Load the IBM Java Examples project by following these steps:

Select the Projects icon in the Workbench toolbar. You could also display the Workbench pop-up menu and select Add Project. As shown in Figure 1.4, the Add Project SmartGuide window opens.

Tip

While in the Workbench, notice that there are often many ways to perform an action. Usually there is a toolbar button and there is also a context-sensitive pop-up menu. Open pop-up menus by pressing and releasing the right mouse button.

Select the **Add projects from the repository** radio button; then select the **Browse** button.

The Add Projects from Repository window lists the projects available from the repository. Select from the list to add a project to your workspace. For this example, select **IBM Java Examples**, as shown in Figure 1.5.

The Editions pane lists all available versions of the project in the repository. Even the Entry edition of VisualAge for Java has a fully functional version-control system.

Select the edition 3.0 checkbox in the *Available editions* list on the right.

Then select the **Finish** button to close this window.

Select the Finish button to load this project into the workspace.

Figure 1.4   Adding a Project.

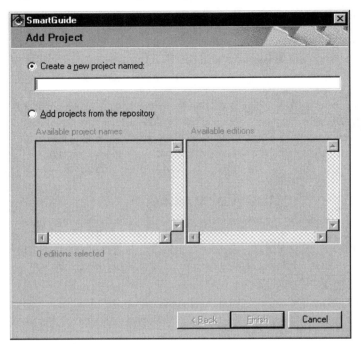

The adding process takes a little bit of time, because the classes are compiled as they are loaded into the workspace, and there are a lot of classes in this project. Whenever you load a large package, the load takes time. This is a case of "pay me now or pay me later." By compiling classes as they are loaded, you avoid waiting when you later run them in the IDE.

While adding this project, pay attention to the progress indicator, shown in Figure 1.6. It provides feedback on the operation being performed.

As the project, packages, and classes are incorporated into the workspace, they are checked against the loaded code to ensure that there are no conflicts. For example, you cannot add a package with the same name as a package already in the Workbench. Instead, you must use the **Replace With** option from the Workbench pop-up menu.

All prerequisite classes are checked for existence in the Workbench. If any required classes or methods in any classes are missing, errors are posted to the Unresolved Problems page of the Workbench, shown in Figure 1.7. These errors are also reported in the progress indicator. You will notice that the JFC Class Libraries project has several errors. You will not use these classes so they will not affect any of the samples in this book. You could delete these classes and they will still be in the Repository if you ever need them, but it is OK to leave them and have errors.

Figure 1.5   Selecting a Project.

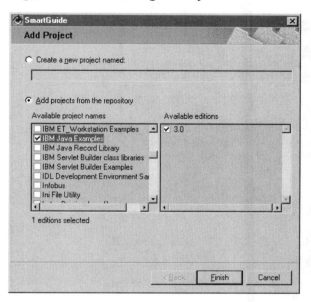

Figure 1.6   Progress indicator.

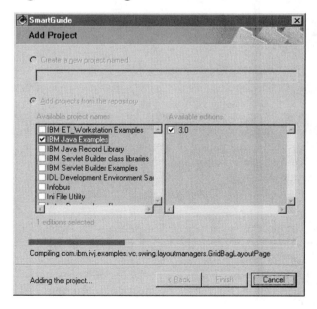

Figure 1.7   Unresolved errors.

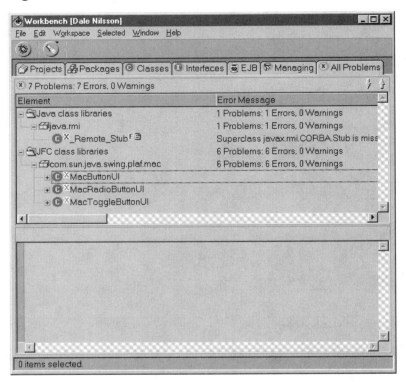

The Unresolved Problems view is the only place where the description of an error appears in its entirety. This is because some error descriptions are very long, and they are displayed in a single line. In this view, you can scroll as far as necessary to see the whole line. You can also see an abbreviated error message in the info area at the bottom of the window.

Running an Applet

Running applets or applications in the IDE is very easy. You select a Java class with the running person icon and then either press the Run button on the IDE toolbar or select Run from the pop-up menu.

Visual cues are displayed throughout the IDE. These cues make it easier to identify the features of program elements in the IDE. The most common ones are shown in Figure 1.8 and Figure 1.9.

Figure 1.8   Visual cues.

Program elements

project

package

class

interface

Java modifiers

Access Modifiers

default access

private

protected

public

Non-Access Modifiers

A abstract

F final

N native

S static

synchronized

T transient

V volatile

Try running one of the Hanoi Java sample that comes with the product as follows:

1. Flip back to the Projects page in the Workbench.
2. Open the IBM Java Examples project.
3. Open the com.ibm.ivj.examples.hanoi package.
4. Select the HanoiApplet class as shown in Figure 1.10. Notice that this class has the executable class icon (running person) besides it.

5. Select the Run button to see the Applet run.

Figure 1.9   More visual cues.

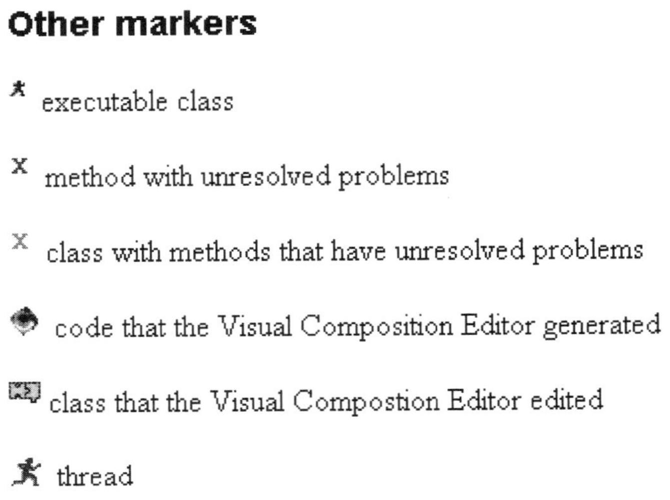

Other markers

*executable class

X method with unresolved problems

X class with methods that have unresolved problems

◆ code that the Visual Composition Editor generated

▥ class that the Visual Compostion Editor edited

🏃 thread

Towers of Hanoi

The puzzle of the Towers of Hanoi is a popular one. Most people are familiar with it. In order to solve the puzzle, all disks have to be moved from the left-hand tower to the right-hand tower. The middle tower is used, as necessary, as a staging area. The rules are no placing a larger disk on top of a smaller one, no moving more than one disk at a time. When all the disks are on the right tower with the largest disk on the bottom, the puzzle is solved. The larger the number of disks, the longer it takes to solve the puzzle.

An applet viewer automatically starts, and you see the Hanoi applet run, as shown in Figure 1.11. When the applet solves the puzzle, it can be restarted from the Applet menu in the applet viewer.

Congratulations! You have completed running your first Java applet inside the VisualAge for Java development environment.

Before proceeding, close the Hanoi applet by selecting the Close button on the applet viewer.

The number of disks used in the Hanoi puzzle is determined by a preset parameter used to run this Applet. You can change this value in the Applet's html *parameter* tag. The parameters for a runnable program are properties of the program. In VisualAge for Java you can change program properties in a special Properties window. Let's change the HanoiApplet properties with the following:

Figure 1.10   Running the Hanoi applet.

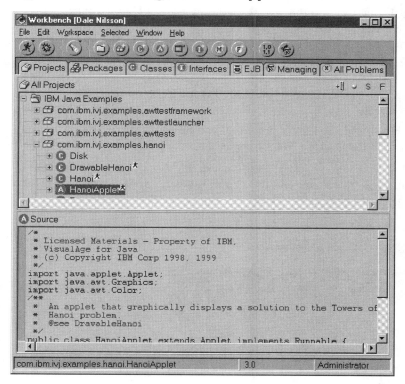

Figure 1.11   Hanoi applet.

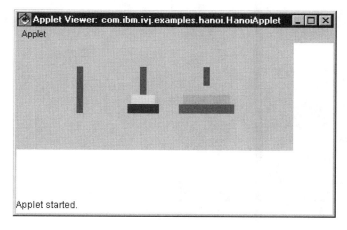

Select the Hanoi Applet in the Workbench and display its pop-up menu.

Then select **Properties** and the Settings window for the Hanoi applet appears. This window can be used to change parameters passed to the applet at run time; in this case, the numbers of disks in the puzzle is changed to 7 as shown in Figure 1.12. You can have this setting saved in the Workbench.

Close this window and try re-running the HanoiApplet to see the changed parameter.

With the HanoiApplet selected, press the Run button and the applet viewer runs and displays the HanoiApplet with the new setting.

You now know how to run Java programs in the VisualAge for Java IDE and how to change their run-time settings. You can also change the applet viewer size from the properties window.

Figure 1.12   Applet parameters.

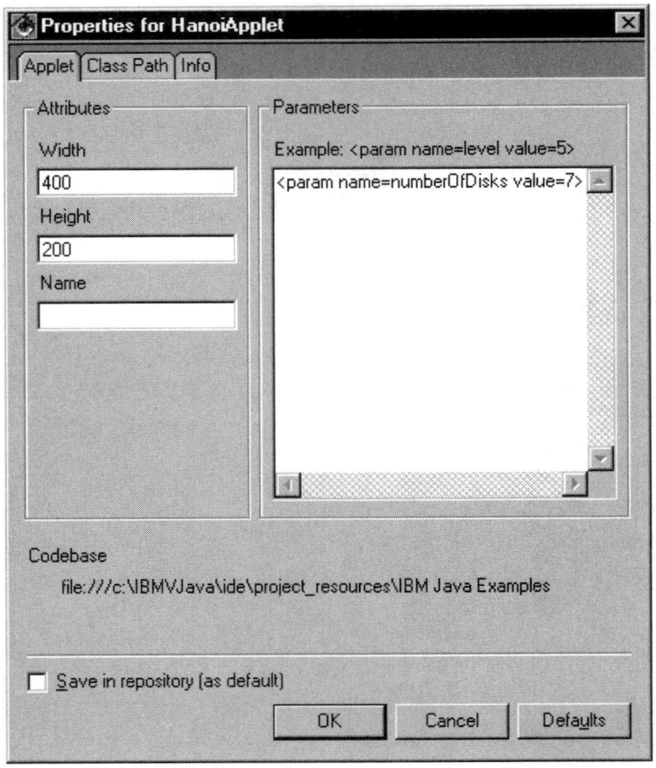

Let's take a closer look at the HanoiApplet class. By pressing the + sign to the left of the class name you can expand the class and see the methods that make it work. The code for the HanoiApplet is shown in the Source window at the bottom of the Workbench. HanoiApplet extends the java.applet.Applet class. Applets do not have a frame of their own; that is why they run either in the applet viewer or, most likely, as part of an HTML page inside of a Web browser.

Applets are subject to the rules of Java applet security. These rules are enforced by code in the Web browser, and they vary from browser to browser. Most notably, applets cannot access system resources like disk files; they can communicate only with the Web server from which they originated.

Because living inside a Web browser is a transitory existence, applets need to know how to initialize, start, stop, and paint themselves. You can see such methods inside the HanoiApplet class. When the applet is first loaded from the Web server, it initializes itself. As a user changes to another page in the browser, the applet is told to stop; when the user returns to this page, the applet is told to start. When the visual contents of the applet change, the applet is told to paint itself.

Selecting each of these methods shows the source code in the bottom pane of the viewer. By far, the most interesting method is **paint**, shown in Figure 1.13.

Tip

Double-clicking the screen area around **Source** and **Comment** maximizes the source pane; double-clicking it again restores it to the original split ratio. This works in most panes in VisualAge for Java that have different labels.

If the applet viewer is still running, close it. Now start it again, but this time, change the parameter **numberOfDisks** to 8. This creates a more complex puzzle, which will take longer to solve and give us time to have some fun.

Once the applet starts, switch back to the Workbench and select the Source pane for the paint method. Locate the statement:

```
g.setColor(background);
```

and change it to:

```
g.setColor(Color.green);
```

Notice that you are changing the code for the paint method while the applet is running in the applet viewer. You can save your changes, either press Ctrl-S or press the right mouse button and select Save from the pop-up menu.

Figure 1.13 Paint method.

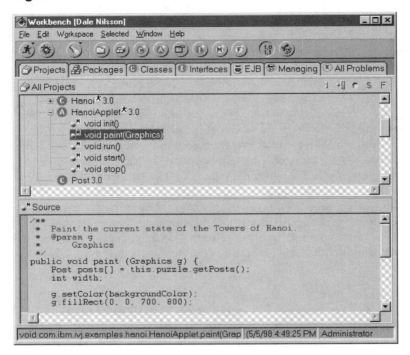

Saving the paint method started an interesting chain of events:

- The source code was saved in the repository.

- A new edition of the paint method was created. An entry in the Log window documented this change.

- The source code was compiled. VisualAge for Java implements an incremental compiler, which compiles each method right after it is modified and saved. Errors, if any, are detected right away. If possible, you should correct any errors before saving. If the nature of the error cannot be corrected at the time (for example, referencing a class you haven't written yet), you can always save the code with the error. Of course, in that case, the method is not compiled.

- As you remember, the applet was running when you made this change. The next move was made, and now it's time to paint the screen with the new disk position. The JVM accesses the newly compiled code of the paint method and executes it. Not only is the next move shown, but also the background color is now green.

As mentioned previously in this section, even the Entry Edition of VisualAge for Java has a fully functional version control system in place. When you saved the changes to the paint method, a new *edition* was created. Editions are created every time you modify a method or class. Editions can be modified. At any point in time, usually when you get something working or when you are about to try something daring, you will create a new version of your code. Once you version a program element, it becomes immutable. You can always go back to a previous version and modify it to create a new edition. But the version itself remains unchanged.

You can go back to any version or edition of your code. You can also compare the current edition with any other version or edition of the same program element. Let's compare the two editions of the paint method of HanoiApplet.

In the Workbench, make sure the paint method of HanoiApplet is selected. Bring up the pop-up menu by pressing and releasing the right mouse button. Select **Compare With** and then **Another Edition** as shown in Figure 1.14. You are then prompted for the specific Edition to compare. Select the version and press OK.

The current edition is compared with the previous edition, and the Comparing window appears as shown in Figure 1.15.

VisualAge for Java displays the difference between the two editions. In this case, there is only one difference; if there were more differences, you could use the arrow buttons to traverse through them. Close the window.

Once you see the differences between editions or versions, you might choose to replace the current edition with one from the repository. From the pop-up menu for the paint method, select **Replace With** and then **Previous Edition** to restore the paint method to the original condition.

The smallest program element that can be versioned is a class. The versioning process takes the current edition of a project, package, or class and creates a read-only version. Use versioning before you make significant changes to a program element or when you are happy with its behavior and want to take a checkpoint. In the Team Edition of VisualAge for Java, you have to version a program element before it can be released to other developers. To version all classes in a package, select the package; to version all the packages in a project, select the project.

Create a new version of the HanoiApplet class by selecting it in the Workbench. Bring up its pop-up menu and select **Manage**, then **Version**.

Figure 1.14   Comparing with the previous edition.

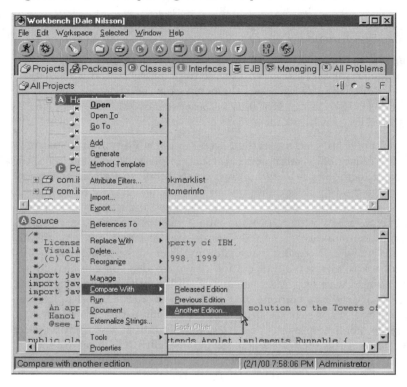

Tip

VisualAge for Java Version 3 has a new toolbar button to version. It is faster to select this new button once you know it's there.

The Version window appears; and now you have three choices for the new version names of HanoiApplet. These choices appear in Figure 1.16.

Automatic assigns the next version number. For example, if the previous version was 1.0, the new version will be 1.1.

One Name assigns the next version name that you enter to the selected item and all of its elements. If you version a package, all of the classes in the package will have this name. For example, you can version a package and call it *beta 1* or *This version works*.

Figure 1.15   Differences between editions.

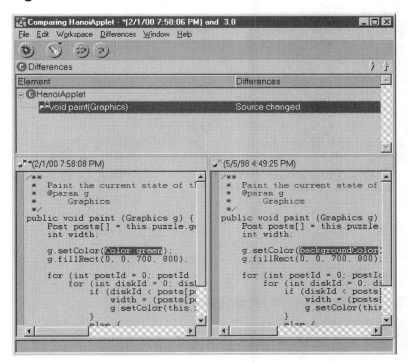

Name Each lets you name the version for the selected item and you can have different names for each of its elements. Additionally, this option gives you a handy list of names already in use.

Figure 1.16   Version naming.

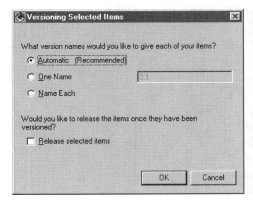

Use the default and select the **OK** button, and the Workbench automatically versions the selected item.

 Use the last set of toolbar buttons on the Workbench to display or hide the version numbers that appear at the end of your program element names.

Tip

When you reversion items, VisualAge for Java can automatically increment the last character. If you name a version **SomeProgram v1** it can automatically name the next version **SomeProgram v1.1**. If you name the version **v1 SomeProgram** the next version will be **v1SomeProgram** because the last character is incremented.

Figure 1.17 HanoiApplet version 1.1.

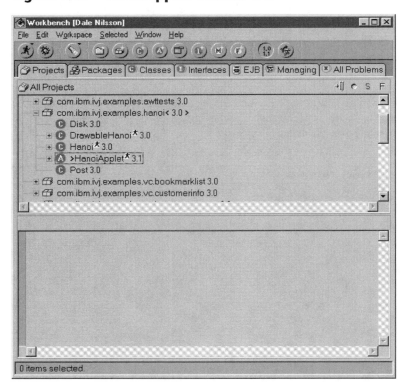

The new HanoiApplet version is now in the Workbench as shown in Figure 1.17. Also note that the package and project no longer have versions; instead they are open editions because the HanoiApplet changed.

Bookmarks

Once you get familiar with VisualAge for Java, you will use the Projects view of the Workbench more and more. In this view, you have a complete picture of what is loaded in the Workbench. During development, you often move from package to package and from class to class to see what is available, check method names, check input parameters for the methods, and so on. You will find yourself jumping back and forth between different program elements. When there is a lot loaded in the Workbench, this jumping around can be slow and confusing as you scroll through many screens to move from one place to the next. VisualAge for Java enables you to set bookmarks throughout the Projects view and then use these bookmarks to jump between points that are of interest to you.

To set a bookmark, use the Set Bookmark icon. Just select the project, package, class, or method you want to bookmark and then select the icon. As you add bookmarks, they are numbered and added to the left of the bookmark icon as shown in Figure 1.18.

Figure 1.18   Bookmarks.

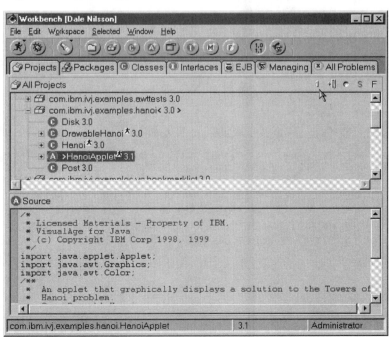

> **NOTE**
>
> Bookmarks are one of the many cool stealth (little known and hard to find) features in the IDE. There is a maximum of nine bookmarks you can set in the Workbench. This is mainly constrained by the available IDE screen space to display the bookmarks.

To move between the program elements represented by the bookmarks, click the corresponding bookmark number. If you forget where a bookmark will take you, just rest the mouse pointer over the number and a help window will open, identifying what program element the bookmark represents. You can also bring up the pop-up menu for a bookmark and select **Go to** or **Remove**.

Summary

In this chapter, you prepared your system to continue with the rest of the book. To do this, you:

- Reviewed the hardware and software requirements for VisualAge for Java.
- Learned how to find information in the online documentation. This will be very helpful when using VisualAge for Java and the AWT class library.
- Learned about the IDE and loaded Java classes from the repository.
- Started the Workbench, tested a sample applet, and determined that everything is working properly.
- Edited Java code, then saved and tested an Applet.
- Changed program properties.
- Learned the basics of versioning classes in the Workbench.
- Used bookmarks in the Workbench to help you find program elements.

Now that VisualAge for Java is installed and working, you are ready to start building Java programs! The instructions in this book don't require you to look in the documentation for help, but if you ever need more information during development, you should consult the online help. As you develop your Java programs, remember to version your Java components as you get them to work.

Building the Hello World Applet

2

What's in Chapter 2

Now that you have all the necessary software installed and have tested VisualAge for Java by bringing up the Workbench and studying its various views and components, you are ready to start visual programming. In this chapter, you build your first VisualAge for Java application, which is a simple Hello World window. Building this application covers the basic elements of visual programming that you will continue to use throughout this book. First you learn to use AWT controls, then later in the book you will learn how to use the JFC controls and other more advanced applications. In this chapter, you will learn how to:

- Set Workbench options
- Create projects and packages
- Work in the Visual Composition Editor (VCE)
- Use simple Abstract Windowing Toolkit (AWT) beans to design an applet
- Make visual connections
- Generate Java source code
- Build and run a program

If you have closed VisualAge for Java, you need to restart it. The simplest way to start VisualAge for Java is to double-click its icon. To make it easier to access VisualAge for Java, you may want to create a *shortcut* of its icon. For convenience, you can place the *shortcut* icon directly on the desktop.

As you remember, when you start VisualAge for Java, the workspace is loaded and any windows or views that were open when you last saved the workspace are reopened. Restoring the workspace to the last saved state can take quite a while, especially if there were many open windows that need to be reconstructed. One way to avoid this slow startup is to close any unnecessary windows and browsers before you close the Workbench.

Workbench Options

There are a number of options you can set in the Workbench to make it work to your liking. VisualAge for Java Version 3 has a lot of new options that were not available in Versions 1 or 2. When VisualAge for Java is installed, all the default options are turned on and assume a beginning user. It is highly recommended that you read this section because it will give you many tips for customizing the VisualAge for Java IDE. Some of the option settings may be unfamiliar to you, and you will probably not change them until you become more familiar with VisualAge for Java. For example, you may want to disable a number of warnings as you become more familiar with Java and VisualAge for Java. Some options change many settings, that are familiar to you, for example, the fonts that are used in the different browsers and editor windows.

All customizable options are grouped together in the Options window. Display the Options by selecting **Window => Options** from the menu bar in any of the VisualAge for Java windows. The window appears as shown in Figure 2.1. The options are displayed in a tree view for editing. The following sections cover some of the options in the Workbench that you will probably want to change.

General Options

First select **General** item in the Options list on the left. You may want to deselect **Expand all problems on problems page**. The Problems page shows all the Java code errors in the Workspace, including syntax, reference, and even deprecated method warnings. It is very helpful to keep the tree view in the Problems page collapsed to save screen space.

You should also leave **Lock log window open** checked. The Log window displays messages from VisualAge for Java as you work on Java classes, such as versioning messages and messages when classes throw exceptions. Locking the window prevents you from closing or killing it. If you close it and VisualAge for Java has one of these development time messages, the Log window is automatically constructed and displayed. This can be annoying and it is a good practice to keep the Log window around but minimized.

You will probably want to deselect **Show welcome dialog on startup** as shown in Figure 2.1. This saves a little time when you start VisualAge for Java by eliminating the startup dialog.

Also on this page, the default behavior is that double-clicking opens a browser for the selected item. This is what most users expect, so you do not need to change this setting, as shown in Figure 2.1.

There is a new option called **Open an item in** that has two options:

1. New browser
2. Current browser

The default setting is the behavior that has always been in VisualAge for Java. When you open a browser or editor for any Project, Package, or Class, the IDE automatically opens a new browser window. This can sometimes create a bit of window clutter. The new option to open an item in the current window dis-

Figure 2.1 General Options.

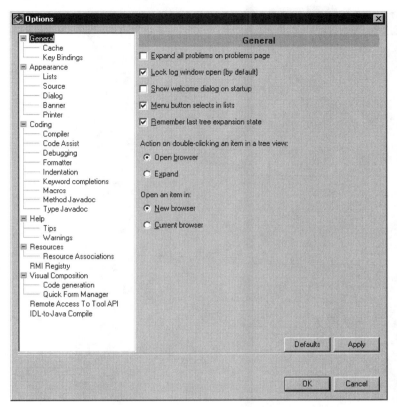

plays the new browser in the client area of the Workbench window. If you use this option, you will get two new buttons on the left end of the toolbar. These arrows allow you to switch between the different browsers contained in the window. The browsers are in memory, but they seem to display much more slowly than when the browsers are in separate windows.

Next, select the *Cache* item in the Options list on the left, and it appears as seen in Figure 2.2. This was a new feature in Version 2, and the default settings should be increased to improve performance. The cache is separate from the system memory cache and will not automatically expand if you have more memory. VisualAge for Java is a heavy weight tool and it can use quite a bit of memory. If you have 128MB or 256MB of memory, you should increase the memory cache to 2000 or 3000 for better performance.

The disk cache option is not very good as it creates a separate file for each cached class in the x:\IBMVJava\ide\cache subdirectory. These small files can con-

Figure 2.2   Cache options.

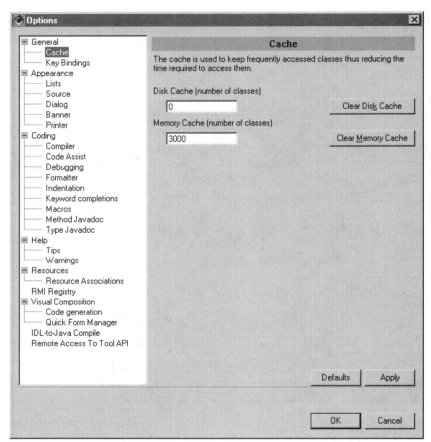

tribute to disk fragmentation and may not improve performance very much, so you may want to set the disk cache to 0 to prevent this. After you make a change to any option, it is a good idea to press the *Apply* button to save the changes.

Appearance Options

Next select the *Appearance* item in the Options list on the left, and these options appear as seen in Figure 2.3. The option to include the type in the field label is selected by default. It is a good idea to select the checkbox to *include return type in method label*. Even though this may cause some scrolling during development, there are so many methods in Java that it is helpful to have the method return type displayed when coding and debugging.

Figure 2.3 Appearance options.

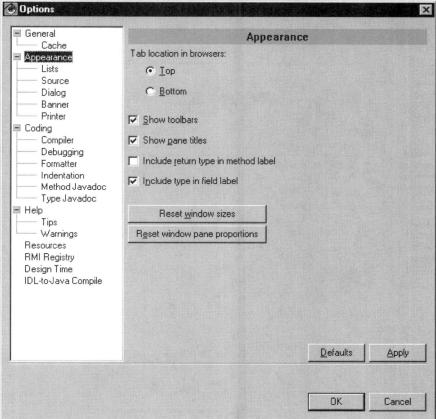

If you prefer the windows in the Workbench showing the Projects and Unresolved Problems views to be split vertically instead of split horizontally, you need to change that setting from the Workbench. You can set this option by selecting **Window => Orientation => Vertical** from the Workbench. You can then adjust the panes in the Workbench and browsers by dragging them to be larger or smaller. The window sizes and positions are saved as part of the Workspace, so when you restart VisualAge for Java, you will get the same user interface layout. All the labs in this book assume that you use the default horizontal orientation.

Changing fonts in the Workbench requires you to set fonts for the different kinds of panes. The font used for the editor and the various colors used for syntax highlighting is set on the Text Editing page shown in Figure 2.4. VisualAge for Java has many different Views or Browsers and all of them can have different font settings.

Figure 2.4   Changing options—fonts.

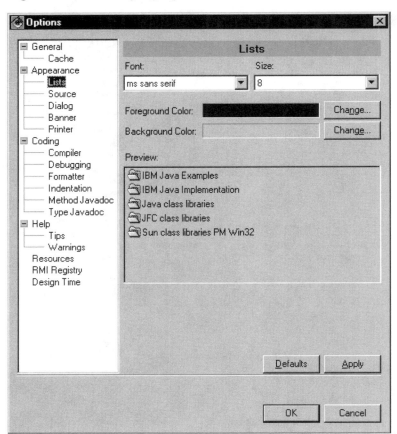

To change the way lists appear in the IDE, such as their font and colors, select the *Source* item in the Options list on the left. The default font size is 8; you may want to increase it for legibility or decrease it to display more code. VisualAge for Java Version 3 does not let you set bold fonts because of cross-platform problems.

Help Options

Next select the *Tips* item in the Options list on the left, and these options are shown in Figure 2.5. Tips are displayed in dialogs during development and require you to close them as you work. The tips can be helpful for new users, but they can become a nuisance for more experienced users. You may want to deselect the tips as shown in Figure 2.5. The Enterprise Edition has more tips; they are all annoying, so you should turn them all off.

Figure 2.5 Help—tips.

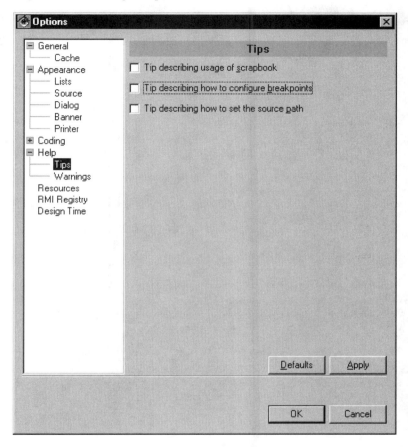

It is a good idea to leave most of the warnings on. These dialogs appear when VisualAge for Java detects a problem or error, so they can be very helpful. More advanced users should turn off the following warnings as shown in Figure 2.6:

- Confirm restarting scrapbook
- Confirm changing workspace owner
- Reminder to release classes when versioning
- Warn when resources need to be manually copied

All of these warnings and reminders are not errors, rather they are common tasks that most developers do on a daily basis. Because these warnings are modal dialog boxes, they interrupt the more advanced developer.

Figure 2.6   Help—warnings.

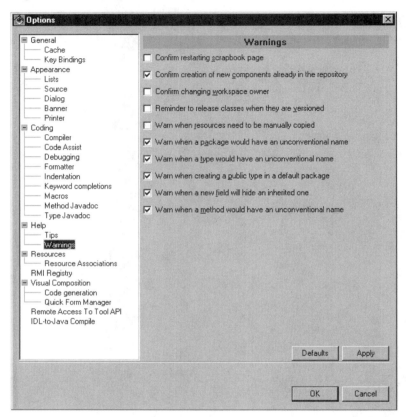

Visual Composition Editor Options

The Visual Composition option allows you to make classpath changes specific to the VCE. This default setting is fine for now. Select the *Code generation* item under Visual Composition. VisualAge for Java Version 3 has new code generation options for the connections in the Visual Composition Editor. Connections can be generated as:

1. **Do not use any inner classes.** The old default generation style that generates a separate method for each visual connection.

2. **Use one inner class for all events.** The new default generation style that generates an inner class with separate methods for each visual connection. This option is a cleaner Java style that hides the connections in an inner class, but it relies on the JVM (Java Virtual Machine) handling the events in the proper order.

3. **Use an inner class for each event—not the default.** It will generate a lot more code and perform more slowly than the other two options. However, this option guarantees that the events are handled properly by the run-time JVM.

The default setting of Use one inner class for all events is fine, and the examples in the book use this setting.

The VCE has information that cannot be expressed in Java code. If you use the VCE and export the generated Java source code, then import the same Java code back into VisualAge for Java, the visual lines will be lost and the position of the JavaBeans in the VCE will be lost. The Generate metadata method feature puts VCE information in a comment in the generated Java code.

It is important that you change the default setting for this option. You need to select the *Generate metadata method* checkbox to enable this function as shown in Figure 2.7. This stores the VCE metadata from now on, whenever you use the VCE. This is one of the times when leaving the default setting unchanged

Figure 2.7   Visual Composition options.

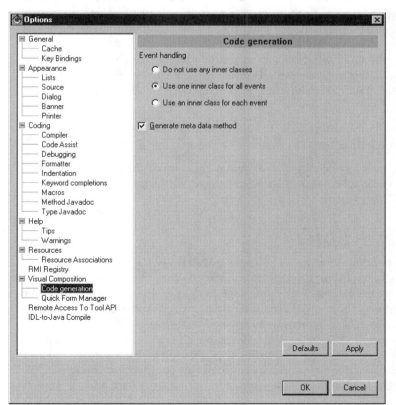

can get you in trouble, because the VCE will not have any connection or position information.

It actually generates a getBuilderData() method the next time you save the class. All the Visual Composition Editor information like the connections and the size and position of the JavaBeans is put in an ASCII string for the tool to use. This method is not generated when you export the class and this is a global setting in the Workbench. There is also a place in the Visual Composition Editor to access this option.

The Generate metadata feature lets you export VCE classes and work on them outside the VisualAge for Java IDE. This can be very helpful when using other tools, keeping your Java code in a file-based versioning system, or making global name changes.

The last VCE option covers Quick Forms, which are new in Version 3. Quick Forms are defined and used in the VCE and they can be registered and managed through this Workbench option.

Other Options

There are many other options that enable you to set additional VisualAge for Java options including options that are Enterprise Edition features and only appear if you have these features installed. For example, if you are developing applets that implement Remote Method Invocation (RMI), you can choose whether or not to start the RMI registry and what port to use. If you installed either the Enterprise or the Professional editions, you can customize which browser to use for displaying the online help. You can also define your IDL compiler as one of these options.

Select the Apply button to save the changes, then the OK button to close the Options window.

The options you have changed are permanently saved only when you exit VisualAge for Java or when you select **File => Save Workspace** from the main menu bar of the Workbench.

Your First Applet

Let's get started building your first applet with VisualAge for Java using the VCE.

 The process for building this applet will use the iterative development method. You develop the applet user interface first, save your work, and test the Java code by running it in the IDE. You iterate by progressively adding more function and user interface elements, saving, and testing again. Every time you save your work while in the VCE, 100 percent pure Java code is generated and compiled. The program automatically runs if you press the Run button instead of selecting **Bean => Save Bean** from the menu bar after compilation is completed. If your program is an applet, the built-in applet viewer starts and loads the applet.

If you are developing an application, the main() method is run. This process enables you to see the results of your work a lot quicker than waiting until you have finished developing the program. Iterating also lets you catch problems before you lose track of what caused them.

> **NOTE**
>
> There are entire books written on the software development process. This book is dedicated to demonstrating how to developing good Java programs, so information on software development techniques is woven throughout the book. Whenever you start to develop a real Java project, you should define and implement a formal software development process.

You can catch a lot of errors right in the IDE. Every time you save a class or method, the code is compiled and any errors are reported right then and there. This may seem annoying at first, especially if you are used to compiling an entire class or program at a time. VisualAge for Java uses an incremental compiler; it compiles only what is necessary. For example, when you change a method, that method is the only thing that gets recompiled. This actually saves a lot of time, enabling you to concentrate on the particular method that you are coding. Sometimes, especially when you are at the early stages of developing a class, this forced-compile-before-saving process can get in the way, reporting problems about unresolved names just because you haven't written that particular part of the class yet. In most cases though, you can save a method even though it has errors. As you continue developing the class, the errors are resolved. Always make sure that there are no unresolved errors in a class before running and testing your programs. VisualAge for Java gives you a visual cue for classes and methods that contain errors. Either a red or a gray X will mark these unresolved errors. Of course, you can also turn to the Unresolved Problems view in the Workbench to see all outstanding errors.

Creating Projects and Packages

By now, you have customized the Workbench, and you are ready to start building your first VisualAge for Java applet. Applet is a Java class in the java.applet package. In VisualAge for Java, all classes must be part of a package (or at least a default package), and all packages must be part of a project. Before you start designing your applet, you need to set up a project and a package. You could use one of the existing projects, but it is not a good idea to mix your Java classes in the projects shipped with VisualAge for Java.

Projects

VisualAge for Java uses projects to organize the packages and classes in the Workbench. Each project has a unique name in the Workspace. A standard for naming projects is emerging: Project names are not Java names; they usually start with upper case and can have multiple words separated by spaces. Before applets or applications can be built using the IDE, a project must be created to contain the package with the beans for the particular applet or application.

With each new project created in the IDE, a subdirectory of the same name as the package is created using the IBMVJava\Ide\project_resources directory as the root. Some file systems don't like spaces or special characters. Be a little careful when defining Project names, but you can easily change the name later. Any packages with resource files in the project also cause the creation of a subdirectory descending from the subdirectory with the name of the project. This subdirectory is where the IDE looks for resource files, like the .gif files needed to display graphics on some types of GUI beans. It also stores any resources it creates in that same directory. This is covered in 8 using the project_resources directory. Note that this subdirectory is only created when you first create a project. It is not created when you import a project from another user or system. In that case, you must create the directory and place any resources there yourself.

Tip

A resource subdirectory is not deleted when you delete a project from the Workbench. If you are tight on disk space you may want to go to the file system and delete old or obsolete subdirectories in the IBMVJava/ide/ project_resources path.

Now let's create a new project for your first application with the following steps:

 In the Workbench, click the right mouse button on the upper pane. Select **Add Project**. You can also create a new project from the menu bar by selecting Selected => Add Project or by pressing the New Project icon.

A SmartGuide to aid you in creating a new project appears as shown in Figure 2.8. Enter **My Project** in the **Create a new project named** entry field. Press the Finish button to create the new project.

A new project called My Project was created in the IDE. The next thing to do is to create a package within this project that will contain all classes of the HelloWorld applet.

Packages

 With **My Project** selected, click the right mouse button on the top pane, and from the pop-up menu, select **Add Package**. You can also press the *New Package* icon from the tool bar.

Figure 2.8   Creating a new project.

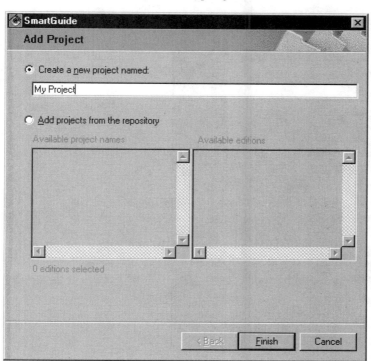

A SmartGuide to help you create a new package appears as shown in Figure 2.9. Enter **helloworld** in the **Create a new package named** entry field. Press the *Finish* button to create the package.

Packages are Java language elements and represent a logical group of classes that provide related services. Package names make up the directory structure of the classes they contain. Naming conventions are still evolving. The current trend is that package names start in lower case. Usually, when developing commercial packages, the company's Universal Resource Locator (URL) is used to make up the package name. The URL is used backwards; for example, IBM's URL is xxx.ibm.com, and any packages names originating from IBM start with com.ibm.xxx. As with most naming conventions, there are exceptions to the rule; that goes for naming conventions as well. You may see some old packages COM.ibm.xxx, with COM in uppercase like the ones used in VisualAge for Java Version 1 and earlier Java classes. This was changed for new packages as a convention starting about October of 1997. If you want to use the latest IBM classes, you will need to reference the new lowercase package names.

Figure 2.9   Creating a new package.

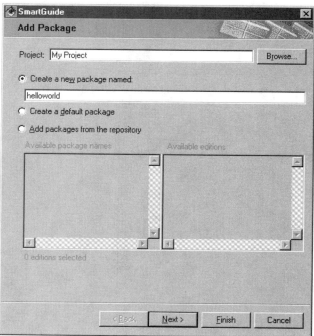

When it comes time to deploy your program, packages can be exported out of the VisualAge for Java environment in a single step. For more information on importing and exporting, see Chapter 7, "Building the Advanced Calculator Logic." Just remember that packages are subdirectories.

After you create the package, the Workbench should look like Figure 2.10.

Making a New GUI Bean

You might have skipped some of the introductory information at the beginning of this book because you already had the product installed. It is a good idea to follow these first few chapters very closely to begin understanding how the VisualAge for Java development environment works. These initial steps are somewhat detailed to help you become familiar with the graphical user interface and the tightly integrated IDE of VisualAge for Java. As you progress through the book, the steps will become briefer.

Next you will construct a simple applet that is just a window with the words *Hello World* and the current date in it. It is probably the simplest program you can build, and it is a good way to familiarize yourself with the IDE and VCE.

Figure 2.10   My Project and helloworld.

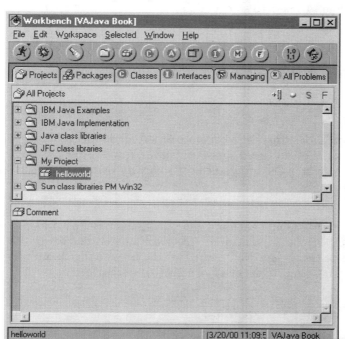

You can also write the Java code by hand, but the purpose of this book is to teach you how to use the many tools in VisualAge for Java. You will use the same steps when building more complex applications. In fact, you use these same steps throughout this book to build the visual components in most of the exercises.

Because you have already defined the project and the package in the IDE, you can start defining the applet. All classes must be in a project and a package. Technically you could skip using a package and this is referred to as a *default* package in Java. VisualAge for Java requires that you define a default package if you want to use one. It is strongly recommended that you use proper packages and not default packages.

The project and package provide the structure for the IDE to contain and catalog your classes (beans) in the repository. First, you will build and run the HelloWorld visual or GUI bean. Later, you will make a few changes to the user interface and add some function using connections, save your changes, and rerun the applet. VisualAge for Java has a new cool SmartGuide in Version 3 that asks a few questions, then generates the proper code for an applet. Initially, Hello World will be developed as a Java Applet, which means it can only run inside a web browser like Netscape Navigator, Internet Explorer or the JDK appletviewer.

To make an applet, the superclass for the HelloWorld class must be Applet, or more specifically, java.applet.Applet. To start building the Hello World applet with the SmartGuide by following these steps:

With the helloworld package selected, click the right mouse button on the top pane and from the pop-up menu, select **Add => Applet....** You could instead select the New Applet icon on the Workbench tool bar.

Tip

To simplify the SmartGuides, there is a separate SmartGuide for creating Interface classes. Interfaces are used heavily in Java. You will be using many of the Interfaces in the JDK and you can design your own Interfaces for business objects.

In the Create Applet SmartGuide, seen in Figure 2.11, enter **HelloWorld** in the Applet Name entry field. You can use the same SmartGuide to create JApplets and other applets. Make sure that the **Browse the class when finished** and the **Compose the class visually** items are selected, as

Figure 2.11   Create Applet SmartGuide.

![SmartGuide - Create Applet dialog box. Fields: Project: My Project; Package: helloworld; Applet name: HelloWorld; Superclass options: Applet (selected), JApplet, Other. Checkboxes: Browse applet when finished (checked), Compose the class visually (checked). Buttons: Back, Next>, Finish, Cancel.]

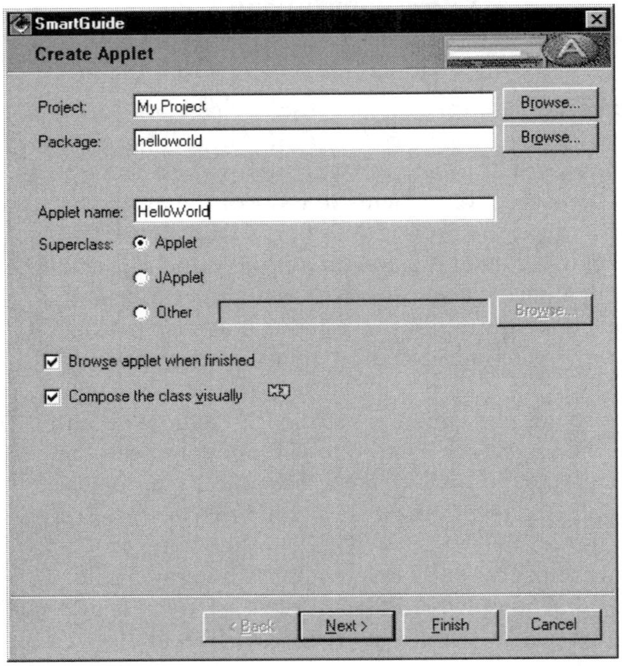

shown in Figure 2.11. These options automatically open the class browser to the Visual Composition Editor. Leave all the other items unchanged and then press Next.

The Applet Properties dialog appears as seen in Figure 2.12. This page gives you some helpful options for your applet. The first option generates the required methods for the applet to act as a WindowListener. The second option can be very useful as it generates the run(), start(), and stop() methods for running as a thread. The HelloWorld applet is pretty simple so this support is not necessary.

Naming conventions for Java classes are well defined. You can get more information on Java styles and conventions in *Sun's Java Look and Feel Design Guidelines,* published in June 1999. Class names start in uppercase, the beginning of each new word is also in uppercase, and no spaces are allowed. The SmartGuide warns you if you don't follow this convention. If you made a mistake entering the class name, the SmartGuide can automatically correct it.

Press the Next button and the Applet Events window displays as seen in Figure 2.13. This dialog generates the appropriate code to support KeyListener,

Figure 2.12   Applet properties.

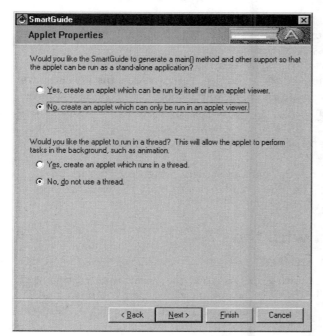

Figure 2.13   Applet Events.

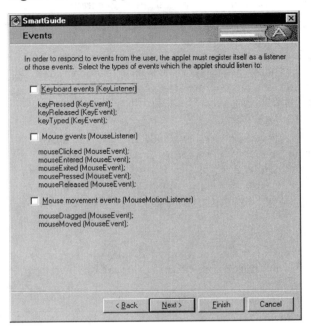

MouseListener, and MouseMotionListener. These can be helpful, but they are not needed for this applet, so press Next and continue.

The Code Writer window displays, as seen in Figure 2.14, providing even more methods that can be generated for an applet. You can press the Finish button and VisualAge for Java will generate an applet to the specifications that you have entered. For Enterprise Edition users, make sure you are working in an open edition of the project and package, and you are a user in the project/package group. You can also press Finish on any of the SmartGuide pages if you don't need any of the additional options.

The Visual Composition Editor opens as shown in Figure 2.15 with an empty HelloWorld applet. This window enables you to place the visual components that make up the HelloWorld applet.

Getting Acquainted with the Visual Composition Editor

The Visual Composition Editor is also referred to as the *Visual Builder*, because it is used to visually build your beans. It is the default view when you open a GUI bean, and it provides a lot of support for creating and modifying beans. You

Figure 2.14   Code Writer window.

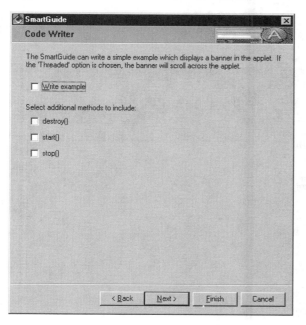

Figure 2.15   Visual Composition Editor.

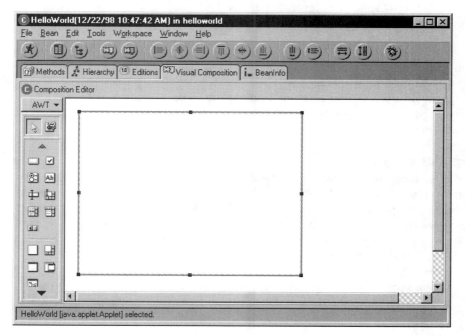

Figure 2.16 Visual Composition Editor areas.

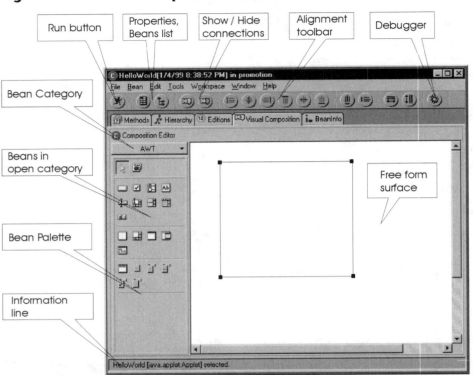

design the entire graphical user interface (GUI) for an application in the Visual Composition Editor.

The VCE is where you combine beans using visual connections to make composite beans and applications. The areas of the Visual Composition Editor are shown in Figure 2.16.

Categories and Beans

The Beans Palette is one column of icons on the left side of the VCE. The top of the column is a dropdown list of *categories* that can be selected. These categories hold beans grouped by common types like AWT, JFC, and so on. The column holds the beans contained in the currently selected category. Each category may contain many beans, so the arrows at the top and bottom of each column enable you to scroll through the category.

Hover help appears when you place the mouse pointer over a bean, and hold it there for a short time. Hover help makes it a lot easier to find the bean you need. A complete list of the default categories and beans is shown in Figure 2.17.

Figure 2.17   VisualAge beans.

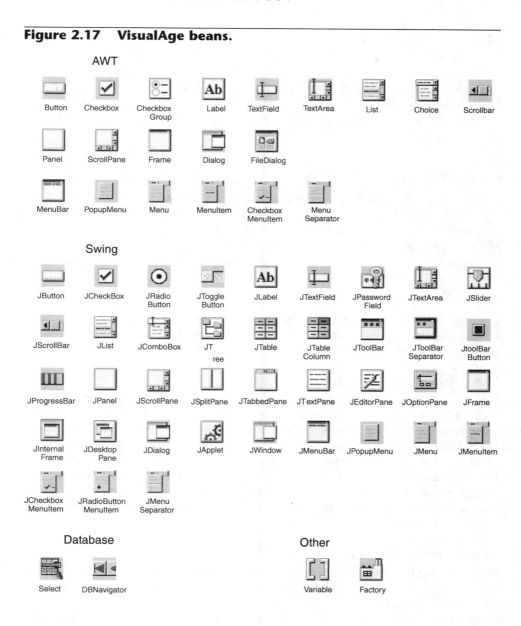

It is a good idea for you to copy it as a handy reference until you become familiar with the available categories and beans.

The Free-Form Surface

The large blank area in the center of the panel is called the *free-form surface*, as shown in Figure 2.16. This is where you construct the user interface for the application and where you add nonvisual beans or logic beans, those that represent business logic of your program. The free-form surface grows as you add more beans. You may have to scroll the free-form surface to reach beans that are not in the current work area.

> **NOTE**
>
> IBM uses the term free-form surface, but you will sometimes hear other terms such as *design area* and *white space*. VisualAge for Java is widely used by many programmers and some of them invent their own terms, especially when they don't read the documentation.

The free-form surface shows GUI beans exactly as they appear at run time. If your main bean is a Frame, its startup position is the same as the position of the window in the free-form surface, unless you write code to change its position.

Using Tool Bars

Just like many of the applications available today, the VCE has tool bars to make it easier for you to select functions. These are first-generation tool bars with very basic functions like showing a group of icons and enabling you to cause actions by pressing the icons. You can choose to hide the tool bar by selecting **Window => Options => Appearance** page. Unfortunately you cannot add your own buttons and functions to the tool bar. Many applications have second-generation tool bars that support drag and drop, have multiple views, and can be modified by the user at run time. However, you can edit and change the categories and folders in the VCE bean palette.

Visual Composition Editor Palette

The menu bar has equivalent items for all the icons on the tool bar, so you can hide the tool bar to save screen real estate. If you need more screen real estate in the VCE, you can also hide the Palette on the left of the window. You can do this by selecting the bar on the right side of the Palette and directly narrow the Palette. The size of the Palette is not saved with the bean, rather it is part of the Workbench settings. The next time you open the bean, the VCE does not display the tool bar. This will magically become the default setting for all VCEs. In the sample illustrations in this book, we use the default setting that shows the tool bar.

Making an Applet

Because you are creating a new GUI bean and you selected Applet as the parent class (or *superclass*), the Workbench opened with an Applet object in the free-form surface, as shown in Figure 2.15.

Applet provides very rich default behavior. The Applet class is a subclass of Panel, as shown in Figure 2.18. Look at the Hierarchy view by selecting the Hierarchy tab on the HelloWorld window. An Applet has all the display functions of a panel along with the ability to be loaded in a browser. Because the applet will run in a web browser, it can't be resized and repositioned at run time.

An AWT Applet acts like a canvas or panel; it is a Container of Components. You can place other AWT components like Buttons, Labels, TextFields, and many other types of GUI elements directly on an applet. The AWT controls are referred to as *heavyweight controls* because they use the native controls in the operating system. The Java Foundation Classes (JFC) are *lightweight controls* and manage their own rendering. Due to this fundamental difference, you will get unpredictable runtime behavior if you mix JFC or Swing components with AWT components. Let's go back to the VCE and start adding components to the HelloWorld applet:

Figure 2.18 HelloWorld hierarchy view.

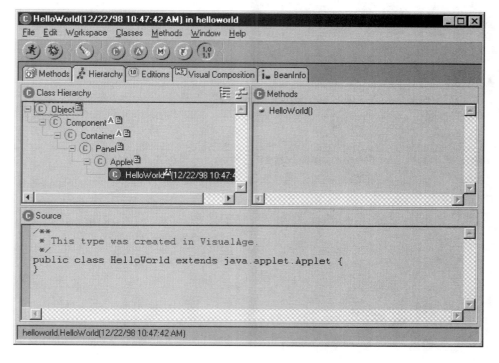

Select the Visual Composition tab on the HelloWorld applet.

Place the mouse pointer in the middle of the Applet and press the left mouse button to select the applet. The name of the selected Applet appears in the information area at the bottom of the VCE.

Java provides several layout managers that are used with containers to control the spacing and alignment of GUI elements. Because the HelloWorld applet is your first project, it is very simple and uses a *null* layout manager, which is technically the same as not using a layout manager. With a null layout manager, you are free to place and size other components on the applet anywhere you wish. Using a null layout manager is highly discouraged and considered poor design. Later, this book covers the standard layout managers by using them in other sample applications.

First HelloWorld is basically an applet with text saying *Hello World*, and then you add a button to display the current date. Because the Applet class inherits from the Container class, it is capable of containing other GUI elements that can display text. The proper class to use for this purpose is the **Label** class. Add a label to the applet with the following steps:

From the AWT category, select the Label icon using the left mouse button.

You have now loaded the mouse pointer with a Label bean to drop on the applet. You can see that it is loaded because the mouse pointer appears as a cross hair as it is moved over the free-form surface. If you picked the wrong bean, just go to the correct icon on the palette and select that icon. You can unload the pointer by selecting the arrow icon (also called the *Selection tool*) on the tool bar.

Move the mouse to the applet and press the left mouse button to place the Label bean.

You now have a Label on the Applet; your VCE should look like Figure 2.19.

Figure 2.19   Adding a Label bean.

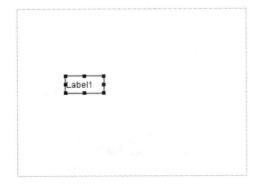

Naming Beans

You can select the various beans on the VCE by clicking the mouse pointer over them. Select the Label bean you have just added. In the information area at the bottom of the screen, the name of the bean, Label1, is displayed. Beans are given default names as they are dropped on the Applet. You should always name your beans using names that describe their function. This becomes very important as the components you build become more complex. The code generator uses the name you give a bean; using good names will help you understand and debug the generated code. To change the name of a bean, you have two options:

- Select the bean and click it with the right mouse button. Select **Change Bean Name** from the pop-up menu. Enter a meaningful name in the window provided.

- Double-click on the bean. This brings up the bean property sheet. In this window, you can change many properties of the bean, one of which is *beanName.*

Using either of these methods, change the name of the Label1 bean to **lbHello.** Usually you don't need to change the default name of a Label or a JLabel because you will not reference it in your Java code; you will use it merely as a label for text.

Editing Text

The default text for the lbHello bean is the same as the generated bean name **Label1.** For this applet, the text should be **Hello World.** To change the text for the label:

Double-click on the Label1 bean. This brings up the bean property sheet. In this window, you can change many properties of the bean, one of which is *text.* See Figure 2.20.

Figure 2.20   Label text changed.

Enter **Hello World** in the text property and press the Enter key to set this new property. You can also see the beanName in the property editor.

Changing Font Properties

> **NOTE**
>
> Direct editing a bean's text is not supported in VisualAge for Java except in Version 1. Direct editing is when you place the mouse pointer on a GUI bean, and press and hold the Alt key and the left mouse button. A small editing window allowed direct editing.

You probably need to stretch the lbHello Label to accommodate the full text. Move the tip of the mouse to any of the black squares in the corners of the selected lbHello bean, press and hold the left mouse button, and stretch the bean to make it bigger. Now, that it looks a little bit better, but it is still pretty plain. Let's change the font size and foreground color to make it look even better with the following:

Select lbHello by clicking once on the words **Hello World.**

Open the property sheet for lbHello by either pressing the right mouse button and selecting **Properties**, or by double-clicking the left mouse button. You can also press the Properties button on the tool bar.

Find the *font* property in the table. Click at the right end of the entry field for *font*. A small button appears; click it. This displays the Fonts window, as shown in Figure 2.21.

Select a font type, size, and style that looks good to you. For example, you could use bold italic style and a size of 24 points.

Select **OK** on the Fonts window to close it; then close the property editor to save your changes.

Your text should look like Figure 2.22. If the words **Hello World** appear clipped when the new font is applied, you have two choices:

- Select the Label bean and stretch the Label by dragging one of the little black boxes or handles on the Label bean until all of the text is displayed.

- Select the Label bean, bring up its property editor, and edit the width in the **constraints** properties to make it big enough to accommodate the text.

Figure 2.21   Changing the font attribute.

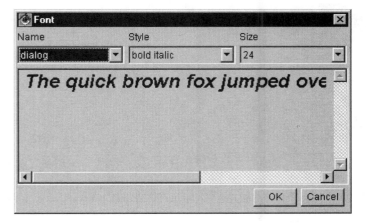

Generating Java Code

The next step is to save the applet and run it. As mentioned before, saving the bean also generates the Java code for all components in the VCE and incrementally compiles the code too.

> Select *Bean => Save Bean* from the menu bar to save the applet. A new edition is created for the bean and stored in the repository; it also becomes the current edition in the workspace. The Java code for the HelloWorld class is generated and compiled.

> To run the Applet, press the Run icon on the tool bar.

Figure 2.22   HelloWorld with changed font.

Figure 2.23 Hello World running.

Pressing the Run button causes the bean to be saved and recompiled if needed. It is equivalent to performing two steps with just one click. The HelloWorld applet runs in the applet viewer as shown in Figure 2.23. There is really nothing spectacular in Hello World, other than you just created your very first Java applet with VisualAge for Java. It compiled and ran without error and you didn't have to write a single line of code! Real VisualAge for Java programs require that you write code and you will have a chance to do this soon. You can rely on VisualAge for Java to generate most or all the code for the user interface and a lot of the high level calls to business logic.

You are probably interested in seeing the generated code. It can be seen in either the Members or the Hierarchy view for the HelloWorld class.

Select the Methods view for the HelloWorld window as shown in Figure 2.24.

You see a number of methods, as shown in Figure 2.24. These methods are:

- `getBuilderData()`
- `main()`
- `getAppletinfo()`
- `getlbHello()`
- `handleException()`
- `init()`
- `paint(Graphics)`

Figure 2.24   Generated methods.

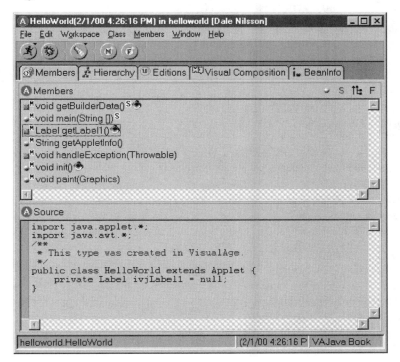

The getBuilderData() method is generated because you set the Workbench option to generate meta data method. This method contains an ASCII representation of the VCE-specific information. Do not edit this information or you will have problems re-importing this class.

Previously, we noted that one of the differences between Java applets and applications is that applets run within a browser and are governed by the security model for applets. Applications have their own frame, run stand-alone, and are not subject to the same security model as applets. Applets start running when the virtual machine (VM) in the web browser constructs the Applet instance and calls the init() and start() methods. Applications start running when a stand-alone virtual machine is started with the name of the class that contains the main() method. After instantiating the object, the main() method is called and execution starts.

You might be wondering why there is a main() method in the generated code of an applet. VisualAge for Java generates this method for all visual components. It exists so components can be tested in a stand-alone environment. Many times you will develop components, such as panels, that cannot be run on their own. In order to test them, you would have to wrap them in an Applet or a Frame. To save you that trouble, VisualAge for Java generates a main() method for them:

```
public static void main(java.lang.String[] args) {
  try {
    java.awt.Frame frame;
    try {
      Class aFrameClass = Class.forName
        ("com.ibm.uvm.abt.edit.TestFrame");
      frame = (java.awt.Frame)
        aFrameClass.newInstance();
    } catch (java.lang.Throwable ivjExc) {
      frame = new java.awt.Frame();
    }
    HelloWorld aHelloWorld;
    Class iiCls = Class.forName
      ("helloworld.HelloWorld");
    ClassLoader iiClsLoader =
      iiCls.getClassLoader();
    aHelloWorld = (HelloWorld)
      java.beans.Beans.instantiate
      (iiClsLoader,"helloworld.HelloWorld");
    frame.add("Center", aHelloWorld);
    frame.setSize(aHelloWorld.getSize());
    frame.setVisible(true);
  } catch (Throwable exception) {
    System.err.println("Exception occurred in
      main() of java.applet.Applet");
    exception.printStackTrace(System.out);
  }
}
```

Let's examine the generated main() method for the HelloWorld a applet in more detail:

- The main() function starts the application.

- A specialized kind of Frame, a TestFrame, is instantiated to hold the Applet. This frame knows how to close itself.

- A new HelloWorld bean is allocated in memory by the **java.beans.Beans.instantiate** call to the class loader.

- The new aHelloWorld instance is added to the center of the frame object.

- The size of the frame is set to the size of the applet.

- The frame is set to be visible and, by doing so, given focus.

- When the frame is closed, the aHelloWorld instance is destroyed.

All of this is coded within the proper, and necessary, try and catch blocks to handle any exceptions that might occur. There will be more on exception handling, the way Java handles errors see Chapter 7.

You can reposition the HelloWorld window on the screen by pointing to the title bar, holding down the left mouse button, and dragging the window. You can also change the size of the HelloWorld window by selecting one of the window edges with the left mouse button and moving the mouse. As the window resizes, the **Hello World** text stays in the same relative position in the window because the applet has no associated layout manager. In a later chapter you learn how to use layout managers to improve this behavior.

Adding More Function to Hello World

Now that you have built a very simple applet, you can add more function and iterate on the Hello World program. Return to the HelloWorld VCE.

You will add function to show the current date in the applet. You will add another Label and a Date class and make a visual connection to complete this function. This is accomplished, without writing any code, using the following steps:

1. Click on the Label icon using the left mouse button.

2. Move the mouse pointer to the applet below the Hello World text, and press the left mouse button to drop the Label bean onto the applet.

3. Name this **Bean lbDate.** (See "Naming Beans" earlier in this chapter.)

This bean will hold the current date read from the system. Stretch this Label bean so that it accommodates all the characters for a timestamp.

Next, you will add a Button bean that will set the Label to display the current date:

1. Click on the **Button** icon using the left mouse button.

2. Move the mouse pointer to the applet below the Hello World text, and press the left mouse button to drop the Button bean on to the applet.

Now the applet has a button. To change the default text of Button1, directly edit the text on the bean:

1. Open the property editor for the Button1 bean by double clicking the mouse over the bean.

2. Enter **Set Date** in the Label property.

3. Name this Bean **pbSetDate.**

> **NOTE**
> Accelerator keys are not supported in Java AWT V1.1; however, they are supported in Java 2 or JDK 1.2.

Figure 2.25   New beans added.

The HelloWorld bean should now look like Figure 2.25.

Selecting Beans

As you have seen, the left mouse button is used to select the beans. To select multiple beans, select the first bean; then press and hold the Ctrl key and click the left mouse button over any other beans you wish to select. The last bean selected is the one used as a reference when aligning all selected beans.

The beans on the applet need to be aligned so that they are centered. The default layout in the VCE is **null**. This means that no alignment or sizing is done within the applet at run time. This can create some serious problems when you run the applet at a different resolution. As mentioned previously, this book covers layouts in later chapters. For now you can use the null layout, but only because you are doing a quick and dirty example.

Using the Ctrl key, select the **lbDate**, the **Hello World** Label, and the **pbSetDate** Button. All of the selected beans have boxes around them, and the last bean selected has black boxes or handles to indicate it will be used as a reference.

 Press the **align center** icon to position the GUI beans in the applet.

There are also buttons to align to the left, right, top, bottom, and middle. You can try these functions to see what they do, but they only work on a null layout.

Making Connections

When the applet runs and the user presses the pbSetDate button, it should set the text of lbDate to the current date. To achieve this without VisualAge for Java, you would need to write some Java code. VisualAge for Java introduces the construction from parts paradigm, that enables you to build event-driven logic by connecting predesigned components. First, add a Date bean to the applet with the following steps:

At the top of the bean palette, select the Choose Bean Button, and the Add Bean window appears.

NOTE

There is no keyboard accelerator, such as control-B, to bring up the Add Bean dialog as there was in Version 1. Send comments to www.software.ibm.com/ad/vajava.

In the Class Name field, enter **Date**, and then select the Browse button. You must fully qualify any Java classes you add to an applet. The **java.util** package is the only currently loaded package with a Date class, so it is highlighted.

Select the OK button to close this window. Enter **aDate** in the Name entry field to properly name this bean as seen in Figure 2.26.

Select the OK button to close the Choose Bean window.

Now the cursor is loaded with the Date bean. Move the mouse to the free-form surface and press the left mouse button to place the Date bean. Notice that because aDate is not a GUI bean, you are not allowed to drop it on top of the Applet.

Make a connection from the **pbSetDate** Button to the **lbDate** bean to set it with the current date when the button is pressed, as follows:

Place the mouse over the **pbSetDate** button, and press the right mouse button to get the context menu.

Figure 2.26   Adding a Date bean.

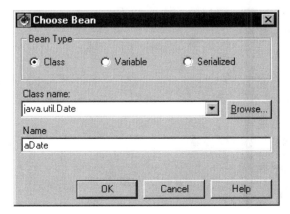

Select **Connect** from the context menu.

This displays the preferred features list for a Button bean seen in Figure 2.27. This is a short list of the most commonly selected connection items. Some items on the preferred list can be disabled or gray. The VCE prevents you from making some types of improper connections by graying out improper or invalid options.

Select the **actionPerformed** Event by clicking the left mouse button. This is the source of the connection.

The mouse pointer changes its shape and looks like a spider attached by its web to the source of the connection. Now select a target for it. The spider needs a place to land.

Move the spider to lbDate in the HelloWorld applet, and press the left mouse button to select the target for the connection. Notice that as the spider pointer moves over the objects on the VCE they receive focus, clearly indicating the object you are about select.

This displays the preferred features list for the Label object shown in Figure 2.28.

Figure 2.27   Selecting the source connection.

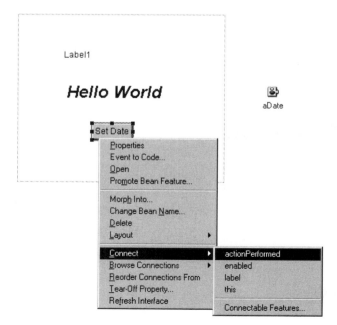

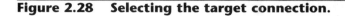

Figure 2.28 Selecting the target connection.

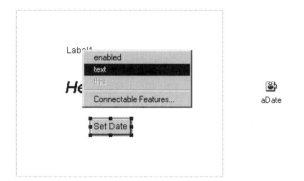

Select the *text* item on the menu. Now you see a dashed line connecting the pbSetDate and the lbDate objects. A dashed line indicates that the connection is incomplete. For now, this is correct, because parameter is missing—we haven't yet told the connection what to set as the text when the button is pressed.

To complete the connection, pass a parameter into the connection with the following steps:

Move the mouse pointer so its tip is on the line representing the connection; press the left mouse button to select the connection. This displays a description of the connection listed in the information area at the bottom of the VCE. This is one way to find out what a connection does. Now make the following connection to pass the current date to the Label:

Select the connection from **pbSetDate** to **lbDate.**

Making sure that the tip of the mouse pointer is not over one of the handles or black squares on the connection, press the right mouse button to display the pop-up menu.

Select **Connect =>value.**

Move the mouse to the aDate object on the free-form surface; then press the left mouse button.

Select **Connectable Features => methods, ;** a dialog appears. Select the methods radio button, and select the **Date()** constructor method to complete the connection and close the connection window. The HelloWorld applet should look like Figure 2.29.

Figure 2.29   Connection completed.

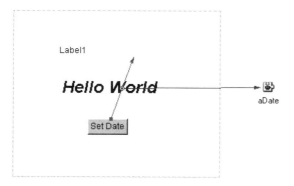

Saving and Running the Improved Hello World Applet

Now you are ready to save and test your changes. It is really easy in the IDE: Just select the Run button on the tool bar. The VCE saves the changes and compiles them into the workspace image. When you run the HelloWorld applet, it looks like Figure 2.30.

When the applet starts, the date does not appear in the lbDate object; you see the default text of Label1. When you press the Set Date button, the date and time replace the default text.

As you can see, it is very easy to create a graphical application with some basic function without writing any code! VisualAge for Java can generate most or all of the user interface code for your applications. Visual connections enable you to call methods in Java classes using event-driven programming.

Applet Properties

You may have noticed that the applet viewer may not show the entire applet and need to be resized. An applet's size is set as parameters to the <applet> in your HTML. These parameters are not part of the Java code so the are stored as properties of the HelloWorld applet class. You can view and edit these properties by the following:

Select the HelloWorld class in the Workbench, and from the pop-up menu select *properties*. The Properties window displays as seen in Figure 2.31. In this window, you can change the applet's width and height, and VisualAge for Java will use these settings when you run the applet. You can still set the applet size in the VCE, but the property setting for the applet tag will determine the display area for the applet. The Properties window is modal, so you must close it before proceeding.

Figure 2.30   Running applet.

Viewing the Generated Code

For this simple sample, you can review the code generated by VisualAge for Java by switching to the Methods or Hierarchy view of the browser. Probably the most interesting piece of code in this applet is the code generated by the connection. VisualAge for Java Version 3 generates different code than Version 2. Note that connections in the VCE are just development artifacts. They are translated into 100 percent pure Java code when the code is generated.

To see the generated code for any connection, the first step is to find out the connection number. You do this by selecting the connection (clicking it with the mouse) and looking in the information area of the VCE. In this case, we are interested in connEtoM1; a corresponding connEtoM1 method can be found in the Members view. Notice that not all connections are translated into code: In this example, there is no method called connPfromM1 for the parameter connection. We are using the new default code generation using one inner class as seen in the following code segment:

```
class IvjEventHandler implements java.awt.event.ActionListener {
  public void actionPerformed(java.awt.event.ActionEvent e) {
    if (e.getSource() == HelloWorld.this.getpbSetDate())
      connEtoM1(e);
    };
  };
```

Figure 2.31 HelloWorld properties.

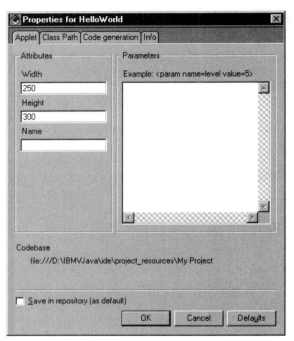

This inner class **IvjEventHandler** does all the dispatching for the applet's events. The only event is the ActionEvent from the pbSetDate button. When this event happens, the connEtoM1() method, shown in the next code segment, is called and executed:

```
private void connEtoM1(java.awt.event.ActionEvent arg1) {
  try {
    // user code begin {1}
    // user code end
    getlbDate().setText(String.valueOf(new java.util.Date()));
    // user code begin {2}
    // user code end
  } catch (java.lang.Throwable ivjExc) {
    // user code begin {3}
    // user code end
    handleException(ivjExc);
  }
}
```

There are a number of interesting points to observe in the code segment for the preceding connEtoM1 method:

- Comments are inserted at the beginning of the class. They are in Javadoc format and can be generated to an HTML file using VisualAge for Java.

- Possible exceptions are handled by generating the appropriate try and catch blocks.

- The code for this method is regenerated every time anything is changed and saved for the HelloWorld applet. Any modifications to this method will be lost the next time code is generated. To preserve your modifications, make them inside one of the user code areas.

```
// user code begin {1}
// Your code here
// user code end
```

- You cannot make your own user code areas, but you will find that they are automatically generated in the appropriate places.

- This line of code does all the significant work in the method getLBDate().

```
getlbDate().setText(String.valueOf(new java.util.Date()));
```

In Java, as in C++ and Smalltalk, messages to an object can be chained as long as the return type of the message is compatible with the next message. In this case, `getlbDate()` gets a reference to the lbDate object. If you look in this method, you will see that if it doesn't exist, the lbDate object is created. The `setText()` method, just as its name implies, sets the text of lbDate.

The next instruction is really the code generated by connPfromM1, the parameter for the connection. The code `String.valueOf(new java.util .Date()`, makes a new Date object, and then asks it for its string representation, which in the case of a Date object is a formatted String with the date and time the object was created. Each time this method is called, it will construct a new Date object. So each time you press the press the *Set Date* Button, the current date is displayed. Pretty cool for not writing any code.

Now you can see why naming your beans is important. Reviewing the generated code would be a lot more difficult with the default bean names.

Attribute Filters

The Members page can get very cluttered with all the methods and fields in a class. VisualAge for Java has a way to control this view called attribute filters. In the Members page, select *Attribute filters* and the dialog opens appears as shown in Figure 2.32. In this window, you can choose to see just the public methods and

Figure 2.32   Attribute Filters.

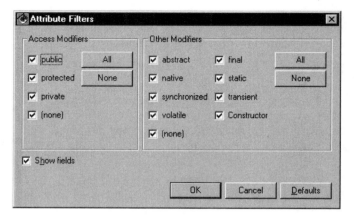

remove fields from this view. You can also use the new attribute filters on the toolbar to quickly screen public methods and fields. Close the Attribute Filters window when you are finished.

When you are done with the HelloWorld window, select the system icon in the upper left corner of the applet viewer and select **Close** to end this applet.

Summary

Well, you are off to a good start. You've built a very simple Java application using VisualAge for Java. In this chapter, you:

- Became familiar with making projects and packages.
- Customized the Workbench with options.
- Learned the basic workings of the Visual Composition Editor using simple beans to design an applet.
- Made some visual connections.
- Edited beans to change their default attributes.
- Saved a JavaBean definition and generated Java code.
- Ran the compiled applet and saw the many default features of the application by using AWT.
- Changed applet properties.

Now that you have learned the basics, you are ready to start building more Java programs in VisualAge for Java.

Making an Adding Machine

3

What's in Chapter 3

You have completed the Hello World applet and probably think programming in Java is very easy. This is one of the simplest Java applications you can develop other than the infamous "to do list" sample. Each chapter of this book increases in difficulty and complexity, and this chapter covers visual programming in more detail. You will build a logic bean and combine it with GUI beans to make an adding machine. You will write some simple Java code for the logic bean to perform the calculation function. This chapter covers the following topics:

JavaBeans basics

- GUI beans
- Nonvisual beans
- Composite beans
- Overview of Layout Managers

Building an Adding Machine

- Using a GridLayout
- Using TextFields
- Setting the tab order of GUI beans
- Adding the contents of two TextFields

As you go through this book, we cover some object-oriented and visual development concepts. Many books exhaustively cover a particular object-oriented methodology or specific design technique. Because this book focuses on implementation, it covers only those object-oriented design concepts necessary to understand the applications you are building. The Adding Machine applet uses the Model-View-Controller design pattern that is common in object-oriented programming. First, you build the view, then you build the model part. This is okay, but in real life you will usually develop the model parts first; then you develop the view parts, because view (or GUI) parts should not influence the implementation of model parts. It is unrealistic to say that view parts have no influence on model parts, but this influence should be minimal.

Now that you have completed a simple HelloWorld applet, it's time to look back at the steps and understand how you built it. Before you go on to more complex programs, you need to understand the different types of JavaBeans. This will help you design and implement your own Java applications. The JavaBeans specification is a fundamental concept of JDK Version 1.1, and you need to understand JavaBeans to fully utilize VisualAge for Java.

JavaBeans Basics

The notion of JavaBeans was introduced in JDK 1.1; VisualAge for Java uses JavaBeans and generates JavaBeans. End users of a program using JavaBeans neither know nor have to care that JavaBeans were used. JavaBeans were introduced primarily to assist Java developers; there are many changes to the JDK to support JavaBeans. In this section, you will learn the basics behind JavaBeans, and in later chapters, you will learn more detailed information about JavaBeans classes and methods. JavaBeans are used throughout this book and in Chapter 14, "Servlets" and Chapter 15, "Using Enterprise JavaBeans," you learn how to use JavaBeans in server-side programming. JDK 1.2 builds on JavaBeans basics and adds methods and new classes, but many of the package names are different.

> **NOTE**
> There is a separate version of VisualAge for Java that supports JDK 1.2 that you need to install if you want to use these new Java features. If you move Java code from JDK 1.1 to JDK 1.2, you will also need to modify the code to reflect the new package names.

Different types of beans or classes are used in the Visual Composition Editor (VCE). There are *GUI* beans, *logic* beans (also called invisible or nonvisual beans), and *composite* beans. This section explains the three types of beans. These JavaBeans terms are used by all Java different tools that support JavaBeans, and they are different from the traditional VisualAge terms that have been used for years. If you are a veteran VisualAge developer, you will recognize that GUI beans are the same as Visual Parts, and logic or invisible beans are the same as Nonvisual Parts.

What Are JavaBeans?

GUI beans and logic beans are Java classes, but there is a bit more to it than that. A comprehensive JavaBeans specification that covers all requirements for a JavaBeans component is available from the Sun web site at www.javasoft.com. There are two key requirements for JavaBeans. First they must have a default constructor that takes no parameters. Classes can have many construcotrs, but the visual builder tools rely on the default constructor to instantiate the class.

Secondly JavaBeans need to be serializable, which means the class declaration needs to implement **Serializable** and implement the appropriate methods. VisualAge for Java does not require that JavaBeans implement serizable as most other Java development IDEs. In Chapter 8, "Deploying Java," you will see how to use nondefault constructors in the VCE.

> **NOTE**
>
> Default constructors can call nondefault constructors, ones that require parameters. You can do this in the constructor code by hard coding default values for the parameters. This may not seem like a good idea, but remember that you just need a JavaBeans instance at development time and you can change properties later.

A few Java books cover the bean specification in great depth, and there are a ton of articles that give various varying overviews of JavaBeans. If you are a Java tool developer, you need to be acquainted with what is needed for JavaBeans. Studying at least one in-depth book on the bean specification is helpful but not required, but it would not hurt. Fortunately, VisualAge for Java generates JavaBeans and therefore insulates you from some of the technical details relating to JavaBeans. However, it is important for you to understand how JavaBeans work.

The entire JDK class library was updated to support JavaBeans, including the new V1.1 event model. You can see how the event model works by examining the code generated by VisualAge for Java. Because the JDK classes implement new methods supporting the new event model, all AWT-based classes inherit these special functions, which support the notification or messaging framework in the JDK class library. Implementation of a notification framework enables beans to notify or send messages to other beans. This critical function is what enables you to build program elements by making connections. As stated previously, this changes the way you develop your Java applications (it is better object orientation), but the end user will not notice any difference.

Deprecated Methods

Java 1.0 classes will work with Java 1.1 run-time support, but the Java 1.0 classes do not use the methods implementing the different event model in JDK 1.1. Although many Java V1.0 classes are beans, they are stale beans that need some refining to be fully compatible with other JavaBeans. A number of methods in the JDK class library were replaced by new methods, and these obsolete methods are referred to as *deprecated methods*. An example of a deprecated method is the

Button **enable**() method, which is replaced with the setEnable(true) method. These old methods work in the compiler and at run time in the virtual machine, but eventually, they will not be supported. It is a good idea to use the new JDK methods.

Types of Beans

The most atomic or granular bean is called a *primitive* bean. GUI and invisible beans can be primitive beans. Examples of primitive beans from the Java class library are Button, which is a GUI bean, and Color, which is an invisible bean. You can change the settings and default properties of primitive beans in the VCE.

Beans can be combined to create *composite* beans. When you combine two or more logic beans, you have a composite logic bean. For example, if you are building the logic component of a Clock bean, you could combine the Timer and Date logic beans in a composite logic bean named **Clock**. The Clock bean would supply the services you would expect from such a bean, such as setting and getting the time and date.

You create a composite GUI bean when you combine a GUI bean with one or more other beans. For example, you can combine the previously discussed logic Clock bean with a user interface bean that displays the time and date and has buttons to perform the various clock functions. You could call this bean a **ClockView** bean as shown in Figure 3.1. In fact, the clock could have multiple views like digital, analog, or a combination, where the date is shown in digital format and the time as a traditional clock with hands ticking.

GUI Beans

GUI beans are user interface controls in the AWT or JFC class library, such as Button, TextField, and JFrame. The VCE generates Java code for all of the GUI beans. GUI beans supplied with the VCE are sometimes called *controls* or *widgets*. The terms *controls* and *widgets* came about because the higher level definitions in the Java AWT essentially map to the underlying graphical API for each windowing system running Java; whereas the JFC controls do not directly map to the operating system graphical controls. When talking about GUI beans in this book, we will refer to them as beans or controls interchangeably.

Figure 3.1   ClockView composite GUI part.

All GUI beans are subclasses of **Component**, which is an abstract base class in the Java class library. The **Component** class sets the base behavior for all user interface controls and for **Container**, too. You can see this inheritance relationship in Figure 3.2.

Finding Beans

You may want to search for other JavaBeans in the Workspace when you are developing Java programs. Let's try searching for *Applet* with the following steps:

 On the Workbench toolbar, select **Search the** button.

The Search dialog appears, as shown in Figure 3.3, allowing you to enter the following:

Enter **Applet** in the Search String field.

Select **Workspace** radio button for the Scope.

Select **Declarations** radio button for the Usage.

Press the **Start** button to begin the search.

If there are no matches to the search string, the short message **No matches found** appears at the bottom of the Search dialog. It's a bit subtle, so be careful because you may think VisualAge for Java is still searching. Also take care not to waste time searching the entire Workspace for a common class reference. You can always click the **Stop** button to end a search that is out of control. Once the Search Results window opens, as shown in Figure 3.4, you can view the declaration and methods in the Java Applet class.

You will often search for a method or a class that is referenced in many places. When the search returns a list, you usually open a view or browser to inspect the class in detail. Open a browser for the Applet by selecting the Applet in the upper left pane, and from its pop-up menu select the **Open** menu item.

When the Class browser opens, select the Hierarchy tab on the view as shown in Figure 3.5.

Figure 3.2   Button inheritance hierarchy.

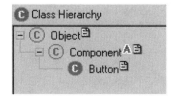

Figure 3.3 Search dialog.

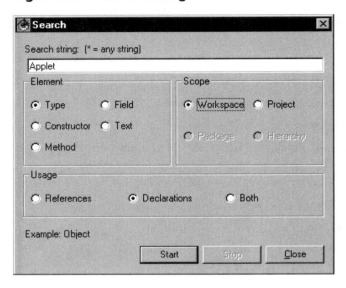

Now that you have found the Applet class, you can browse its definition and learn more about the class and its superclasses. If you ever need information about a bean, the search feature in the IDE is a fast way to get to that information. It will also verify whether the class is loaded in the Workspace and available to use.

Figure 3.4 Search results.

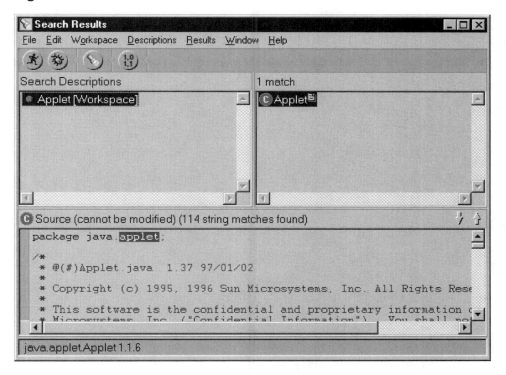

Scoping a Search

VisualAge for Java Version 3 has a new search feature called a *Working Set*. When you are working on certain projects or packages in the IDE, you can define a Working Set that uses these project or packages for a search. Searching a Working Set is much faster than searching the entire Workbench for a class definition. Let's set up a Working Set with the following steps:

Press the Search button and the Search Dialog displays as shown in Figure 3.6.

Select the **Working Set** radio button, and press **Choose,** and the Choose dialog displays.

Select the **New** button on the Choose dialog and another dialog displays.

Enter **Hanoi** for the Working Set name.

Figure 3.5 Applet hierarchy.

Select the com.ibm.ivj.examples.hanoi package in the tree view on the left side of the window as shown in Figure 3.7.

As you can see from Figure 3.7, a Working Set can have a number of projects or packages. You can now use the Hanoi Working Set to easily limit searches to that package. The Working Set definition is saved with the Workspace and can be revised or deleted in the future. When you are finished, close the Search dialog.

Logic Beans

Logic or nonvisual beans contain business logic, such as mathematical computation, data access functions, and application logic. The JDK class libraries come with a number of logic beans that are very helpful in building applications. Most of these beans are designed for general-purpose use, and in many cases, they need to be subclassed to add application-specific function. Figure 3.8 shows the composition of the ClockView application, combining both GUI and logic beans.

Figure 3.6   Search Working Set.

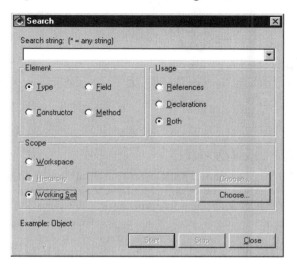

Logic JavaBeans are part of good object oriented design because they allow the use of Model-View separation. This allows you to isolate or encapsulate the logic from its view or visual representation. The logic beans can be reused with other views and can be moved to a server.

Figure 3.7   New Working Set.

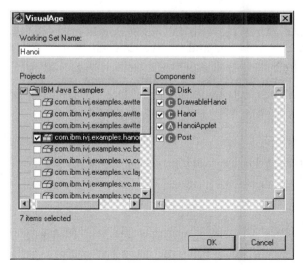

Figure 3.8   ClockView composite with logic beans.

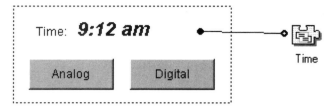

Building an Adding Machine

In this chapter, you will build an Adding Machine application that combines GUI and logic beans. First, you will construct the GUI bean, CalculatorView, and then you will develop a logic bean, Calc, that you will use in combination with the GUI bean to perform the calculations.

The Adding Machine enables you to enter two numbers, press a button to add the contents of the two TextFields, and display the result in the output field. The application window has:

Three TextFields, two for accepting the numbers to be added and one to display the result

Three Labels for the TextFields

A Button for the Add function

A logic bean, which performs the addition and signals that the operation has been performed and that the result property in the Calc bean has changed

Let's begin by making a new applet in the Visual Composition Editor to build the view of the Adding Machine. You will build and test the CalculatorView GUI bean before building the Calc logic bean. This is a new application, so you should make a new package before starting the new class. By creating the new package, you keep the classes, methods, and ultimately the files for the different applications separate. If the VisualAge for Java Workbench is not started, restart it now.

Creating a New Package

First, create the new package for this program in the project used for the Hello World applet.

In the Workbench, move to the upper pane and select the **My Project** project.

If you skipped Chapter 2, "Building the Hello World Applet," you need to create a new project in the Workbench. From the menu bar, select

Figure 3.9 Add Project SmartGuide.

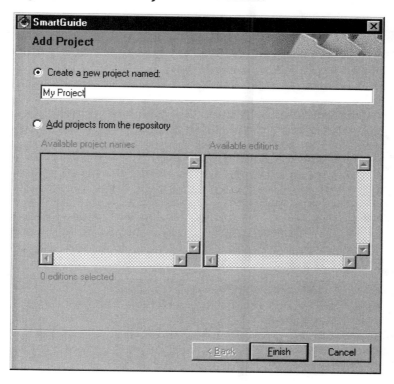

Selected => Add => Project, or else select the **Project** icon on the tool bar. This displays the project SmartGuide, as shown in Figure 3.9, where you can enter the project name. Once you have a project to add new classes, you can proceed.

The next thing to do is to create the package, which will contain all the components of the Simple Adder applet.

With My Project selected, right-click on the top pane, and from the pop-up menu select **Add Package**.

In the **Create a new package named** entry field, enter **calculator** and click. Press the **Finish** button to create the package, as shown in Figure 3.10.

After the calculator package is created, your Workbench should look like Figure 3.11.

Creating a New Class

Now that you have defined the project and the package in the IDE, you can start defining the beans that will make up the Simple Adder. The project and package

Figure 3.10   Add Package SmartGuide.

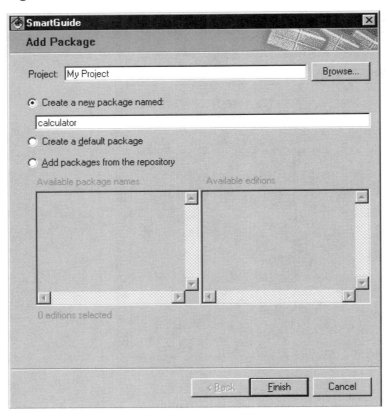

Figure 3.11   Workbench with My Project and calculator package.

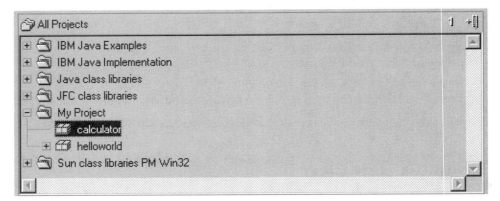

Figure 3.12 Create Class SmartGuide.

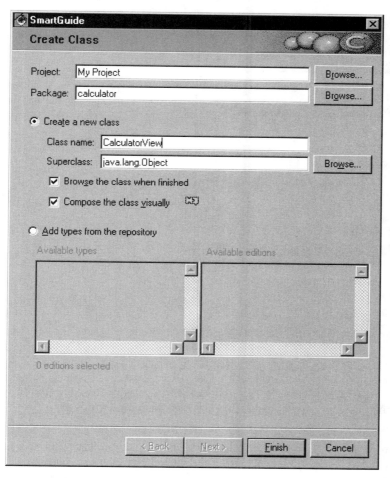

provide the structure for the IDE to contain and catalog your beans in the Workspace. Packages are also used when exporting your Java classes. To begin building the CalculatorView with the following steps:

With the calculator package selected, right-click the top pane, and from the pop-up menu select **Add => Class**.

In the Create Class SmartGuide shown in Figure 3.12, enter **CalculatorView** in the **Class name** entry field.

Make sure you capitalize the class name. It is a Java convention to capitalize class or bean names, and this is for a very good reason. Beans have constructors

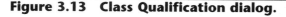

Figure 3.13 Class Qualification dialog.

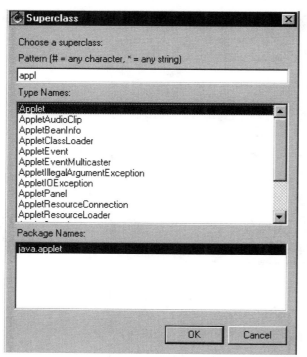

that are essentially methods with no return value. Capitalizing bean names makes it is easy to identify constructors, because they are capitalized methods with the same name as the bean.

Press the **Browse** button opposite the **Superclass** entry field, and type the word **Applet** to select the Applet class from the java.applet package. Notice that as you type in the SuperClass Dialog, the choice of class names is narrowed down as shown in Figure 3.13. You may need to use the scroll bar in the *Type Names:* list to see the Applet class listed at the top.

Once the Applet bean is selected, press the **OK** button to save this selection, and close the Class Qualifications Dialog.

Make sure that the **Design the class visually** radio button is selected on the Smart Guide, as shown in Figure 3.12. This radio button is merely a convenience; it causes the browser to automatically open to the VCE.

Press the **Finish** button to complete the specifications for the applet so VisualAge for Java can generate the code to create the **CalculatorView**

Figure 3.14 Visual Composition Editor.

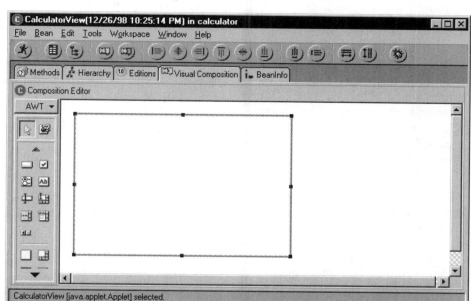

class. You can use the standard class SmartGuide for simple applets. Later you will use this same SmartGuide to make logic JavaBeans.

The VCE now opens, enabling you to place the visual components that make up the CalculatorView, as shown in Figure 3.14. The browser for the CalculatorView class automatically opens to the VCE page because you told the SmartGuide that you wanted to design this class visually. This is primarily a convenience—you can simply open a visual class in the Workbench and flip to the VCE page at any time. As you develop Java programs using the VCE in this book, many of the screen captures in the VCE will show the design surface and omit the toolbar and other areas when they aren't used.

Layout Managers

The HelloWorld applet was built using no Layout Manager; actually, it had a Layout Manager set to *null*. Using a null layout is not a good design, because it uses pixel coordinates to position the controls. This creates a new variation for Java applications: write once and run anywhere, but it will look different with different browsers and various screen resolutions. The net effect is that a perfectly aligned applet on your screen may appear jumbled and ugly elsewhere. Java

Layout Managers are provided to handle the run-time alignment and positioning of GUI JavaBeans. Layout Managers are properties of Java **Containers**, so the Layout Manager can be easily set in the property sheet.

Tip

There is a real cool stealth feature in VisualAge for Java Version 3.0 that transforms a null Layout to a GridBagLayout automatically. You will see how this feature works in Chapter 6, "Building the Advanced Calculator GUI." This feature provides one way to use a good GridBag layout, but you still should become familiar with the different layout managers and their behavior.

Containers can use one of the Layout Managers in the JDK or you can also make your own Layout Managers. This means that Frames, Applets, and Panels can all have their own Layout Managers. In this chapter, you will use GridLayout; later, when you build the Advanced Calculator, you will use multiple panels with different Layout Managers. When you combine Containers with different Layout Managers, you must be careful, because the different Layout Managers can produce conflicting behavior that will not provide the result you expect. This program is an Applet, and because an Applet is a Container, it will have its own Layout Manager.

Layout Managers are used to align, space, and size controls placed on an Applet, Panel or other Container. There are several types of Layout Managers, and only experience will make you comfortable using them. Following are some of the basic Layout Managers in the JDK:

- BorderLayout
- BoxLayout
- CardLayout
- FlowLayout
- GridBagLayout
- GridLayout

Each Layout Manager provides its own behavior and can be customized within the VCE. Each standard Layout Manager subclasses Object and implements either the LayoutManager or LayoutManager2 interface. Many Containers have a default Layout Manager if no Layout Manager is specified. It is best to specify the Layout Manager to insure your Container will perform as you expect. There is also a layout called *null*, which forces the positions of GUI beans to be fixed in the Container. In later chapters, you will use other Layout Managers like the Border, Flow, and GridBag layouts.

Custom Layouts

The VCE lists all the Java Layout Managers in a Container's property sheet. Version 3 includes all user-defined Layout Managers loaded in the Workspace. If you create your own Layout Manager, it can now be used in the VCE.

The VCE always generates a setLayout() method in the init() method of an Applet. The code for the init() method is shown in the next section. You would enter the code for the setLayout() method in a user code area provided in the generated code. All of the other code is regenerated, so you should put code here at your own risk. You can see the warning in the code that this method will be regenerated, and you will lose changes to the source code.

You can change the comment heading for regenerated methods. This can be found in the Workbench Options dialog. You can also add comments to the user code areas. The following code for the CalculatorView init() method, viewable from the Methods page, shows some user exits for Java code:

```
/**
 * Handle the Applet init method.
 */
/* WARNING: THIS METHOD WILL BE REGENERATED. */
public void init() {
  super.init();
  try {
    setName("CalculatorView");
    setLayout(null);
    setSize(300, 203);
    // user code begin {1}
    // user code end
  } catch (java.lang.Throwable ivjExc) {
    // user code begin {2}
    // user code end
    handleException(ivjExc);
  }
}
```

Using a GridLayout

For the Adder applet, you will use GridLayout, which is used when you want to align a number of same-sized beans. This layout is frequently used for entry forms, because it can keep TextFields and Labels aligned.

Place the mouse over the applet and open its property sheet.

Select the **layout** field, which then displays a button.

Select the Layout Manager drop-down list, and select GridLayout from the list as shown in Figure 3.15.

Figure 3.15 Layout properties.

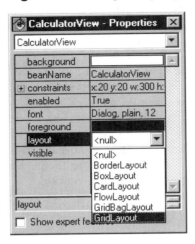

Now that you have changed the layout to GridLayout, some properties for the GridLayout are displayed in the property editor. The Visual Composition Editor assumes 1 row and 0 columns. You will usually need to change these properties to achieve the results that you want instead of what the default GridLayout behavior. Use the following steps to set properties for GridLayout:

Expand the layout + in the property editor.

Set the **columns** to **1**.

Set the **rows** to **7**.

Close the property sheet to save these changes. The Applet will not look any different, because the Layout Manager will only affect the GUI beans placed on it, and currently the Applet has no GUI beans.

Adding GUI Beans to a GridLayout

The Simple Adder needs the GUI beans for the user interface. Add the needed GUI beans to the GridLayout with the following steps:

First, make the Applet smaller by resizing it. Select the Applet with the left mouse button, select one of the handles (the black squares in the corners), and drag the handle to resize the Applet.

Place three **Label** beans alternating with three **TextField** controls on the GridLayout on the applet. See Figure 3.16 for suggested placing of controls. You may need to drag and drop some of the controls until you like the Applet's appearence. The ability to dynamically reposition GUI JavaBeans is very helpful in designing user interfaces.

Figure 3.16   Applet with GUI beans.

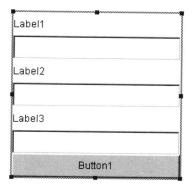

Tip

VisualAge for Java Version 1 had a **Sticky** checkbox to make it easier to drop multiple controls of the same type. Version 3 does not have the Sticky checkbox—you need to press the Ctrl key when you select the icon in the VCE palette. You can also use the clipboard copy/paste features to copy several of the same controls. You can even use copy/paste to copy JavaBeans between different VCE windows.

 Select a **Button,** move the mouse pointer to a position near the bottom of the dashed box on the VCE, and press the left mouse button to drop the Button.

Setting the Text Property

Many GUI JavaBeans have a *text* property that is a Java String that holds the value of the characters displayed on the GUI bean. But Buttons are special; they have a *label* property for the same purpose. You need to edit these properties in the CalculatorView Applet with the following:

Open the property for the Button and change the *label* property of the Button to **Add.**

Edit the *text* properties for the Label controls to describe the TextFields below them. Use **First number, Second number, Result** for the respective Labels. When you finish the CalculatorView, it should look like Figure 3.17. You can also edit the Label text in the property sheet.

Figure 3.17   Beans placement.

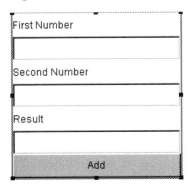

Naming Beans

Each bean you drop has a default name. The first TextField control you drop is
called TextField1. In addition, the first TextField you drop on the next composite
you build will also be named TextField1. You can see that the proliferation of
beans named TextField1 could cause a debugging nightmare. Changing the name
to something more meaningful will help you follow the generated code, and it
will provide some level of documentation for the code. So give the beans appropriate names. Change the bean names with these steps:

> Point to a GUI bean, click the right mouse button, and select **Change
> Bean Name** from the pop-up menu.

> Change the names of the TextFields to **tfNum1, tfNum2,** and **tfResult.**

> Change the name of the Button to **pbAdd.**

Read-Only TextFields

Because the result of the calculation will be supplied by a logic bean that is yet to
be built, the result TextField should not allow keyboard input. One way to
achieve this is to set the *editable* property to **False.**

> Double-click on the tfResult TextField to open its property sheet.

> Select the **editable =>** field; from its pull-down menu, select **False.**

> Close the property sheet to save the change.

If you make any changes to a control in a property sheet and decide you do
not like the changes, there is an easy way to go back to the old settings. After you
close the property sheet, you can go to the **Edit** menu of the Visual Composition
Editor and select **Undo.** You can step back through the changes until you get the

Figure 3.18 CalculatorView applet running.

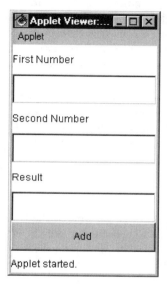

bean back to the way you want it. Remember that **Edit/Undo** is your friend. There is also a **Redo** function if you go too far in your undoing.

Testing an Applet

Now you are ready to run this applet for the first time. From the upper tool bar of the VCE, press the **Run** button. This generates run-time code for the applet.

Once compilation ends, the appletviewer window appears using the default size and parameters for the applet. The appletviewer starts and runs the CalculatorView applet, as shown in Figure 3.18.

You can move between the first two fields, enter values, and press the **Add** button (of course, nothing happens yet). Nothing can be entered in the **Result** field because you made it noneditable. If you use the mouse to increase or decrease the window size, the GUI beans stay centered in the applet and the GUI beans expand, thanks to the GridLayout. It is usually good to have TextFields expand, but Buttons should not expand in the user interface. Close the applet viewer when you finish testing it.

Naming Conventions

Before you begin building the application is a good time to have a short discussion of naming conventions. When developing applications, it is prudent to adopt some consistent naming conventions. Java is a case-sensitive, type-specific language, which means that each class, method, and data field must have a unique name and a defined type. Use descriptive names to make your beans more usable. A good guideline is to have a set of prefixes and suffixes that can ensure consistent naming. For example, the Hello World application used the *pb* prefix for Buttons. Most people have their own naming conventions as well as coding style conventions. In this book, the names of class instance variables start with a lowercase character.

Each word in the name of a class or bean also starts with an uppercase character. For example, the adding machine view is called CalculatorView. Any properties of a class or bean start with a lowercase character. Each subsequent word in the name of the property starts in uppercase. For example, the property that holds the result of the calculation is called *result*. The convention for instances of a class is the same as for properties. For example, the instance of the entry field that displays the calculation result is called *tfResult*.

When you create an instance of a class, you should try to identify the type of class you are instantiating. For example, you can use *tf* as the beginning of the instance name for an entry field. Adhering to these simple suggestions makes it easier to follow and understand the generated code, as well as to understand the connection messages that are issued by the program at run time. It also improves debugging, in the rare event that you make a programming error.

What Are Tab Stops?

Tabbing is a useful feature in user interfaces that improves screen navigation. The term *Tab stop* describes the position or location where the cursor goes when you press the Tab key. Each control placed on a canvas can be designated as a Tab stop. This designation determines the cursor position after the user presses the arrow or Tab keys.

Pressing the Tab key moves the cursor from its current position to the next control that has been designated a tab stop. The tabbing sequence is determined by the order in which the controls occur in the generated Java code. This order is determined by the order that controls are placed in the container. This order can be easily viewed and changed visually.

Setting the Tab Order

This section describes how you can define Tab stops and tabbing order. By default, AWT GUI beans have tabbing function automatically at run time. Tabbing order can be determined from the Applet's pop-up menu. To see an Applet's current tabbing order, select the Applet. Make sure the tip of the mouse pointer is not over one of the GUI beans; it should be at the bottom of the Applet in the small gap between the Button and the Applet. If the container is completely covered by GUI components, you will need to use the Beans List described in the next section.

Figure 3.19 Beans List for the applet.

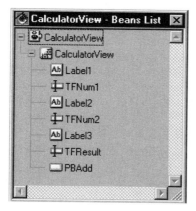

Using the Beans List

As you can see, selecting some beans like Containers can be difficult. Sometimes the GUI beans are hidden or covered by other beans. In the case of Containers, controls can fill the Container bean so you can't access it. A special window enables you to select and work on beans. The Beans List shows all the JavaBeans in the VCE and all the visual connections that are listed at the bottom. Let's use the Beans List window to view the Tab Stops with the following steps:

From the menu bar, select **Tools => Beans List.** The Beans List window appears. You could also use the **Beans List** icon on the tool bar to open this window.

Expand the CalculatorView by pressing the expansion (+) icon as shown in Figure 3.19.

This window is very helpful for accessing beans in a Container; it provides a graphical tree view of all beans associated with this composite bean. This window lists all beans in this Applet, so you can easily select a bean and access all functions on its pop-up menu, like Properties, Delete, Open, and also the visual connections at the bottom. You can also drag and drop components in this window to put them in the desired order. The VCE will then generate the code with the components in the new order. If the TextFields and Buttons do not appear in the proper order, you can drag and drop them into the proper sequence by:

Selecting a control.

Using the mouse to drag the control to the proper position.

Releasing the mouse button to drop the control and set its position.

Figure 3.20   Setting Tab stops.

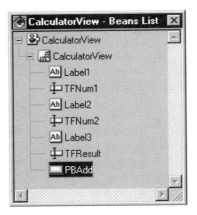

Now you are ready to see the tab stops for the Applet by following these steps:

Select the second **CalculatorView** item and press the right mouse button to get the pop-up menu.

Select **Set tabbing => Show Tab Tags** to see the tabbing order as shown in Figure 3.20.

Tip

After you have finished adjusting the Tab tags, you can hide them using the same process. When the Tab tags are showing, the pop-up menu item for the applet shows **Hide Tab Tags**.

The VCE now shows the Applet with little yellow tab tags on each control in the Applet. The number in the tab tag indicates the sequence that the cursor will follow when you press the Tab key. If the TextFields and Buttons do not appear in the proper order, you can drag and drop the tab tags in the proper sequence. Set the tabbing order so the tabbing sequence starts with **tfNum1** and then goes to **tfNum2, tfResult,** and **pbAdd,** as shown in Figure 3.19, with these steps:

Select one of the tags.

Drag the tag to the proper position.

Drop the tag to set its position.

Continue dragging and dropping the tab tags until they are in the proper order.

Figure 3.21 Running the Adding Machine.

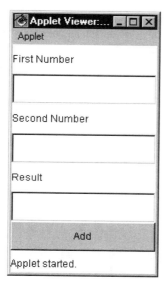

The new tabbing order will be saved when you save the applet. The tab tags show only at development time, not at run time. You can hide the tags with these steps:

From the Beans List, select the pop-up menu for CalculatorView.

Select **Set Tabbing => Hide Tab Tags**.

Close the Beans List window because it is no longer needed.

Running the Updated Adding Machine

You have completed the user interface for the CalculatorView applet. Now it is time to save and run the updated applet.

 Select the Run tool bar button to save, generate, compile, and run the applet.

When the applet starts, it should look like Figure 3.21. The user interface looks like it did the last time you ran the Adding Machine. You can enter numbers in the TextFields, and the tabbing works correctly. When you are finished reviewing the running applet, you can leave the applet running. In the next chapter you will add the logic to the applet, and you will be able to use that function by merely reloading the applet.

Summary

This was a little tougher than the Hello World application, but it was still pretty easy. You still need to make a logic bean with the add function, which is covered in the next chapter. In this chapter you learned the following:

VisualAge JavaBeans Basics including:

- Composite beans
- GUI beans
- Logic beans

How to Search in the IDE and define a Working Set

How to build the Adding Machine application user interface that included:

- Using a GridLayout
- Adding TextField, Label and Button beans
- Setting Tab order

These are the very basics of GUI design programming. In the following chapter, you will create a logic bean with the add function, complete the CalculatorView, learn another important aspect to JavaBeans; namely bean features, and define JavaBeans properties and methods.

MAKING LOGIC BEANS

4

You have completed the user interface for the CalculatorView, and you have worked with a number of basic GUI beans. The next step is to develop a logic bean to hold the business logic for the applet. Before you develop the logic bean, we will cover another aspect of beans, namely JavaBeans features. We will cover the essential aspects of JavaBeans features in enough detail for you to feel confident in developing basic logic beans. There are reference books that cover the JavaBeans specification and its features in far greater detail. The standardization of the Java class interface in the JavaBeans specification is a key reason that beans are open and extensible.

Understanding JavaBeans Features

In the previous chapter, we described JavaBeans and covered the basic types of beans. Remember that beans are Java classes, and just like classes, beans have a public interface. The public interface comprises JavaBeans features that other beans can call or address. There are three kinds of features: *properties*, *methods*, and *events*. Each feature has a Java type (for a method, it is a return type), so when you define a feature, you must specify a type. In this chapter, we describe these features and then show you how to define them in VisualAge for Java.

Java Types

When you first studied Java, you probably learned about the different types in the Java language and the JDK class library. There are both primitive types (like *int*, *float, boolean*), and beans that encapsulate them (like *Integer, Float*, and *Boolean*). When you specify the **type** for a property, remember the big difference between an *int* and an *Integer*. If you accidentally set a property to the wrong type, there is no SmartGuide to help you.

> **NOTE**
>
> Because Java has primitive types, it is not a purely object-oriented programming language. You could build a Java program and use only classes, but most beans, including those in the JDK class library, use primitive types.

What Are Properties?

In moving to a better object-oriented design, the JDK 1.1 class library adopted *properties*. VisualAge products have had the notion of properties for quite a while, but they are referred to as *attributes*. Properties are basically class variables, or *fields*, with a formalized interface to store data. In good object-oriented programming, you should not directly access variables, so properties are variables with a *get* and a *set* method as accessors. If you define a property named *foo* in VisualAge for Java, the SmartGuide generates a foo variable, a setFoo() method, a getFoo() method, and a foo property in a BeanInfo class. The Java convention is to use lowercase names for properties; also by convention, the Visual Composition Editor capitalizes the first character of the property name when it generates names for the get and set methods.

    Properties can be *bound* or *constrained*. Bound properties set the new value then signal an event by calling a firePropertyChange() method whenever the property changes value or state. Constrained properties first signal the event, but the events are vetoable by the *listeners*. A later section on events describes listeners and how they work. If the event is vetoed, the new value is not assigned.

Properties can also be *indexed*; that is, they have an array type. Examples of indexed properties are int[] and String[]. Indexed properties are not widely used, but they can be very helpful in special circumstances.

Properties need to have the same type in the getter, the setter, the instance variable, and the property. If you decide to change a property's Java type, you must change the type in all four items. If the types don't match, VisualAge for Java will indicate the error as a type mismatch.

What Are Methods?

This question may seem rhetorical, because as a Java developer, you are very familiar with methods. Methods must be covered as part of the definition of JavaBeans features. Method features are part of the public interface of the bean, so this implies that *method features* are public class methods.

Another term for public class methods that is used in other VisualAge products is *actions*. With so many new terms associated with JavaBeans, it's nice that Java uses one term for methods. But this sometimes causes confusion in VisualAge for Java, because there are two places you can enter class methods. Just remember that method features are *public* methods that are in the BeanInfo file.

What Are Events?

There are a number of improvements to the event model in JDK 1.1. These changes support a better object-oriented implementation through additional methods and classes. There are many *events* in Java. Events can be caused by user actions, like pressing a button or closing a frame. The AWT class library is full of events and VisualAge for Java makes it easy to take advantage of this function. Events can also be caused by the system or by other logic beans. For example, in the Enterprise Edition, the data access beans send a *connected* event whenever a Java program that uses the data access beans successfully connects to a database.

Events have a *source* and can have *listeners*. The source is the bean that signals the event. The listener is a bean that receives the event signal. Two methods control the registration of listeners: addListener and removeListener. For example, properties use addPropertyChangeListener() and removePropertyChangeListener(). It is a good practice to implement these methods so they can automatically work with other beans.

The other VisualAge products such as VisualAge for C++ also use events. Although the concept is the same, the implementation is completely different. Java events work with Java only.

Although events are messages, they are entirely different from Java *exceptions*, which are used for error detection. Exceptions are handled by using a Java *try/catch* block, where the code in the *catch* block is executed whenever the appropriate exception is caught. On the other hand, nothing happens when an event occurs unless the event has registered listeners. If your Java program isn't behaving the way you expect, make sure that events are actually being signaled and that the target classes are registered listeners.

> **NOTE**
> If you are coming to Java and VisualAge for Java with experience in another programming language or VisualAge product, one of the key hurdles is understanding the Java lingo. The JDK class library uses a number of terms for classes and methods that are different from the class libraries that you may already know. Fortunately, once you know Java and the JDK classes, you can speak a universal language with other Java developers.

The BeanInfo Class

As mentioned earlier, beans are designed to make Java tool development easier. So when you make a bean, additional information about the bean that is required at development time is stored in a BeanInfo class. This class in not needed at run time, so it is not deployed with the Java program. The Visual Composition Editor automatically generates the BeanInfo class whenever you add or change a bean feature. After you add features to a bean, you can review the generated BeanInfo class, but you should never edit the BeanInfo class. There is no reason to do so, because the Visual Composition Editor can always generate a BeanInfo class that matches the bean. If you do edit the BeanInfo class, it may get out of sync with the bean that it represents. Or if you edit the Java code that effects bean property definitions, the property definitions in the BeanInfo class will not match.

Finishing the Adding Machine

VisualAge for Java generates pure JavaBeans, so all the background information on JavaBeans is very helpful. This information is not specific to VisualAge for Java, but is part of Java 1.1 and is used by Java development tools available from many of the leading software development tool providers. Additionally, many smaller firms sell specialized beans for specific purposes, and these beans can be used in any of the tools that support JavaBeans. This is a great example of a truly open development environment.

What Are Logic Beans?

JavaBeans that contain business logic are referred to as logic or nonvisual beans. They are often subclasses of **Object**, which is an abstract base class in the Java class library. You can see this inheritance relationship in the *Date* bean, shown in Figure 4.1. Logic beans can have many different functions, like managing the user interface, accessing a database, providing communications and print support, and running business logic. Logic beans encapsulate Java function in a separate bean, which helps you keep this function separate from the user interface or GUI beans.

Figure 4.1   Date inheritance hierarchy.

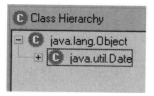

VisualAge for Java comes with a number of logic beans, such as the Select bean for database access. The Enterprise Edition has additional code generators that create logic beans to access other data and transaction sources, such as SAP, MQ, and CICS. You can use VisualAge for Java to generate your own specialized logic beans with properties, events, and methods.

Creating Logic Beans

Now let's use this knowledge of JavaBeans features to build the logic bean for the CalculatorView. If the VisualAge for Java Workbench is not started, restart it now. You will build the **CalculatorLogic** JavaBean, then you will combine it with the **CalculatorView** GUI bean previously built. You will use the same project and package for the logic bean.

Select the package in the project used for the CalculatorView Applet. The workbench should look like Figure 4.2.

Now that you have selected the project and the package in the IDE, you can start defining the logic bean for the Simple Calculator. It is not necessary to have the package selected, but it is helpful. When you create a new bean, you must specify the project and package that contains the new bean. By selecting the package, it will be passed to the SmartGuide. You could put your math or calculation beans in another package, but for convenience, it is better to use the same package. So get started making a new bean with the following steps:

With the **calculator** package selected, click the right mouse button on the top pane and from the pop-up menu select **Add/Class**. This will cause the Create Class SmartGuide to display.

In the Create Class or Interface SmartGuide as shown in Figure 4.3, enter **CalculatorLogic** in the **Class Name** text field.

Leave the superclass as the default **java.lang.Object**, which is at the top of the Java class hierarchy.

It is not necessary to have the *Compose the class visually* checked, so make sure this box is blank.

Figure 4.2 Workbench with My Project and calculator.

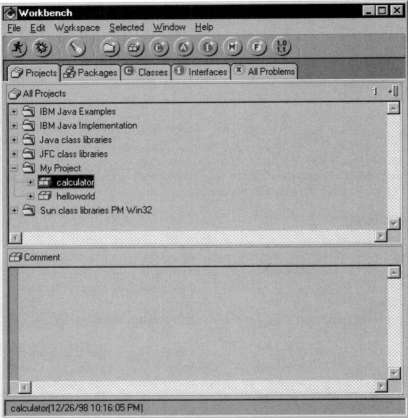

Also, have the *Browse the class when finished* blank this time. Sometimes it is convenient to automatically open a browser.

You have entered all the information needed to generate the CalculatorLogic bean, but let's look at the other pages of the SmartGuide to see the additional information that could be used to generate a bean.

Press the **Next** button to see the second page of the SmartGuide, as shown in Figure 4.4.

This page enables you to select a number of options for a bean. First, there is a list box to specify any **import** statements for the bean. You may feel it is easier to type these in the code, and you can always add import statements to the generated source code later. The SmartGuides are aides that help with the initial code

Figure 4.3   Create Class SmartGuide.

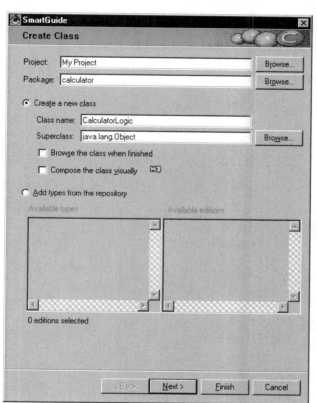

generation. This dialog is very helpful, because a handy browser make it easy for you to correctly specify the class or package you want to import.

You can specify additional modifiers for the class, including *abstract* and *final*. Abstract classes contain method declarations with no implementation. An abstract class cannot be instantiated at run time, primarily because it is lacking method definitions. The implementation must reside in a subclass of the abstract class. By specifying the final modifier, you prevent a class from being subclassed. If you add either of these modifiers to a method, you see additional visual cues in the IDE. VisualAge for Java uses an **F** for final and **A** for abstract.

There are a number of common methods that many classes implement. Some of these methods are listed on the SmartGuide page as options for the method stubs to be generated, as shown in Figure 4.4. The Visual Composition Editor generates the method definition, and you must enter the specific implementation code for each method. The equals(), finalize(), hashCode(), and toString() methods all have a default implementation of calling the same method in the parent or

Figure 4.4 Class definition2.

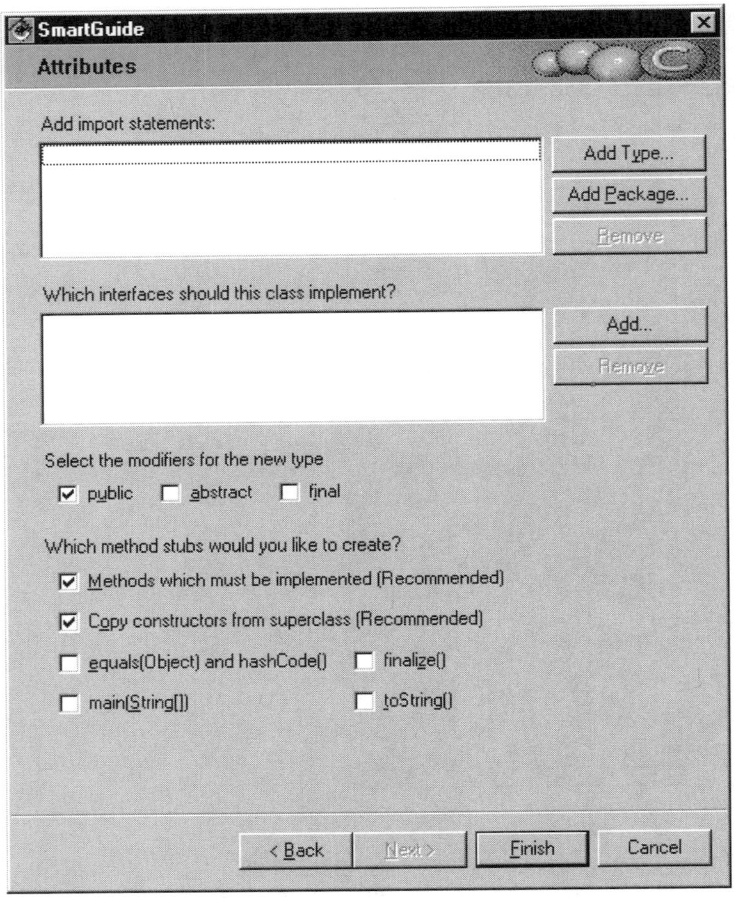

superclass. The CalculatorLogic bean does not need any of these methods, so you do not need to select them.

This second page of the SmartGuide also enables you to add interfaces to the classes. Remember that interfaces are a way that Java gets around multiple inheritance. When you add interfaces to the bean, VisualAge for Java generates the correct code in the class definition. You can always edit the source code and add *implements* to the bean definition. This is the last page of the SmartGuide; you are finished specifying the bean.

You can select additional modifiers for a bean on this page. These are the standard Java modifiers that you should recognize. By selecting any of these modifiers, VisualAge for Java adds them to the class definition. For this bean, you can use the default modifier *public*.

There are also a number of method stubs you can have VisualAge for Java generate for you. This is very helpful if you initially know that you will need a certain method like toString() in the bean. You still need to write the implementation code for the generated stub. Later in this chapter, you will learn how to add methods to a bean.

The SmartGuides are an easy way to specify information for the VisualAge for Java generator. This only happens when you are creating a new item. If you ever want to change an item, you need to modify the source code.

Press the **Finish** button to create the class.

The SmartGuide closes, and VisualAge for Java saves the bean, generates the code, and compiles it. Focus goes back to the Workbench, and the new bean is highlighted. The Workbench should look like Figure 4.5.

Figure 4.5 Added CalculatorLogic class.

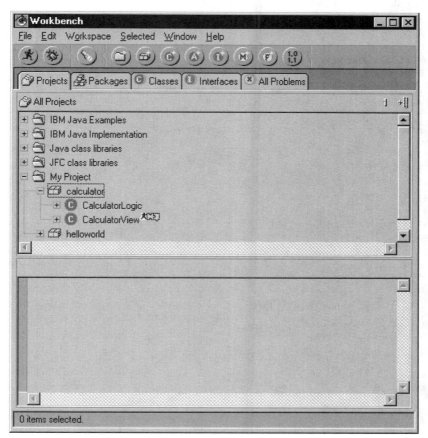

You can see that the CalculatorLogic bean was added to the Workbench in the calculator package. You can add methods and variables (also known as *fields*) to the code for the bean in the Source pane. You can also edit or **open** the bean, which opens another view or window that enables you to work on the class. It is best to open a separate view for editing the class, because this frees the Workbench for browsing the other classes loaded in the workspace. You can still make changes to a class in the Workbench, but opening the bean gives you a lot more tools to help you work on it. Usually, you will find that you only make small changes to a bean in the Workbench.

Editing a Bean

Double-click the mouse while it is over the bean if you have set the **Double Click in the Workbench** preference. If you are using the default setting, click the right mouse button on the top pane, and select **Open** from the pop-up menu.

The class browser opens for you to continue developing this bean as seen in Figure 4.6. By default it opens to the *Methods* page. This browser looks like the

Figure 4.6 Class browser.

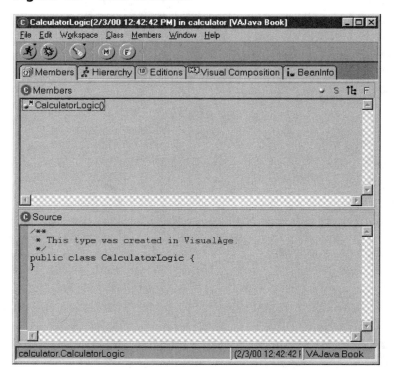

Workbench, but it is very different. The browser can only work on this bean. This browser has five pages and each has its own special functions. These pages are:

Members. Helps you work with the methods and fields for the bean. You can also enter or edit public methods, but public methods are bean features and should to be entered in the BeanInfo class so that tools can work with them. This page is also used to work with fields or variables for the bean. Just like methods, public fields should be properties and should be entered in the BeanInfo page.

Hierarchy. Shows you all superclasses of the bean.

Editions. Shows all editions. You create new editions when you version the beans.

Visual Composition. Shows a bean's visual representation. All beans have a Visual Composition page in VisualAge for Java even if they have not visual representation. You can use the Visual Composition Editor for both GUI beans and logic beans.

BeanInfo. Helps you create and edit bean features, namely properties, methods, and events. You can also generate and edit the BeanInfo file from this page.

If the tabs on a browser are displayed as icons with no text, only as shown in Figure 4.7, there is a reason this happened and an easy way to fix it. You probably resized the browser and made it smaller to conserve screen space. The text on the tabs of the notebook was automatically removed, leaving just the icons. You can increase the size of the browser window, and the text will magically reappear.

> **NOTE**
>
> You may wonder why the JavaBeans icon on the BeanInfo page is blue instead of brown, as in the Sun samples. The reason is that this page is for IBM generated beans, so the icon for the beans is blue. Actually, a JavaBean is a JavaBean, no matter what tool creates it.

Defining Properties

The CalculatorLogic bean needs three integer properties to hold the two operands and the result of the calculation. Because we will be using this bean in the Visual Composition Editor, these properties must be enabled to send and receive notifications so that the GUI and logic representation of the values are synchronized. In other words, when the user enters a number in the user interface or changes the value of one of the numbers, the corresponding property in the logic bean must

Figure 4.7 Icons on tabs.

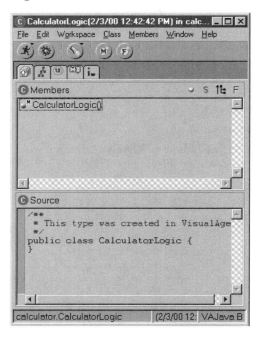

be notified of this change. To do this, properties for the class should be defined in the **BeanInfo** page of the class/interface browser.

Select the **BeanInfo** page of the class/interface browser as shown in Figure 4.8.

Notice the class browser tool bar buttons change on every page. This page has the familiar cut, copy, and paste buttons, along with the Debugger and Search. There are three more tool bar icons, as shown in Figure 4.9 that indicate the special functions in this page. These tool bar buttons represent properties, events, and methods, and selecting these buttons starts a SmartGuide to help you create the desired bean feature.

Let's create a property and see how this works. Follow the next steps:

Right-click on the Features pane (top left) and select **New Property Feature** from the pop-up menu.

Enter **num1** in the **Property name** entry field.

Select **int** for the **Property type**, as shown in Figure 4.10.

The **Readable** and **Writeable** check boxes are selected by default. VisualAge for Java automatically generates a *get* method and a *set* method for the property.

Figure 4.8 BeanInfo page.

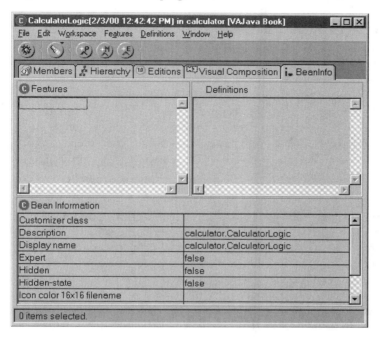

NOTE

When you enter Java types, the Visual Composition Editor provides the Browse button on many of the SmartGuides. The browse function lets you search for the fully qualified name for a class including its packages. Since the browse function searches for classes, you cannot find the Java primitive types. If you need to enter a primitive type, you will need to select it from the initial dropdown list, or merely enter it in the field.

The *get* method returns an object of this type and the *set* method is passed an object of this type. If you want the property to be read-only, you can deselect the **Writeable** check box, and there will not be a set method. The properties in the

Figure 4.9 Property, event, and method icons.

CalculatorLogic bean need to have both get and set methods generated, so leave both check boxes selected.

It is very important to ensure that the **bound** check box is selected. This insures that the property will emit a propertyChange whenever it changes. Bound properties are easier to use when making connections in the Visual Composition Editor.

You could press **Finish** at this time and accept the defaults for the remainder of the settings. You could also press **Next** to further define the interface of the property. Selecting defaults in the SmartGuide is generally okay, but in this case, select **Next** to see what else is available.

On the next page of the SmartGuide, as shown in Figure 4.11, add a display name and a short description of the property. Enter **operand1** for the Display name.

When you enter a display name, it is used in the connections pop-up menu in the Visual Composition Editor; otherwise, the property name is used. This property is a primitive type, so it does not need a special property editor. These settings cause the Visual Composition Editor to generate code for a property descriptor method in the BeanInfo class, which creates a *PropertyDescriptor* class for each property in the bean. The PropertyDescriptor class has a number of methods to get and set information about the bean. The specific methods for these descriptions are setDisplayName(String) and setShortDescription(String).

Figure 4.10   Adding a Property Feature.

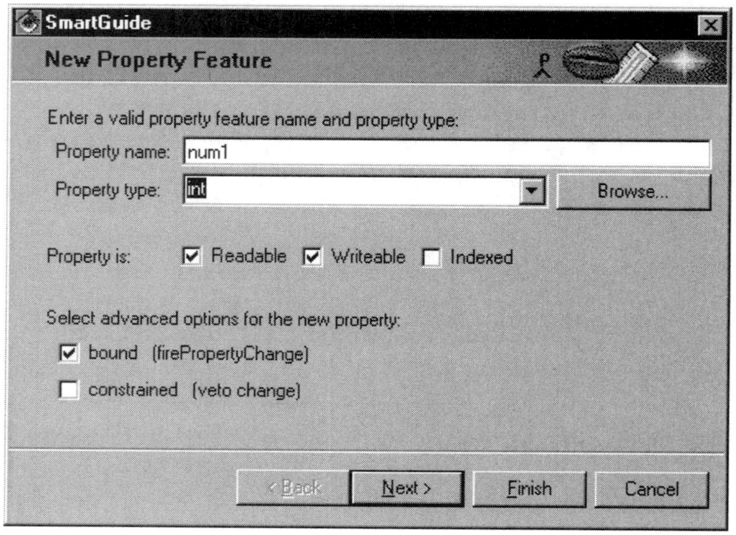

Expert and Hidden Features

You will notice check boxes for *expert, hidden, and preferred*. The methods in the PropertyDescriptor class for this information are setExpert(boolean) and setHidden. Expert features are those deemed by the bean developer to be advanced or seldom used features. There are checkboxes in VisualAge for Java that give developers the option to screen expert features. The JDK classes have a number of expert features, such as the *enabled* property of a TextField.

Hidden features are those that the bean developer deems should not be used by a Java tool. So although they are in the class, they are hidden from you in the tool, Preferred is a VisualAge for Java specific setting for the Visual Composition Editor. It lets bean features appear in the connections pop-up menu. Using preferred features saves mouse clicks, so it is a good idea to set frequently used features as preferred.

If the property you have added needs a specialized editor to set its value, you can specify the class name of the editor in this window. This is not required for common or primitive types such as **int**, but is frequently needed for user-defined types or composite types, like Font and Color. The method in the PropertyDescriptor class for this information is setExpert(propertyEditorClass). This means you need to construct a propertyEditorClass with all the needed settings and required data.

The SmartGuide has enough information, so press the **Finish** button.

> **NOTE**
>
> There is no hard-and-fast rule about what features are expert; in fact, you may find that you will frequently use many of these expert features. The Visual Composition Editor shelters you from many of these bean API details by generating the BeanInfo class with all its methods.

Finish defining the other properties for this bean by creating two more **bound int** properties, using the steps that you used to make the **num1** property. Name these two properties **num2** and **result**.

Notice that as you add properties to the bean, the BeanInfo Editor adds the properties to the Features list in alphabetical order, not the order in which you define them. The BeanInfo Editor automatically generates the get and set methods to access the properties.

Where Is the BeanInfo Class?

The *Features* pane in this window, as shown in Figure 4.12, lists all bean features. Actually, it lists the bean features that are in the BeanInfo class. The properties have some trailing characters that were discussed in Chapter 3, "Making an

Figure 4.11   Property SmartGuide.

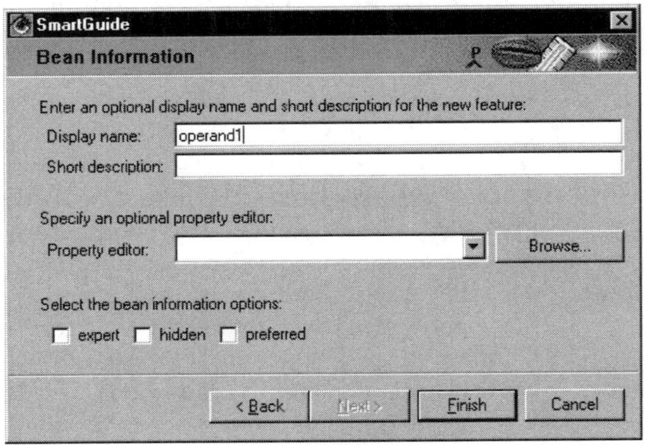

Adding Machine." These characters are a shorthand notation to help you identify the characteristics of the property. These characters came from the options in the SmartGuide when the property was generated, and they are:

R = Readable, has a get() method

W = Write, has a set() method

B = Bound, can fire a property change event

E = Expert, screened from the developer

H = Hidden, hidden from developers

Any method created on the *Methods* page, or directly added in the source code, is not automatically added to the BeanInfo class. The Features pane has its own pop-up menu with the functions that apply to bean features.

The *Features* pane is actually a view into the BeanInfo class for this bean.

The lower pane on the BeanInfo page is used as two different editors—a BeanInfo editor when a bean *Feature* is selected, and a source code editor when a bean *Definition* is selected. As mentioned earlier, you should not edit the generated BeanInfo class. VisualAge for Java, which uses the java.lang.reflect functions to access information about the bean, can generate the BeanInfo class. This package contains the *Class* class, which is another addition to JDK 1.1. The Class class contains the information about the class, and it has a number of methods to access this information.

The *Definitions* pane of the BeanInfo page is used to display the methods and beans associated with each bean feature. Let's look at the generated methods for the **operand1** property with the following steps:

Figure 4.12 Bean information.

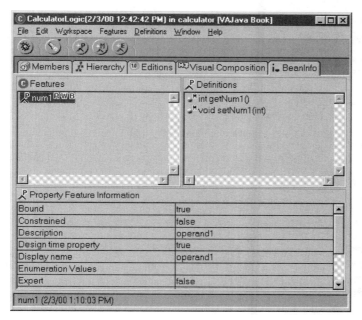

Select a property feature in the Features pane; the corresponding get and set methods are displayed.

Select the **setNum1(int)** method; the lower pane is now the **Source** pane for the set method as seen in Figure 4.13.

If you define the property as a **String** type, you see a String class (or String bean) in the Definitions pane. This is the default type in the SmartGuide, so you may have accidentally set one of the properties to String instead of **int**. This will not work correctly in the CalculatorLogic bean, because the add() method will add the properties, and the result of adding Strings is different than adding ints. Check the property types with the following steps:

Select the **num2** property.

Select the **getNum2()** method in the Definitions pane.

The BeanInfo page Source pane should look like Figure 4.14. The definition for the num2 Property is:

```
public int getNum2() {
```

The num2 property is correct because it returns an **int**. Check the other properties and insure that they return an **int**.

Figure 4.13   Source pane for setNum1.

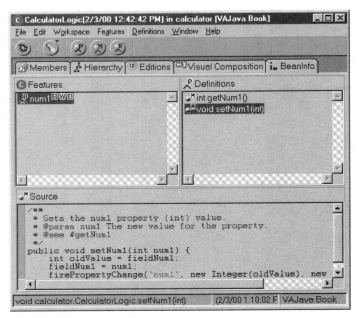

If any of the properties are of type **String,** you need to change the type to int. Because a property usually consists of a get and set method, a class variable, and the property in the BeanInfo class, changing a property's type means editing a lot of code. You could do this, or you can follow the steps in the following section (Changing a Property's Type). Even if the properties have the correct type, you should review this section, because you will probably need to do this sometime.

Changing a Property Type

If you ever want to change or delete a bean property, your first inclination may be to start editing the code. You must change all four type references for the property, or else there will be errors. There is also code in the BeanInfo class for the property descriptors. Unless you have added code to either the set or the get method of the property, it is much easier to delete the property and create a new one if you want to change its type. If you have a **num1** property that is a String and you really want a **num1** property as an **int,** you need to follow these steps from the BeanInfo page:

> With the property selected, from the popup menu select *delete.* The
> Delete features Dialog opens with the selected feature. The list shows the
> getter and setter methods, and the field that will be deleted, if they are
> selected. In VisualAge for Java 3.0, these items are selected by default. If

Figure 4.14   Property types.

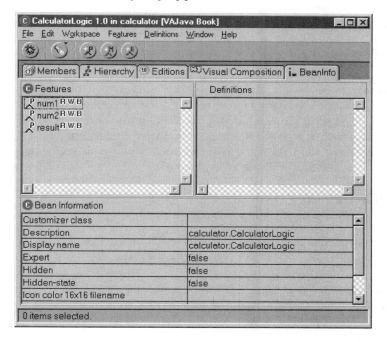

you forget to select them, they will still be in the bean and you will need to delete them individually.

Save the class.

Go back to the BeanInfo page, create the new property, and carefully select int as the property type.

You may wonder how the fieldText1 variable got in the class. When VisualAge for Java generates code for a property, it generates the appropriate accessor methods, and a variable to represent the property. The code generator creates a variable name by adding *field* before the property name. Let's see the properties in the generated class code for the CalculatorLogic class with these steps:

Select the Workbench page to view all the classes.

Select the Calculator View class. The code displays in the Source pane as shown in the following:

```
/**
 * This class was generated by a SmartGuide.
 *
 */
```

```
public class CalculatorLogic {
  protected transient java.beans.PropertyChangeSupport
  private int fieldNum1 = 0;
  private int fieldNum2 = 0;
  private int fieldResult = 0;
}
```

This is another way to verify that the properties are the correct type. You can look at the class code and check the type of the fields corresponding to the properties. Of course, it helps to know what you are looking for. VisualAge for Java is a great tool for working with JavaBeans, but you need to understand JavaBeans and the generated code. As you can see in the previous code segment, fieldNum1, fieldNum2, and fieldResult are all type int.

Defining Methods

Next, create a method to perform the addition operation:

While still on the **BeanInfo** page of the class browser notebook, right-click on the upper left pane, and select **New Method Feature** from the pop-up menu.

Type **add** as the **Method name**, leave the method type as **void** and the **parameter count** as 0, as shown in Figure 4.15.

Press the **Finish** button. VisualAge for Java saves the new method, generates the code, and compiles it.

Figure 4.15   Creating the add method.

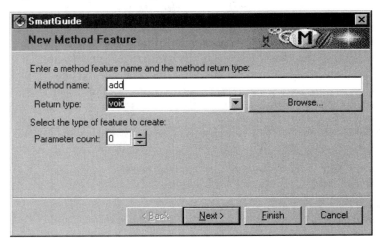

Figure 4.16 Choosing the Calculator bean.

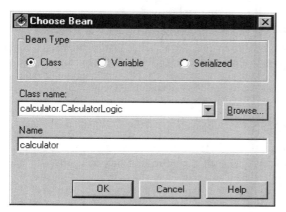

Using JavaBeans in the Visual Composition Editor

Now the only thing left is to bring the logic bean into the Visual Composition Editor for the CalculatorView and make the connections.

Switch back to the browser showing the CalculatorView, and make sure the Visual Composition tab is selected.

 From the beans palette of the Visual Composition Editor, select **Choose Bean**. The Choose Bean window appears.

Select the **Browse** button to show the list of available beans.

Type **CalculatorLogic** and press **OK** to choose this bean.

Figure 4.17 Calculator logic bean added.

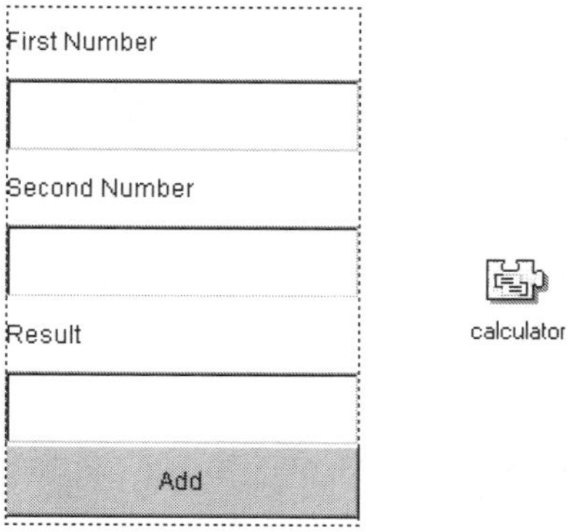

Enter a name for this bean (use **calculator**) as shown in Figure 4.16.

Press **OK** to load the cursor with the CaculatorLogic class.

Move the mouse pointer outside of the dashed box and over the free-form surface and click the mouse to drop the bean. You should now have a bean that looks like a jigsaw puzzle piece and is available for connections, as shown in Figure 4.17.

Types of Connections

You have already used visual connections in the HelloWorld applet in Chapter 2. The Visual Composition Editor provides a number of connections to help you build Java programs:

Event-to-Method

Event-to-Property

Event-to-Code

Property-to-Property

All connections that start with an event are shown in green with an arrow pointing to the target. These different event connections are essentially the same. An event-to-property connection actually calls the set method for the property, and an event-to-code connection actually calls a class method that has Java code. Code connections call methods in the Parent class and they are good for methods that need access to references at the class level. Code connections are commonly used for calling other-than-public methods, though they can be used to call public methods also.

Property-to-Property connections are bi-directional: a change in one property can cause a message or event to be passed to the other property. These are very powerful connections, because they signal a **propertyChange** event. For example, in a TextField, a propertyChange event can occur every time you type a key. Because of this potentially intensive messaging, beans with property-to-property connections create tightly coupled beans. There are many situations where tightly coupled beans are necessary, and there are other situations where they can be limiting. A tightly coupled bean cannot be easily moved to another system for distributed processing, which is a common requirement when using Remote Method Invocation (RMI).

You can also make connections to connections. This is used to pass parameters into connections like in the HelloWorld applet, where the **Date** is passed to the **setText()** method of the Label bean.

This is a lot of information about connections if you are new to VisualAge for Java. You will become familiar with these different connections as you complete the samples in this book.

> **NOTE**
>
> It is better object-oriented design to pass objects instead of primitive Java types as parameters. Many beans, including those in the Java class libraries, accept primitive typed parameters, but this is usually only done for efficiency.

Property to Property Connections

When the CalculatorView runs, the values entered in the TextFields need to be copied to the logic bean. You can do this using property-to-property connections from the TextFields to the corresponding properties you defined in the CalculatorLogic bean.

The connection menu can be accessed by selecting the bean, pressing the right mouse button, and selecting **Connect** from the pop-up menu. The cascade menu contains the *preferred* properties, methods, and events available for connections. Preferred features have been used in the different VisualAge products and can be modified by the developer. However, the JavaBeans specification does not provide for preferred features, so there is no way to save them in the BeanInfo class. VisualAge for Java provides some default features in the preferred features list for the JDK classes loaded in VisualAge for Java. As shown earlier, you can add bean features as preferred in the BeanInfo editor and they will appear on this list.

The **Connectable Features** selection at the bottom of each connection menu displays a window containing all possible features for this bean. You should use **Connectable Features** to access the features that you need for connections, because the Connectable Features window contains the properties, events, and methods in separate lists. These separate lists help ensure that you pick the desired feature for the connection.

> **NOTE**
>
> To improve usability, the **Connectable Features** menu item in the Visual Composition Editor will only display valid connection types. For example, if you pick a property as a connection source, the Visual Composition Editor will show only properties as targets for the connection.

Now create the connections in the following steps:

Start the connection by opening the pop-up for the **tfNum1** text field and select **Connect**, which displays the preferred features menu.

From the preferred features menu, select **text**. Now you see a line, which originates from the selected control and follows the mouse movements.

Take the end of the connection to the **calculator** bean and click the left mouse button. Another pop-up menu appears; it belongs to the **calculator** bean. To complete the connection, select Connect, Connectable Features, and operand1 or num1 property (depending on whether you chose an optional display name).

This establishes a blue connection from tfNum1(text) to calculator(num1), as shown in Figure 4.18.

> **NOTE**
>
> You do not get a warning that the source and target types are incompatible, even though the *text* property of the textfield is type **String** and the *result* property is type **int**. The Visual Composition Editor will generate the proper conversions to match the types at run time.

Connect tfNum2 (text) to calculator(num2 or operand2).

Connect calculator(result) to tfResult(text).

Connect pbAdd(actionPerformed(java.awt.event.ActionEvent)) to calculator(add). Remember to select the **Connectable Features** choice from the pop-up menu, so that you can select the **add**() method to complete the connection.

You have made all the connections needed for the applet. It should look something like Figure 4.19.

Figure 4.18 Property-to-property connection.

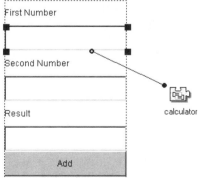

Figure 4.19   Completed connections.

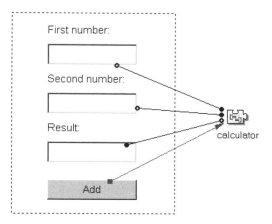

Finding Connections

There is another really helpful feature in VisualAge for Java. The connections you make are displayed in the Beans List as shown in Figure 4.20. Remember that visual connections represent program logic, and you will need to locate specific connections for editing and debugging. In Chapter 5, "Debugging Beans," you will learn how to rename connections, another new feature in VisualAge for Java 2.0.

Figure 4.20   Connections in Beans List.

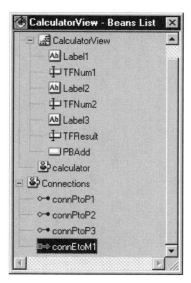

Testing the Calculator

There is quite a bit of function completed on the CalculatorView applet, so this is a good time to test it. Press the Run button to save and run the applet.

When the applet starts, it should look like Figure 4.21. You should notice that the Result TextField is magically set to 0. Actually, the magic comes from the connection to the Result TextField. This connection was drawn from the CalculatorLogic bean to the Result TextField. The result property in the CalculatorLogic bean is an int, so it is initialized to be 0. Therefore, the value of the result property in the CalculatorLogic bean gets passed to the Result TextField.

Enter a number in each text field and press the **Add** button. The Result field should show the value of adding the two numbers. Test this and enter **123** in the first field and **456** in the second field.

Press the **Add** button on the applet: nothing happens.

There is nothing wrong; the applet is not finished. You still need to do two things:

- As characters are typed in the TextFields, the events are not passing to the CalculatorLogic bean.
- The **add()** generated by the SmartGuide needs the logic to do the adding.

Figure 4.21 Running CalculatorView.

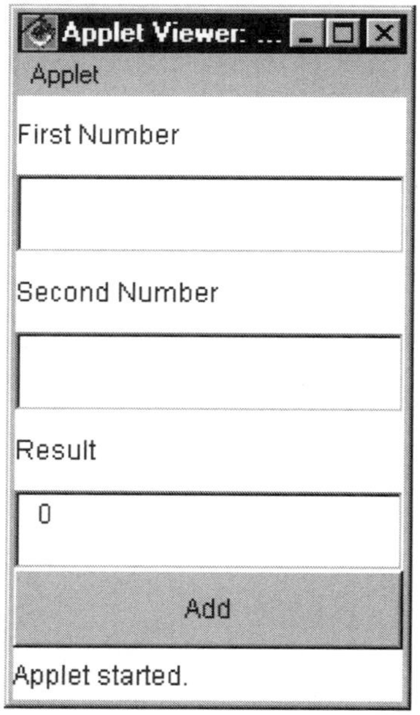

![Applet Viewer window showing CalculatorView with fields for First Number, Second Number, Result (0), and an Add button. Status bar reads "Applet started."]

With these two changes, the CalculatorView applet is complete.

Property Events

As discussed previously, when a property changes, it passes an event. Some beans, like TextField, have a number of different events that can be passed at run time. The Visual Composition Editor does not know what event you might want to pass from a TextField, so you must set this during development. You set the event in the property sheet for the property-to-property connection with the following steps:

Open the property sheet for the connection. Either double-click on the blue connection line, or use its pop-up menu and select **properties**.

Set **Source Event** to **textValueChanged(java.awt.event.TextEvent)**. This tells the connection to fire whenever the text value of the source object (the num1 text field) changes, as shown in Figure 4.22.

In a similar fashion, make the following property-to-property connections:

Connect num2 (or operand2) (text) to calculator(num2) and set the source event.

Connect calculator(result) to result(text).

Adding Code to Methods

When the SmartGuide generates a method, it generates *stub* code consisting of the following:

Figure 4.22 Property-to-property connection.

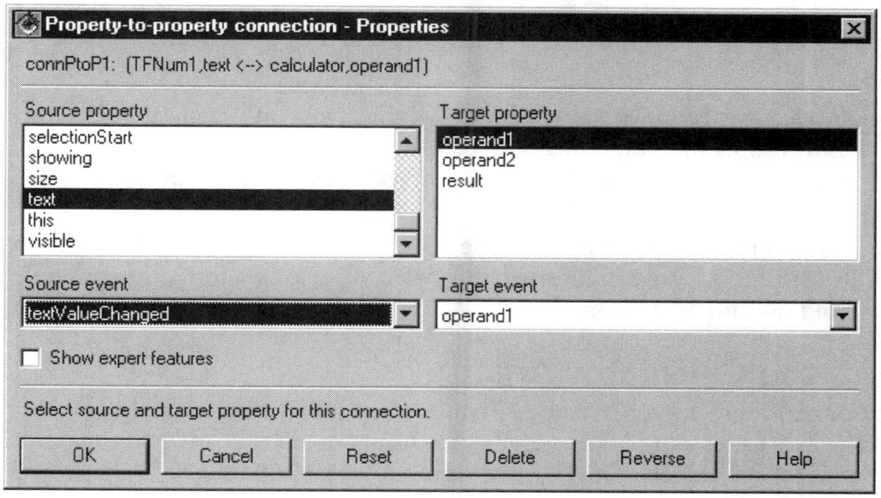

A comment

The method definition

Another comment

The *return* for the method

The add() method for the CalculatorLogic bean looks as follows:

```
/**
 * Performs the add method.
 */
public void add() {
  /* Perform the add method. */
  return;
}
```

This stub code allows you to call the method and then continue after it returns. This particular method has no return. You need to add the logic as Java code to the methods you generate:

Select the **add()** method in the Definitions pane (top right) to display the code for the method in the bottom pane.

Enter the following code to perform the calculation as shown in Figure 4.23:

```
setResult( getNum1( ) + getNum2( ) );
```

This code sets the *result* property on the **CalculatorLogic** bean with the sum of the values of **num1** and **num2**.

Right-click on the bottom pane and select **Save** to save and compile the code for the **add()** method.

Any errors are reported now. You can also use Ctrl-S to save and compile the bean.

If you select the **result** property on the Features pane and then select the **setResult(int)** method on the top pane, you will see how the notification is sent to inform interested parties that the value of the *result* property changed.

You have completed creating the logic bean, which will perform the addition for you. In Chapter 5, you will improve this bean to perform subtraction, multiplication, and division operations.

Testing the Calculator Again

Now it is a good time to verify that everything is working in the CalculatorView applet. The TextFields can pass the event data to the logic bean and the add() has code to perform the calculation. Test it with the following steps:

Figure 4.23   Code for add() method.

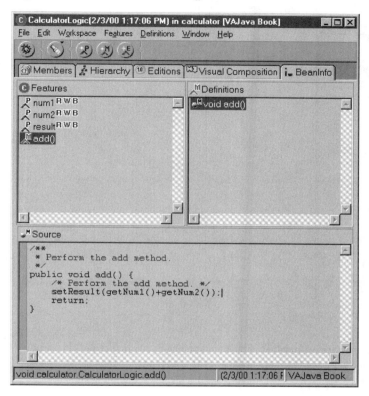

Press the Run button on the Visual Composition Editor tool bar to save and run the applet.

Try again by entering a number in each of text fields and pressing the **Add** button. The Result field should show the value of adding the two numbers. Test the applet again: enter **123** in the first field and **456** in the second field, as shown in Figure 4.24.

Select the **Add** Button, and the **Result** field should show **579**.

When you have finished testing the CalculatorView, close the applet.

If you were coding this by hand, you might have just added an add() method to the CalculatorView class and put the necessary code in this method to do the adding. In addition, this applet does not have many refinements that are needed

Figure 4.24   Completed CalculatorView.

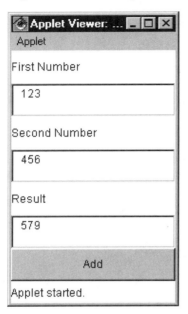

for a real applet that you could deploy. The next sample you build will be much more complete.

Documenting Classes

There are three ways to document the classes that you develop in VisualAge for Java:

> Print screen captures of the Workbench. This is cumbersome and impractical.

> Print the classes with the new Print feature in the IDE. This is pretty straightforward and you should try this on your own. You can select a class in the IDE, then from the pop-up menu, select *Document, Print*.

> Generate Javadoc for the class. This is a real cool feature and you can learn how this works with the next steps.

Generating Javadoc

As you have seen, VisualAge for Java has a number of code generators that help you develop Java programs. The generated code includes comments that record the purpose of classes and methods, along with other information about the Java program. If you select the main() method in the CalculatorView applet, you see the following comment and the top of the method:

```
/**
 * main entrypoint - starts the part when it is run as an application
 * @param args java.lang.String[]
 */
```

What Is Javadoc?

Javadoc is a Java documentation technique for generating the documentation as an HTML (Hypertext Markup Language) file from the comments in the code. Javadoc uses /** to start a comment and */ to end a comment, as shown in the previous code sample. Because Javadoc generates HTML, you can insert HTML tags in the Java comments, and they will be passed to the generated HTML file. There are also a number of Javadoc tags that can help you document the code.

Figure 4.25   Javadoc window.

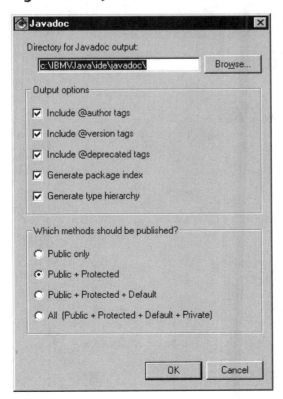

The previous code sample shows the **@param** tag. The JDK includes a Javadoc generator, and there is one included in the VisualAge for Java IDE. Let's try generating the Javadoc for the CalculatorView Applet with the following steps:

Go to the Workbench.

Select the **CalculatorView** bean.

Display the pop-up menu and select **Document, Generate javadoc,** which is at the bottom of the menu.

When the **Javadoc** window opens as shown in Figure 4.25, you can accept the default values and press the **OK** button.

Figure 4.26   Viewing Javadoc in a browser.

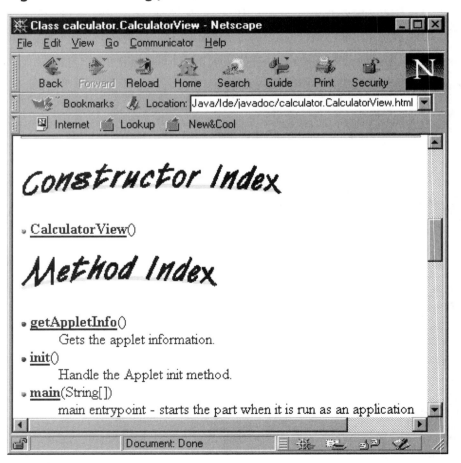

After the HTML files are generated, focus returns to the Workbench. You can view these HTML files in your browser. Figure 4.26 shows the Calculator HTML loaded into Netscape Navigator. In this HTML page, you can see the hierarchy map of the bean and all of its parents, and you can review all the fields, methods, and constructors for the bean. This is a very fast and easy way to document your Java programs. Because this function is integrated into VisualAge for Java, you can easily generate Javadoc while you are working on a Java program.

Summary

This Java program was a little tougher than the Hello World applet, but it was still pretty easy. You learned about JavaBeans features and how to use a SmartGuide in the BeanInfo page to define your own logic beans. In this chapter, you learned the following:

- How to create logic beans
- Defining properties
- Defining methods
- Adding user code to logic beans
- Connecting logic beans in the Visual Composition Editor
- Generating Javadoc

These are very basic elements in visual programming. In the following chapters, you build on these basic elements and learn how to build more complex Java applications with VisualAge for Java.

DEBUGGING BEANS

What's in Chapter 5

This chapter provides you with an introduction to using the debugging aids available in the VisualAge for Java development environment. You will learn about:

- Adding trace information to your programs
- The Scrapbook window
- The methods in the **com.ibm.uvm.tools.DebugSupport** class
- The VisualAge for Java integrated source-level debugger

These are very helpful tools for debugging applications. Because VisualAge for Java generates a lot of code for you, it may give you a false sense of security, as though the software VisualAge for Java knows what you want it to do. We all know, however, that there will always be little bugs in our programs that we need to find and fix.

This is the only chapter that covers debugging tools and techniques. You should use what you learn here in the other chapters and as you encounter problems with your programs.

In the first few chapters of this book, you learned the basics about using beans to build simple programs with VisualAge for Java. You built and tested the Hello World and Calculator applications, which are fairly simple and not very error-prone. They were meant to introduce you to the basic user interface controls and the mechanics involved in composing, building, and running an application using the Building from Beans paradigm. You were also introduced to the world of connections and how you can use them to make things happen in an event-driven program.

Introduction to Debugging

In this chapter, you will learn about several debugging tools and techniques that will help you find logic, flow, and other problems in your Java programs. We will cover some debugging principles, which you probably already know from your experience with other programming languages and environments, by showing you how to apply them in VisualAge for Java. We will also cover the debugging tools and features that are exclusive to VisualAge for Java.

Using System.out.println()

If you have a C or C++ background, you have probably used the printf() function to examine variables and print messages as a program is executed. Other languages have equivalent functions to print the execution position or the run-time status of your program's variables to a console or trace file. This technique is one of the simplest ways to obtain information from your program at run time. In Java you can use the same approach using the System.out.println() method.

You can insert System.out.println() method calls anywhere in your code to send messages to yourself and to examine variable and state information.

The println() method is defined in the **java.io.PrintStream** class. The PrintStream object is accessed on the System class through a class variable named **out**. Using println() is very versatile because of its extensive overloading; here are all the parameters it supports:

- println(boolean)
- println(char)
- println(char[])
- println(double)
- println(float)
- println(int)
- println(long)
- println(java.lang.String)
- println(java.lang.Object)

When passing a **java.lang.Object** to println(), the toString() method of that object is called and returns a string representation of that type of object.

All objects have the toString() method defined. In fact, this method is defined at the top of the Java class hierarchy in the **Object** class. The default toString() method returns a string of the form *className@hashcode*. As you develop your own classes, it is good programming practice to override the default toString() method and supply your own string representation of your object.

Debugging Connections

By now, you are probably beginning to understand that programs generated using the VisualAge for Java Visual Composition Editor are event-driven and rely on the underlying event model provided by Java 1.1.

In traditional programming, when you receive unexpected results while executing your program, you examine the code, analyze the logic flow and operations, and often use the debugger to step through the program execution step-by-step.

Visual programming introduces a new level of complexity when debugging connections, partly because the connections are actually generated methods in the bean. There are at least three things that can go wrong with connections:

- The connection does not execute.
- The connection executes at the wrong time (out of sequence).
- The wrong connection executes.

When debugging connections, it is a good idea to verify that the connection is being executed. This also helps you determine not only that the connection has executed, but also the sequence in which it executed in relation to other connections in the program. When you program visually, it is very easy to create connections that execute in the wrong order.

As mentioned before, in other programming languages, you probably used some type of tracing to send messages to yourself and to examine variables and state information at run time. When debugging complex connection problems it may be necessary to use this technique again. You need to have the ability to "see" the connections executing in order to help you determine what the problem is. You can easily add traces to a program at strategic places in the code. Use the **System.out.println**() method to send messages to the Java console at the appropriate time.

Using the Console

In VisualAge for Java, the console provides a multiple-pane window where you can view messages sent to standard out (System.out) and standard error (System.err). You can also provide keystrokes for programs waiting for input from standard in (System.in). The top pane, **All Programs**, displays all threads from the programs running in VisualAge for Java. As you select the particular thread or program you are interested in, the **Output** and **System In** panes change accordingly to remain in sync with the selected program. See Figure 5.1.

You can stop any running thread, select it, and press the **Terminate** tool bar button. You can also select the thread and press the right mouse button, then from the pop-up menu select **Terminate**. You can remove console output for non-running threads, simply press the right mouse button on the All Programs pane and from the pop-up menu select **Remove All Terminated**.

You can access the console at any time from the **Window** menu. The console also comes up automatically when a message is sent to it, and it remains visible until closed. These messages can result from a deliberate action, like executing System.out.println(), or from the program or the JVM executing exception code. In general, any message sent to System.out, System.err, or System.in causes the console to open.

When code is generated for a connection, a description is included in the comments for the method that implements the connection. If you look at the code

Figure 5.1　Console window.

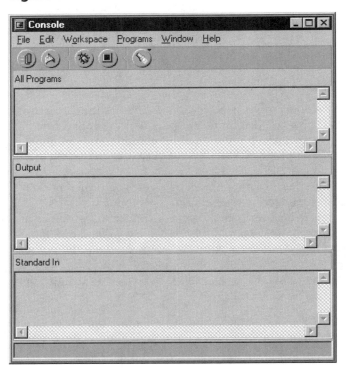

that implemented the connection between the PBSetDate Button and the LBDatebel Label in the Hello World example, you will see the connection's description:

```
/**
 * connEtoM1:  (PBSetDate.action.actionPerformed
 *   (java.awt.event.ActionEvent) --> LBDate.text)
 * @param arg1 java.awt.event.ActionEvent
 */
/* WARNING: THIS METHOD WILL BE REGENERATED. */
private void connEtoM1(java.awt.event.ActionEvent arg1) {
  try {
    // user code begin {1}
    // user code end
    getLBDate().setText(String.valueOf(new java.util.Date()));
    // user code begin {2}
    // user code end
```

```
   } catch (java.lang.Throwable ivjExc) {
     // user code begin {3}
     // user code end
     handleException(ivjExc);
   }
 }
```

To add a trace point just before the code for the connection executes, insert the following line:

```
   ...
   // user code begin {1}
   System.out.println(
     "connEtoM1:(PBSetDate.action.actionPerformed
       (java.awt.event.ActionEvent)-->LBDate.text)");
   // user code end
   ...
```

The actual string passed to System.out.println() was copied and pasted from the comments of the method.

Tip

Add your own code only between the lines designated as //**user code begin{1}** and //**user code end**, so it will be preserved when VisualAge for Java regenerates code. Code added elsewhere in the method is lost the next time VisualAge for Java generates the method.

You can easily monitor the value of your program variables because System.out.println() is so versatile. For example, to monitor the value of a variable int j as you execute a *for* loop, you could write the following code:

```
   ...
   for (int j=0; I < 10; I++)
   {
      // do something
      System.out.println("The value of j is " + j);
   }
   ...
```

Notice how you can combine a String and an int into a single argument to System.out.println().

As your program executes, messages appear in the Standard-out pane of the console. Contents of this pane can be cleared by selecting **Clear** from the pop-up menu, the Edit menu, or pressing the **Clear** button on the tool bar.

The handleException() Method

The Java compiler requires that every invocation of a method that contains the **throws** keyword in its definition must be enclosed in a try/catch block. To be compiled successfully, code generated by VisualAge for Java must follow this rule.

In every catch block generated by VisualAge for Java, you will find a call to the handleException() method. See the following code segment from the Hello World applet:

```
/**
 * connEtoM1:   (PBSetDate.action.actionPerformed
(java.awt.event.ActionEvent) --> LBDate.text)
 * @param arg1 java.awt.event.ActionEvent
 */
/* WARNING: THIS METHOD WILL BE REGENERATED. */
private void connEtoM1(java.awt.event.ActionEvent arg1) {
  try {
    // user code begin {1}
    // user code end
    getLBDate().setText(String.valueOf(new
      java.util.Date()));
    // user code begin {2}
    // user code end
  } catch (java.lang.Throwable ivjExc) {
    // user code begin {3}
    // user code end
    handleException(ivjExc);
  }
}
```

In many cases, it is acceptable to do nothing in a catch block. In that case, only the handleException() method will execute. The code in this method is all commented out. In most cases, this is fine. However, if you are getting strange results from your program or if it ends abruptly, you may want to remove the comments from handleException and see if an exception that is not handled. See the following code with comments removed:

```
/**
 * Called whenever the part throws an exception.
 * @param exception java.lang.Throwable
 */
private void handleException(Throwable exception) {

  /* Uncomment the following lines to print
     uncaught exceptions to stdout */
```

```
System.out.println("--------- UNCAUGHT EXCEPTION
                     ---------");
exception.printStackTrace(System.out);
}
```

Every class has its own handleException() method, so depending on the complexity of your program, you might have to remove comments from code in one or more of the classes in the program path that is executing when the exception is thrown.

Introduction to the Scrapbook

You can access the Scrapbook window from the **Window** menu on the menu bar of the Workbench or any of the browsers, as shown in Figure 5.2.

You can use the Scrapbook to try out segments of code without having to write a method in a class. You can enter fairly complex code segments in the Scrapbook's window and execute them to prove a concept, verify the syntax of a method, or just observe the behavior of a few lines of code in isolation.

Figure 5.2   Scrapbook window.

You can save and load code entered in the Scrapbook from the File menu on the window. These files are saved as text and can be manipulated outside the VisualAge for Java environment by any text editor. By contrast, you can use the Scrapbook to edit text files, even those that are not necessarily Java source files.

Most commonly, code debugged and tested in the Scrapbook ends up being copied and pasted back into a method in a class. The reverse is also true when code that is not giving the predicted result is copied from a method and pasted on the Scrapbook for further testing and debugging.

Scrapbooks can have multiple independent pages. You add pages by selecting **New Page** from the Page menu or by pressing the **New Page** button on the tool bar. There is no interaction or interdependence between pages. Each page executes in its own context.

Execution Context

The execution context of a Scrapbook page can be set to any class in the workspace. The default context is the **Object** class. Code in the Scrapbook is treated as though it is a method in the class of the designated context. It has access to other methods and fields in that class and also classes in the same package. Classes in other packages must be fully qualified with their package names.

Each page in the Scrapbook can have a different execution context. To change the context of the current page, select **Run in** from the **Page** menu. From the Class/Interface Browser, pick the desired context.

Using the Scrapbook

You can run any valid Java expression in the Scrapbook. If you attempt to compile and run an invalid expression, you get an error message indicating the problem. Error messages appear in-line with the line of code that produced the error. Error text is highlighted and can be removed by pressing the Backspace, Delete, or space-bar keys.

While the code in the scrapbook is running, and depending on how long the process is, you see one of the icons on the page tab as shown in Figure 5.3. If the contents of the Scrapbook was loaded from a file, or if you saved the contents to a file, the file name appears in the page tab.

Running code in the Scrapbook is as easy as selecting the code you want to run and pressing the **Run** button. You can also bring up the pop-up menu by

---

Figure 5.3   Scrapbook page icons.

page is not associated with a file   page is busy running code

file for the page is modified and not saved   page is busy running code

file for the page is saved   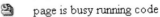 page is busy running code

right-clicking the mouse and selecting Run. You can select a portion of a line, a complete single line, or multiple contiguous lines. Depending on what code runs, you may or may not see anything output on the screen. Typically, you will **Display** the value of an expression or **Inspect** the contents of a variable. Open a Scrapbook window and enter the following lines of code:

```
int a;
a = 4 + 23;
```

Start by selecting 4 + 23, swipe the mouse pointer over the text while holding down the left mouse button. Press the Run button. The equation is compiled and run, but nothing is displayed.

To see the result of the calculation, highlight the same code, but this time press the **Display** button. You will see the answer (int) 27 highlighted right besides the equation. Press the **Backspace** key to remove the answer.

If you select the whole line and press the Display button, you get an error, because the code that defines the int a variable, on the line above, did not execute. To avoid the error, select both lines of code and then press the Display button.

Inspector Windows

Sometimes you need to examine the value of a more complex object, such as an array. Enter the following code in the Scrapbook:

```
int a[] = { 0, 4+23, 5, 12 };
return a;
```

Select both lines of code and press the Display button; all you get this time is the internal representation of the array object, [I@b55. This number is the reference to the array in memory and it will be probably be different each time it is executed. To see the contents of array, you must press the Inspect button instead. Select the code again and press the Inspect button. An inspector window opens as shown in Figure 5.4.

In the case of the int array, you can see the value of each element. You can also change the value of any element in the array by selecting it on the Fields pane and over-typing a new value on the Value pane. Once you change the value of a field, you have to save it. You can select **Save** from the Edit menu, or press the right mouse button over the right pane and from the pop-up menu select **Save**.

Inspector windows are very powerful; they let you get right in and inspect complex objects. Let's instantiate a **Frame** object and use an Inspector window to manipulate the object. In the Scrapbook, enter the following lines of code:

```
Frame f =
  new Frame("This is where the title goes");
return f;
```

Set the context of this page to be the java.awt.Frame class. Select the lines above and press the Inspect button. The code compiles and runs. When the line

Figure 5.4   Inspector window.

containing `return  f` is reached, an Inspector window is opened. The return statement triggers the Inspector to open; the object to be inspected is the object returned.

This Inspector lets you inspect and act on the `Frame  f` object that is displayed in the window as shown in Figure 5.5.

As you can see, an object of type **Frame** is pretty complex. In this Inspector, you can explore all of the Frame's properties. You can even open other Inspectors for the properties that represent objects, or open a browser for any of the typed properties in Frame. To do this, select the property you are interested in, bring up the pop-up menu, and select either **Inspect** or **Open type**. You can also choose to see all fields or only the public fields of the object.

In the Value pane, you can inspect variables and also send messages to this particular object.

The first thing you will notice is that the Frame is nowhere to be seen on your screen. This is because Frames are created in a hidden state. In order to see the actual Frame, you need to call its show() method. Type **show()** in the Value pane, select the text, and press the Run button. Somewhere in your display, you should see a frame window with the title you entered on the code in the Scrapbook.

Try to send a few more messages to the Frame. Here are some ideas:

- setSize(200,200)
- setBackground(Color.green)
- width
- title
- dispose()

Figure 5.5   Inspector for Frame f.

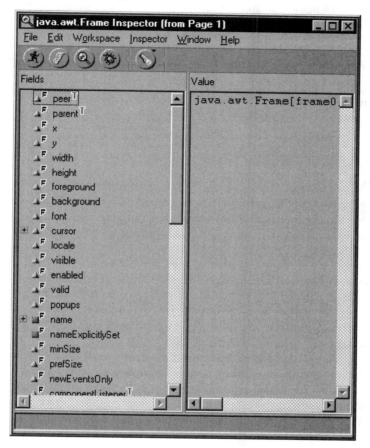

Both width and title should be selected in the Fields pane. Their value is displayed and can be changed in the Value pane. They are properties of the Frame, so it does not make any sense to run them.

Tip

Be careful when you enter commands in the Value pane. You should not have any selected items in the Fields pane. If you do, the command in the Value pane will fail when it is executed. To deselect an item in the Field pane, press and hold the Ctrl key and click the left mouse button on the selected item. Now you can continue entering and executing commands in the Value pane.

There are more advanced topics to learn about Inspector windows; we will cover some of them in the Debugger section. You will also discover new features as you begin to use them while debugging your own programs.

The com.ibm.uvm.tools Package

Included with VisualAge for Java is a package in the IBM Java Implementation project called **com.ibm.uvm.tools**. In this package, you will find the **DebugSupport** class, which has methods very useful for debugging your programs. They are:

- bell()
- halt()
- inspect(java.lang.Object)

These are all static methods implemented in native code.

You can place **com.ibm.uvm.tools.DebugSupport.bell()** in your code when you want an audible indication that you have reached a certain spot in your program.

To force the debugger window to display at a specific instruction in your program, use the **com.ibm.uvm.tools.DebugSupport.halt()** method. Execution pauses after the halt() instruction, giving you a chance to test your code in the debugger. This is the only way to set up a breakpoint while you are executing code in the Scrapbook. You will rarely use halt() inside a method, because you can always set up a debugger breakpoint in a method of a class.

The last method in this package allows you to inspect the value of a variable on the fly. As the JVM executes the **com.ibm.uvm.tools.DebugSupport.inspect(java .lang.Object)** method, an Inspector window opens with the current state of the object passed as the argument. Execution of the program does not stop, so the variable you are inspecting may be out of scope by the time you see it in its inspector, but you can still look at it as a snapshot of the way it was at the time the Inspector opened.

Introduction to the Debugger

Sometimes studying the output of trace information or exercising a portion of code in the Scrapbook does not provide enough insight to determine what is causing a program to go haywire. At other times, you want to better understand a complex function or algorithm. For these cases, you need to examine the code more closely, perhaps by setting a breakpoint at a particular instruction and monitoring state variables, or single stepping through the program. The source-level debugger, that is part of VisualAge for Java is an excellent tool to use when the going gets tough.

Importing the Switcher Package

Before you can start using the debugger in this chapter, you need to import the switcher package into the repository from the CD-ROM and then move it into the workspace. In the CD accompanying this book, you will find the **answers.dat** file. This file contains a buggy version of the Switcher program. The classes in this package will help you learn how to use the source-level debugger in VisualAge for Java.

Importing the answers.dat file into the workspace is a two-step process. First you import the package into the repository; then, you add the package from the repository into the workspace. Once the package is in the workspace, you can start working with it.

Importing into the Repository

Import the answers.dat file into the repository by following these steps:

Select the My Project project.

From the File menu, select **Import**. The Import SmartGuide appears as shown in Figure 5.6.

Figure 5.6   Import SmartGuide.

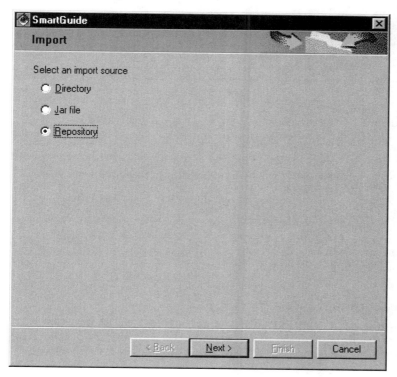

Figure 5.7   Import from another repository SmartGuide.

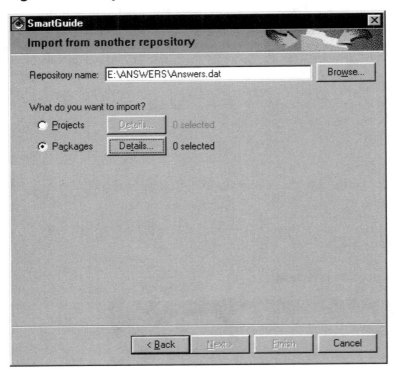

Select **Repository**. Press the **Next** button. The Import from another repository SmartGuide appears as seen in Figure 5.7.

Repository files are used to share projects and packages between programmers. Only versioned projects and packages can be exported as repository files.

Enter the location of the answers.dat file, or press the **Browse** button to locate it.

Because answers.dat contains multiple packages, select the **Packages** radio button, press the **Details...** button and select the switcher package from the Package import dialog. See Figure 5.8.

Adding a Package from the Repository

VisualAge for Java imports repository files into the repository. The next step is to bring the switcher package from the repository into the workspace. For details on performing this action, see Chapter 1, "Breaking Open the Box." For a shorter set of instructions, follow these steps:

Figure 5.8   Selecting Package to import.

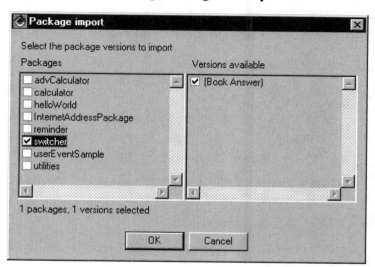

Select the My Project project, right-click, and from the pop-up menu, select **Add, Package…**.

In the New Package SmartGuide, select the **Add package(s) from repository** radio button.

Select the switcher package from the **Available package names** list. Select the Book Answer edition from the list of **Available editions**. Depending on what work you have already done on this package, the list might have more than one entry.

Press the **Finish** button on the SmartGuide to complete the operation. See Figure 5.9.

Switcher Class Description

The switcher package contains several classes that implement a very simple program you can use to get acquainted with the debugger. Similar in construction to the Calculator project, the Switcher program is built following a model-view-programming paradigm.

The view is built on a Panel using a GridBagLayout and is implemented in the **SwitcherPanel** class. The model is coded in the **SwitcherModel** class. The SwitcherPanel bean contains:

- Two Label beans
- Two TextField beans
- One Button bean

Figure 5.9   Adding Package from repository.

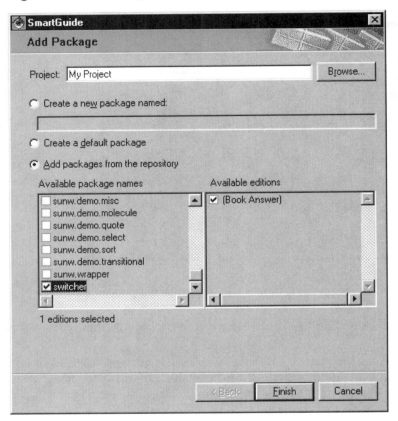

Each of the beans is placed on a Panel with a GridBagLayout; each has its own GridBagConstraints to control its placement and other properties on the GridBag. You can use the property sheet for each bean to find out more about these settings.

The purpose of the Switcher program is to switch the values of the **First word** and **Second word** fields when the **Switch now** button is pressed. The logic to perform this operation is contained in the model bean, **SwitcherModel**.

Usually, model or domain beans have views associated with them. The views represent part of the model and, therefore, have some of the same properties. In this case, the Switcher model has two String properties representing **word1** and **word2**. The view has corresponding entry fields. The model has the logic to perform the switching of word1 and word2 in a public method called **switchNow()**. The view has the **Switch** button, which, when pressed, calls the switchNow() method to perform the operation.

The SwitcherPanel bean contains a SwitcherModel bean, which is named switcher. The proper connections have been made, as shown in Figure 5.10. Feel free to open these beans in the VisualAge for Java browsers and observe the implementation details.

The SwitcherPanel bean can be run on its own within the VisualAge for Java development environment, because the code generator always creates a main() method for testing. However, before you can run it in a Web browser, you need to place it inside an Applet. If you want to run it as an application, you need to place it inside a Frame. We have provided implementations for both options in the classes **SwitcherApplet** and **SwitcherApplication,** respectively.

Both classes are very straightforward, where the SwitcherPanel is just placed in the center of an Applet or Frame with a BorderLayout.

A connection gives focus to the **First word** field when the program completes its initialization. In the Applet, this is very easy; you just connect the init() event of the Applet to the requestFocus() method of the SwitcherPanel.

The only complication is that the features of the SwitcherPanel are encapsulated in the bean and are not accessible once it is placed on the Applet. To resolve this problem, promote the requestFocus method of the word1 TextField. You learn more about promoting bean features, see Chapter 9, "Building the Internet Address Applet."

Because Frames don't generate init() events, you need to find another way to signal that the application has completed its initialization phase. The **windowOpened** event is generated when the frame opens. You will use this event to call the requestFocus method of the word1 TextField.

Figure 5.10   SwitcherPanel bean.

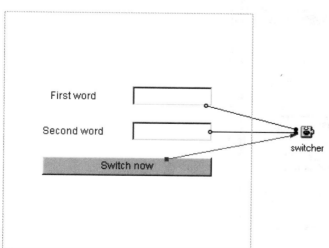

Debugging the Switcher Program

Now back to the problem at hand. Select either the SwitcherApplet or the SwitcherApplication and run the program. Enter a distinct word in each of the text fields, for example, Justin and Jessica as shown in Figure 5.11.

Press the **Switch now** button and observe the change. The expected result is that Justin and Jessica will switch places, with Jessica will be on top and Justin will move to the bottom field. What really happens is that you end up with Jessica in both text fields, as shown in Figure 5.12.

Even though the switch operation did not produce the expected result, you have ascertained several facts:

- Pressing the button fired an actionEvent.

- A method was executed.

- Something in that method acted on the fields.

Setting Breakpoints

The next step is to step through the code and see what is actually happening. If you open the Composition Editor for the SwitcherPanel bean, refer to Figure 5.10, and click on the connection from the button to the model part, you will see in the information area that this connection is named **ConnEtoM1**, or the English translation: **Connection Event to Method 1**.

Figure 5.11   Switcher application before switch.

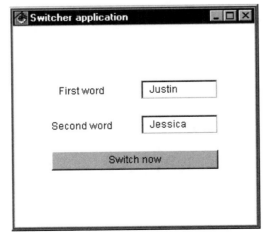

Figure 5.12   After switching.

Select the Members tab of the browser for SwitcherPanel and find the **ConnEtoM1** method. Click on it to display its source in the bottom pane of the browser as shown in Figure 5.13.

The gray column at the left of the source pane is used to manipulate debugger breakpoints. Place the mouse pointer on the dark column to the left of the source pane, aligned with the source line where the **switchNow()** method is invoked, and double-click the left mouse button. Notice that a blue sphere appears next to the line indicating that a breakpoint is set and enabled. Breakpoints can be set at any valid executable line of code. Resetting the breakpoint is accomplished the same way, just double-click on the blue sphere.

Figure 5.13   Setting a breakpoint at ConnEtoM1.

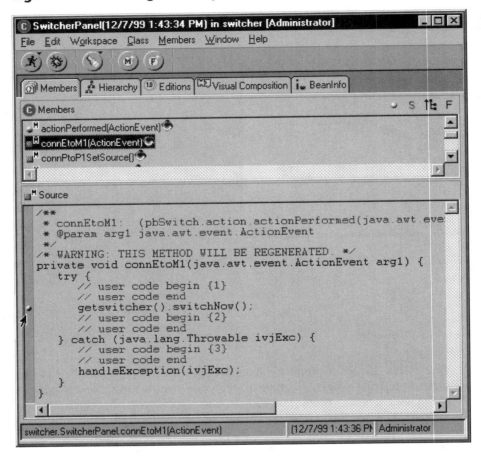

Tip
Avoid setting breakpoints in the bean constructor created in the Visual Composition Editor. These constructors are run in order to render the visual bean in the composition surface. A breakpoint in the constructor stops this process by bringing up the debugger.

Setting Breakpoints in External Files
You can set breakpoints on code that is currently not loaded in the VisualAge for Java workspace. To set a breakpoint on an external class file press the **External**

Figure 5.14 Setting external breakpoints.

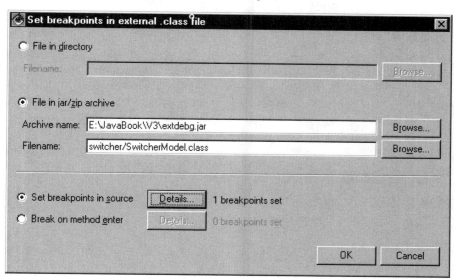

.class file breakpoints tool bar button on the Breakpoints page of the debugger's window. Follow the prompts of the SmartGuide to select either a class or an archive (jar or zip) file from the file system. You can then select method names in the selected files for the debugger to stop when the method is entered. If the source for the method is available, you will also be able to set breakpoints on any valid line of code, just as if the code was locally available on the workspace. See Figure 5.14.

Stopping When an Exception Is Thrown

If your code is throwing a certain exception and you would like to stop program execution when the exception is thrown, you can set a breakpoint at any of the exception classes currently loaded into your workspace. Switch to the **Exceptions** page on the debugger's window. From there you will see a selection list of all the eligible exceptions. There are toolbar buttons to see the exceptions in different views. You can sort the exceptions by Class, Package or Hierarchically. Other toolbar buttons assist you set a single breakpoint on an exception class, or multiple breakpoints on a class and all of its subclasses. See Figure 5.15.

Enabling and Disabling Breakpoints

You can manage breakpoints as a group from the Breakpoints page of the Debugger window. From this window, you can temporarily enable, disable, or remove breakpoints in the workspace, as shown in Figure 5.16.

Figure 5.15   Setting a breakpoint at an exception.

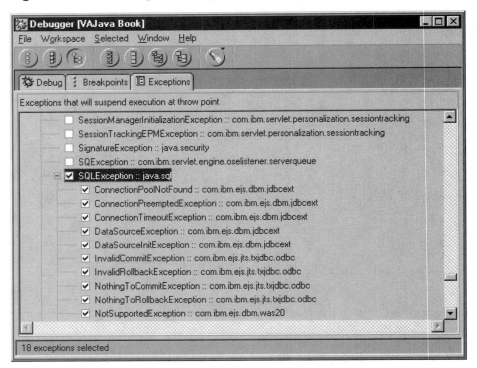

Integrated Source-Level Debugger

Now that the breakpoint is set, run the program again. Ensure that you are viewing the SwitcherPanel class and press the Run button. Enter text in each field and press the **Switch Now** button. The program runs until it encounters the breakpoint; the debugger automatically comes up as shown in Figure 5.17.

The Debugger presents a complex window made up of many panes as shown in Table 5.1.

You can size panes by sliding the separator frames between them. You can maximize any pane by double-clicking its title. To restore it to its original size, double-click its title again.

The All Programs/Threads pane lets you switch between threads that are stopped at their own breakpoints. This pane also shows how you got to this particular breakpoint by displaying the call stack. You can work your way back to examine the source code and variables at each point of execution. You can even restart execution from a particular point on the call stack by selecting it, pressing the right mouse button, and from the pop-up menu selecting **Drop Selected to Frame**.

Figure 5.16   Breakpoints window.

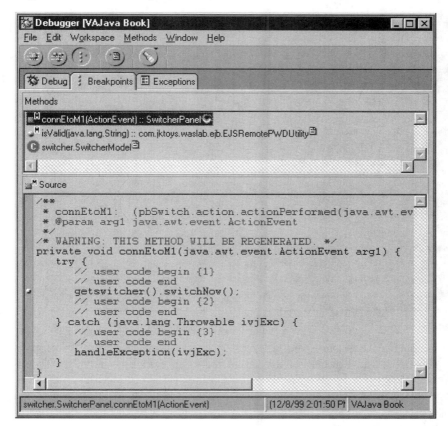

Table 5.1   Debugger Window Panes

Pane	Displays/Function
All Programs/Threads	Lists the programs and threads available for debugging and the call stack for the selected thread
Visible Variables	List of variables you can inspect
Value	Value of the currently selected variable
Source	Source code for the selected method

Figure 5.17   Debugger stopped at breakpoint.

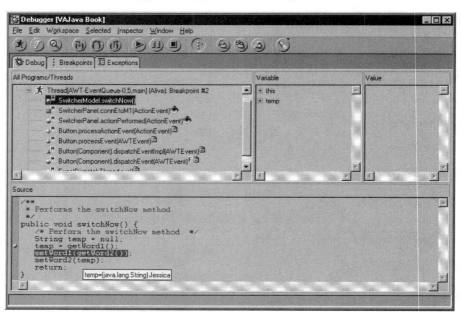

The Visible Variables pane and Value pane are very similar to an Inspector window. You select the variable you are interested in and examine its value. To change a variable's value, over-type the current value and from the pop-up menu selecting **Save**. Notice that sometimes this option is grayed out, or unavailable. This happens if the variable is immutable (for example, a String object) or if the variable you want to change is out of scope.

As long as you are stopped at a breakpoint, you can change the source code in the Source pane. Save your changes by selecting **Save** from the pop-up menu or by pressing Ctrl-S. Saving will sometimes reset the breakpoints in the modified method. Changes to the code take effect immediately after saving. After a modified method is saved, the execution pointer is moved to the first instruction of the method, allowing you test it again.

Debugger Tool Bar

The last six buttons of the debugger tool bar control the execution of the program while the debugger is in control, as shown in Table 5.2.

More Debugging

The debugger window opens, and the next statements to be executed are:

getswitcher() - press the **Step over** button

Table 5.2 Debugger Tool Bar Buttons

Button	Function key	Function	Description
	F5	Step into	Steps into the highlighted method.
	F6	Step over	Executes method without debugging into method.
	F7	Run to Return	Executes until the return statement of the method.
	F8	Resume	Resumes execution until next break-point or program end.
	NA	Suspend	Suspends the currently running thread at the next opportunity. It can then be resumed.
	NA	Terminate	Terminates execution of the current thread.

switchNow() - press the **Step into** button

Even though the statement at the breakpoint is a compound expression (getswitcher().switchNow();), each method call is executed and can be traced individually.

Now you have reached the switchNow() method and can analyze what is causing the two strings to switch incorrectly.

```
/**
 * Performs the switchNow method.
 */
public void switchNow() {
    /* Perform the switchNow method. */
    setWord1( getWord2());
    setWord2(getWord1());
    return;
}
```

At this point, verify that the String variables hold the same value as the fields in the view bean. This proves that the connections between them are firing properly.

Click on the plus sign next to the *this* variable in the middle pane.

It expands, and you see the two String variables, **fieldWord1** and **fieldWord2**. VisualAge for Java assigned these names as a result of the String property names defined in this bean. If you select each of them, you can see their contents in the Value pane. They contain the same string as the field on the screen.

Examining the code shows that this is obviously a beginner's error. Every programmer knows that two variables cannot be switched without first storing one of the values in a temporary variable. You can change the code right in the debugger Source pane so that the two strings are switched properly.

```
public void switchNow() {
    /* Perform the switchNow method. */
    String temp;
    temp = getWord2();
    setWord2( getWord1() );
    setWord1( temp );
    return;
}
```

Press Ctrl-S to save and compile the method.

Quick Display of Variable Contents

When you are debugging a Java program, you can get a quick look at the contents of a variable by resting the mouse pointer over the name of the variable. Let the mouse pointer hover over the variable name without moving it, and soon a pop-up window will open and show you the value of the variable.

Make sure you have executed enough of the method so that the variable has a valid value. Also, make sure that you have not clicked anywhere on the source pane. Doing so activates the text cursor and disables the pop-up window. See Figure 5.18.

Press the Resume button to continue executing the program. The two fields switched properly: Justin moved to the bottom and Jessica to the top field.

It is important to use the set method to set a new value into the bean's properties. Because these are instance variables, you could access them directly, for example:

```
fieldWord2 = fieldWord1;
```

This is a very bad idea, especially with bound properties. The code to fire propertyChange events is in the set method. If you assign values directly, the set method does not execute, and therefore property-changed events do not execute. The result is that no other components are notified that the property changed. See the following code segment:

```
public void setWord2(String word2) {
    /* Get the old property value for fire property
```

Figure 5.18 Quick variable content display.

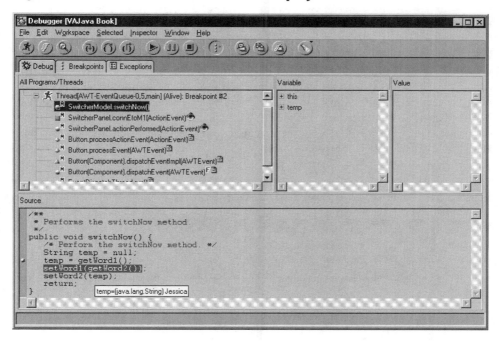

```
    change event. */
 String oldValue = fieldWord2;
/* Set the word2 property (attribute) to the new
   value. */
 fieldWord2 = word2;
/* Fire (signal/notify) the word2 property change
   event. */
firePropertyChange("word2", oldValue, word2);
 return;
}
```

Conditional Breakpoints

Sometimes you need to set a breakpoint in your program, but you do not want to stop executing the program every time the breakpoint is reached. Instead, you want to stop only if a certain condition is met.

The integrated debugger allows you to set a condition that is evaluated when a breakpoint is reached. If the condition is met, you can choose to stop the program and present the debugger window.

To set a conditional breakpoint, place the mouse pointer over the blue sphere, which signifies an active breakpoint, press the right mouse button, and from the pop-up menu select **Modify...**. The dialog shown in Figure 5.19 opens.

The default condition consists of a single line containing the boolean **true**. This signals the debugger to pause the execution of the program and display its window. Other conditions that evaluate to a boolean can be placed in this window.

You can also place other valid Java statements in the window followed by either **true** or **false**, depending on whether you want execution to stop or continue respectively. For example, you may want to display a message to the console when a certain point in the program is reached, and depending on the state of a variable, bring the debugger window up.

Figure 5.19   Setting a conditional breakpoint.

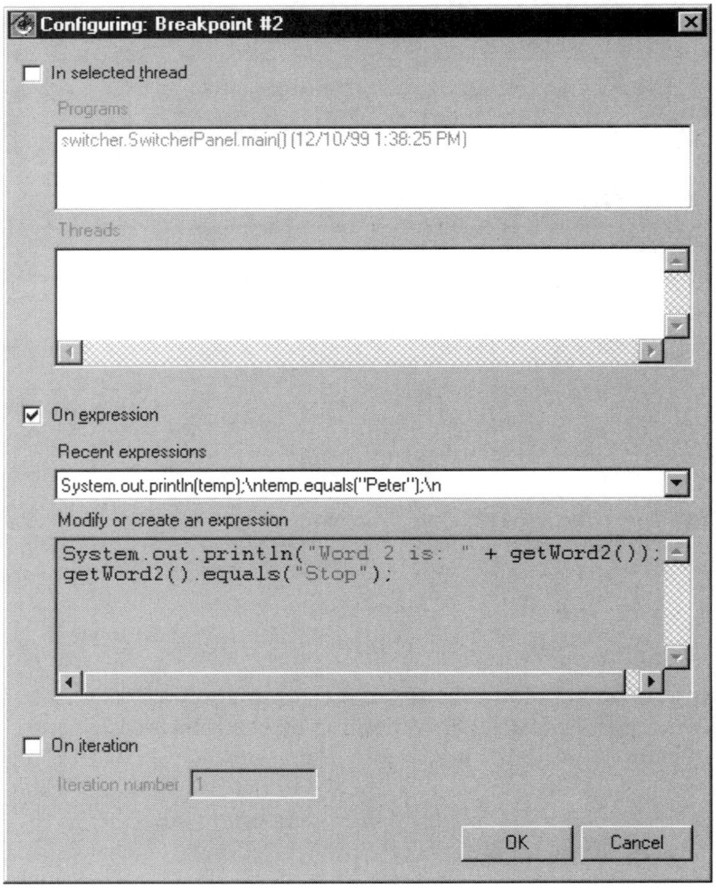

Open the source for the **switchNow()** method of the **SwitcherModel** class. Set a breakpoint on the line where the temp variable is assigned the value of word2. Place the mouse pointer on top of the breakpoint's blue sphere and press the right mouse button, from the pop-up menu select **Modify...**, and make sure the **On expression** box is checked.

Replace the word **true** with the following lines:

```
System.out.println("Word 2 is: " + getWord2());
getWord2().equals("Stop");
```

Run **SwitcherApplet** and try several values in the **Word 2** text field. Notice that each time you press the **Switch now** button, a line showing the content of the second text field is printed to the console. Now enter the word **Stop** on the Second Word and make the switch. The word **Stop** prints on the console, the expression above evaluates to **true**, the debugger window comes up, and the program stops at the breakpoint.

For a list of the ten most recently used expressions, go to the **Configuring Breakpoints** dialog box and click on **Recent Expressions**.

You can also set a conditional breakpoint that will cause the debugger to stop program execution after a predetermined number of iterations through the code. The iteration count can be reset at any time by pressing the right mouse button over top of the breakpoint indicator and selecting **Reset Iterations Count.**

Visible Variables, Watches, and Evaluation Area

There are three more ways to examine variables in the VisualAge for Java Version 3 debugger. You may use these panels in different debugging situations.

You may want to detach the Variables and Values pane from the main debugger window to give yourself more room or to place this new window in a more convenient place of screen real estate. See Figure 5.20. The Visible Variables window can be reattached to the debugger window by closing it.

The Watches window allows you to set up expressions and variables, which will be evaluated and displayed every time the debugger stops or executes a step. This is a convenient way to monitor a set values without having to reselect them all the time. See Figure 5.21.

Tip

Beware that if the expression or variable in the Watches window goes out of scope, its value is no longer updated, in fact you may see some type of error indication in the Value column instead of an indication that the expression is out of scope.

Figure 5.20   Visible Variables window.

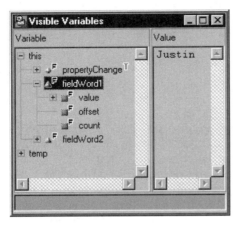

To enter a variable or expression on the Expression column, just double click on an empty row. To Edit or Delete an entry, right mouse click and select the appropriate action from the popup menu.

The Evaluation Area window is very similar to the Scrapbook covered earlier in the chapter. The main difference is that code executed in the Evaluation Area runs in the current class context.

See Figure 5.22. The first line in the figure can be selected and evaluated because it requires no context—it is just a formula. The second line will not evaluate because **getBalance**() is not a method of the **SwitcherModel** class, which is the class the debugger is stopped on. The third line evaluates properly because **getWord2**() is a method in SwitcherModel.

There are subtle differences between the Scrapbook window and the Evaluation window. There is no menu bar on the Evaluation window, so code

Figure 5.21   Watches window.

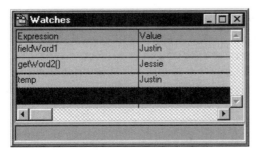

Figure 5.22 Evaluation area window.

typed in this window cannot be readily saved to a file, though you can always cut and paste. The other main difference is that the execution context of the Evaluation window cannot be changed.

Killing Active Programs

It is possible to close the debugger while the program being debugged is stopped at a breakpoint. The program being debugged remains visible but does not respond to keyboard and mouse events, and the program cannot be ended from the frame controls of the window.

 In these cases, you can bring up the debugger and kill your program's thread. Another option is to resume execution from the breakpoint. If you find yourself in this situation, press the Debug button. The debugger window opens and shows a list of the running threads for all the programs.

You can attempt to determine which thread belongs to your program by selecting each one individually and studying the call stack for that thread. When you find the thread you want to kill, select it and press the **Terminate** button to end the thread.

Other VisualAge for Java Debuggers

In addition to the integrated debugger, VisualAge for Java Enterprise Edition offers three other debuggers that allow you to debug your code outside of the VisualAge for Java environment. They are:

- The Workstation Debugger, which lets you debug programs running on Windows, OS/2, or AIX
- The AS/400 Cooperative Debugger
- The OS/390 Debugger

To use any of these debuggers, you must export the code for your program to the file system of your target platform. In order to debug your programs using one of the external debuggers, you must select the **Include debug attributes in .class files** checkbox when you export your class files.

Remote debugging is also supported. You can run a program on its intended target platform and debug it remotely from another workstation.

It is beyond the scope of this book to describe in more detail the operation of these debuggers. If you have VisualAge for Java Enterprise Edition, you can read more about them by searching the help system using the following phrase: **"Choosing the right debugger for your program"**

Conclusion

This completes the introduction to debugging using VisualAge for Java. As you develop your own beans and combine them to form applets and applications, you will have lots of opportunities to hone the skills you started to develop in this chapter.

The integrated debugger brings an unprecedented level of debugging when working on server-side applications. The debugger, along with the VisualAge Development Environment, lets you debug your servlets and Enterprise JavaBeans within the IDE. This is achieved by running a Web server and IBM's WebSphere Application Server inside VisualAge for Java.

Summary

In this chapter, you were introduced to the trace and debugging facilities of VisualAge for Java. You learned how to:

- Add trace information to a program by entering your own trace statements in the code.
- Use the Java console to display trace information and provide keyboard input.
- Use the handleException() method to display uncaught exceptions.
- Test segments of code in the Scrapbook.
- Use the com.ibm.uvm.tools.DebugSupport class.
- Load a program from a repository file and bring it into the workspace.
- Debug the Switcher application to fix a logic error.
- Set conditional breakpoints.

You should use the debugger to debug and inspect the Java programs that you develop. Debugging OO programs forces you to dive deep into the code, so don't be shy—you must do this to get your programs working properly.

BUILDING THE ADVANCED CALCULATOR GUI

What's in Chapter 6

This chapter builds on the topics already covered in this book. You will build on what you learned in making the Adding Machine and improve it in a number of ways. The new application will have a much more sophisticated user interface and you will add more math functions. You will also work on the user interface to support these new functions. This chapter covers the following topics:

- Copying beans in the IDE
- Using GridBagLayout
- Setting TextField and Label properties
- Setting GridBagConstraints properties
- Using the init() method
- Implementing the clear function with an Event-To-Code connection

---

Based on your previous experience with the Simple Adder, you will now construct a better calculator. This version will be able to perform operations to add, subtract, multiply, and divide two floating-point numbers. It will also provide a Clear function and be able to detect an attempt by the user to divide by zero.

If you have closed VisualAge for Java, restart it. The simplest way to start VisualAge for Java is to double-click its icon.

Your Next Applet

Let's get started building the next applet with VisualAge for Java using the Visual Composition Editor. You will use the iterative development method, just as you did on the previous programs. You will develop the applet's user interface first, save your work, and test the Java code by running it in the IDE. You will iterate by adding more function and user interface elements, saving and testing again.

Packages

With the My Project project selected, right-click on the top pane, and from the pop-up menu select **Add Package.** You can also press the New Package icon from the tool bar.

Enter **advcalculator** in the **Create a new package named** entry field. Press **Finish** to create the package.

After creating the package, your Workbench should look like Figure 6.1.

The Advanced Calculator builds on the Simple Adder developed in previous chapters. It is much easier to start with the Simple Adder than to begin building the Advanced Calculator from the beginning. This section covers copying beans, one of the most common forms of reuse.

Copying Beans

When copying a bean, first select the bean that you want to copy in the Workbench, then copy the bean using the pop-up menu. There is no other easier way to copy beans without exporting them.

Figure 6.1   Advcalculator package.

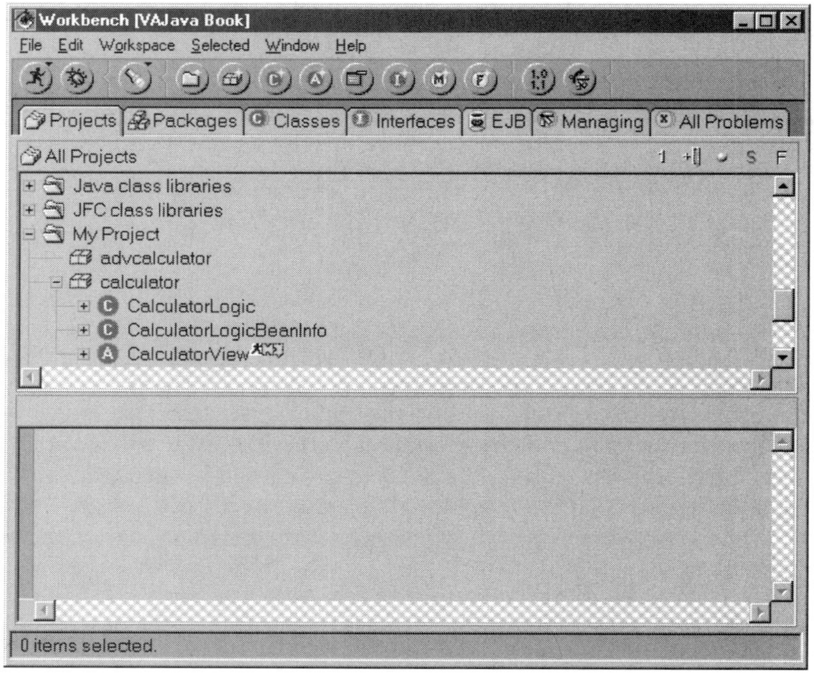

In the Workbench, select the **CalculatorView;** then display the pop-up menu.

Select **Reorganize** and then **Copy,** and the **Copying types** dialog opens.

Enter the package name for the Advanced Calculator, **advcalculator,** as the target package in the **Copy to** field as shown in Figure 6.2.

You can always use the **Browse** button to select the package name from the packages known in the workspace. The window prevents you from selecting an invalid package name by disabling the **OK** button until you select a valid package name. It is not necessary to rename this bean.

Deselect the **Rename** check box, and press the **OK** button to start copying the bean. At any time you can rename a JavaBean using the rename function, but for illustration purposes this book keeps the name CalculatorView.

Tip

If you copy a bean from one project to another, you get a warning message, as shown in Figure 6.3. This message warns you that the classes being copied might not be able to find resource files (like bitmaps or icons) associated with GUI beans. The resource files are located in a subdirectory named like the project that contains the bean. When you copy beans, the resource files are not automatically moved to the target project. After you have seen this message a few times, it may become annoying. To suppress it, you can use the menu item Window/Options/Help/Warnings. There is more information on working with resource files later in this book in the Chapter 8.

Figure 6.2   Copy dialog.

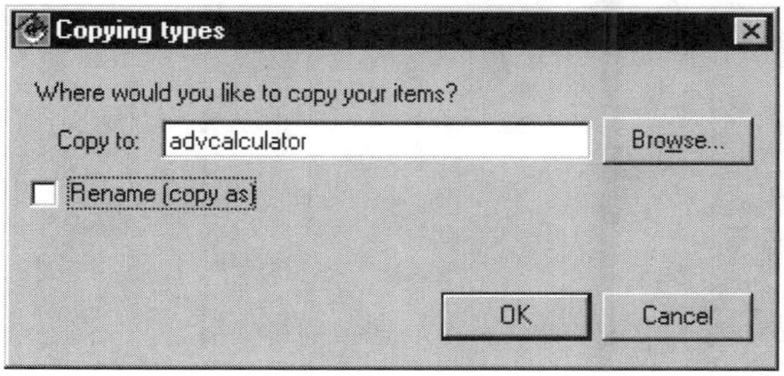

Figure 6.3   Copy warning.

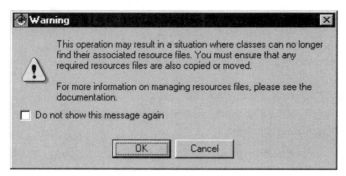

CalculatorView appears in the advcalculator package in the Workbench, as shown in Figure 6.4. While the class copies, a progress indicator appears. There are now two CalculatorView JavaBeans in the Workbench, each in a different package. For the rest of this chapter you will work on advcalculator.CalculatorView, and for

Figure 6.4   Workbench with copied CalculatorView.

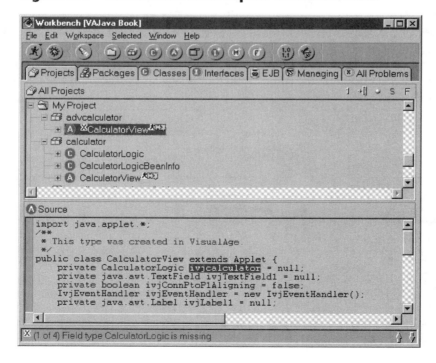

brevity, instructions will not use the fully qualified class name that includes the package name.

Notice the red X next to the CalculatorView bean in the Workbench. You only copied the bean, why does it suddenly have errors? Did you copy it incorrectly? The error message in the info area at the bottom of the Workbench reads:

```
Type for field: private Calculator ivjcalculator, is missing
```

This is generated code, but let's look at it to see how to fix the problem. You need to look at the source code for the class that defines the variables. If you select the CalculatorView in the Workbench, you see the following:

```
private CalculatorLogic ivjcalculator = null;
```

By looking at the code, it is clear that the **ivjcalculator** has a type of **CalculatorLogic**. There is no qualification for the CalculatorLogic type. So the type for the field is not missing, but maybe it is out of scope in the workspace. Let's quickly review Java access conventions to see why this type may be out of scope.

Access Rules

Java has the same access modifiers for methods and fields as C++, as follows:

Private. Access is limited to the class

Protected. Access is limited to the class, all of its subclasses, and all the classes in the same package

Public. Access is not limited

Java allows another type of access when you do not specify an access modifier for the method or variable. This access, called *default* access, is a very loose level of access control because it is implied. Default access allows any class in the package to access the method or variable.

When you refer to objects and methods, you refer to them by name, which can be either unqualified or fully qualified. Fully qualified names include the specific packages that contain the referenced item. Fully qualified names can be very long, so it is common to use unqualified names. When you move a bean to another package, the unqualified names become out of scope.

Fixing Generated Code

As discussed earlier, there is no qualification for the CalculatorLogic type. So the type relies on the fact that CalculatorLogic is in the same package. When you copy the class to another package, this assumption is shattered. There are a number of ways to fix this error and correctly reference the variable. Three options are:

- Edit the generated code to fully qualify the reference to CalculatorLogic
- Edit the generated code and add an import statement to resolve the reference

- Have the Visual Composition Editor regenerate the code with the correct reference

The last option is a little easier, and if there are any other invalid references, the Visual Composition Editor should fix those references, too. You can use the Visual Composition Editor to force regeneration and fix the applet with these steps:

Go to the Visual Composition Editor for the new CalculatorView in the advcalculator package.

There are two options to force regeneration:

- Select Bean/Save Bean, so you can regenerate the code for the applet. If the Save Bean option is disabled, you can make a trivial change to the applet like moving the applet or the CalculatorLogic bean in the workspace, or resizing the applet. This enables the save function. From the menu bar select **Bean**, then **Save Bean** to save and generate the correct code.
- Use the menu item that code re-generates the code. Select **Bean=>Re-generate Code** to accomplish this. If this menu item is disabled, select **Bean=>Save Bean**.

When the Visual Composition Editor finishes saving the bean and generating the code, the red Xs disappear. You can look at the regenerated code in the Workbench or on the Members page of the browser or in the Workbench. The Visual Composition Editor regenerates a fully qualified reference, as shown in the following code:

```
private calculator.CalculatorLogic ivjcalculator
     = null;
```

This is an example where the internal model of the class in VisualAge for Java has the correct information and can regenerate the code to match.

The Generated main()

The Visual Composition Editor automatically generates another method in the advanced version of the CalculatorView. When you define an applet in a SmartGuide, the Visual Composition Editor generates a main() method. Following is the code for the generated main():

```
/**
 * main entrypoint - starts the part when it is run as an application
 * @param args java.lang.String[]
 */
public static void main(java.lang.String[] args) {
    try {
```

```
            java.awt.Frame frame;
            try {
                Class aFrameClass =
    Class.forName("com.ibm.uvm.abt.edit.TestFrame");
                frame =
      (java.awt.Frame)aFrameClass.newInstance();
            } catch (java.lang.Throwable ivjExc) {
                frame = new java.awt.Frame();
            }
            CalculatorView aCalculatorView;
            Class iiCls =
    Class.forName("calculator.CalculatorView");
            ClassLoader iiClsLoader =
    iiCls.getClassLoader();
            aCalculatorView =
    (CalculatorView)java.beans.Beans.instantiate
    (iiClsLoader,"calculator.CalculatorView");
            frame.add("Center", aCalculatorView);
            frame.setSize(aCalculatorView.getSize());
            frame.setVisible(true);
        } catch (Throwable exception) {
            System.err.println("Exception occurred in
    main() of java.applet.Applet");
            exception.printStackTrace(System.out);
        }
    }
}
```

The Visual Composition Editor only generates the main() method once. If you intend to always use the program as an applet, there is no need for main(). If you ever want to run it as an application, you need to edit the main() method. When you copied the bean, the reference to the bean did not change. Look at the code and you can see the following:

```
aCalculatorView =
  (CalculatorView)java.beans.Beans.instantiate
  (iiClsLoader,"calculator.CalculatorView");
```

The main() method creates an instance of the CalculatorView in the old *calculator* package. After you have made a number of changes to the new CalculatorView, you still see the old CalculatorView when you run it. You would probably find this problem by tracing the code, but it can be very confusing because it is the same class in different packages. Since you only use the Advanced Calculator as an applet, you do not need to edit the main() method.

Tip

The Visual Composition Editor only generates the main() method one time. If you copy or rename the class, you need to edit the main() method so that it refers to the new class name. If you forget to edit main(), it tries to instantiate the old class when it runs. This can be very frustrating as you work on the new class. Whenever you test the new class, the main() will instantiate the old class.

Improving the CalculatorView

Now that the CalculatorView is all cleaned up (or rather, it doesn't have any errors), you can start improving it with the following:

From the Workbench, open the **advcalculator** package; then open a browser to edit the **CalculatorView** class.

The Visual Composition Editor opens, enabling you to modify the applet and place the additional GUI beans.

The first thing to improve in the CalculatorView is the Layout Manager. For this applet, the GridBagLayout helps keep the GUI beans properly aligned at run time, and it is better suited for this applet. After you change the Layout Manager, you add the additional Buttons for the new calculator functions.

GridBagLayout

You built the Simple Adder using the applet in GridLayout to place other GUI beans. GridLayout kept the GUI beans in the correct place, and the applet could be resized at run time. However, when you resized the applet, the TextFields and the Button got bigger. This is not a good design for a user interface; you would do better with GridBagLayout.

Building the Advanced Calculator involves using the applet with its own GridBagLayout Manager. The applet has the same TextFields and Labels that you used in the Simple Adder. The applet also has a separate panel with a FlowLayout Manager that contains the buttons for the calculator. You add this panel to the applet as a component in the GridBagLayout.

GridBag Basics

As you learned earlier, Layout Managers are used to align, space, and size controls placed on a Container. GridBagLayout is a fairly complex Layout Manager. It is far more complicated than FlowLayout, which is the default Layout Manager for applets. The GridBag is also much better than the Grid because components can span more than one grid, and the grids can have different sizes and properties. The

GridBag is organized in rows and columns, and numbering starts in the upper left corner. Rows and columns are addressed using integers, with the upper left cell having the address of row 0 and column 0, as shown in Figure 6.5. The GridBag properties for location are *gridX* for the column and *gridY* for the row.

Once you place a Java Component on a Container that has a GridBagLayout, the component has a new property. GridBagConstraint is a class in the java.awt package, and it holds properties for the behavior of the bean within the GridBag. The cells or coordinates in the GridBag are referred to as grids. The GridBag has the following properties:

anchor. Determines the location in the GridBag cell in which the GUI bean anchors itself. Directional values for this property are center, north, northeast, east, southeast, south, southwest, west, and northwest.

fill. Specifies which directions the GUI bean fills or grows as the GridBag is resized. Valid settings are NONE, BOTH, HORIZONTAL, and VERTICAL. The default value is NONE.

gridHeight and **gridWidth.** The number of grids that the GUI bean spans or occupies. By default, the GUI bean is in one grid.

gridX and **gridY.** The GridBag x and y coordinates for the bean.

insets. The padding outside the GUI bean, specified in pixels. There are separate insets for top, bottom, right, and left.

ipadx and **ipady.** The padding inside the GUI bean, specified in pixels. These are frequently used to increase the size of a GUI bean.

weightX and **weightY.** Specify how extra space is used by the GUI bean.

As you can see, there are a lot of different properties you can set in GridBagConstraints. You can set these properties individually or in combination, thus adding to their complexity. The Visual Composition Editor generates default values for all of these properties, but you need to modify the default settings to get the desired results.

Figure 6.5   GridBagLayout addressing.

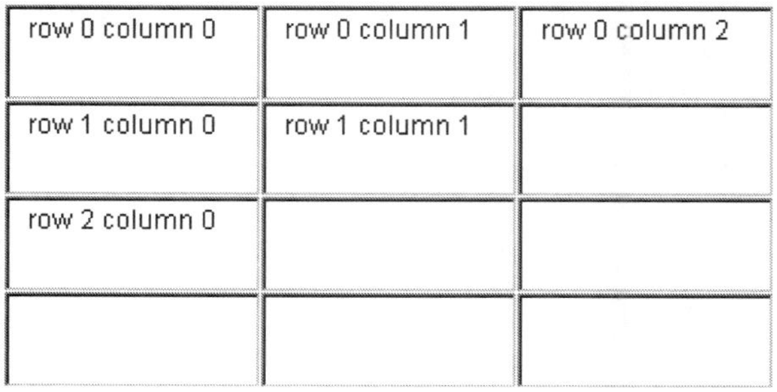

row 0 column 0	row 0 column 1	row 0 column 2
row 1 column 0	row 1 column 1	
row 2 column 0		

Using the GridBagLayout

The Visual Composition Editor makes it easy to work with more complex Layout Managers. The GridBag Layout provides a lot of flexibility, allowing more control of the user interface. VisualAge for Java Versions 1 and 2 let you to set any Layout Manager in the Visual Composition Editor. But these older versions did not handle the GridBag automatically, and they required you to move the GUI components and adjust their properties. Let's change the Layout Manager for the CalculatorView to GridBagLayout with the following steps:

Select the CalculatorView from the Beans List, and open its property sheet as shown in Figure 6.6.

Select the *layout* property from the list and open its drop-down list where you can select layouts.

Select **GridBagLayout** from the drop-down list and press the Enter key to save the new layout property.

NOTE

Earlier versions of VisualAge for Java did not have the same support for the GridBag Layout. After changing to the GridBag, the GUI components in the Applet appear on one line after you change the Layout Manager. The Visual Composition Editor does not know where to place the GUI beans in the new Layout Manager, so it places all the GUI beans in one long row with grid locations –1 and –1. If this happens, you should upgrade to the latest version of VisualAge for Java.

When you switch to the GridBag Layout, The Visual Composition Editor puts all the GUI beans into grids in the GridBag, retaining their size and location. It looks just as it did with the Grid Layout. To do this, the Visual Composition Editor adds padding and insets to the GridBag Constraint properties. This is a real cool stealth feature that makes using the GridBag very easy, especially helpful when you are creating a new user interface. But now you are revising an existing Grid Layout user interface, and you can't resize the GUI beans because they are padded out. There are two ways to get the job done:

- Set the layout to *null*, do all the arrangement in the *null* layout, then set the layout to GridBag.

- Edit the individual padding and inset properties for each GUI bean, and then do all the arrangement.

The first way is a little easier, and if there were a lot of GUI beans it would save a lot of time. So use the first option and move the GUI beans to a better arrangement with the following steps:

Figure 6.6   Setting the Applet Layout Manager.

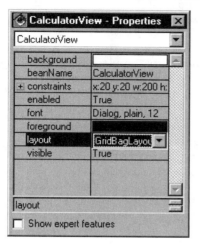

Set the applet layout manager to *null*.

Drag and drop the GUI beans in the Applet so they align in columns in the proper order as shown in Figure 6.7.

You need to resize the GUI beans and you may use the alignment functions. To do this, select multiple GUI beans by using the Control key and pressing the left mouse button. Then from the menu bar, select Tools, Match Width, or Align Left.

Set the applet layout manager to GridBag.

If you drag additional GUI beans over the GridBag, you see artificial lines that indicate the grids. Since the GUI beans are fully padded, additional GUI beans are added to new grids. The arrangement of the GUI beans is good, but

Figure 6.7   GUI beans arranged.

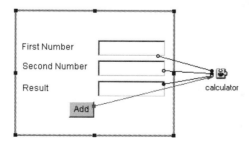

there are some GridBag Constraints that can improve the appearance of the Applet. You will fix these after a quick test of the applet.

Tip

When you drop GUI beans in the GridBag, it is possible to place two GUI beans in the same grid. If you do this, the Visual Composition Editor generates the code successfully, then compiles and runs without errors. You will not get errors that prevent you from doing this; but when the program runs, the GUI on top will obstruct the other GUI bean. You may think this is a bug, but technically you can do this in Java.

Test Iteration One

Let's test the applet with GridBag layout to see how it works:

Run the CalculatorView by pressing the Test button; the applet should look like Figure 6.8.

Change the size of the applet; notice how the controls reposition according to the behavior of the Layout Manager. The TextFields and the Button do not grow bigger as you resize the applet; instead, they stay in the center of the applet.

Try to enter numbers in the TextFields, then use the *Add* Button. It should still work.

After you finish testing, close the applet so you can continue improving it.

Figure 6.8   Running the GridBag layout.

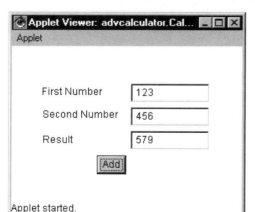

Setting TextField Properties

You need to change specific properties of the TextFields. The paint() method manages many GUI beans. You can manage the TextField's size with its *columns* property, which specifies the number of characters that the TextField displays. Increase the *columns* property with the following steps:

Open the property sheet for the tfNum1 TextField.

The *columns* property is currently set to 0, which is why you can't enter numbers in the TextFields. You can set the number of characters for the *columns* property so the TextField works properly:

Enter **10** for the *columns* property as shown in Figure 6.9. Also change the *columns* property for tfNum2 and tfResult to 10.

Check the contraints, insets, and ipadX and make sure they are all 0.

Tip

You can keep the property sheet open when you need to change the properties of a number of beans. Just select the next bean in the Visual Composition Editor; the property sheet refreshes itself with the properties for the new bean. This is a very handy feature that makes it a lot easier to edit bean properties. You can also select another bean from the drop-down list at the top of the property sheet.

Figure 6.9   TextField columns properties.

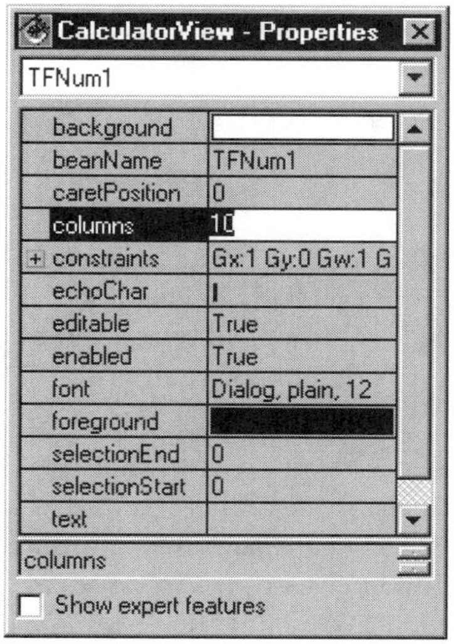

Figure 6.10   Property sheet for alignment.

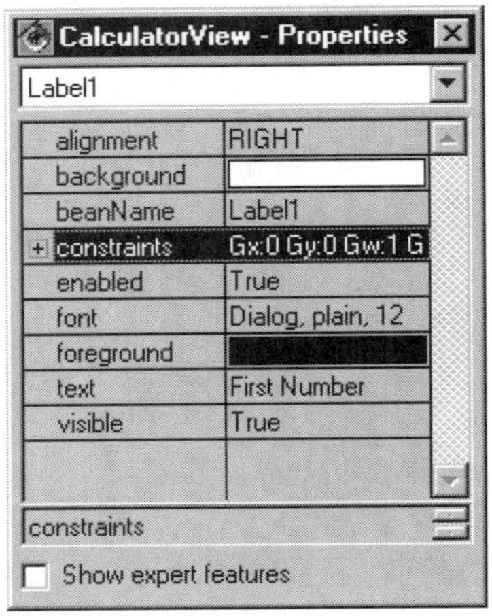

Label Alignment

You can also change the Labels and right-align them next to the TextFields. You can change the alignment of a Label through its GridBag Constraint or its own properties. In some cases, you need to use multiple GridBag Constraint properties to get the desired result. Change the Labels with the following steps:

Select the *First Number* Label and bring up its property sheet.

The default alignment setting is LEFT. It looks better if you right-align the Labels so they align with the TextFields.

Select **RIGHT** in the drop-down list for the **alignment** property, as shown in Figure 6.10.

Change the alignment to RIGHT for the other two Labels.

When you complete these changes to the properties, the text is right-aligned, as shown in Figure 6.11, but it is not right-aligned within the grid. This is not quite what you need, but there is another setting to make all the GUI beans right aligned. The GridBag Constraints let you make property settings for each grid.

Setting GridBagConstraints Properties

If you look closely at Figure 6.11, you see that the Labels are readable but would look more polished if they were truly right-aligned with a little space between the GUI beans. You learned about the many different GridBag constraints in a previous section. Now you have a chance to use what you learned about the GridBag.

Figure 6.11   Right-aligned TextFields.

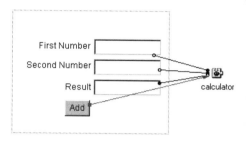

Using the Anchor Property

The Visual Composition Editor padded out the grids, so the GUI beans are fixed in the grids. The *anchor* is the location where the bean is attached or the direction in which it is oriented. The Labels in the Advanced Calculator are different lengths, and the default anchor is *CENTER*. If the user interface has Labels and TextFields, they should be consistently aligned either to the right or to the left. Since it is not, you should adjust the anchor property of the GridBag Constraint with the following steps:

Select the *First Number* Label and open its property sheet.

Select *constraints,* the *anchor* property, and set it to **EAST** in the drop-down list as shown in Figure 6.12.

Repeat the previous steps for the *Second Number* and *Result* Labels.

Figure 6.12   TextField anchor properties.

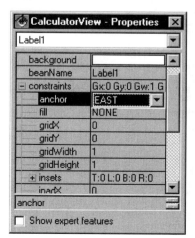

Figure 6.13   Right-aligned East-anchored TextFields.

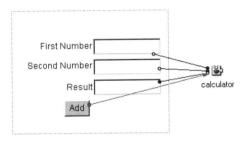

When you finish setting the properties, close the property sheets. The Labels appear nicely right-aligned as shown in Figure 6.13.

Using Insets

The insets properties of the Label are the number of pixels on the top, bottom, left, and right of the bean. The Visual Composition Editor has generated insets for some of the positions. You should set the correct inset for each of the beans so they appear consistently. Make these changes with the following steps:

Select the tfNum1 Label and open its property sheet.

Select **constraints, insets,** and look at each Label's *right inset*. Make sure that the *right insets* are the same for all labels, for example 5, as shown Figure 6.14.

When you finish setting the properties, close the property sheets.

All the components in the applet have the correct settings. The Visual Composition Editor shows the applet as shown in Figure 6.15.

Tip

You can set properties for more than one bean at a time. For example, you can select multiple TextFields, then go to the property editor and edit any common properties. Any properties that are different, like the bean name, will be disabled and cannot be changed.

Building a Sub-Panel

The Advanced Calculator needs four more Buttons for the Subtract, Multiply, Divide, and Clear functions. You could add the additional buttons directly to the applet, but each button needs to be in a separate grid. The buttons should behave

Figure 6.14 Setting an inset.

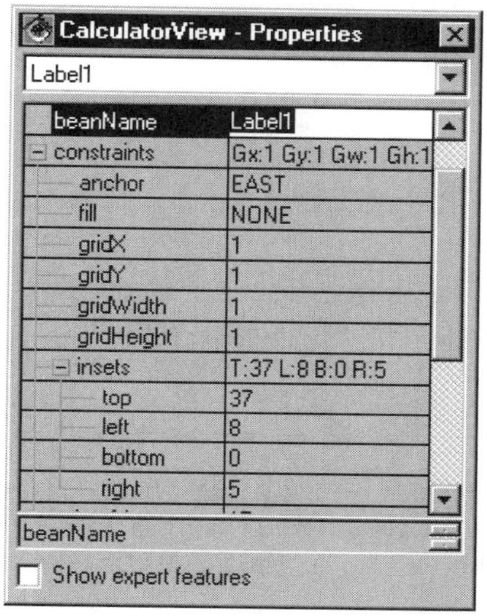

CalculatorView - Properties
Label1
beanName
Label1
constraints
Gx:1 Gy:1 Gw:1 Gh:1
anchor
EAST
fill
NONE
gridX
1
gridY
1
gridWidth
1
gridHeight
1
insets
T:37 L:8 B:0 R:5
top
37
left
8
bottom
0
right
5
beanName
Show expert features

separately from the TextField GUI beans. They should stay together in a group and not increase in size or move around the user interface. Users like to rely on the location of buttons in the user interface.

It is better to combine multiple buttons on a Panel. An AWT Panel is a subclass of Container and it can have its own layout manager. You can add the panel to another Container like an applet or a frame. Build the buttons Panel with the following steps:

In the CalculatorView Visual Composition Editor, select the Container category on the beans palette.

Figure 6.15 Labels with a right inset.

First Number
Second Number
Result
Add
calculator

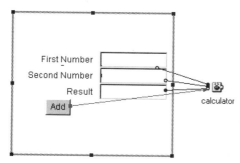

Select a **Panel** bean and temporarily drop it on the free-form surface outside the Applet instance, as shown in Figure 6.16.

Select the pbAdd Button in the applet and drag it to the new Panel.

Drop four AWT Buttons on the Panel you have just added to the free-form surface.

Tip

VisualAge for Java Version 1 had a Sticky button that kept the cursor loaded. A new stealth feature replaces this. You can keep the cursor loaded with the AWT Button bean by pressing Control and the left mouse button when you select it from the Beans Palette.

Notice how the buttons stay where you drop them on the Panel. That is because this Panel has a null Layout Manager. FlowLayout would keep the Buttons neatly displayed in different screen resolutions. To set the Layout Manager for the button Panel:

Double-click inside the dashed box that represents the Panel instance, and open its property sheet.

This time, set the layout to FlowLayout, and close the property sheet. Now the buttons align, flowing one after the other.

Figure 6.16   Sub-panel on free-form surface.

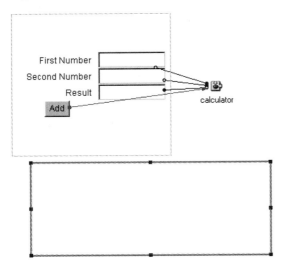

Figure 6.17   Buttons panel.

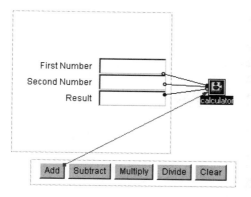

Edit the *label* property of the new buttons to read **Subtract**, **Multiply**, **Divide**, and **Clear**.

Adjust the size of the Panel until it is just big enough to hold all the buttons in one row, as shown in Figure 6.17.

Warning

You must set the Panel to any kind of Layout Manager before placing the Panel in a Container. If you place a panel with a null layout in a Container, the Panel disappears in the Visual Composition Editor. This is another good reason to avoid using null layout. Some people might call this a bug, but the politically correct term for this behavior is to call it a "feature."

Adding a Panel to a Container

The sub-panel is a component of the applet, and as a component, it initially resides in one grid.

Drag and drop the buttons Panel onto the lower section of the Applet instance, just under the Result Label.

Notice that as you mov the mouse pointer over the top of the Applet, distinct areas appear as dashed boxes inside the Applet. These are *drop zones*, and they show the GridBag cells in the Applet. These lines appear only at development time, when a GUI bean is moving over the GridBag. Your CalculatorView should now look like Figure 6.18.

Figure 6.18   CalculatorView with buttons panel.

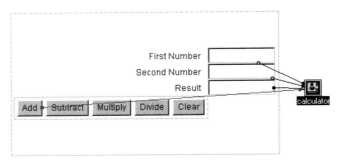

Spanning Multiple Grids

The ability for GUI beans to span multiple grids is a unique feature of the
GridBag layout. The Panel1 panel is a large GUI bean and it should span multiple
grids, which you can easily change in the GridBag Constraints. Change Panel1 so
that it spans three grids with the following steps:

Select the Panel1 panel and bring up its property sheet.

Select *constraints* and open its property sheet.

Select *gridWidth* property and set it to 3 as shown in Figure 6.19.

When you finish setting the properties, close the property sheet.

Figure 6.19   Buttons panel, spanning grids.

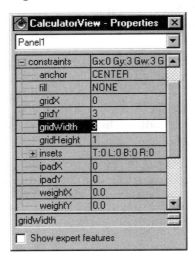

Figure 6.20 All GUI beans are aligned.

First Number
Second Number
Result
Add
Subtract
Multiply
Divide
Clear
calculator

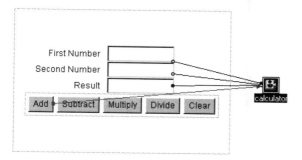

The updated Advanced Calculator applet looks like Figure 6.20. All the GUI beans align properly and the buttons panel visibly spans multiple grids.

Test Iteration Two

Run the **CalculatorView** by pressing the Test button. It should look like Figure 6.21.

Change the size of the applet and notice how all the GUI beans reposition according to the behavior of the Layout Managers.

The GridBag Code

You have completed the user interface for the advanced calculator. You used the GridBag Layout with a number of GUI beans, and you made a lot of property

Figure 6.21 Running iteration two.

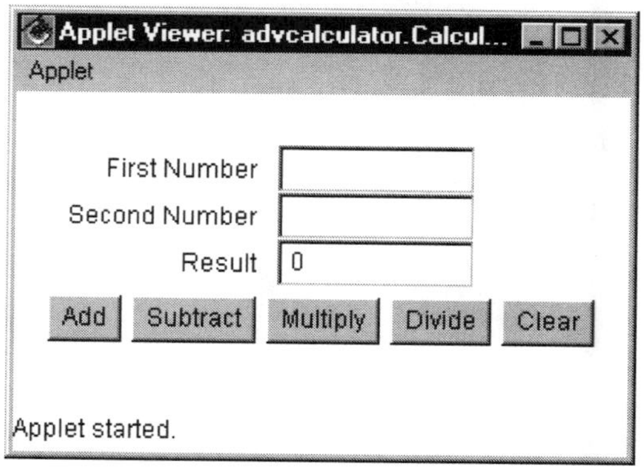

Applet Viewer: advcalculator.Calcul...
Applet
First Number
Second Number
Result
0
Add
Subtract
Multiply
Divide
Clear
Applet started.

settings. Let's look at all the generated code for the applet using a GridBag. This code is a little better than the code generated in previous versions of VisualAge for Java. This code is added to the applet in the init() method as shown in the following code segment:

```
/**
 * Handle the Applet init method.
 */
/* WARNING: THIS METHOD WILL BE REGENERATED. */
public void init() {
  try {
    super.init();
    setName("CalculatorView");
    setLayout(new java.awt.GridBagLayout());
    setSize(273, 185);

    java.awt.GridBagConstraints constraintsLabel1 = new
       java.awt.GridBagConstraints();
    constraintsLabel1.gridx = 0; constraintsLabel1.gridy = 0;
    constraintsLabel1.anchor = java.awt.GridBagConstraints.EAST;
    constraintsLabel1.ipadx = 15;
    constraintsLabel1.ipady = 4;
    constraintsLabel1.insets = new java.awt.Insets(37, 8, 0, 5);
    add(getLabel1(), constraintsLabel1);

    java.awt.GridBagConstraints constraintstfNum1 = new
       java.awt.GridBagConstraints();
    constraintstfNum1.gridx = 1; constraintstfNum1.gridy = 0;
    constraintstfNum1.insets = new java.awt.Insets(41, 2, 0, 11);
    add(gettfNum1(), constraintstfNum1);

    java.awt.GridBagConstraints constraintsLabel2 = new
       java.awt.GridBagConstraints();
    constraintsLabel2.gridx = 0; constraintsLabel2.gridy = 1;
    constraintsLabel2.anchor = java.awt.GridBagConstraints.EAST;
    constraintsLabel2.ipady = 4;
    constraintsLabel2.insets = new java.awt.Insets(1, 9, 2, 5);
    add(getLabel2(), constraintsLabel2);

    java.awt.GridBagConstraints constraintstfNum2 = new
       java.awt.GridBagConstraints();
    constraintstfNum2.gridx = 1; constraintstfNum2.gridy = 1;
    constraintstfNum2.insets = new java.awt.Insets(6, 2, 1, 11);
    add(gettfNum2(), constraintstfNum2);
```

```
java.awt.GridBagConstraints constraintsLabel3 = new
   java.awt.GridBagConstraints();
constraintsLabel3.gridx = 0; constraintsLabel3.gridy = 2;
constraintsLabel3.anchor = java.awt.GridBagConstraints.EAST;
constraintsLabel3.ipadx = 51;
constraintsLabel3.ipady = 4;
constraintsLabel3.insets = new java.awt.Insets(2, 9, 3, 5);
add(getLabel3(), constraintsLabel3);

java.awt.GridBagConstraints constraintstfResult = new
   java.awt.GridBagConstraints();
constraintstfResult.gridx = 1; constraintstfResult.gridy = 2;
constraintstfResult.insets = new java.awt.Insets(5, 2, 4, 11);
add(gettfResult(), constraintstfResult);

java.awt.GridBagConstraints constraintsPanel1 = new
   java.awt.GridBagConstraints();
constraintsPanel1.gridx = 0; constraintsPanel1.gridy = 3;
constraintsPanel1.gridwidth = 2;
constraintsPanel1.fill =
   java.awt.GridBagConstraints.HORIZONTAL;
add(getPanel1(), constraintsPanel1);
initConnections();
// user code begin {1}
// user code end
} catch (java.lang.Throwable ivjExc) {
// user code begin {2}
// user code end
handleException(ivjExc);
}
}
```

As you can see, the Visual Composition Editor generates a lot of code—about 60 lines of pure Java. The generated code is more compact and better-organized in Version 3. Each property that you set in the Visual Composition Editor generates the appropriate code for the GridBag. The Visual Composition Editor is a great help in generating code for the more complex GUI beans.

Naming the GUI Beans

Each control you use has a default name. The first TextField control you drop is called TextField1. Remember that changing the name to something more meaningful is a good idea. It helps you follow the generated code and provides some level of documentation to the code.

Change the names of embedded beans by clicking the right mouse button on the bean and selecting **Change Bean Name** from the pop-up menu. Change the name of the buttons to **pbSub, pbMult, pbDiv,** and **pbClear** respectively.

You don't need to change the names of the TextFields, because they retain the names tfNum1, tfNum2, and tfResult. Just like the Simple Adder, the result of the calculation comes from the AdvCalculatorLogic bean (yet to be built), and the tfResult TextField should not allow keyboard input. You set the tfResult TextField as uneditable in the Simple Adder, so you do not need to reset it.

Using the init() Method

When a browser loads an applet, the init() method executes. After the init() method completes, the init event is sent. The init event is very good for triggering initial behavior in your beans. You might have noticed that when the applet runs, you must use the mouse and select a TextField in order to enter data. By default, focus is not set in an applet. You can easily set the initial focus to a specific TextField with a simple visual connection.

Setting Focus

When you tested the Advanced Calculator, you placed the mouse in the TextField in order to enter numbers. When a window or an applet displays, it is very helpful to set the focus. In this case, you should set focus to the tfNum1 TextField. You can accomplish this by adding code in the init() method or by making a connection in the Visual Composition Editor. Usually, you should not make user interface settings with visual connections, so this is a good place to use the init() method. You will make a connection from the applet's init() method, access the applet's features from the pop-up menu on the free-form surface. Make this connection with the following steps:

Move the mouse to the free-form surface and open the pop-up menu.

Select **Connect** and then **Connectable Features**.

Select the *init* event as the source for the connection. If you can't find it, select the **Show expert features** check box at the bottom of the connection window as shown in Figure 6.22. Close the connection window.

Tip

You learned about expert features previously when we described JavaBeans in Chapter 3. Unfortunately, there are a number of frequently used JavaBeans features that are expert features. If you can't find a feature in a class, remember to check the expert features.

Figure 6.22   Selecting the expert init event.

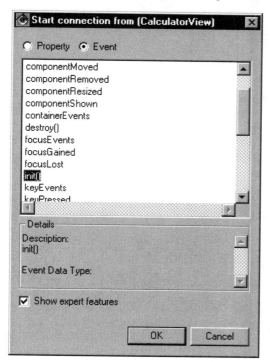

Move the mouse to tfNum1 and bring up the connection menu. Select **Connectable Features.**

On the connections window for tfNum1, select the requestFocus() method. This is another expert feature.

As indicated by the green line, this is an event-to-method connection, and it requires no parameters, as shown in Figure 6.23. You can accomplish the same result by adding the following line of code directly to the applet's init() method:

```
gettfNum1().requestFocus();
```

It is far more efficient to write a line of code in the init() method than to use the visual connection. But the visual connection is much easier to see and change in the Visual Composition Editor. If you want to change the initial focus, you could merely drag the connection to another TextField or Button, and then the Visual Composition Editor will generate the correct code.

Figure 6.23   Applet init() connection.

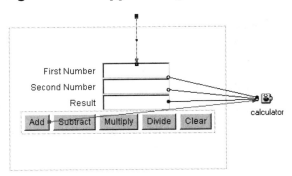

Test Iteration Three

The CalculatorView is good enough to test. Run the applet by pressing the Test button.

The user interface for the Advanced Calculator is much cleaner than that for the Simple Adder. Resizing still works as in the previous tests. When the applet starts, the cursor appears in the first field.

When you finish testing, close the applet viewer.

Adding a Clear Function

Another function that is common to calculators is a Clear function. There are several ways to implement this function:

1. Set the text properties in the GUI beans with connections from the Clear Button, as shown in Figure 6.24.

2. Set the num1, num2, and result properties in the Calculator logic bean, which in turn sets the GUI beans.

3. Create a method in the Calculator logic bean that sets the properties.

4. Create a class method in the applet that sets the text properties for the GUI beans.

Options 1 and 2 require three connections that technically work. However, they are not good options because each connection generates a new method in the class and adds visual clutter and more code, and slows execution. More importantly, however, each additional TextField in the user interface requires an additional connection for the **Clear** button. Additionally, option 2 doesn't really clear the fields, rather it sets them to 0 (zero).

Figure 6.24 Too many connections.

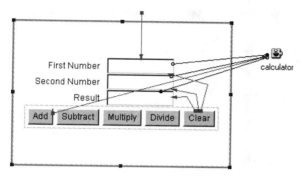

Option 3 is less costly, but it puts GUI behavior at the model or logic bean level. It is usually better to place this GUI function with the applet bean. This is not a hard and fast rule—in some cases it is better to keep this type of function with the logic bean.

Adding Another Applet Method

For this applet, option 4, creating a class method in the applet, is a good option to implement. Add the clear function to the applet bean with the following steps:

Go to the *Clear* Button on the applet and open the pop-up menu.

Select Connect, actionPerformed.

Go to the free-form surface and bring up the pop-up.

Select Connect, Event to Code, and the Event to Code dialog opens as shown in Figure 6.25.

Enter the code needed for the clear method as shown in bold in the following code segment:

```
/**
 * Comment
 */
public void pBClear_ActionPerformed
   (java.awt.event.ActionEvent actionEvent) {
  gettfNum1().setText(null);
  gettfNum2().setText(null);
  gettfResult().setText(null);
}
```

Figure 6.25 Event to Code dialog.

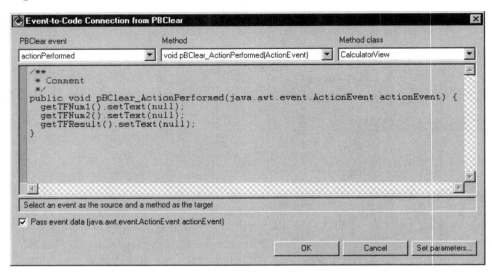

Save these changes to the code by selecting **Save** from the pop-up menu in the Source pane.

Close the Event to Code dialog and the Visual Composition Editor shows this new connection, as shown in Figure 6.26.

Test the applet by pressing the run button. When you type text in the TextFields and press the Clear Button, the TextFields are cleared.

Although this is not the only way to clear the values for the Advanced Calculator, it is one of the best ways. It requires only one connection that creates one method. Adding additional code in the method can easily extend it. This technique is even more efficient with user interfaces that have many properties to set. Each property change is merely another line of code. If you delete or rename a TextField, you will need to edit this code, because it will have an invalid reference. There is a better way.

The Better Clear Method

What about making a generic method that looks for any TextFields and clears them? With JavaBeans, it's pretty easy. You can ask a Container for all its Components. The Applet is a container and TextFields subclass Component. For this applet, option 4 is a good option to implement. Edit the clear function in the applet bean with the following steps:

Figure 6.26 Event to Code connection.

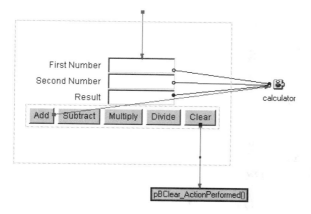

Go to the new connection from the Clear Button to the free-form surface.

Open the property editor for this Event-to-Code connection and the dialog appears as shown in Figure 6.27. You could also edit this method on the Methods page.

Delete the three lines with explicit calls to tfNum1, tfNum2, and tfResult.

Figure 6.27 Event to Code dialog.

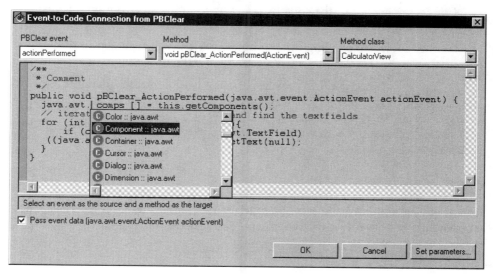

Enter the code needed for the clear method as shown in bold in the following code segment:

```java
/**
 * Comment
 */
public void pBClear_ActionPerformed
   (java.awt.event.ActionEvent actionEvent) {
  java.awt.Component comps [] =
     this.getComponents();
  // iterate through the components and find textfields
  for (int i=comps.length-1;i>=0;i--){
      if (comps[i] instanceof java.awt.TextField)
    // set the TextField to null
    ((java.awt.TextField) comps[i]).setText(null);
  }
}
```

Tip

When typing Java code in the editor, you can use the Control-Space keys while on a dot (.) to get the code assist functions as shown in Figure 6.27. This cool feature shows all available methods for a given context. It is handy for finding methods and preventing typos.

Save these changes to the code by selecting **Save** from the pop-up menu in the Source pane.

Test the applet by pressing the run button. When you type text in the TextFields and press the Clear Button, the TextFields clear.

Though this is not the only way to clear the values for the Advanced Calculator, it is probably the best way. It requires only one connection and it always clears all TextFields in the Applet. It is very good for maintenance, because this technique works whether you add, delete, or even rename any of the TextFields.

Summary

In this chapter, you have completed a much more complicated user interface, and improved the Simple Adder in many ways. You learned how to:

- Copy beans and deal with invalid references.

- Understand GridBagLayout.
- Set TextField and Label properties.
- Use GridBagConstraints and properties.
- Use the init() method to set initial focus.
- Create the clear function with an Event-To-Code connection.

The applet now has the GUI beans for the Advanced Calculator, and it is ready for you to add the additional function for the CalculatorLogic bean. This is a much better user interface, like the ones used in real life.

BUILDING THE ADVANCED CALCULATOR LOGIC

7

What's in Chapter 7

In this chapter, you will continue to improve the Advanced Calculator. The new application will have a much more sophisticated user interface and more math functions. You will also add user interface controls to support these new functions. In this chapter, you will learn how to:

- Extend logic beans
- Incorporate Exception handling
- Use a message box
- Modify the beans palette
- Use a numeric-only TextField

You will apply all of these concepts in completing the Advanced Calculator applet. After you have finished this chapter, you will have a better understanding of what it takes to develop more complex Java programs.

Based on your previous experience with the Simple Adder, you will now construct a better Calculator with improved functions. This version performs operations to add, subtract, multiply, and divide two floating-point numbers. It also provides a function that detects when the user to divide by zero, then it displays a warning message. If you closed VisualAge for Java, restart it. The simplest way to start VisualAge for Java is to double-click its icon.

Extending a Logic Bean

Let's continue and construct the **AdvCalculatorLogic** logic bean. Although you reused the CalculatorView for this application, for the Advanced Calculator you will make a new logic bean. The CalculatorLogic used in the Simple Adder had properties of type *int*. The AdvCalculatorLogic bean also has three properties, but they are of type *float* so they can hold bigger numbers that include decimal values. Start building the logic bean with the following steps:

> From the Workbench panel, select the **advcalculator** package, right-click, and select **New Class**.

Name the class **AdvCalculatorLogic** and leave the superclass for this class as the default java.lang.Object, which is the topmost class in the Java class hierarchy.

Select the **Browse the class when finished** check box. Press the **Finish** button to create the class as shown in Figure 7.1.

The Class/Interface browser opens for you to continue developing this class. This bean needs three properties of type **float** to hold the two operands and the result of the calculation. Because you will use this bean in the Visual Composition Editor, you must enable the properties to send and receive notifications so that the visual and logical representations of the values are kept synchronized. In other words, when the user enters a number in the user interface and changes the value of an existing number, the corresponding property in the logic bean is notified of the change. To do this, you define properties for the class in the BeanInfo page of the Class/Interface Browser. Use the following steps to make the properties:

Select the BeanInfo page of the class browser.

Right-click on the Features pane and from the pop-up menu select **New Property Feature.**

Figure 7.1   Added AdvCalculatorLogic class.

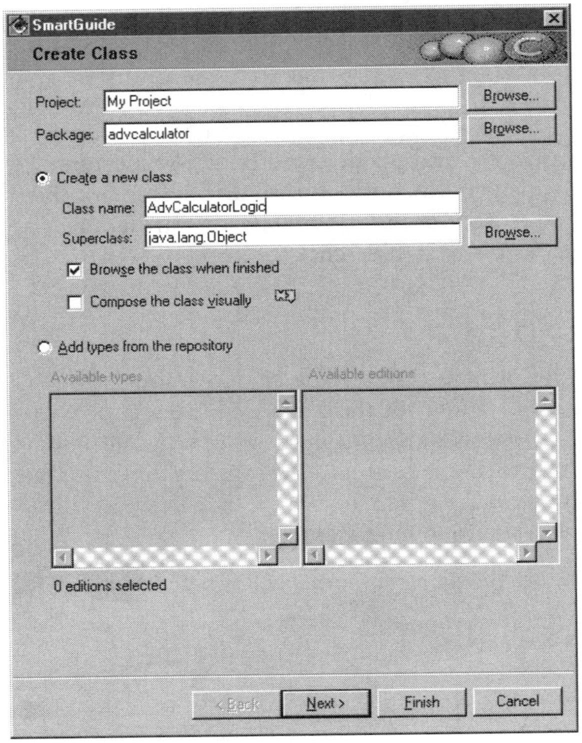

Enter **num1** in the **Property name** entry field; select **float** from the **Property type** list. It is very important to ensure that you select the **bound** check box if you will be using this property in a connection in the Visual Composition Editor, as shown in Figure 7.2. If you accidentally set the wrong type, delete the property and then go to the source code for the class and delete the variable for the property.

> **NOTE**
>
> Be very careful to make sure you use little *float*, which is a primitive Java type, and not big *Float*, which is a Java class. Float is referred to as a *wrapper class* , as it "wraps" a primitive type. There are wrapper classes for all the primitive types. You can perform arithmetic operations such as add, subtract, multiply, and divide on primitives directly, but the code for these operations on classes is a lot different.

At this time, press **Finish** and accept the defaults for the remaining settings, or press **Next** to further define the *num1* interface property with a display name and preferred setting.

Figure 7.2   Adding properties.

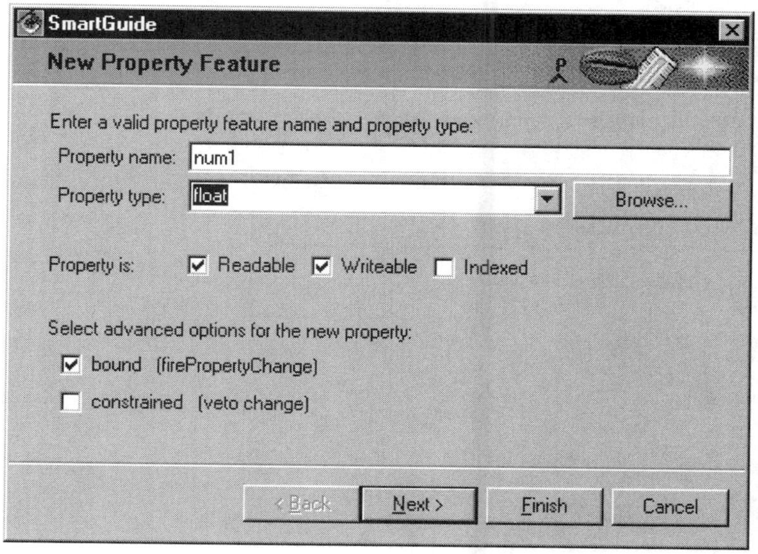

Repeat the previous steps and create the *num2* and *result* properties. Make them both of type **float** with **bound** properties.

Next, create the methods in the bean that perform the calculator operations, as follows:

Right-click on the Features pane and from the pop-up menu select **New Method Feature,** as shown in Figure 7.3.

Type the method name **add.** Press the **Finish** button.

Repeat these steps to add new method features for the **subtract, multiply,** and **divide** operations.

The SmartGuide generates stubs for the user-defined methods you created in the BeanInfo page. You need to add the code to perform the added math functions in the AdvCalculatorLogic bean, just as you did with the CalculatorLogic bean. Enter the code to perform the calculation in the bottom pane, as shown in Figure 7.4. This code sets the *result* property in the AdvCalculatorLogic bean with the sum of the values of *num1* and *num2*.

Select the *add* property in the Features list; then select the add() method in the Definitions list.

Enter code for the add() method.

Right-click on the bottom pane and select Save to save and compile the code for the add method. Any errors are reported now. You can also use Ctrl-S to save and compile.

Enter the code for all operation methods in the AdvCalculatorLogic bean as shown in Table 7.1:

Figure 7.3   Creating the add method.

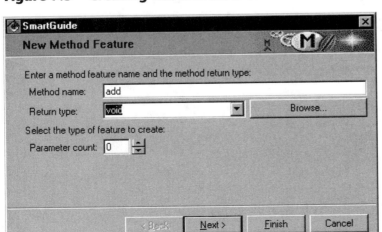

Figure 7.4 Code for the add method.

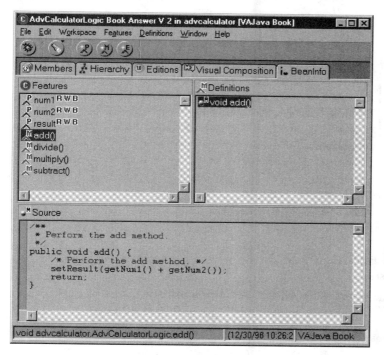

Adding the GUI Bean to the Visual Composition Editor

You have finished adding the math functions to the logic bean that performs operations for the calculator. Now, bring the logic bean into the Visual Composition Editor for the **CalculatorView** and make the necessary connections with the following steps:

Switch back to the class browser that shows the **CalculatorView** class, and make sure you select the Visual Composition tab.

Table 7.1 Code for AdvCalculatorLogic Bean

Method	Code
add()	setResult(getNum1() + getNum2());
subtract()	setResult(getNum1() – getNum2 ());
multiply()	setResult(getNum1() * getNum2 ());
divide()	setResult(getNum1() / getNum2 ());

Figure 7.5   New logic bean.

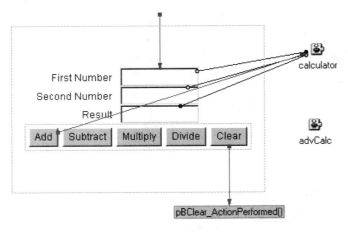

Select **Choose Bean**; then select the **Browse** button to show the list of available classes.

Enter the name of the adder bean, **AdvCalculatorLogic**, and select **OK**.

Enter a name for this bean, for example **advCalc,** and select **OK**.

Move the mouse pointer outside of the dashed box and over the free-form surface; click the mouse to drop the bean. advCalc should be near the old calculator bean on the free-form surface.

You now have a bean that looks like a jigsaw puzzle piece available for connections. Now you are ready to connect the GUI beans to this logic bean, as shown in Figure 7.5.

Advanced Calculator Connections

One of the benefits of visual programming is that you can see method calls between classes. You can also quickly and easily modify any of these method calls by modifying the visual connections. Once the program has visual connections, you can changing the source event or the target method of the connection. You can also move the source or target of the connection to a different bean in the Visual Composition Editor.

Moving Connections

The connections for Advanced Calculator are very much like the ones used in the Simple Adder. In fact, the AdvCalculatorLogic bean is designed similarly to the CalculatorLogic bean, so you can move the existing connections from the

CalculatorLogic bean to the corresponding properties in the AdvCalculatorLogic bean. Move the connections to AdvCalculatorLogic bean with the following steps:

Select the property-to-property connection from the **tfNum1** TextField to the CalculatorLogic bean.

The selected connection has black handles for moving and positioning. Verify that you have the correct connection. The information area at the bottom of the window indicates the selected item. It should read:

```
connPtoP1: (tfNum1,text <->calculator, operand1) selected.
```

Place the tip of the mouse on the end of the connection handle on the calculator bean; press and hold down the left mouse button.

With the mouse button still down, move the end of the connection to the **advCalc** bean and release the left mouse button, as shown in Figure 7.6.

Because the CalculatorLogic bean and the AdvCalculatorLogic bean have the same *num1* property, the connection automatically completes. If the properties were not an exact match, the Visual Composition Editor would prompt you with a list of properties to select.

The other two TextFields need their connections moved to the AdvCalc bean. In a similar fashion, move the following connections:

- **tfNum2** (text) connection to AdvCalc *num2* property
- **tfResult** (text) connection to AdvCalc *result* property

---

Figure 7.6   ConnPtoP1 moved to advCalc.

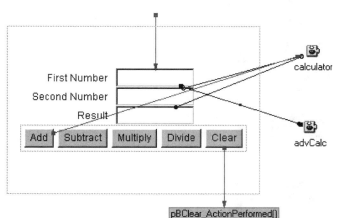

Automatic Type Conversion

When you move these connections, the Visual Composition Editor does not warn that the source and target types are incompatible. However, the *text* property of the TextField is of type String, and the *result* property is of type float. The Visual Composition Editor correctly generates the proper conversions to match the types at run time, when the connection is initially made. Let's look at the generated code for this connection, connPtoP1(), to see how this is handled. This connPtoP1() is the default generated name for the connection, and these names are used throughout this book.

Tip

The generated name connPtoP1 means that it is a property-to-property connection. You can easily change the connection name to something more meaningful in the connection's pop-up menu. The generated code for properties is tighter and more efficient than in previous versions of VisualAge for Java.

First, save these changes by selecting **Bean, Save Bean** or **Bean, Re-generate Code** from the Bean menu. The applet is saved, and the code is regenerated.

To view the class code, you can go to the Workbench or the Methods page of the class browser. Refer to the following code segment:

```
/**
 * connPtoP1SetSource:   (tfNum1.text <--> advCalc.num1)
 */
/* WARNING: THIS METHOD WILL BE REGENERATED. */
private void connPtoP1SetSource() {
  /* Set the source from the target */
  try {
    if (ivjConnPtoP1Aligning == false) {
        // user code begin {1}
        // user code end
        ivjConnPtoP1Aligning = true;
        gettfNum1().setText(String.valueOf
          (getadvCalc().getNum1()));
        // user code begin {2}
        // user code end
        ivjConnPtoP1Aligning = false;
    }
  } catch (java.lang.Throwable ivjExc) {
     ivjConnPtoP1Aligning = false;
    // user code begin {3}
    // user code end
```

```
        handleException(ivjExc);
    }
}

/**
 * connPtoP1SetTarget:   (tfNum1.text <--> AdvCalc.num1)
 */
/* WARNING: THIS METHOD WILL BE REGENERATED. */
private void connPtoP1SetTarget() {
    /* Set the target from the source */
    try {
        if (ivjConnPtoP1Aligning == false) {
            // user code begin {1}
            // user code end
            ivjConnPtoP1Aligning = true;
            getadvCalc().setNum1(new
                Float(gettfNum1().getText()).floatValue());
            // user code begin {2}
            // user code end
            ivjConnPtoP1Aligning = false;
        }
    } catch (java.lang.Throwable ivjExc) {
        ivjConnPtoP1Aligning = false;
        // user code begin {3}
        // user code end
        handleException(ivjExc);
    }
}
```

The property-to-property connections generate two methods; one method sets the source and the other method sets the target. As you can see in the code setting the source, when the setTest() method is called, it is passed a Java String parameter derived by using the valueOf() method. This method converts the float to a String. The SetTarget method uses the floatValue() method to convert a Java String into a float.

Property Events

Remember from the CalculatorView that TextFields have a number of events that can be passed via property-to-property connections. You set these events when you built the CalculatorView. You do not need to reset these events in the AdvCalculatorView. However, it is a good idea to verify that these events are set correctly:

Open the connection's property sheet for the previous connections, as shown in Figure 7.7. Either double-click on the blue connection line, or use its pop-up menu and select **properties**.

Figure 7.7   Verifying connection properties.

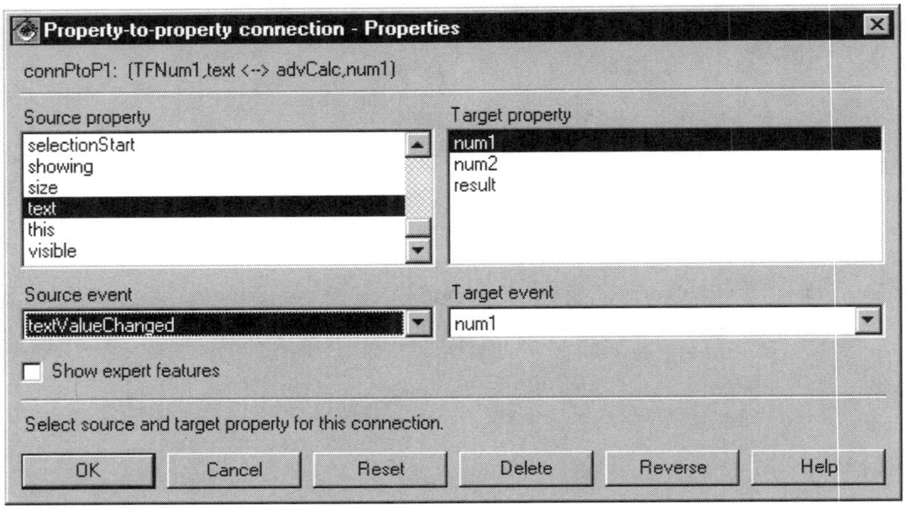

Look at the corresponding event drop-down list and verify that it is set to **textValueChanged**.

Close the connection's property sheet when you have verified the correct event settings.

Moving Method Connections

Now you need to move the add() method call to the new logic bean. It is the same process as moving the previous connections, only it's easier now that you have already done it a few times. Move the connection as follows:

Select the green connection between the pbAdd Button and the calculator bean.

Move the end of the connection from the calculator bean to advCalc.

When you have moved all the connections, the applet design in the Visual Composition Editor should look like Figure 7.8.

Testing the Add Function

There are enough changes in the Advanced Calculator to test it. Execute the following steps:

Press the Run button on the upper tool bar of the Visual Composition Editor to generate and run the applet.

Figure 7.8   All calculator connections moved to advCalc.

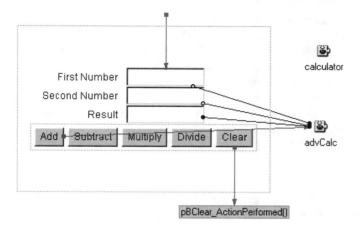

Enter values in the TextFields and try all the operations of the calculator.

The **Result** field should show the correct value of the addition operation on the two numbers, as shown in Figure 7.9. If it does not add the two numbers correctly, use the debugger to trace the values in the AdvCalc bean and check the add() method execution. Make sure that you have set the textValueChanged events for the TextField connections.

When you are finished testing, close the applet viewer.

Figure 7.9   Running the Advanced Calculator.

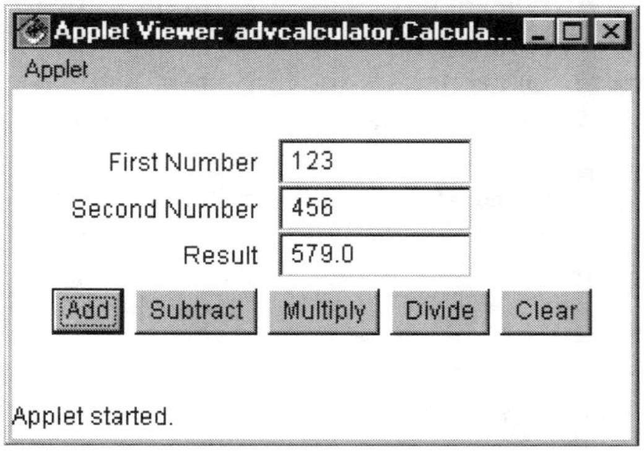

Tip

Notice how the **Result** field displays 0.0 when it starts. This is because the connection for this TextField starts at the AdvCalc bean as the source and points to the tfResult TextField as the target. The source value sets the target value when the objects are instantiated at run time. The float property in the AdvCalc bean is initialized to 0.0, so this value sets the value in the tfResult TextField. tfNum1 and tfNum2 do not have 0.0 as their initial value, because both TextFields are sources for the connections. They are of type String and they set the appropriate values in the AdvCalc bean.

Deleting Beans

The Advanced Calculator ran fine when you tested it. There were two logic beans that provide calculation functions, but only one of the logic beans is called by the applet. The logic beans placed on the free-form surface are instantiated or NEWed at run time. The Visual Composition Editor generates the call to the constructor of the bean using its default constructor. After you have moved all the connections to the AdvCalc bean, there is no need to keep the old calculator bean on the free-form surface. Delete this bean as follows:

Select the calculator logic bean from the free-form surface of the AdvCalculatorView applet.

Either press the Delete key, or point the mouse at the calculator logic bean and from the pop-up menu select **Delete**.

More Connections

Now that you have made a number of connections in the Visual Composition Editor, the instructions in the book for making connections are much briefer. These shorter instructions indicate the source bean and its feature, followed by the target bean and its feature. Try to use **Connectable Features** and ensure that you are selecting the proper feature for the connection. Also, verify that you have the correct connections by referring to the screen captures that follow a number of connection instructions.

Each math function in the AdvCalc bean needs to be called when the corresponding button is clicked. Make the following connections from the math buttons on the applet to their corresponding method in the logic bean, as shown in Figure 7.10:

pbSub (actionPerformed(java.awt.event.ActionEvent)) to advCalc (subtract)

Figure 7.10   All math buttons connected.

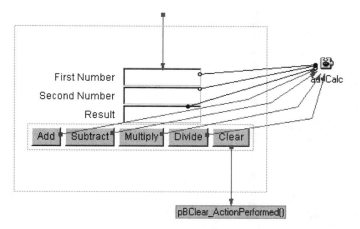

pbMult (actionPerformed(java.awt.event.ActionEvent)) to advCalc (multiply)

pbDiv (actionPerformed(java.awt.event.ActionEvent)) to advCalc (divide)

Tip

The previous example shows one of the better ways to minimize connections in the Visual Composition Editor. It may seem ironic, but connections need to be used sparingly to get the best performance results. By using connections only for higher-level functions, the Visual Composition Editor view of the bean has fewer lines, and is easier to understand and debug. This minimizes what is referred to as *visual spaghetti*.

Testing the Math Functions

Now that all the math functions are complete, it is a good time to iterate and test the applet.

 Press the Run button on the upper tool bar of the Visual Composition Editor to generate and run the applet.

Enter numbers in the TextFields and try all the operations of the calculator. The **Result** field should show the correct value of the selected operation on the two numbers.

Figure 7.11   Multiply function.

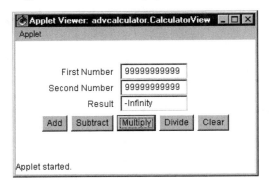

Try multiplying two really big numbers. The result will be *infinity*—a special Java term used for arithmetic results. Hopefully, it will be needed to calculate our book royalties.

Try multiplying a really big number and a really big negative number. The result will be *-infinity*, as shown in Figure 7.11. This is another special Java term used for arithmetic results. This new term is possibly anticipating future calculation of the national debt.

Try to divide a number by 0. What happens? The result is *NaN*, the Java term for *Not a Number*. The traditional math term for this is undefined, but at least Java translates a divide-by-zero error into something you can use.

Try the clear function: It should still work as in Chapter 6 and set all the fields to blank or null.

When you are finished, close the applet viewer.

All the basic functions for the Advanced Calculator are complete. The Layout Manager works well, the focus is initially on the first TextField, all the math functions operate, and the clear function works.

Exception Handling

What happens if you enter 0 in the **Second Number** field and press the **Divide** button? The result of NaN is not very useful to most endusers. It would be much better to intercept this error and handle it programmatically. *Exceptions* are the standard way to handle errors in Java. You should place all method calls that can throw an exception in a *try/catch* block. If the method throws an Exception, the code after the *catch* is executed.

The connections in the Visual Composition Editor generate try/catch blocks for all methods that call targets. The following code segment shows the code that calls the divide() method:

```
/**
 * connEtoM5:  (pbDiv.action.actionPerformed
   (java.awt.event.ActionEvent) --> advCalc.divide()V)
 * @param arg1 java.awt.event.ActionEvent
 */
/* WARNING: THIS METHOD WILL BE REGENERATED. */
private void connEtoM5
   (java.awt.event.ActionEvent arg1) {
  try {
     // user code begin {1}
     // user code end
     getadvCalc().divide();
     // user code begin {2}
     // user code end
  } catch (java.lang.Throwable ivjExc) {
     // user code begin {3}
     // user code end
     handleException(ivjExc);
  }
}
```

Why does the program keep running after an Excpetion is thrown? That is because even though you are throwing the exception in the logic for the divide function, nobody is catching the exception. It is being handled by the handleException() method, as shown in the following code segment. This is a generic method that lets you see Exceptions at run time. Under normal execution, nothing happens, because all the code has been commented out. The last two commented out lines must be uncommented to see the Exception information in the Output window of the VisualAge for Java Console window.

```
/**
 * Called whenever the part throws an exception.
 * @param exception java.lang.Throwable
 */
private void handleException(Throwable exception) {

   /* Uncomment the following lines to print uncaught exceptions to
      stdout */
   // System.out.println("--------- UNCAUGHT EXCEPTION ---------");
   // exception.printStackTrace(System.out);
}
```

Using Exceptions

The console is good for debugging, but for running the application an appropriate action is to display a message to the user to tell the user about the problem. You can easily incorporate this action into the CalculatorView by performing the following steps:

You must change the declaration of the divide() method to indicate that it can throw an exception if the user attempts to divide by zero. Go to the Methods page of the AdvCalculatorLogic class and edit the divide() method declaration to be:

```
public void divide() throws java.lang.ArithmeticException {
```

The code for the divide() method needs to test if the second operand, num2, is zero. If it is, an exception is created and thrown as shown in the following code segment. Make sure that your version of the method looks exactly as shown in the following code segment:

```
public void divide() throws java.lang.ArithmeticException {
if( getNum2() == 0 )
    throw( new java.lang.ArithmeticException
      ("Divide by zero not allowed"));
else
  setResult( getNum1() / getNum2());
return;
}
```

If you select the setResult(float) method from either the BeanInfo tab or Methods tab of the class browser, you will see how the notification is sent to inform interested parties that the value of the *result* property has changed.

Importing a Bean

There are a few ways to notify the user of the exception message. You could have the computer beep, but that can be annoying. It is usually good to display an error message, either in an information area or in a message box. Let's use a message box in the Advanced Calculator applet.

You could use the generic java.awt.Dialog bean, but it is not suited to easily display exceptions. An OKDialog bean that is designed to display exceptions is provided on the CD-ROM with this book. It is in the answers.dat file and you can import it into the repository. If you have already imported the answers.dat file, you can skip to "Loading the utilities package." Follow these steps to add the answers from the CD-ROM:

From the Workbench, select **File, Import**.

From the Import window, select Repository and press the **Next** Button.

Select the correct path for the answers.dat file in the Repository name field, as shown in Figure 7.12.

Figure 7.12   Import from repository SmartGuide.

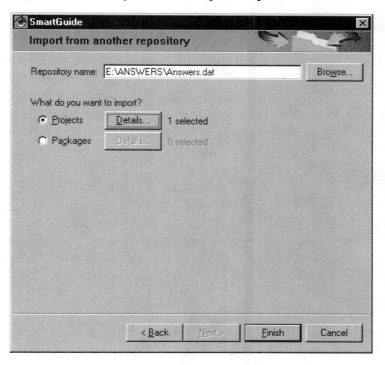

Press the Projects **Details** Button, and select the version to import. Then press the Finish Button and the Project import begins.

Loading the Utilities Package

Now that the classes are in the Repository, you can add them to the Workspace with the following steps:

Select the Add Package Button and the SmartGuide displays as shown in Figure 7.13.

Select **Add packages from repository,** and select the **utilities** package.

Press the **Finish** button to load this package into the Workspace.

The OKDialog class uses the MultiLineLabel class to display the exception message. You must import both classes for it to work properly.

Using a Message Box

Once the utilities package is in the Workbench, you can use the OKDialog bean with Java programs. You use it in the Advanced Calculator to display the exception to the user. Add the OKDialog bean as follows:

Figure 7.13   Add package SmartGuide.

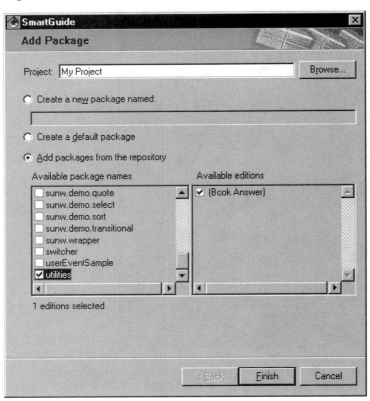

Go back to the class browser for the Advanced CalculatorView. On the VCE page, select **Choose Bean** from the beans palette.

On the Choose Beans window, select or enter **OKDialog** and press the **OK** button.

Place OKDialog on the free-form surface for Advanced Calculator. Call it errorDialog.

The OKDialog is instantiated at run time, so all you need to do is call it when the AdvCalc bean throws the exception. All the connections in the Visual Composition Editor are generated as methods. The method calls inside the connections are placed in a try/catch block. You will see examples of this convention later in this chapter when we review the code for connections. When an exception is thrown inside a try/catch block, the code after the catch is executed. This is the standard Java and C++ method for handling exceptions.

The connection from the pbDivide Button to the AdvCalc divide() method is executed in a try/catch block. The Visual Composition Editor enables you to make a connection with a connection. You can intercept exceptions or return values from methods in connections. In this case, you will make a connection to intercept the exception and display a warning message. You will make a connection from the pbDivide Button connection to the OKDialog bean. Connect the OKDialog bean with the following steps:

Click on the pbDivide,actionPerformed → calculator,divide() connection to select it.

Right-click on the selected connection; from the pop-up menu, select **Connect** and then **exceptionOccurred**, as shown in Figure 7.14.

Move the mouse to errorDialog and select **Connectable Features, showException(java.lang.Throwable)** method.

Notice that this a dashed or broken connection, which means that it is a method call requiring one or more parameters. This connection merely displays the message box without any information. The exception object holds message text for the specific exception. You should pass this exception object as the parameter to the showException() method. You can easily accomplish this in the Visual Composition Editor with the following steps:

Now open the properties for this new connection and select the **Pass event data** check box, as shown in Figure 7.15.

Select the **OK** button to save this change and close the property sheet.

This causes the Exception object to be passed as the parameter to the showException() method. Note that Exception is a subclass of Throwable, so it's a valid parameter type. The completed Advanced Calculator should look like Figure 7.16.

Figure 7.14 Connecting from an exception.

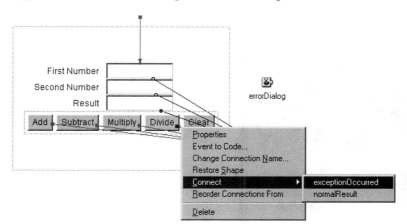

Figure 7.15   Exception connection properties.

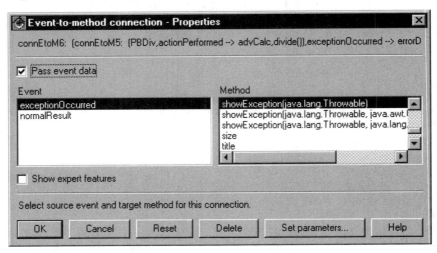

Testing Exception Handling

Let's see if this works. Save these changes and test it with the following:

Press the Run button on the upper tool bar of the Visual Composition Editor to generate and run the applet.

Run the applet and test the new connections by performing a calculation that divides by zero.

Figure 7.16   Completed connections.

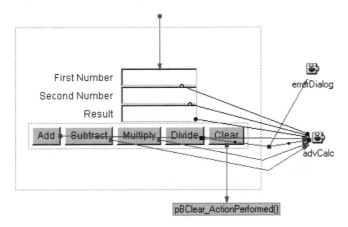

Figure 7.17   Message box display.

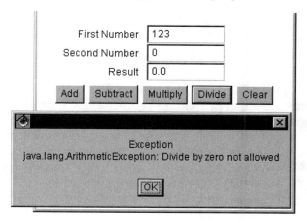

The exception is thrown and caught. The message box appears as shown in Figure 7.17, telling the user of the error.

Close the message box, and close the applet when you are finished testing.

As you can see, it is very easy to work with exceptions using VisualAge for Java. However, it can become very tedious to add connections for all the exception handling. When you are developing larger applications, you need to consider developing an exception handler bean to handle the exceptions caught for the application.

How Does the Exception Work?

This may seem like magic—how do the connections handle the exception? Let's look at the code for the connections to see how it works. As discussed earlier, each connection is a method that is generated by the Visual Composition Editor. Each connection method is automatically named by the Visual Composition Editor as *connXtoY*(), where X is the source feature and Y is the target feature. For example, connEtoM1 means Event-to-Method1. These are just default names that can be changed. You can see all the connections on the Methods page of the Advanced Calculator.

Analyzing Connections

First, you need to find out the connection name for the **Divide** button connection. The information area in the Visual Composition Editor displays the connection name. Let's find out the name of the Divide connection by the following:

From the Visual Composition Editor for the Advanced Calculator, select the Divide connection.

Look in the information area at the bottom of the Visual Composition Editor, as shown in Figure 7.18. The Divide connection is connEtoM5, which means that the Visual Composition Editor generates a connEtoM5() method in the CalculatorView bean.

NOTE

Your connection names may be different than those in this book. You may have made the connections in a different order, you may have changed connections, or you may have deleted a connection. All of these actions can affect how connections names are assigned, so your method may have a different name different.

If you go to the Members page, you can select and view the code for connEtoM5(). The following code segment shows the method for the **Divide** button:

Figure 7.18   Divide connection.

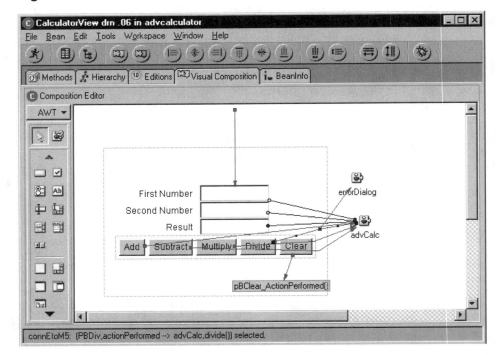

```
/**
 * connEtoM5:  (pbDiv.action.actionPerformed
(java.awt.event.ActionEvent) --> advCalc.divide()V
 * @param arg1 java.awt.event.ActionEvent
 */
/* WARNING: THIS METHOD WILL BE REGENERATED. */
private void connEtoM5
  (java.awt.event.ActionEvent arg1) {
  try {
    // user code begin {1}
    // user code end
    getadvCalc().divide();
    // user code begin {2}
    // user code end
  } catch (java.lang.Throwable ivjExc) {
    // user code begin {3}
    // user code end
    connEtoM6(ivjExc);
  }
}
```

As you read the code it makes good sense. The connection method calls the AdvCalc divide() method inside a try/catch block. The exception is caught. The Visual Composition Editor generates a method call to another connection method, in this case connEtoM6, which passes the exception as a parameter. Let's look at the code for connEtoM6 in the following code segment:

```
/**
 * connEtoM6:  ( (pbDiv,action.actionPerformed
   (java.awt.event.ActionEvent) -->
   advCalc,divide()V).exceptionOccurred -->
   errorDialog.showException(Ljava.lang.Throwable;)V)
 * @param exception java.lang.Throwable
 */
/* WARNING: THIS METHOD WILL BE REGENERATED. */
private void connEtoM6(Throwable exception) {
  try {
    // user code begin {1}
    // user code end
    geterrorDialog().showException(exception);
    // user code begin {2}
    // user code end
  } catch (java.lang.Throwable ivjExc) {
    // user code begin {3}
    // user code end
```

```
        handleException(ivjExc);
    }
}
```

This connection method calls the errorDialog showException() method, passing the exception as a parameter. In this case, the Visual Composition Editor generates all the code to catch the error and display it to the user. You could circumvent this connection by editing the code to add a call to the errorDialog showException() method after the catch statement in the Divide connection method.

Modifying the Beans Palette

As described earlier in the book, the beans palette on the left side of the Visual Composition Editor contains standard AWT beans supplied with VisualAge for Java along with a separate category for JFC Swing beans. You may want to add other frequently used AWT beans or your own beans to the beans palette. The OKDialog is very helpful; you may want to use it in other programs for displaying exceptions. Try adding this bean to the palette as follows:

Select the Visual Composition page of the class browser for the Advanced Calculator.

From the Beans menu, select **Modify Palette**.

The Modify Palette window appears as shown in Figure 7.19, where you can specify the information for the bean as follows:

Figure 7.19   Add to palette window.

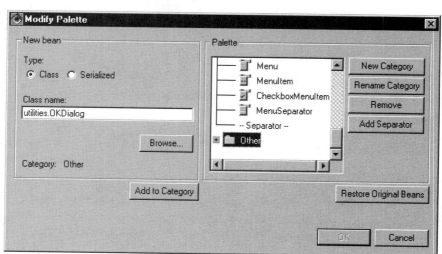

This is a Class, not a Serialized bean, so leave the **Class** radio button selected.

Use the **Browse** button to specify the fully qualified path for the OKDialog bean.

Select the **Other** category from the **Palette** list.

Press the **Add to Category** button and the OKDialog is added.

Press the **OK** button when you are finished.

If you select the **Other** category and scroll to the bottom of the list, you can see the OKDialog bean. The modified palette is saved with the Workbench when you exit. When you open the class browsers for other beans, the OKDialog is in the **Other** category of the beans palette for you to use.

It is also possible to add new bean categories, add menu separators, delete beans and categories that you rarely use, and restore the palette to its original bean configuration. The beans are retained in the repository; the beans palette just refers to beans that are loaded in the workspace.

Making a Numeric-Only TextField

The Advanced Calculator user interface uses the same AWT TextField GUI bean that you used in the Simple Adder. When you tested the Advanced Calculator, you might have found that you could use alphabetic characters and other non-numeric characters in the TextFields. It would be good if the TextFields prevented the user from entering characters other than valid numerals. This is referred to as field-level validation. Other techniques are used to validate data from multiple fields.

Importing More Java Files

A bean called **IntTextField**, provided on the CD-ROM with this book, can help solve this problem. IntTextField has a number of constructors and methods, so you load this prebuilt bean instead of building it. It is in the utilities package, so you can use it with this Applet.

Using a Filtered TextField

Now that the IntTextField is loaded in the workspace, you can add it to the Advanced Calculator with the following steps.Select the **Choose Bean** Button.

Select **IntTextField** using the **Browse** button in the Choose Bean window, as shown in Figure 7.20.

Name it InttfNum1.

Then press the **OK** button to load the cursor with the IntTextField bean.

Move the mouse to the free-form surface and drop the IntTextField bean.

Switching GUI Beans

One of the neat things about working in the Visual Composition Editor is that it is pretty easy to update your programs by switching beans. In this section, you replace the standard AWT TextFields with the recently imported IntTextField. Switch the beans with the following steps:

Select the tfNum1 TextField and drag it to the free-form surface.

Move the IntTextField to the grid where tfNum1 used to be.

After you have substituted the IntTextField for the TextField, set the IntTextField *columns* property to 10.

The substituted IntTextField in the Advanced Calculator should look like Figure 7.21. You might need to resize the applet to get the IntTextField to display showing 10 columns. As you can see, switching beans takes a lot of steps and it might be simpler to do it in code. You can switch JavaBeans a lot easier and you will switch tfNum2 TextField using morphing.

Morphing JavaBeans

There is another really cool feature that makes this much easier. The Visual Composition Editor has a new function called *morphing* that helps with migrat-

Figure 7.20   Choose bean window.

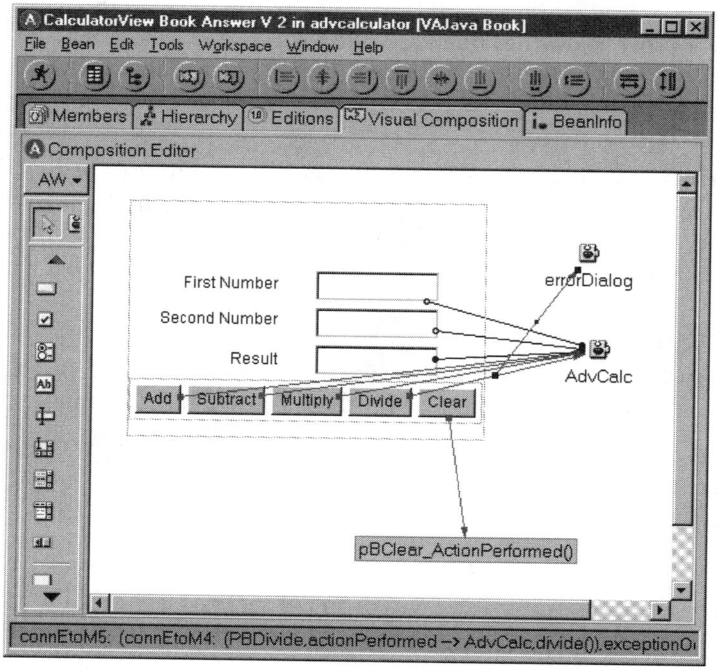

Figure 7.21   Substituting an IntTextField.

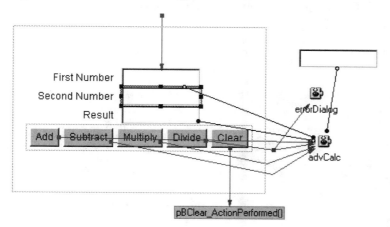

ing to Swing. You can point to any bean in the Visual Composition Editor and the pop-up menu has the *Morph into* option. Technically, you can morph any bean into any other bean.

When you morph a bean, you can have the invalid connections automatically deleted. Connections represent some of the high-level logic in your program, so deleting connections can have adverse effects on the program. When the bean is morphed, the new bean type may not have the same bean features (properties, events, and methods). So for any connection that does not have the same bean feature in the new morphed bean, the connection is invalid. It is good that the Visual Composition Editor cleans up the morphed bean by deleting these invalid connections, especially if you plan on doing a lot of redesign with new connections. It is better to inspect the connections and modify the ones that require changes. Usually the morphed bean connections merely need a different source event.

There is a limitation to morphing; you cannot morph the parent bean. This means that you cannot use the Morph function for any Containers like Applets, Panels, or JFrames that you defined as a Visual Composition Editor class in the Workbench. The **Morph Into** menu item displays for the component beans, but not for the parent bean in the Visual Composition Editor. To morph a parent part, you must go to the source code for the class definition and change the superclass to the desired superclass. When converting from AWT to JFC, you should first edit the Panels and change them to JPanels. Then you can open a JPanels in the Visual Composition Editor and morph the AWT components into their JFC replacements.

Although the examples for morphing beans usually show morphing GUI beans, it is just as easy to morph nonvisual or logic beans like the AddCalculatorLogic bean. Morphing is a cool new function in VisualAge for

Java, and it can save you time once you are familiar with its capabilities. Try morphing the second TextField with the following steps:

Morph the tfNum2 AWT TextField into an IntTextField.

Change its bean name to InttfNum2.

NOTE

The tfResult TextField does not accept input, so it does not really need to be changed to be an IntTextField. If you do not change the tfResult field, the Advanced Calculator still runs correctly. For consistency, you may want to use the IntTextField for the result.

Changing Connections

You can move connections between beans just as you did when you replaced the CalculatorLogic bean with the AdvCalculatorLogic bean. You can drag either end of a connection to a new source or target:

Select the connection from InttfNum1 to the *num1* property.

Move the TextField end of the connection to the corresponding IntTextField in the Applet.

You don't need to do this for InttfNum2 TextField because the morphing function preserved the connections. It's magic.

It is not necessary to substitute the tfResult TextField because it is a read-only field. It does not make any sense to change this GUI bean.

Tip

Sometimes it is easier to redraw simple connections. If you have problems moving these simple connections you may want to redraw them. However, you will find that connections with a number of parameters are much easier to move than to redraw.

Delete any unused TextFields that are on the free-form surface.

When all the TextFields are replaced with the IntTextFields, the Visual Composition Editor looks like Figure 7.22. The applet looks just as it did before you added the IntTextFields.

Figure 7.22 All TextFields replaced.

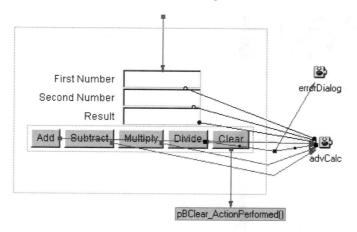

Testing the IntTextFields

Let's see if this works. Save these changes and test the applet with the following:

Press the Run button on the upper tool bar of the Visual Composition Editor to generate and run the applet, as shown in Figure 7.23.

Run the applet and try entering numbers in the TextFields. All the calculation functions should work.

Try entering alphabetic characters in the TextFields. You should not be able to enter characters in the IntTextFields.

When you are finished testing the applet, close it.

How Does the IntTextField Work?

Because you did not develop the IntTextField bean, you probably want to see how it works. This section shows you the classes used to make the IntTextField and how the code works.

IntTextField Hierarchy

If you open the IntTextField, you see its superclasses as shown in Figure 7.24. IntTextField is a subclass of FilteredTextField, which is a subclass of TextField. FilteredTextField is an abstract class that defines behavior for the IntTextField bean. We could have directly subclassed the TextField, but it is a much more flexible design to subclass the FilteredTextField.

Figure 7.23   Running advanced calculator.

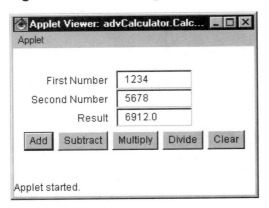

After you have reviewed the code for the IntTextField bean, you are prepared to make other subclasses of the FilteredTextField class, like an AlphaTextField or an UpperCaseTextField. Use the browser to review the constructors and methods for both the IntTextField and FilteredTextField beans.

IntTextField Source Code

The key method in the IntTextField bean is the filter() method. The code for the filter() method is shown in the following code segment:

```
/**
 * filter method comment.
 */
protected void filter(java.awt.event.KeyEvent e) {
   String allChars = "0123456789";
   String allSigns = "-+";
```

Figure 7.24   IntTextField hierarchy.

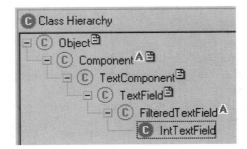

```java
char aChar = e.getKeyChar();
if(e.isActionKey() == true) {
  return;
}
if(((int)aChar == KeyEvent.VK_DELETE) ||
  ((int)aChar == KeyEvent.VK_BACK_SPACE))
  return;
else
if( (allSigns.indexOf((int)aChar) != -1 ) &&
  (getCaretPosition() == 0) ){
  return;
}
else
if( (aChar == '.') && (getText().indexOf('.')
  == -1)){
  return;
}
else
if( allChars.indexOf((int)aChar) != -1) {
  return;
}
else {
  e.consume();
}
}
```

Two Strings (allChars and allSigns) hold the allowed characters for the IntTextField. The *if* statement handles the different types of characters that may be entered. As each valid character is parsed, the method *returns*. Finally, all invalid characters are consumed at the end of the *if* statement. This is the preferred design for filtering characters in TextFields, because the consume() method prevents the characters from displaying.

You can use this sample to make your own TextField that screens certain characters. It is very common to have an upper-case or a lower-case TextField. You can also limit the number of characters entered in the TextField.

Summary

Well, this chapter covered a lot of topics. You built a Java program with a bit more function using VisualAge for Java. In this chapter, you learned how to:

- Extend logic beans with additional methods.
- Add exception handling to an applet.

- Import JavaBeans into VisualAge for Java.
- Use a message box to display an exception.
- Modify the beans palette.
- Use a numeric-only TextField.
- Switch beans and connections in the Visual Composition Editor.
- Use the morphing function.

Each chapter has built on the information used in the previous chapters. This is about all you will do to the Calculator applet, although there is still room for additional function. In the next chapters, you will create new programs using VisualAge for Java and use other tools. You will learn additional tips and techniques that will help you build beans with VisualAge for Java.

DEPLOYING JAVA

What's in Chapter 8

Now that you have used VisualAge for Java to build several applications and applets, you are ready to distribute the programs to others. This chapter shows you how to deploy your applet to the World Wide Web or your application to the desktop. Additionally, you will learn how to share your code with other developers by:

- Exporting code from the IDE
- Running applets outside of the IDE
- Running applications outside of the IDE on the Desktop
- Distributing beans

V isualAge for Java is a powerful tool for building applets, applications, and servlets in Java. However, to fully realize the fruit of your labors, you will want to make your work available to both end users and other developers. With VisualAge for Java, you have several options for deploying and sharing your code. The following sections show you how to place your applets on a Web server and your applications on a user desktop. Additionally, this chapter discusses and gives advice on how to effectively share code with other developers without compromising source code integrity.

Exporting from VisualAge for Java

When you are working in the IDE, all source code is stored in a monolithic repository. Using this repository allows you to version, compare code across versions, and apply complex configurations to your code for multiple customer situations. For more information on the repository, see Chapter 2. While there are many benefits to using the repository, you must export the code from the repository at some point if you want to enable others to use or share the code. VisualAge for Java offers several procedures and file formats for exporting. You can export your work from VisualAge for Java to the following:

- byte-code
- Java source code

- .jar files, Java Archive files
- .dat Repository or Repository files, a VisualAge-specific format

Exporting Java Byte-Code (.class Files)

When using VisualAge for Java, the compiled source code (byte-code) is stored in the workspace. In order to use the code outside of the IDE, you must export to the file system. One option is to export the byte-code as .class files.

Why Export Java Byte-Code?

In order to use the application, applet, servlet, or bean outside of the VisualAge for Java IDE, you must export it to the file system. Exporting byte-code, or .class files, is an excellent choice for initial attempts at deployment. By exporting each Java class as a .class file, you can make modifications to individual classes and then re-export only those classes that changed. Once you have successfully deployed a set of .class files, you will probably want to examine the use of .jar files.

A .class file can be re-imported into your VisualAge for Java workspace, or given to other VisualAge for Java developers for importing. However, doing so makes only the byte-code available and essentially hides the source code.

When exporting byte-code as .class files from VisualAge for Java, you can export projects, packages, classes, and interfaces. You may not export classes or interfaces that contain unresolved problems, classes that were previously imported as .class files, or individual methods.

Tip

It is possible to have two different versions with the same name in the repository at the same time. It is much better to have a unique name for each version for easy identification. You should reversion the items with unique names to reduce confusion.

An Example of Exporting Java Byte-Code

You can use an IBM-supplied sample, com.ibm.ivj.examples.vc.todolist, to learn how to export byte-code (.class files) from VisualAge for Java. You can find this sample in the **IBM Java Examples** project.

If not already started, start the VisualAge for Java IDE.

Select the program elements that you want to export. For this example, select the **com.ibm.ivj.examples.vc.todolist** package.

Select **Export** from the File menu, as shown in Figure 8.1.

Figure 8.1   Exporting byte-code.

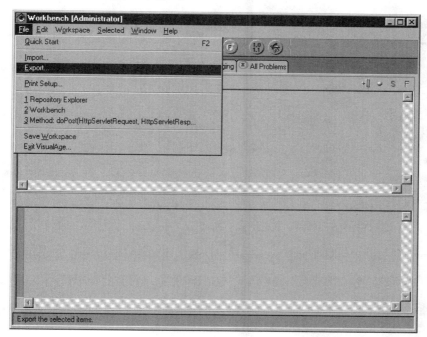

The Export SmartGuide appears with the **Directory** radio button selected. Depending on the type of program elements that you selected, some radio buttons might not be available, as shown in Figure 8.2.

Keep the **Directory** radio button selected.

Select the **Next** button to specify the target directory, the directory where you want to place your exported .class files.

As shown in Figure 8.3, ensure that only the **.class** check box is selected. Then select the **Browse** button to open a file dialog.

Use the file dialog, as shown in Figure 8.4, to locate the target directory. For this example, create a subdirectory under C:\ called **myexports**. Use the New Folder button in the top right-hand corner of the file dialog to create a new folder named myexports.

Close the file dialog by clicking the **OK** button.

Click the **Details** button to select the classes to export. As shown in Figure 8.5, select the **IBM Java Examples** project and the **ToDoList::com.ibm.ivj.examples.vc.todolist** class.

Figure 8.2 Export SmartGuide: byte-code.

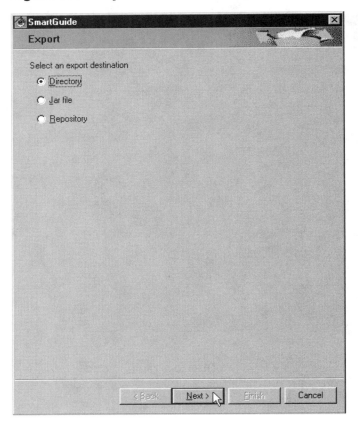

Click the **OK** button and then click the **Finish** button on the Export SmartGuide.

VisualAge for Java exports the .class files for the classes in the selected package to the C:\myexports directory.

> **NOTE**
> VisualAge for Java created a directory for each part of the package name. If the directories already exist, the export function reuses the existing directories. For example, the package you exported (COM.ibm.ivj.examples.vc.todolist) created the directory tree under C:\myexports as shown in Figure 8.6.

Figure 8.3   Export to files options: byte-code.

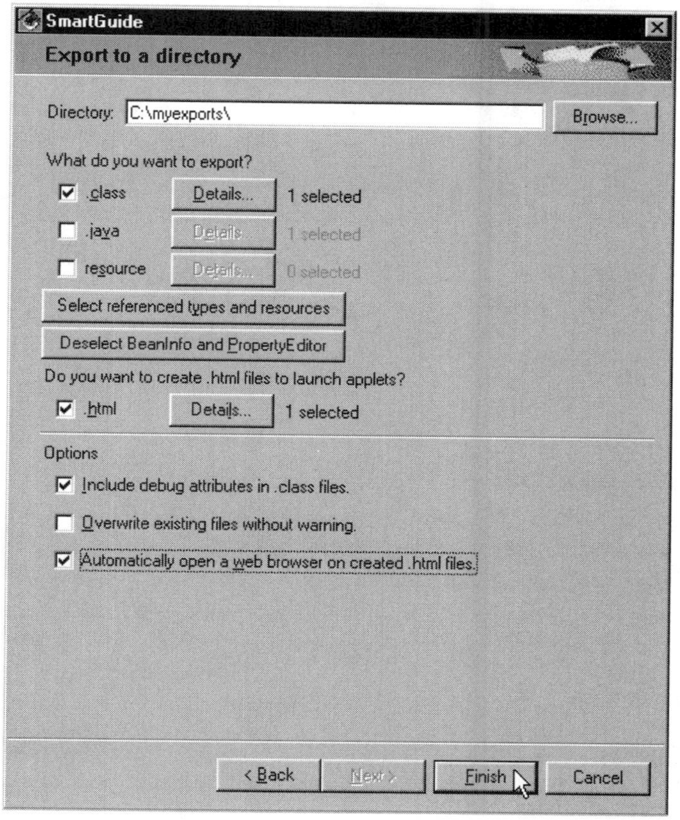

To run the ToDoList applet, you can use the Sun JDK *appletviewer* tool. You must supply an .html file with an applet tag. If you want VisualAge for Java to generate the .html file, select the **.html** check box on the SmartGuide. Select the **Automatically open a Web browser on created .html files** check box to open a Web browser to launch the applet. The ToDoList applet references classes in the swingall.jar file and may not work without additional preparation. Later in this chapter we discuss in more detail how to run applets outside the IDE. When running a JFC-based applet or application, you will want to refer to the correct .jar file in your CLASSPATH. For more information, see Running Applets Outside of the IDE, later in this chapter.

Figure 8.4   File dialog.

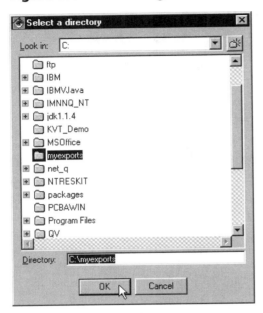

Figure 8.5   .class export dialog.

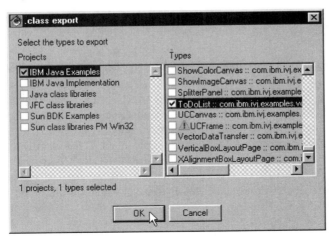

Figure 8.6   Directory structure for a package.

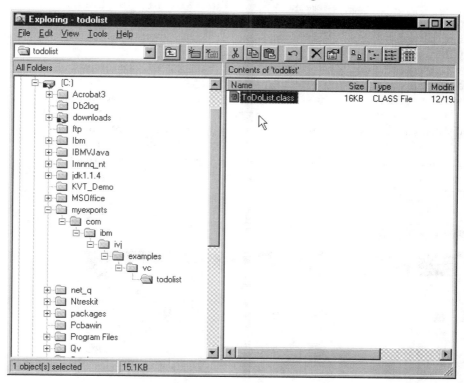

Exporting Java Source (.java Files)

When building beans, applets, or applications in VisualAge for Java, the source code is stored in the repository. In order to share the source code with developers who use tools other than VisualAge for Java, you must export to the file system in the form of **.java** files.

Why Export Java Source?

There are many reasons for exportingJava source code (including beans) outside of VisualAge for Java:

> Incorporate the code into a build system.
>
> Add the code to a file-based code maintenance system.
>
> Backup the code for safekeeping.
>
> Exporting Java source (.java files), and Java archive (.jar) files are the way to share source with non-VisualAge users and tools.

Java source files can be re-imported into the VisualAge for Java repository. Additionally, you can give these .java files to other VisualAge for Java developers for importing. When you import .java files, the VisualAge for Java IDE creates another edition of the class, stores the source code in the repository, and compiles the byte-code in the workspace.

An important consideration when exporting to .java files is the use of the Visual Composition Editor. By default, Java source files do not contain VisualAge for Java connection information. Therefore, you should not export classes built with the Visual Composition Editor as .java files if you want to share them with other VisualAge for Java developers. If you want to share connection information or JavaBean information from the Visual Composition Editor, you must check the **generate meta data method** check box on the Code generation Options window, as shown in Figure 8.7. This option will increase the size of your java source files by approximately 30 percent.

Figure 8.7   Exporting Visual Composition Editor source code.

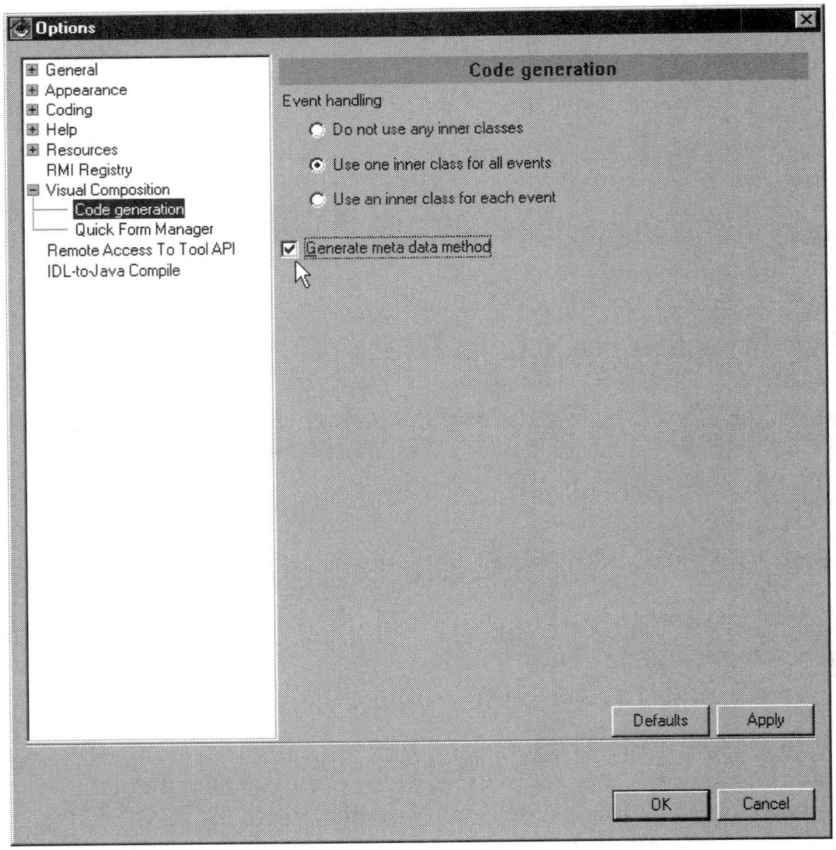

When exporting Java source code as .java files, you can export projects, packages, classes, and interfaces. You can also export as .java files any classes and interfaces with unresolved problems. You may not export individual methods or classes that were previously imported as .class files.

An Example of Exporting Java Source

You can use an IBM-supplied sample, com.ibm.ivj.examples.vc.todolist, to learn how to export Java source (.java files) from VisualAge for Java. You can find this sample in the **IBM Java Examples** project.

If VisualAge for Java is not already started, start the IDE.

Select the program elements that you want to export. For this example, select the **com.ibm.ivj.examples.vc.todolist** package.

Select **Export** from the File menu, as shown in Figure 8.8.

Figure 8.8   Exporting Java source code.

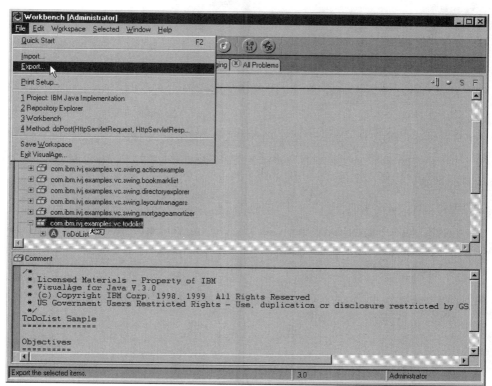

Figure 8.9   Export SmartGuide: source code.

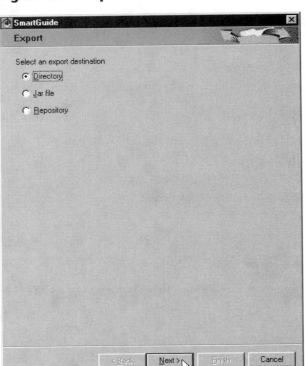

The Export SmartGuide appears with the **Directory** radio button selected, as shown in Figure 8.9. Depending on the type of program elements that you selected, some radio buttons might not be available.

Select the **Next** button to specify the directory where you want the exported .java files to go.

Make sure that the **Directory** check box is still selected.

As shown in Figure 8.10, ensure that only the **.java** check box is selected. Then select the **Browse** button to open a file dialog. Use the file dialog shown in Figure 8.11 to locate the target directory; the directory where you want to place your exported .java files. For the example, use the c:\myexports directory.

Close the file dialog by clicking the **OK** button.

Click the **Details** button to select the .java source classes to export.

Figure 8.10   Export to files options: source.

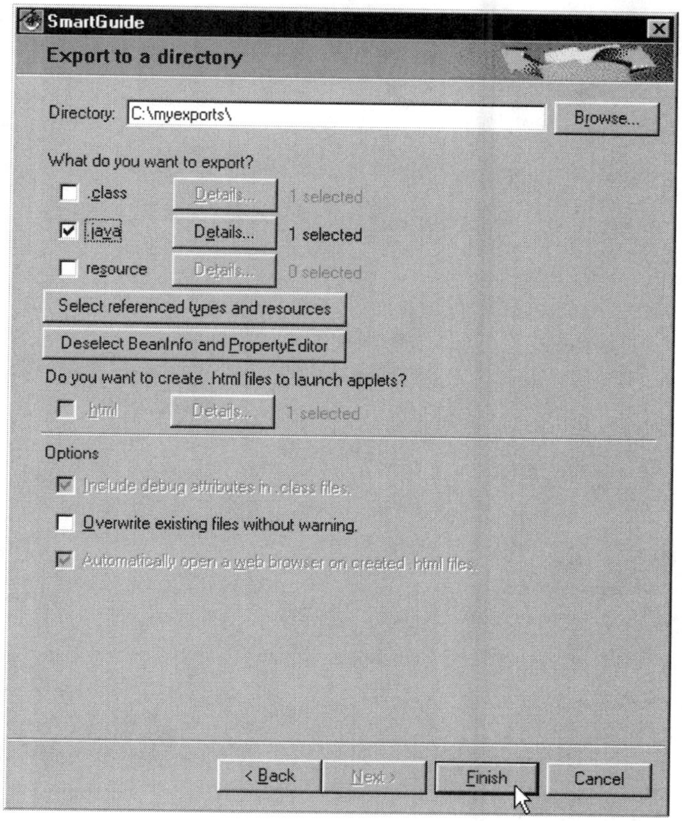

As shown in Figure 8.12, select the **IBM Java Examples** project and the **ToDoList::com.ibm.ivj.examples.vc.todolist** class.

Click the **OK** button and then click the **Finish** button on the Export SmartGuide.

NOTE

VisualAge for Java creates (or reuses, if it already exists) a directory for each part of the package name. For example, the package you exported (COM.ibm.ivj.examples.vc.todolist) created the directory tree under C:\myexports as shown in Figure 8.13.

Figure 8.11   File dialog.

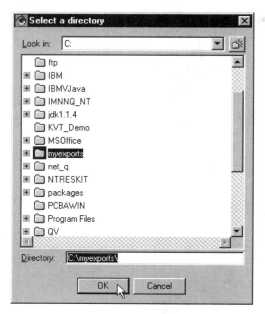

Figure 8.12   .java export dialog.

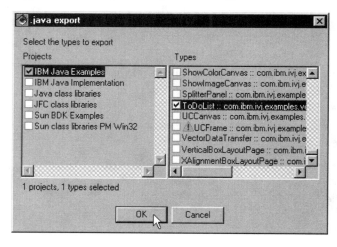

Figure 8.13   Directory structure for a package.

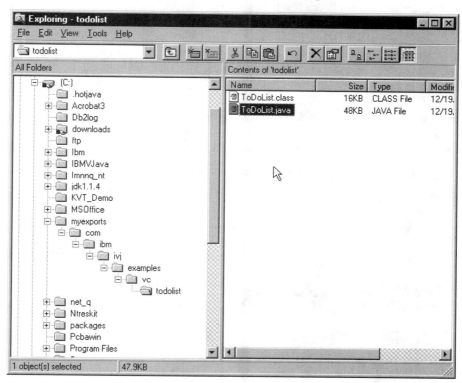

Java Archives (.jar Files)

JAR files, more precisely known as *Java Archives*, were new to the JDK 1.1 specification. JAR files enable you to package byte-code as well as resource files into a single, compressed file. Resource files are files that are necessary for proper execution of your application or applet, such as audio files, image files, video files, and other files used by your applet or application.

Why Export Java Archives?

In order to use the application, applet, or bean outside of the VisualAge for Java IDE, you must export it to the file system. Exporting Java Archives, or .jar files, is an excellent choice for final deployment. By exporting your Java classes in a .jar file, your byte codes and resource files are compressed for performance and faster network transport. Exporting .jar files also enables you to export beans to give to colleagues.

While you typically use .jar files to hold byte-code and resource files, you can put anything into a .jar file. You can use .jar files as portable source archives by exporting your code from VisualAge for Java to .java files and then using the .jar utility outside of VisualAge for Java to assemble the .jar file.

You can re-import a .jar file into your VisualAge for Java workspace. You can also give the .jar files to other VisualAge for Java developers for importing. In fact, .jar files are the mechanism of choice for sharing beans with other developers. You can export an individual package, class, interface, or method.

Exporting a Java Archive

You can use a sample supplied with VisualAge for Java, sunw.demo.juggler.juggler, to learn how to export a .jar file from VisualAge for Java. You can find this sample in the **Sun BDK Examples** project.

If VisualAge for Java is not already started, start the IDE.

Select the project to export. For this example, select the **Sun BDK Examples** project.

Select **Export** from the File menu or the pop-up menu.

Figure 8.14   Export SmartGuide: Java Archive.

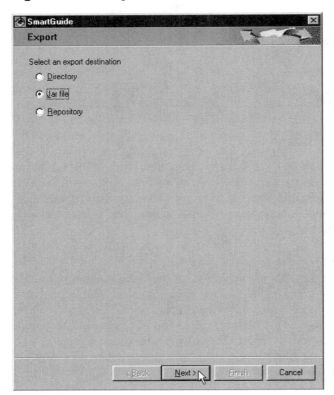

The Export SmartGuide appears with the **Directory** radio button selected. Depending on the type of program elements that you selected, some radio buttons might not be available.

Select the **Jar File** radio button, as shown in Figure 8.14. Then select the **Next** button.

Select the **Browse** button to open a file dialog, then select the .jar file to export to, as shown in Figure 8.15.

Use the file dialog to locate the target directory and file where you want to place your exported .jar files. For the example, use the **c:\myexports** directory. Name the file **juggler.jar** as shown in Figure 8.16.

From the SmartGuide, select the **.class** check box to select the classes to place in the .jar file. From the class dialog, select the Sun BDK Examples project and the Juggler::sunw.demo.juggler type as shown in Figure 8.17, and press the **OK** button.

Figure 8.15   Export .jar file options.

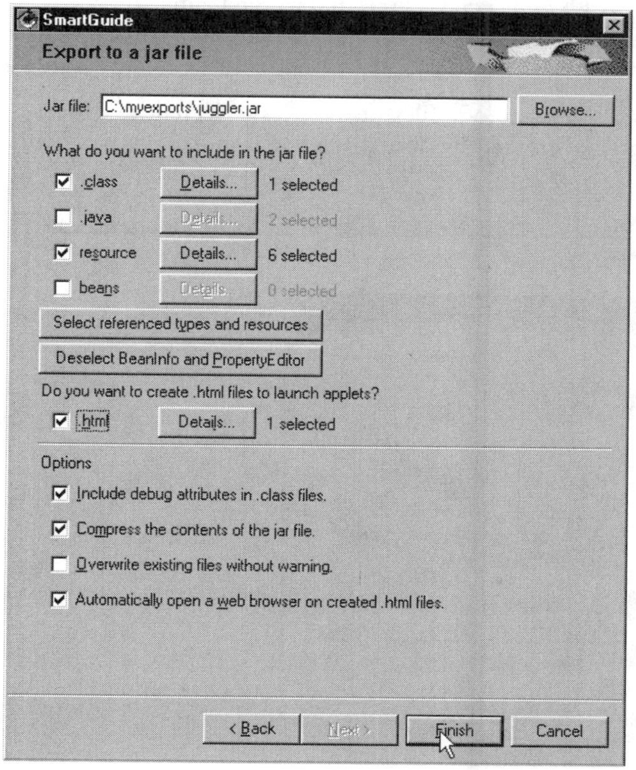

Figure 8.16   File dialog.

This returns you to the SmartGuide window. Build the .jar file by clicking the **Finish** button on the SmartGuide.

VisualAge for Java exports all of the classes selected to the C:\myexports\ juggler.jar file. Exporting and compressing the .jar file can take some time.

The .jar file includes Java the byte-code files (.class files) selected, resources for the project, and a manifest file created by VisualAge for Java.

Figure 8.17   Class dialog.

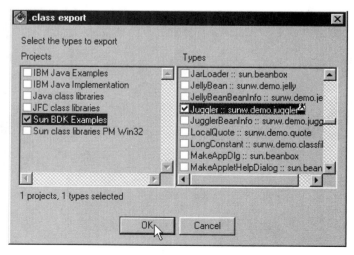

Figure 8.18   Juggler applet in applet viewer.

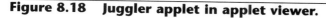

After exporting the .jar file, you need an .html file to run the juggler object from the .jar file. VisualAge for Java can generate the .html file for you. To do so, select the **.html** check box on the SmartGuide.

Figure 8.18 shows the running juggler applet. It juggles the JavaBeans.

How VisualAge Uses Resource Files

VisualAge for Java stores resource files in the file system, not in the repository or the workspace. VisualAge for Java creates a resources directory for each project you create, but it does not create, edit, manage, or delete resource files for you. You must manage the project resources directory, subdirectories, and resource files yourself. In the resources directory for a project, you can leave the files at one level or group them into subdirectories. If you group them, your code must specify a path that is relative to the project's resources directory.

When you import a project from a .jar file, VisualAge for Java extracts any resource files stored in the .jar file and copies them to the project's resources directory. When you export a project as a .jar file, VisualAge for Java copies the resource files from the project's resources directory and includes them in the .jar file with their directory structure intact.

When you run a program that uses resource files, the program can access them in several ways:

- The getResource() method can be used to get resources. If the program specifies a ClassLoader, it can specify where to look for resource files. If the program does not specify a ClassLoader, it looks for resource files on the CLASSPATH. If the program is an applet being run by the applet viewer, it looks for resource files first in the CLASSPATH and then in the code base as specified in environment variables or .html parameters.

- The getSystemResource() method can get system-level resources. The program looks for resource files on the CLASSPATH.

- If the program is an applet, there are two ways to access resources: getAudioClip() and getImage(). The applet looks for resource files in the code base. If a bean inside the applet needs resource files, it looks for them in the bean's code base.

If you export the applet as a .class file and the applet uses resource files, you must copy the resource files to the directory where you export the applet files. If the applet uses resource files, they must be in the project_resources directory for the project that contains the applet class. Copy the resource files to the same directory where you placed the exported applet class.

VisualAge Repository Format (.dat Files)

VisualAge for Java provides a common format for exchange of source code between multiple VisualAge for Java environments. The same source management architecture is used by many popular Smalltalk environments such as VisualAge for Smalltalk and ParcPlace Smalltalk. An Repository file is one way to share visual connection information with other developers. If you export a class built using the Visual Composition Editor as a .java or .jar file, you can lose all of the Visual Composition Editor connection information. To preserve the connection information, export the class to a Repository file, or to a .java source file with the **Design time option: generate meta data method** turned on.

You can export an entire project or individual packages in a format that can be imported easily into another VisualAge for Java workspace. Repository files do not include resource files. The Repository file includes:

- Program elements (including project and package comments)

- Applet settings

- Information that the Visual Composition Editor uses (connection information)

Tip

The resource files for the beans in a project are kept in a subdirectory with the Project's name. You need to copy these resource files and distribute them with the program. You should also back up the resource files in case of hardware problems.

You can only export editions of entire projects or individual packages that have been versioned. However, these projects or packages may contain elements that have unresolved problems. You cannot export individual classes, interfaces, or methods, or a project or package that is an open edition.

Exporting a Repository File

You can use an IBM-supplied sample, com.ibm.ivj.examples.vc.todolist, to learn how to export to an Repository (.dat) file from VisualAge for Java. You can find this sample in the **IBM Java Examples** project.

If VisualAge for Java is not already started, start the IDE.

Select the program elements that you want to export. For this example, select the **com.ibm.ivj.examples.vc.todolist** package.

Select **Export** from the Workbench File menu.

The Export SmartGuide appears with the **Directory** radio button selected. Depending on the type of program elements that you selected, some radio buttons might not be available.

Select the **Repository** radio button as shown in Figure 8.19.

Figure 8.19 Export SmartGuide: Repository file.

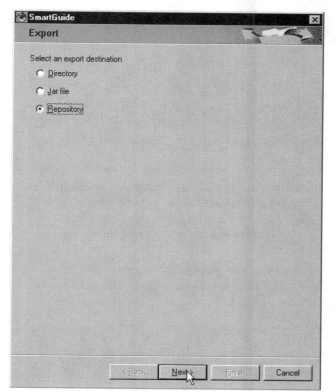

Figure 8.20   SmartGuide.

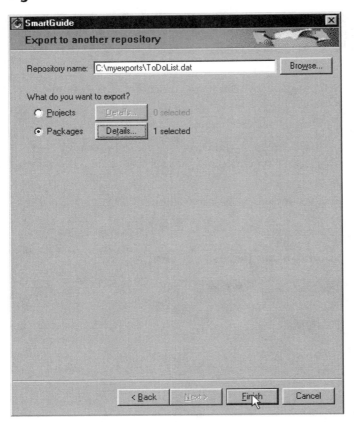

Select the **Next** button and then select the **Browse** button to open a file dialog. Use the file dialog to locate the target directory, the directory where you want to place your exported .dat file. For this example, use the subdirectory under C:\ called **myexports**. The name of the Repository file is **ToDoList.dat**.

On the SmartGuide, select the **Packages** radio button and then the **Details** button to select the **com.ibm.ivj.examples.vc.todolist** package. As shown in Figure 8.20, click the **Finish** button on the SmartGuide.

NOTE

If you leave off the .dat extension, VisualAge for Java will create it without an extension (even though it looks for .dat files in the SmartGuides).

VisualAge for Java exports the .dat file for the classes in the selected package to the C:\myexports directory.

Running Applets Outside of the IDE

When you export an applet, you need to export all of its dependent packages as well. You do not need to export the Sun Java class libraries; the Web browser should include these. When you export .jar files, VisualAge for Java does not require you to find all the dependent classes, but you must ensure that you have exported all dependent packages in order for you applet to work properly.

Additionally, you must ensure that you placed all resource files used by the applet in the appropriate directory. Exporting to a .jar file helps to ensure that resource files are placed in the right place. However, these options work only if you have previously placed the resource files in the **project_resources** directory for the project that contains the applet class.

Making HTML Files

Deploying your applet requires you write an .html file. You can use VisualAge for Java to generate it for you. Table 8.1 shows a listing of basic .html required to run your applet.

```
<APPLET
  CODE = applet-filename
  WIDTH = pixel-width
  HEIGHT = pixel-height
  OBJECT = serialized-applet-filename
  ARCHIVE = comma-separated-jar-filename-list
  CODEBASE = applet-url
  ALT = alternative-text
  NAME = applet-name
  ALIGN = alignment
  VSPACE = pixel-vertical-margin
  HSPACE = pixel-horizontal-margin
>
<PARAM NAME = parameter VALUE = value>
<PARAM NAME = parameter VALUE = value>
. . .
alternate-text
</APPLET>
```

If your applet is specified in a .jar file, remember that although a .jar file is compressed, the entire file is always downloaded. You need to ensure that you place in the appropriate .jar file only those items that need to be together in the appropriate .jar file, or your applet will download classes that are not needed.

Table 8.1 Basic HTML for Running an Applet

Tag	Description
APPLET	Specifies the applet to be loaded and run. If the applet viewer or Web browser does not recognize Java applets, text after the ALT tag is displayed.
CODE	Required attribute specifies the .class file containing the applet class. Must be relative to the CODEBASE or the document URL.
CODEBASE	Optional attribute specifies the base URL of the applet. Should be a directory, not a file. If not specified, the URL of the document is used.
WIDTH	Required attribute specifies the initial width in pixels that the applet uses.
HEIGHT	Required attribute specifies the initial height in pixels that the applet uses.
OBJECT	Required attribute specifies the .class file containing a serialized applet class. Must be relative to the CODEBASE or the document URL.
ARCHIVE	Optional attribute specifies a comma-separated list of .jar files to be preloaded by the applet viewer or Web browser. Must be relative to the CODEBASE or the document URL.
ALT	Optional attribute specifies alternate text to be displayed by a web browser that does not support Java applets.
VSPACE	Optional attribute specifies vertical margin in pixels.
HSPACE	Optional attribute specifies horizontal margin in pixels.
NAME	Optional attribute specifies the name of the applet instance.
ALIGN	Optional attribute specifies the alignment of the applet on the web page.

Exporting .class files provides your applet with what you need. However, the .class file is not compressed, and the browser must initiate a separate URL request to the server for each .class file.

Running Applications Outside of the IDE

When you export the application .class files, you need to export all of the dependent packages as well. You do not need to export the Sun Java class libraries; the local JVM provides these. When you export .jar files, VisualAge for Java does not require you to find all the dependent classes, but you must ensure that you have exported all dependent packages in order for your application to work properly.

If you do not export the application as a .jar file and if the application uses resource files, you must copy the resource files to the directory where you exported the application files. If the application uses resource files, they are in the project_resources directory for the project that contains the application.

It is essential that you set the CLASSPATH environment variable to a default directory where your Java applications will run. When distributing the applications across the enterprise, you may want to create a batch file to set the CLASSPATH variable for each application. Or you could use the '.' current directory indicator in your CLASSPATH to use the current directory as the starting point for finding the applications. You will also have to explicitly list each .jar file in your CLASSPATH.

Tip

If your applet or application is having difficulties finding resources, make sure your resources can be found in your CLASSPATH. You can place them in the same directory as your applet or application.

Distributing Beans

Exporting .jar files enables you to share beans with other developers. When you create a .jar file, you get the manifest file built for you by VisualAge for Java or by the JAR utility. Earlier you exported a .jar file for the Sun Demo Examples project. The juggler.jar file had one bean marked for export. The **manifest.mf** file identifies the beans exported. Figure 8.21 shows a partial listing of this file and the bean marked in the export we did earlier.

To demonstrate sharing beans, you can re-import the juggler.jar file and place the juggler bean on the beans palette of the Visual Composition Editor.

Delete the **Sun BDK Examples** project from the workspace. You can reload it later from the repository if desired. The errors found during the deletion will be fixed when we import.

Figure 8.21 MANIFEST.MF file listing.

```
Manifest-Version: 1.0

Name: sunw/demo/juggler/Juggler.class
Java-Bean: True
Digest-Algorithms: SHA MD5
SHA-Digest: cJQCmvpQeDZVsPq7AHrhKPRVCKQ=
MD5-Digest: MoQ9yiRXseVv7FtUUUbBDQ==
```

Figure 8.22   Importing the juggler.jar file.

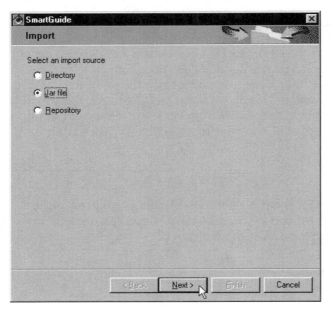

Select **File** and **Import** from the Workbench.

Select the **Jar file** radio button on the SmartGuide and click the **Next** button as seen in Figure 8.22.

Enter the **Sun BDK Examples** project and click the **Browse** button on the SmartGuide as seen in Figure 8.23. Select the **C:\MyExports\juggler.jar** file from the file dialog and click the **Open** button, as shown in Figure 8.24.

Click the **class** check box and press the **Details** button as shown in Figure 8.23.

From the Class Import window, select the Juggler class and the JugglerBeanInfo class. Click the **OK** button, as shown in Figure 8.25.

Click the **resource** check box.

Press the **Details** button as shown in Figure 8.23.

Select the **juggler0.gif** through **juggler4.gif** files and the **jugglerIcon.gif** file.

Click the **OK** button, as shown in Figure 8.26.

Figure 8.23   Import SmartGuide: archive.

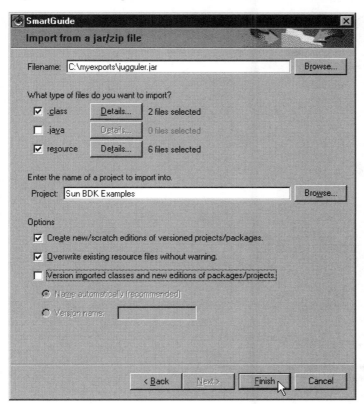

Figure 8.24   Import file dialog.

Figure 8.25   Class import.

Figure 8.26   Resource import.

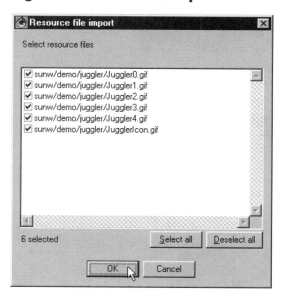

Figure 8.27   Category selection.

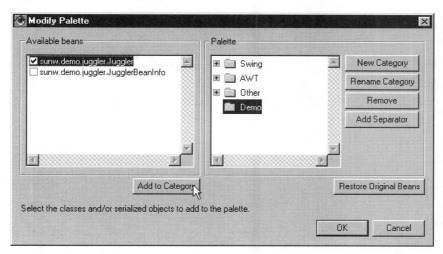

When importing classes into VisualAge for Java, you can have the class placed on the Visual Composition Editor palette. As shown in Figure 8.27, click the **sunw.demo.juggler.Juggler** check box. Click the **New Category**

Figure 8.28   Modify palette.

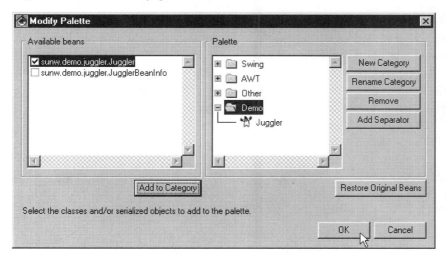

Figure 8.29   Bean on palette.

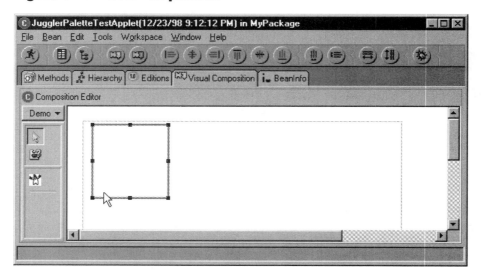

button and enter **Demo** for the new category. Click the **Add to Category** button to add the **sunw.demo.juggler.Juggler** class to the **Demo** category. The list box on the right is updated, showing the Juggler class in the Demo category, as shown in Figure 8.28. Click the **OK** button on the **Modify palette** window.

Finally, import the juggler.jar file by clicking the **Finish** button on the SmartGuide, shown in Figure 8.23.

To see if the juggler bean is on the beans palette, create a new class as a subclass of applet in MyProject and open the Visual Composition Editor. Scroll to the bottom of the categories and click the **Demo** category. Click the **juggler** bean and place it on the applet, as shown in Figure 8.29.

Summary

In this chapter you learned how to export the various forms of source code and byte-code from the VisualAge for Java repository to the file system. To do this you:

- Exported a sample as .class, .java, .jar, and .dat (Repository format).
- Learned about resource files.

- Ran exported code both from a web page and as a stand-alone application.
- Learned what html tags are needed to test an applet.

Now that you can deploy your code in a variety of forms, you can share your beans, applets, and applications with colleagues. Deploying and testing your Java programs outside the development environment is a very import step in completing the program.

BUILDING THE INTERNET ADDRESS APPLET

> **What's in Chapter 9**
>
> Now that you have learned about the Visual Composition Editor and JavaBeans, you are ready to take advantage of object technology through visual layering and bean reuse. In this chapter, you build a VisualAge for Java applet that enters Internet address information for users and reformats the information in a list bean. In this chapter, you learn how to:
>
> - Build panels that can be layered to give the desired appearance and reused across applets and applications
> - Promote bean features that can be accessed by other beans
> - Use tear-off properties and Variables to simplify bean communication
> - Use Factories to produce object instances visually
> - Use CardLayout to simulate a notebook bean

VisualAge for Java enables you to extend object technologies through the visual programming of beans and their reuse across applets and applications. Building the Internet Address Applet shows you how to reuse panels using layering, Factories, and Variables. You develop the applet model or domain classes, paint the user interface, connect the beans, and test the Java code by running it in the IDE. Figure 9.1 shows the first card in the running applet.

The pace of this chapter is much quicker than previous chapters. In each section, you will see a picture of the running program and then you will build that component.

Figure 9.2 shows the second card in the running applet. In this chapter, you will build this applet using the CardLayout manager to manage the two cards. The cards contain GUI subbeans that you will build as separate beans. You will then use visual layering to combine the subbeans.

The **User Info** and **Additional Info** buttons enable the user to switch between two cards (or panels) and enter information about the Internet address. After typing information in the text fields, the user can select the **Add** button to add the information to the list. When the user selects an item from the list, the information appears in the corresponding text fields of the InternetUserInfoPanel and InternetAdditionalInfoPanel beans. When the user selects an item in the list, information can be changed in the text fields and updated with the **Update** button. The user can delete selected items from the list by clicking the **Delete** button.

Figure 9.1   InternetAddressFinalApplet first panel.

Figure 9.2   InternetAddressFinalApplet second panel.

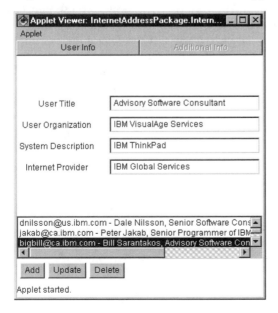

The steps required to build the Internet Address Applet are:

1. Create a model, or the InternetAddress domain class, to hold information about the user's Internet address information.
2. Add bean properties to the InternetAddress class.
3. Create the InternetAddress panels, which contain the user interface for the applet.
4. Create the InternetAddressTestApplet class, which contains the panels, model class, and other invisible beans of the applet.
5. Create the InternetAddressFinalApplet class, which contains reused panels, the model class, and other invisible beans to perform a final test of the applet.

Creating the InternetAddress Class

The domain objects are a central part of your applet or application. These beans represent business objects and interface with GUI beans, broker beans, and controller beans. Domain objects are invisible beans that run on the client or on the server. Start building the domain object with the following steps:

If you have closed VisualAge for Java, restart it.

Select the **My Project** project in the Workbench.

VisualAge for Java offers many ways to do the same task. You can use the tool bar to create the package; this time, use pop-up menus.

In the Workbench, click the right mouse button to open the pop-up menu. Select **Add** and then **Package....**

Use the SmartGuide to enter the package name, internetaddress, and click the check box labeled **Create a new package named**.

Now you are ready to create the InternetAddress class. It contains information about the Internet address (state), as well as functions to get, format, and set Internet address information (behavior). It does not need to inherit behavior from any other classes, so its superclass is the Java Object class. Create the new class using the following steps:

Select InternetAddressPackage on the Workbench list and click the right mouse button to add the new class.

From the pop-up menu, select **Add** and then **Class....** In the SmartGuide, as shown in Figure 9.3, enter **InternetAddress** as the class name.

Leave the default values for all other information and select the **Finish** button to create the class.

Figure 9.3 Class SmartGuide.

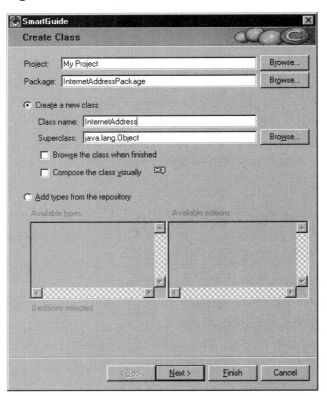

VisualAge for Java generates the InternetAddress class and shows the new class in the package of the Workbench window, as shown in Figure 9.4. If you are

Figure 9.4 Workbench with InternetAddress class.

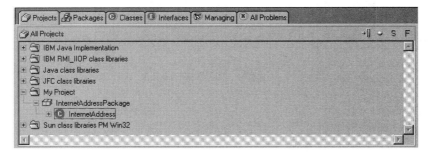

developing a number of classes, you can create all of them before defining the features. Once the classes display in the Workbench, you can add the features to each class. This method is very helpful when you are developing in a team. After you have defined the different classes, each team member can work on completing their individual classes. For this program, you develop the features for the InternetAddress class before creating the other classes needed for the applet.

Adding Bean Properties to the InternetAddress Class

Next, you need to add properties and methods to the InternetAddress class to support communication with other beans, as shown in Figure 9.5. Objects contain both fields and methods that access data and provide object behavior.

From the Workbench, move the mouse pointer over the InternetAddress class and click the right mouse button. Select **Open To** and then **BeanInfo** as shown in Figure 9.6.

The browser for the bean opens with the BeanInfo page displayed.

From the InternetAddress BeanInfo page, place the mouse pointer within the features list, click the right mouse button, and from the pop-up menu select **New Property Feature....**

The SmartGuide - New Property Feature window opens, prompting you for information about the added property. Type **firstName** as the property name and select the **Finish** button as shown in Figure 9.7.

Figure 9.5   InternetAddress Class.

InternetAddress Class

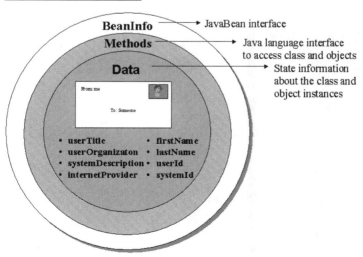

Figure 9.6 Opening the BeanInfo page.

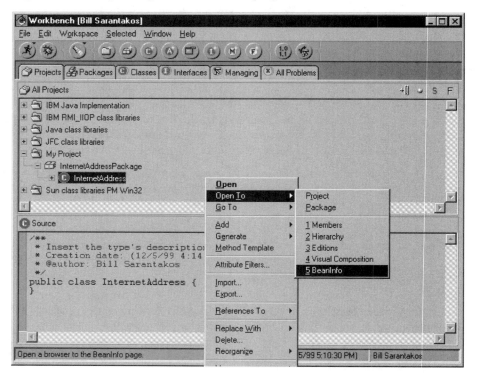

Figure 9.7 New Property SmartGuide.

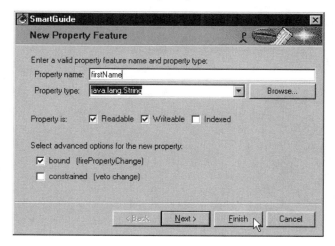

In the same way, add the following properties to the InternetAddress class:

lastName

userId

systemId

userOrganization

userTitle

systemDescription

internetProvider

You also need to create a method feature to format the userId, systemId, and user name for display purposes. Click the right mouse button over the features list and from the pop-up menu select **New Method Feature....**

From the SmartGuide - New Method Feature window, enter the method name, **getFormattedName**, into the Method name field. Select **java.lang.String** from the Return type combo box and then select the **Finish** button as shown in Figure 9.8.

VisualAge for Java generates the method for you. Modify the generated getFormattedName() method to return a formatted string of the property features. Add the code shown in bold face, as follows:

```java
/**
 * Performs the getFormattedName method.
 * @return java.lang.String
 */
public String getFormattedName() {
    /* Perform the getFormattedName method. */
    String fieldFormattedAddress = new String();
    try {
        fieldFormattedAddress =
            getUserId().trim() + "@" +
            getSystemId().trim() + " - " +
            getFirstName().trim() + " " +
            getLastName().trim() + ", " +
            getUserTitle().trim() + " of " +
            getUserOrganization().trim();
    } catch (java.lang.Throwable exception) {
        System.err.println("Exception creating formattedName");
    }  return fieldFormattedAddress;
}
```

Figure 9.9 shows the BeanInfo page for InternetAddress.

Figure 9.8   New Method Feature SmartGuide.

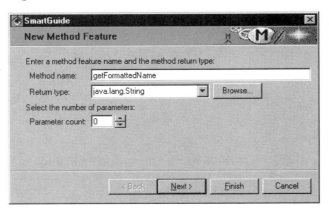

Finishing Off the InternetAddress Class

The toString() method is required to return a formatted string of InternetAddress. The toString() method calls getFormattedName() to do its job. It is very common to use a toString() method for converting object information into a Java String that can be used by other beans.

Add the toString() method to the InternetAddress class. This method returns a java.lang.String, the result of the call to the getFormattedName() method.

Figure 9.9   BeanInfo properties.

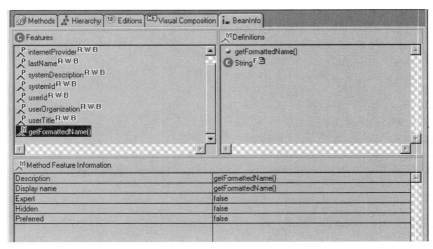

Creating User Interface Panels

Now that you have created the domain class, it is time to create the user interface for the applet. The InternetAddress Applet contains four panels that allow the user to enter Internet address information:

- **InternetUserInfoPanel** enables entry of user information.
- **InternetAdditionalInfoPanel** enables entry of additional information.
- **InternetFormattedInfoPanel** enables the selection of an address for update or deletion.
- **InternetButtonPanel** contains buttons that enable the user to add, update, and delete Internet address information from InternetUserInfoPanel and InternetAdditionalInfoPanel in the InternetFormattedInfoPanel list.

InternetUserInfoPanel

InternetUserInfoPanel enables the user to enter the Internet user's first and last name, user ID, and system ID, as shown in Figure 9.10.

Figure 9.10   InternetUserInfoPanel.

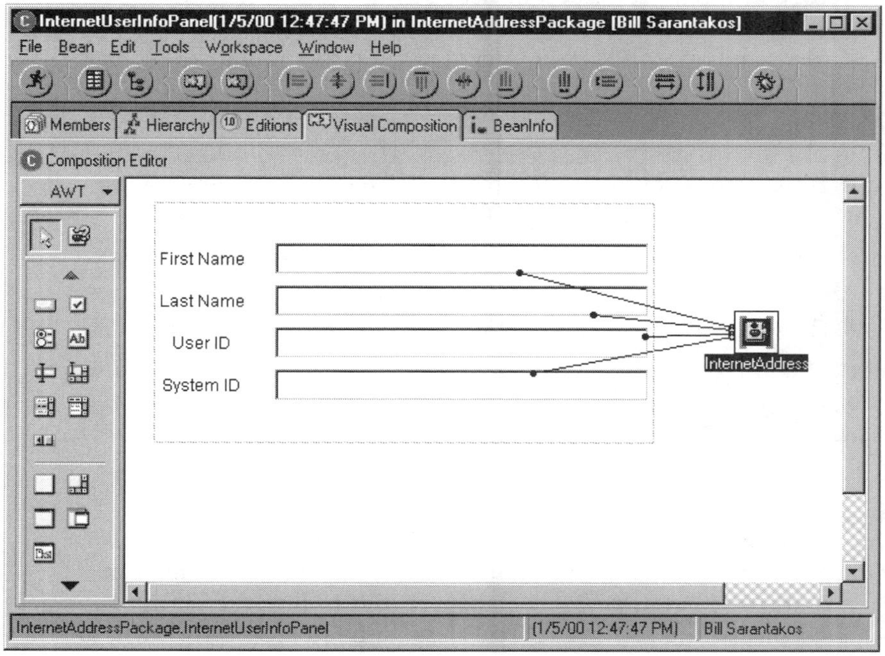

Create the InternetUserInfoPanel class in the internetaddress package using java.awt.Panel as its superclass.

You will use the GridBagLayout for the InternetUserInfoPanel. Set the Layout Manager for the panel as follows:

In the Visual Composition Editor, press the left mouse button to select the panel; then press the right mouse button to display its pop-up menu.

Select **Properties** and then open the drop-down list of the *layout* property.

Select **GridBagLayout** and then close the window.

The GridBagLayout can prove challenging when you are adding beans to a Panel or Frame. You have already used it in the Advanced Calculator in Chapter 6, so this is another chance to practice with this powerful Layout Manager. When you add Labels and TextField beans to the Panel, GridBagLayout groups the beans in the center of the Panel. You may set the component beans' GridBag constraint weights to gain needed vertical space between rows or horizontal space between columns.

Continue building the panel by doing the following:

Add four *java.awt.Label*s to the panel vertically in the first column.

Add four *java.awt.TextField*s to the panel vertically in the second column.

It is good practice to give the beans in your composite bean names that you recognize when you inspect or debug the generated code. In this case, you should rename the TextField beans to FirstNameText, LastNameText, UserIdText, and SystemIdText in order from top to bottom.

In order to get the right size and position for the TextField, set its properties using the following steps:

With the left mouse button, select the UserIdText bean; then with the right mouse button, display its pop-up menu. Select **Properties**.

UserIdText should show only 8 characters of input. Set the UserIdText bean *columns* property to 8.

Similarly, set the *columns* property for the other three TextFields to 30.

Set the UserIdText GridBagConstraints *anchor* property to *West*. To set it, expand the *constraints* property from the TextField property sheet and then select **West** for the *anchor* attribute, as shown in Figure 9.11.

VisualAge Variables

VisualAge for Java supports a special type of invisible bean called a *Variable* bean, which refer to specific instances of a certain type. In this example, a Variable bean dropped on the free-form surface next to InternetUserInfoPanel represents an instance of the InternetAddress class. In InternetUserInfoPanel, drop a Variable bean on the free-form surface with the following steps:

Select the **Other** category from the category pull-down menu, which is located at the top edge on the left side of the free-form surface.

Select the Variable icon from the beans palette. The mouse pointer changes to a crosshair. Move the mouse pointer to the free-form surface and press the left mouse button to drop the Variable bean.

The Variable bean used for this panel represents the instance of the InternetAddress accessed by the user. The Variable bean name is InternetAddress, and its type, or class, is InternetAddress. You can set both the name and type of the variable by placing the mouse cursor over the Variable bean and pressing the right mouse button. You can select **Change Bean Name...** and **Change Type...** from the pop-up menu to change the bean name and Variable bean type, respectively. The bean name can be any valid Java identifier, whereas the bean type, in addition to being a valid Java identifier, must be a valid class in the workspace.

Property-to-property connections connect the Variable properties to the TextField beans' *text* properties. The source of the connections is the Variable bean. These connections update the InternetAddress referred to by the Variable bean when the user types information into the TextFields. The connections also update the text in the text fields when a new instance of InternetAddress is placed in the Variable.

Don't forget that once you have created the property-to-property connections, you need to edit the connection properties and change the **Target event** from **<none>** to **textValueChanged**. If you forget to do this, the InternetAddress bean will not receive notification that the values in the TextFields have changed. Therefore, any application that uses the Panel will probably not work properly.

Using the *this* Feature and Promotion

You must promote the *this* feature of the Variable so the instance in the Variable can be accessed from Internet Address applet. The *this* feature is merely a reference to a class, and it assumes the class is instantiated. Promote the *this* feature of the Variable bean using these steps:

Select the Variable bean with the right mouse button. From the Variable pop-up menu, select **Promote Bean Feature....**

Select the *this* property on the **Promote features from: InternetAddress** window as shown in Figure 9.12. After selecting the *this* feature, select the **>>** button to promote the feature. This makes the feature public to other beans.

Select the **OK** button to close the window.

Now you can access the Variable from the Applet or other beans.

Figure 9.11   InternetUserInfoPanel properties.

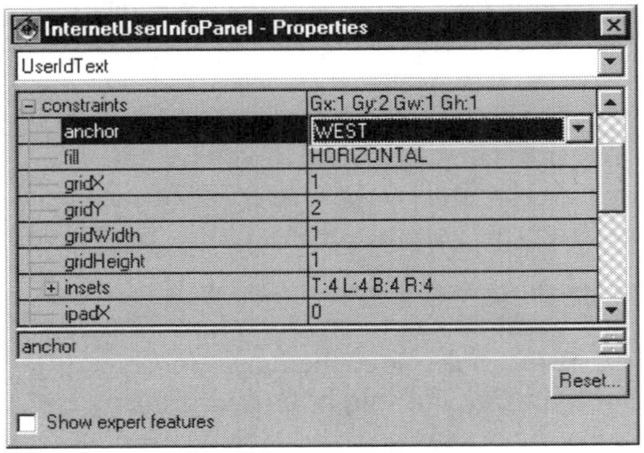

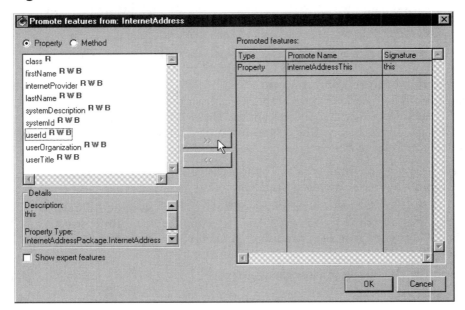

Save the InternetUserInfoPanel bean so you can use it later.

The next step is to continue developing components and create InternetAdditionalInfoPanel.

Figure 9.12   Promote Bean Feature window.

Unpromoting a Feature

Sometimes you need to remove or undo the promotion of a feature. You may need to do this because you made a mistake in the feature you actually wanted to promote or because you have removed or renamed a feature that you previously promoted. To unpromote a feature, do the following:

Switch to the BeanInfo page for this class.

For each promoted feature, a "new" feature with a name based on the original feature is also listed in the Features list. The name corresponds to the name listed in the promoted features window when the feature was originally promoted. Delete the promoted feature using its pop-up menu.

In the Workbench, select the corresponding BeanInfo class and clean up any method that now has an error listed against it by removing the unresolved or unknown variables or references in the method. The references are usually found within an array initialization list. You have the choice of working directly in the Workbench to do this or opening the class browser for the BeanInfo class.

> **NOTE**
>
> You can always delete the promoted methods anywhere in VisualAge for Java. You should always check the BeanInfo file for the class to insure that all references are deleted. Promoted methods may have names that are not obvious because they were given a name other than the default when they were promoted.

You may also be able to delete other support classes that were generated into the package if the feature that was unpromoted was the last of a certain type (property, method, or event). It will not be a problem if you leave some of these classes—they will just not be used.

InternetAdditionalInfoPanel

InternetAdditionalInfoPanel enables the user to enter the Internet user title, the user organization, the system description, and an Internet provider. Create InternetAdditionalInfoPanel as shown in Figure 9.13 with the following beans and properties:

- GridBagLayout to manage the position of the GUI beans.

- Label and TextField beans to enable entry of the user title, the user organization, a system description, and the Internet service provider. These TextFields should have a *columns* property of 30.

Figure 9.13   InternetAdditionalInfoPanel.

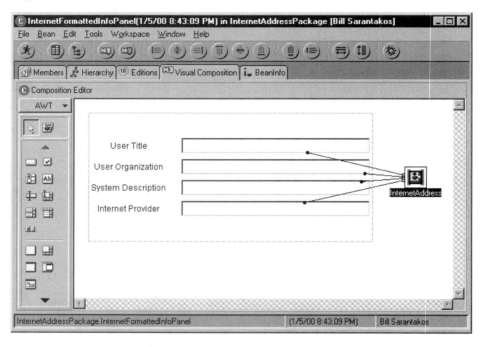

- A Variable to represent the instance of the InternetAddress being worked on by the user. The Variable should have a type of InternetAddress and a bean name of InternetAddress. Promote the *this* feature of the Variable.

- Connections between the source InternetAddress Variable properties and the target text properties of the TextFields. The specific connection events used are significant.

After visually programming the Panel, save your work and continue to the next section, where you create the InternetFormattedInfoPanel. If you need any help in working with GridBagLayout, setting bean properties, creating a Variable, or making the necessary connections, review the work you did for the InternetUserInfoPanel.

InternetFormattedInfoPanel

InternetFormattedInfoPanel, shown in Figure 9.14, formats the information entered on the InternetUserInfoPanel and InternetAdditionalInfoPanel and displays the formatted information in a list of String items. The user can select items in the list for update or deletion. When the user opens the applet, and then adds, updates, or deletes an Internet address, the **refreshListBoxItems()** method is called to retrieve the Strings from a Vector. Start building the panel by doing the following:

Figure 9.14   InternetFormattedInfoPanel.

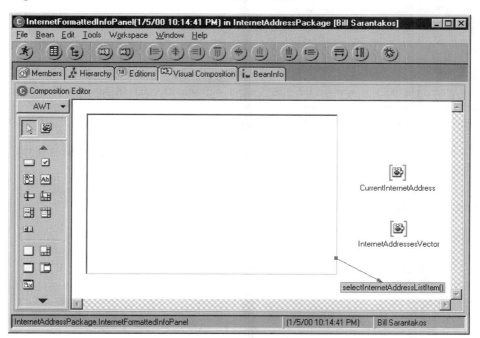

Create InternetFormattedInfoPanel by deriving it from java.awt.Panel as you did for the first two panels.

Change the layout of the panel to *BorderLayout*.

Drop a java.awt.List bean into the *Center* region of the panel. Name the List bean *InternetAddressListBox*.

Now, create the **refreshListBoxItems** method containing the code below. Don't worry if there are unresolved references when you save the code; they will be resolved when you finish creating the rest of the panel.

```
/**
 * This method was created by a SmartGuide.
 */
public void refreshListBoxItems ( ) {

  getInternetAddressListBox().removeAll();

  // iterate thru the Vector and set the items of
  // the list box
  for (int i = 0; i < getInternetAddressesVector().size(); i ++){
```

```
        getInternetAddressListBox().
          add(getInternetAddressesVector().
          elementAt(i).toString());
        }
    return;
    }
```

When the user selects an item in the list, the **selectInternetAddressListItem()** method is called to place the selected item into the CurrentInternetAddress Variable. When this event happens, each field is copied to a Java Vector that holds the items for the list. Create the method in the BeanInfo page.

Add the following code to this new method. Again, don't worry about unresolved references for now.

```
/**
 * This method was created by a SmartGuide.
 */
public void selectInternetAddressListItem ( ) {
  // set the current InternetAddress properties
  // based on the list item selected
  int i = getInternetAddressListBox().getSelectedIndex();
  if (i >= 0) {
    InternetAddress vectorIntAddr =
    (InternetAddress)getInternetAddressesVector().elementAt(i);

    InternetAddress currentIntAddr =
      (InternetAddress)getCurrentInternetAddress();
    currentIntAddr.setFirstName(vectorIntAddr.getFirstName());
    currentIntAddr.setLastName(vectorIntAddr.getLastName());
    currentIntAddr.setUserId(vectorIntAddr.getUserId());
    currentIntAddr.setSystemId(vectorIntAddr.getSystemId());
    currentIntAddr.setUserTitle(vectorIntAddr.getUserTitle());

currentIntAddr.setUserOrganization(vectorIntAddr.getUserOrganization())
;

currentIntAddr.setSystemDescription(vectorIntAddr.getSystemDescription(
));

currentIntAddr.setInternetProvider(vectorIntAddr.getInternetProvider())
;
  }
  return;
  }
```

InternetFormattedInfoPanel contains two Variables. **CurrentInternetAddress** represents the current Internet address being worked on by the user. **InternetAddressesVector** represents a Vector of all InternetAddress objects added and modified by the user, as shown in Figure 9.14. After adding the two variables, be sure to promote their *this* attribute.

The CurrentInternetAddress variable should have its type set to InternetAddress. Set the type for InternetAddressesVector to java.util.Vector.

When the user selects an item in the list, the itemStateChanged event is signaled and the **selectInternetAddressListItem**() method is called. This is an event-to-code connection. Make this connection as follows:

Select the List and bring up its connection menu (by selecting the *Connect* item from its pop-up menu).

Select the **itemStateChanged** event as the source.

Move the mouse to the free-form surface and press the left mouse button. Select the **Event to Code...** menu item. The *Event-to-Code Connection from InternetAddressListBox* dialog displays for the connection properties, as shown in Figure 9.15.

Select the **selectInternetAddressListItem**() entry from the *Method* choice box and select the OK button to complete the event-to-code connection.

Figure 9.15   itemStateChanged connection.

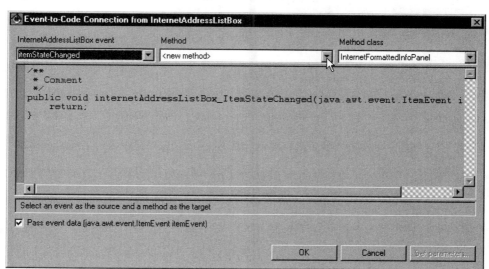

When the user updates the InternetAddress item selected in the list, the **updateInternetAddress()** method will be called. Create this method as follows:

```
/**
 * This method was created by a SmartGuide.
 */
public void updateInternetAddress ( ) {
// set the vector InternetAdress properties
// based on the curent internet address
int i =
 getInternetAddressListBox().getSelectedIndex();
if (i >= 0) {
  InternetAddress vectorIntAddr =
  (InternetAddress)getInternetAddressesVector().
   elementAt(i);
  InternetAddress currentIntAddr =
  (InternetAddress)
  getCurrentInternetAddress();

 vectorIntAddr.setFirstName
  (currentIntAddr.getFirstName());
 vectorIntAddr.setLastName
  (currentIntAddr.getLastName());
 vectorIntAddr.setUserId
  (currentIntAddr.getUserId());
 vectorIntAddr.setSystemId
  (currentIntAddr.getSystemId());
 vectorIntAddr.setUserTitle
  (currentIntAddr.getUserTitle());
 vectorIntAddr.setUserOrganization
  (currentIntAddr.getUserOrganization());
 vectorIntAddr.setSystemDescription
  (currentIntAddr.getSystemDescription());
 vectorIntAddr.setInternetProvider
  (currentIntAddr.getInternetProvider());
 }
return;
}
```

Finally, you need to promote *selectedIndex* property of the InternetAddressListBox. This allows other beans to access the currently selected index in the list box. It is required for the delete function that you will add later.

> **NOTE**
>
> The List fills the entire panel. If you would like to set up a border around the List, first change the panel *LayoutManager* to *GridBagLayout*. Next change the InternetAddressListBox constraints of weightX and weightY to 1.0. Now experiment by setting each of the inset attributes of the constraints to 10. If that is not visually appealing, try another value.

InternetButtonPanel

The **InternetButtonPanel** contains buttons for add, update, and delete. This Panel contains the buttons in the shape and size required to fit in the South border of the applet, as shown in Figure 9.16. Create the initial panel much like you did for the previous panels. Continue by doing the following:

Change the layout manager to *FlowLayout*. At the same time, change the *alignment* attribute (of the layout manager itself) to *LEFT*.

Add three *java.awt.Button* beans to the panel.

Figure 9.16   InternetButtonPanel.

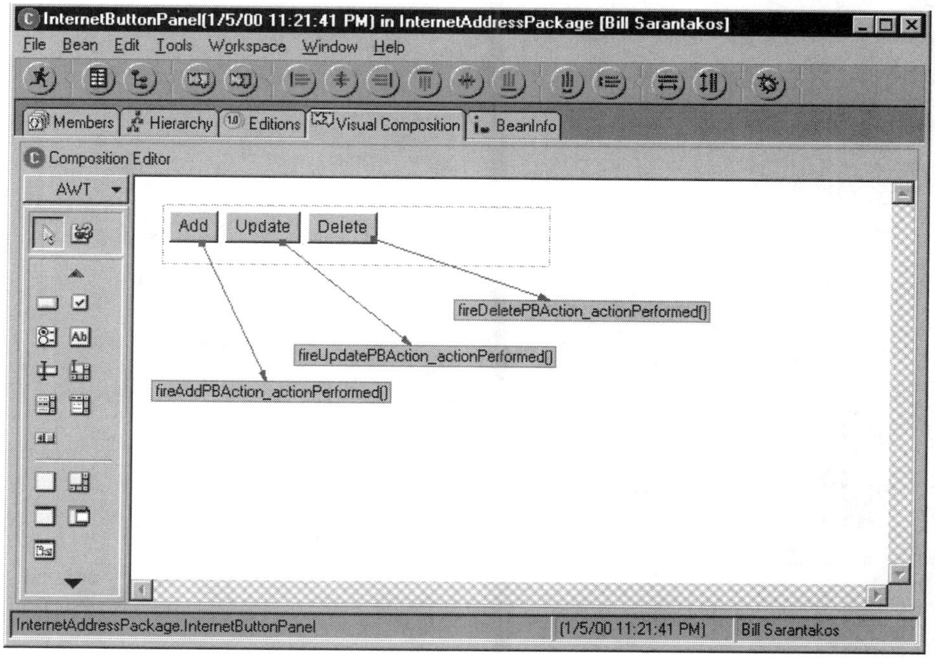

For this GUI, you will use a different naming convention. No convention is perfect, but you should always change the default bean names. Change the names of the button beans to pbAdd, pbUpdate, and pbDelete, and the text on the buttons to **Add**, **Update**, and **Delete**, respectively.

Now you need to promote the actionPerformed event for each of the buttons. Promoting the event makes the feature available to other beans. Promote the events as follows:

Select a Button with the left mouse button and press the right mouse to display the pop-up menu.

Select **Promote Bean Feature...**

Select the **Event** radio button.

From the Event list, select actionPerformed and then select the **>>** button. For the pbAdd button, this generates a feature named pbaddAction_actionPerformed(java.awt.event.ActionEvent).

Finally, select the **OK** button as shown in Figure 9.17.

Figure 9.17   Promoting actionPerformed.

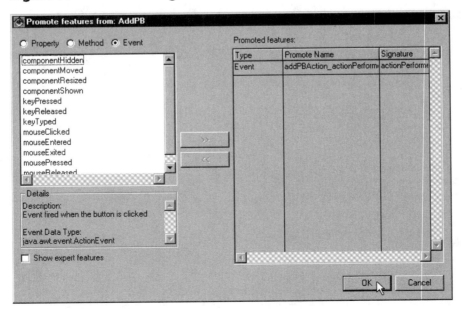

Testing the InternetAddress Panels

The applet is tested in two steps. At this point, you can test to see if the InternetUserInfoPanel and the InternetFormattedInfoPanel work together. Figure 9.18 shows the end result of the applet test. You will construct this applet with the panels you have created.

InternetAddressTestApplet uses BorderLayout as follows:

- InternetButtonPanel is in the South border cell.

- InternetUserInfoPanel is in the North border cell.

- InternetFormattedInfoPanel is in the Center border cell.

Figure 9.19 shows the Visual Composition Editor for InternetAddressTestApplet.

InternetAddressTestApplet uses the beans in Table 9.1.

Create an InternetAddressTestApplet class that subclasses Applet.

After dropping the Panels on the Applet, and the Variables and beans on the free-form surface, you make connections between these beans. Next, connect the Panel Variables to the Applet beans as follows:

Connect the *this* property of the CurrentInternetAddress bean on the free-form surface to the promoted *InternetAddress* feature (internetAddressThis) of the InternetUserInfoPanel1 panel.

Figure 9.18   InternetAddressTestApplet

Table 9.1   InternetAddressTestApplet Beans

Bean	Description
CurrentInternetAddress	Bean that represents the instance of the InternetAddress manipulated by the user
InternetAddressesVector	Vector that contains a collection of InternetAddress instances
InternetAddressObjectFactory	Factory used to generate an instance of InternetAddress when user adds an InternetAddress to the list

Connect the *this* property of the CurrentInternetAddress bean on the free-form surface to the promoted *CurrentInternetAddress* feature (currentInternetAddressThis) of the InternetFormattedInfoPanel1 panel.

Connect the InternetAddressesVector *this* property to the promoted *this* property of the InternetAddressesVector (internetAddressesVectorThis) of the InternetFormattedInfoPanel1 panel.

Figure 9.19   InternetAddressTestApplet in the Visual Composition Editor.

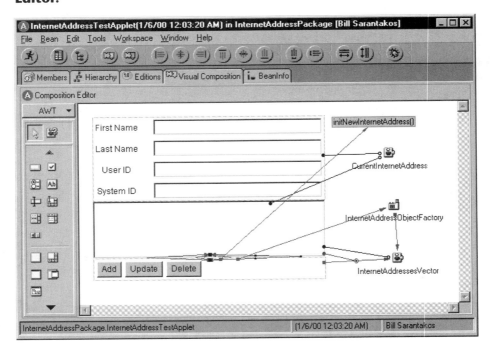

Now make the connections required to add an InternetAddress instance to the list of InternetFormattedInfoPanel. The event-to-code connection constructs a new instance of the InternetAddress class and refreshes the contents of the list. The constructor uses the TextFields *text* properties as parameters.

Connect the InternetButtonPanel1 panel pbaddAction_actionPerformed event to the InternetAddress() constructor of the InternetAddressObjectFactory factory.

Connect the InternetButtonPanel1 panel pbaddAction_actionPerformed event to the free-form surface to the initNewInternetAddress() method (as an event-to-code connection). Add the following code to the method:

```
/**
 */
public void initNewInternetAddress() {
  InternetAddress newAddr =
    getInternetAddressObjectFactory();
  InternetAddress curAddr =
    getCurrentInternetAddress();

  newAddr.setFirstName(curAddr.getFirstName());
  newAddr.setLastName(curAddr.getLastName());
  newAddr.setUserId(curAddr.getUserId());
  newAddr.setSystemId(curAddr.getSystemId());
  newAddr.setUserTitle(curAddr.getUserTitle());
  newAddr.setUserOrganization
    (curAddr.getUserOrganization());
  newAddr.setSystemDescription
    (curAddr.getSystemDescription());
  newAddr.setInternetProvider
    (curAddr.getInternetProvider());
}
```

Connect the InternetButtonPanel1 panel pbaddAction_actionPerformed event to the InternetFormattedInfoPanel1 panel refreshListBoxItems() method.

Continue by adding the instance generated by the InternetAddressObjectFactory constructor to the InternetAddressesVector:

Connect the *this* event of InternetAddressObjectFactory factory to the InternetAddressesVector addElement(java.lang.Object) method.

Open the properties of the event-to-method connection you just created in the previous step and enable the **Pass event data** check box.

Make the connections to delete an entry in the InternetFormattedInfoPanel1 list and to refresh the list:

Connect the InternetButtonPanel1 pbdeleteAction_actionPerformed event to the InternetAddressesVector removeElementAt(int) method.

Connect the InternetFormattedInfoPanel1 promoted *selectedIndex* property (internetAddressListBoxSelectedIndex) to the *index* property of the previous connection.

Connect the InternetButtonPanel1 pbdeleteAction_actionPerformed event to the InternetFormattedInfoPanel1 refreshListBoxItems() method.

Make the connections to update and refresh the InternetFormattedInfoPanel list:

Connect the InternetButtonPanel1 pbupdateAction_actionPerformed event to the InternetFormattedInfoPanel1 updateInternetAddress() method.

Connect the InternetButtonPanel1 pbupdateAction_actionPerformed event to the InternetFormattedInfoPanel1 refreshListBoxItems() method.

Your test applet is now complete. Save your work and run the applet from the Visual Composition Editor. After you are satisfied with the results of your applet, close the applet viewer. Then you are ready to build the final applet, using all of the panels you have created.

> **NOTE**
>
> If any of the targets of the connections being attempted don't appear to be there, you may have missed a step earlier either in promoting a bean attribute or event, or in making a method a bean feature (check the BeanInfo page).

Creating InternetAddressFinalApplet

The InternetAddressFinalApplet demonstrates the following:

- Reuse of Panel beans
- Use of CardLayout

Figure 9.20 shows the applet running from the VisualAge for Java applet viewer.

InternetAddressFinalApplet reuses all of the beans, panels, and Variables found in InternetAddressTestApplet. Other panels are used for the CardLayout, along with the use of InternetAdditionalInfoPanel to enable the user to enter data about the user and system. The CardLayout layout manager is used to alternate among a deck of panels.

You build the two applets with a common InternetButtonPanel panel. This panel actually does very little and may end up generating more code than if you built the panel directly in the bean where it is used. It is done this way to show you the level of reuse you can attain when building your applications. Whether you choose to build a reusable button panel in a particular situation depends on a number of factors. Here are a few:

- Is the panel reusable in one or two other beans, or many? Reuse makes sense for many.

- If there is potential for reuse, will the button (or other) panel be reused in the same way or will there be variations in use? Reuse makes sense when it is used consistently.

- Can you generalize the panel to make it more useful? A well-designed panel can be used not only in the particular application it is created, but also in future applications that haven't yet been designed or even anticipated.

You can apply these factors to any bean you are designing or developing.

CardLayout

CardLayout arranges components in a linear depth sequence similar to a notebook or deck of cards. Each component forming the deck is called a *card*. You add components to the CardLayout parent, and VisualAge for Java adds them to the top of the deck, making the first bean the bottom card. To move through the deck or to perform tasks on the covered cards in the **Beans List**, select **Switch To** from the pop-up menu for the Panel containing the CardLayout.

Using CardLayout

First, create an InternetAddressFinalApplet class that subclasses Applet.

Provide visual access to the layout manager interface with the following steps:

Place a java.awt.Panel bean named **CardPanel** into the Center region of the InternetAddressFinalApplet main panel (with the layout manager set to BorderLayout). You can either drop it directly into the main panel or drop it on the free-form surface and then drag it into the center region of the border panel.

Change the **layout** property of the CardPanel panel to **CardLayout**.

Drop a Variable on the free-form surface to the right of the CardPanel panel.

Change the type of the Variable to java.awt.CardLayout.

Figure 9.20   InternetAddressFinalApplet.

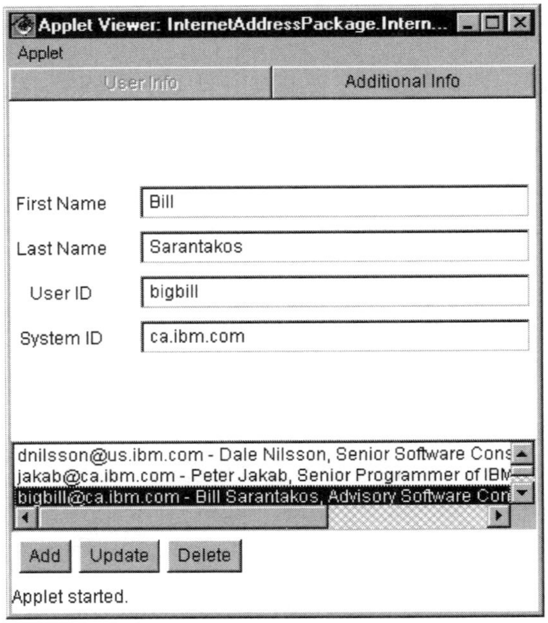

Change the name of the Variable to CardLayoutManager.

Connect the *layout* property of the CardPanel panel to the *this* property of the CardLayoutManager Variable. You can now connect to the features of the Variable bean.

Before you use the CardPanel panel, you must build the panel through the layering of other Panels to obtain the appearance of the Applet. Figure 9.21 shows the reuse and layering of Panels to achieve the desired appearance.

You can create panels as separate beans or on the applet free-form surface in the Visual Composition Editor. Table 9.2 describes how each panel is put together. When you build the CardButtonPanel, be sure to disable the pbUser button in the Visual Composition Editor.

After building the Panel layers for the InternetAddressFinalApplet, connect the beans. Figure 9.22 shows the Visual Composition Editor for InternetAddressFinalApplet.

In the Visual Composition Editor, InternetAddressFinalApplet looks very much like InternetAddressTestApplet. All of the same invisible beans from the InternetAddressTestApplet appear on the InternetAddressFinalApplet free-form surface. There is one additional Variable and a few additional connections to discuss:

Figure 9.21   Panel reuse and layering.

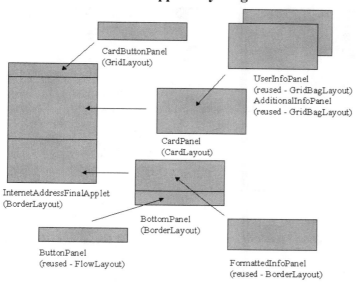

InternetAddressFinalApplet Layering

CardButtonPanel
(GridLayout)

UserInfoPanel
(reused - GridBagLayout)
AdditionalInfoPanel
(reused - GridBagLayout)

CardPanel
(CardLayout)

InternetAddressFinalApplet
(BorderLayout)

BottomPanel
(BorderLayout)

ButtonPanel
(reused - FlowLayout)

FormattedInfoPanel
(reused - BorderLayout)

Table 9.2   Putting Panels Together

Panel Name	Description
InternetAddressFinalApplet	Primary bean. Uses BorderLayout with CardButtonPanel in the North, CardPanel in the Center, and BottomPanel in the South.
BottomPanel	Built on InternetAddressFinalApplet free-form surface. Uses BorderLayout with ButtonPanel in the South and FormattedInfoPanel in the Center.
ButtonPanel	Reused InternetButtonPanel.
FormattedInfoPanel	Reused InternetFormattedInfoPanel.
CardButtonPanel	Built on InternetAddressFinalApplet free-form surface. Uses GridLayout. Used to switch between the CardLayout Panels.
CardPanel	Used to hold cards. Uses CardLayout.
UserInfoPanel	Reused InternetUserInfoPanel.
AdditionalInfoPanel	Reused InternetAdditionalInfoPanel.

Figure 9.22 InternetAddressFinalApplet in the Visual Composition Editor.

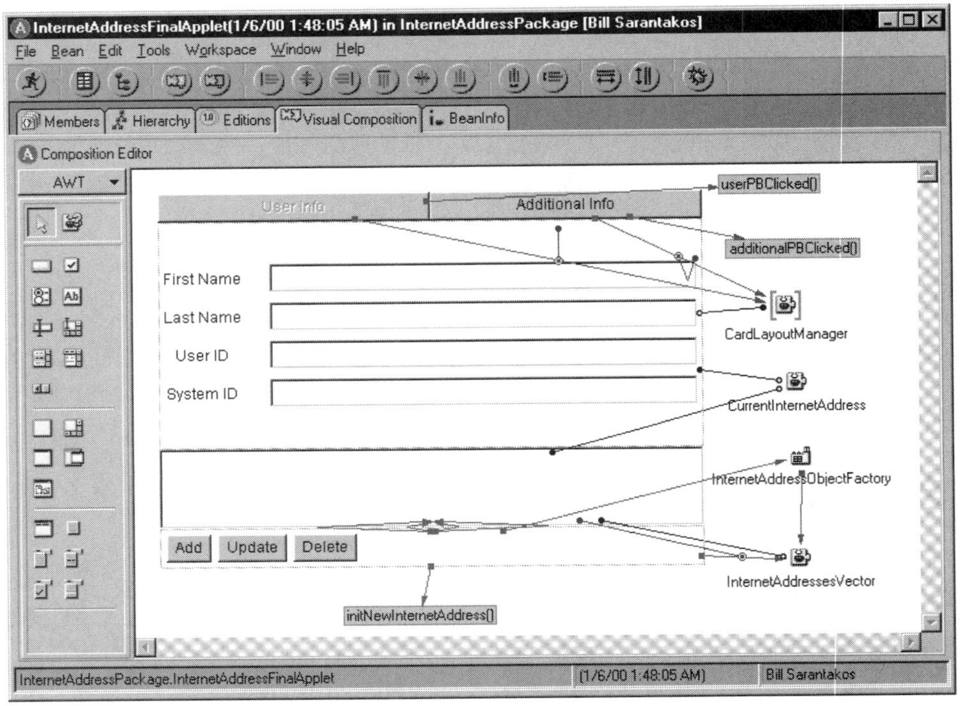

> **NOTE**
>
> It is common to use a Tab GUI bean to get the look of a notebook. The Tabs blend into each card of the notebook for a seamless look. The AWT 1.1 class library does not include a Tab GUI bean, so we use a Button. There are many Tab GUI beans available from bean providers on the Web. You can also develop one using the JFC controls with a JTabbedPane to get a similar result.

The CardLayout of CardPanel switches the card showing within the Panel. Add the CardLayout Variable to the free-form surface and connect the *layout* property of CardPanel to the *this* property of the CardLayout Variable.

Additional connections are required to switch to the first card when the user clicks the **User Info** button. The pbuserClicked() method is also called to enable and disable the appropriate buttons:

Connect the pbUser button *actionPerformed* event to the first(java.awt.Container) method of the CardLayoutManager variable.

Connect the *this* property of CardPanel to the *parent* property of the previous connection.

Connect the pbUser button actionPerformed event to the pbuserClicked() method of InternetAddressFinalApplet. Code for this method follows:

```
/**
 * This method was created by a SmartGuide.
 */
public void pbuserClicked ( ) {
  getpbUser().setEnabled(false);
  getpbAdditional().setEnabled(true);
  return;
}
```

You must create connections in order to switch to the last card when the **Additional Info** button is clicked. The pbadditionalClicked() method is also called to enable and disable the appropriate buttons:

Connect the pbAdditional button actionPerformed event to the last(java.awt.Container) method of CardLayoutManager variable.

Connect the *this* property of CardPanel to the *parent* property of the previous connection.

Connect the pbAdditional button event to the pbadditionalClicked() method of InternetAddressFinalApplet. Code for this method follows:

```
/**
 * This method was created by a SmartGuide.
 */
public void pbadditionalClicked ( ) {
  getpbUser().setEnabled(true);
  getpbAdditional().setEnabled(false);
  return;
}
```

Make the remaining connections in the same way you made them for the InternetAddressTestApplet. Note that instead of entering the body of the **initNewInternetAddress()** method again, you can select the method from the InternetAddressTestApplet and, from the pop-up menu, select **Reorganize >> Copy** item to copy the method to this class. Don't forget to uncheck or reset the **Rename (copy as)** check box if you do copy the method.

In addition, don't forget to use the **Switch To** pop-up menu item so that you can make connections to panels that are currently not displayed. Note that any connections to panels in a CardLayout are visible if and only if the panel itself is visible. There is another way to make visual connections to objects that are obscured or covered. You can use the Beans List to make connections just like you do in the Visual Composition Editor. Just select the source bean and start the connection from the pop-up menu, then point to the target bean in the Beans List and set the target feature for the connection.

If you have problems building this applet, you can load a complete version of the applet that is provided on the CD-ROM. This visual program has a lot of connections, and many of them are critical to the applet's successful completion.

Testing the InternetAddressFinalApplet

Let's test the applet and see how it works. Save these changes and run the applet by doing the following:

Press the Run button on the tool bar of the Visual Composition Editor to generate and run the applet. When the applet starts, it looks like Figure 9.23.

Try entering data in the first page as shown in Figure 9.23. You can use the Tab key to move from field to field.

Figure 9.23 Testing the first card.

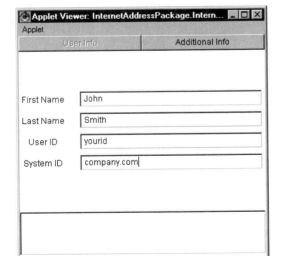

Figure 9.24   Testing the second card.

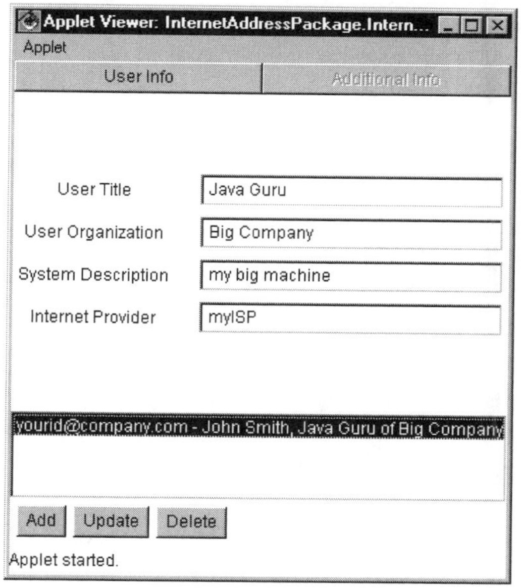

Press the **Additional Info** button and the second card displays as shown in Figure 9.24.

Try entering sample data in the TextFields. Add the new InternetAddress to the list by pressing the **Add** button. The new InternetAddress displays in the Listbox.

Try adding other InternetAddresses to the List.

Try updating some data for one of your entries in the List. Notice how the selected item in the List fills the TextFields with the appropriate data.

Try deleting a selected item from the List.

When you are finished testing the applet, close it.

This applet demonstrates a good example of how to use the CardLayout manager. It has a lot of the common features that you would expect to see in a program. There are a number of different ways you could have implemented this applet, and there are a few improvements that could be made to it. However, the applet does the job that is required and it is time to learn more new features of VisualAge for Java.

The InternetFormattedInfoPanel does not display all the information contained within the InternetAddress class. You should not be alarmed or concerned about this situation. In this case, the InternetFormattedInfoPanel displays the entry found very quickly, usually by displaying a unique portion of the data. Once the user selects the entry, all the information contained in the object appears. In this case, the information is split across two panels. To change the displayed information for the InternetAddress applets, modify the toString() method of the InternetAddress class. Try it yourself!

Summary

In this chapter, you built a more complex applet using the Visual Composition Editor and some new AWT GUI beans. This chapter showed you how to:

- Reuse Panels to test your Applet connections before you completed the final Applet.

- Use a CardLayout with Panels to achieve a notebook appearance, helping you maximize window real estate.

- Use Variables to represent object instances, helping you pass an object from one Panel to another.

- Layer Panels to mix layouts, giving elements of your Applets the appropriate size and position.

- Use Factories to generate instances of your domain classes, minimizing code and simplifying your application.

It is good to know how to use the CardLayout, because it is a common user interface container that you can use in many of your Java programs. The use of Factory Objects and Variables is essential for you to get the most benefit from the Visual Composition Editor. Finally, using feature promotion helps you implement better OO layering in Java programs.

Working with JFC

What's in Chapter 10

In this chapter, you will learn about the new GUI JavaBeans called the Swing Components in JFC, which are a very powerful advance for Java programming and have a lot more function than the previous AWT components. You will learn how to use the Swing components in VisualAge for Java by building a JApplet. Then you will learn how to create user-defined events. This chapter covers the following topics:

- Overview of the Swing and the JFC components
- Constructing a simple application using JFC JApplet, JLabel, and JButton
- Creating a user-defined Event
- Using the user-defined Event in the Visual Composition Editor

You will apply all of these concepts in completing the Bank Account Applet. These are critical concepts and they will help prepare you to create your own Java programs. After you have finished this chapter, you will have a better understanding of what it takes to develop event-driven Java programs.

Swing GUI controls are part of the Java Foundation Class (JFC) API. The overall goal for the Swing project was to build a set of extensible GUI components that enable developers to rapidly develop powerful Java front ends for commercial applications. Sun created Swing controls to alleviate Abstract Windowing Toolkit (AWT) restrictions. The intent of the AWT was to provide platform independent user interfaces. AWT controls were implemented using a peer component design, as shown in Figure 10.1, and AWT peer classes were implemented with native platform code. In order to achieve a common look and feel across all GUI platforms, the least common denominator of user interface behavior was implemented. Peer design hinders extensions to other platforms, because presentation and behavior are passed to the native control.

Swing classes are layered on the AWT class hierarchy and rendered using 100 percent Java code, as shown in Figure 10.2. Swing controls are lightweight; they do not require a peer class written in the native operating system GUI in order to be rendered. Swing classes give a consistent look and feel across all GUI platforms. So there are a lot more GUI JavaBeans in Swing and they are more sophisticated

Figure 10.1 AWT peer component design.

awt.List
addItem
removeItem
awt.ListPeer
remove
addItem
Native List Control

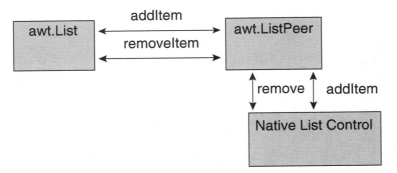

GUI beans. However, there is a price to pay for this additional function. Unfortunately, Swing controls are usually slower than their AWT counterparts.

As with most classes in the JDK, there are a number of differences between the Swing 1.03 and the Swing classes in JDK 1.2. There are many examples of these differences, such as some changed package names, additional methods, and new function. This section discusses the most common Swing components available in the base Version 1.03. If you want to use the features in JDK 1.2, you need to install the version of VisualAge for Java that supports JDK 1.2, which is discussed in a later chapter.

Swing Parts

There are three main Swing parts:

Figure 10.2 Swing architecture.

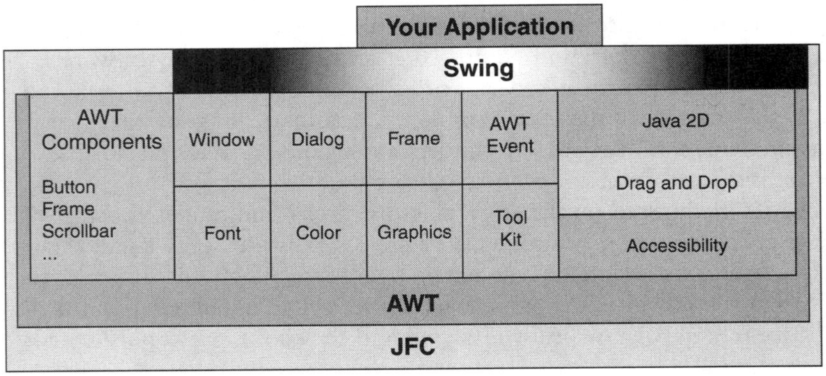

Your Application
Swing
AWT
Components
Button
Frame
Scrollbar
...
Window
Dialog
Frame
AWT
Event
Java 2D
Drag and Drop
Font
Color
Graphics
Tool
Kit
Accessibility
AWT
JFC

Swing components subclass from JComponent. These are the visible components of Swing, and their class names all start with J.

Support classes, also called services. These classes do not create visible Swing components that appear on the computer screen, but they do provide vital services to the Swing API and to your Swing applications. Examples: ToolTipManagers and FocusManager.

The set of **Swing-related interfaces** is implemented by Swing's component classes and support classes. Swing's event classes and model classes are examples of logic classes, like the TableModel and the TreeModelListener.

Swing visual classes extend JComponent, which provides a number of functions:

Pluggable look and feel across different GUI platforms

Extensibility

Smart trapping of keyboard events like tabbing

Customization of component borders

Easy resizing of components

Tool Tips or Hover Help

Autoscrolling

Support for debugging

Support for localization

Swing Components

There are a lot of new and updated components in Swing and they are preloaded in VisualAge for Java. The Swing components are on a separate Palette in the Visual Composition Editor, because you need to keep AWT and Swing components separate. The Swing components are divided into five groups:

Buttons. Select mutually exclusive items or invoke actions are shown in Figure 10.3.

Data entry. Get data from the user in the form of a narrative or labeling data are shown in Figure 10.4.

Lists. Show choices to select from are shown in Figure 10.5.

Containers. Hold other GUI objects are shown in Figure 10.6.

Menu elements. Show menu selection items and invoke menu actions are shown in Figure 10.7.

Figure 10.3   Swing buttons.

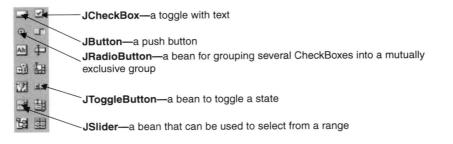

JCheckBox—a toggle with text

JButton—a push button

JRadioButton—a bean for grouping several CheckBoxes into a mutually exclusive group

JToggleButton—a bean to toggle a state

JSlider—a bean that can be used to select from a range

Figure 10.4   Swing data entry.

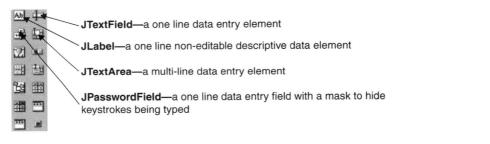

JTextField—a one line data entry element

JLabel—a one line non-editable descriptive data element

JTextArea—a multi-line data entry element

JPasswordField—a one line data entry field with a mask to hide keystrokes being typed

Figure 10.5   Swing lists.

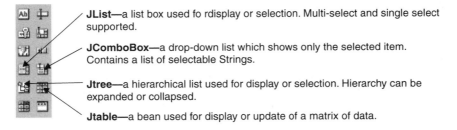

JList—a list box used fo rdisplay or selection. Multi-select and single select supported.

JComboBox—a drop-down list which shows only the selected item. Contains a list of selectable Strings.

Jtree—a hierarchical list used for display or selection. Hierarchy can be expanded or collapsed.

Jtable—a bean used for display or update of a matrix of data.

Migrating to Swing

As you can see, the AWT GUI beans have Swing equivalents that start with a J. The AWT Label is a Swing JLabel. This was done to make migrating to Swing easier. But moving to Swing is much more complex than adding Js to the beginning of all your GUI classes.

The Swing classes have more properties, and you must set many of them in order for your Java Swing programs to run correctly. For example, a JLabel has an opaque property that you must set to true in order to see changes in the background color. The AWT Label bean does not have this property. and it is not necessary to set this property. You use the JLabel and set this property in the next exercise.

Figure 10.6   Swing containers.

Menus supported include
- **JMenuBar** - Displayed in a JFrame and contains many menus
- **JCheckBoxMenuItem** - an item on a menu that is a check box
- **JRadioButtonMenuItem** - an item on a menu that is radio button
- **JSeparator** - a line that separates menu items visually
- **JPop upMenu** - a floating menu

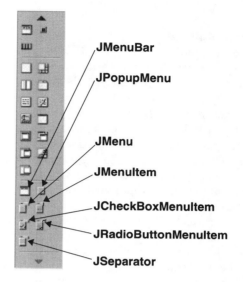

The new package names in JFC affect the fully qualified references throughout your code. Additionally, you will need to update the import statements in you code.

You should remember never to mix AWT and Swing when developing Java programs. If you do, you will get unpredictable or unreliable results. This is not a

Figure 10.7   Swing menu items.

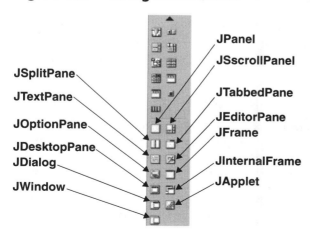

good trait for software that you develop. When you convert a program from AWT to Swing, you must convert all the AWT GUI beans to Swing beans.

Morphing JavaBeans

The Visual Composition Editor has a real cool function called *morphing* that helps you migrate to Swing. You can point to any bean in the Visual Composition Editor and the pop-up menu has the *Morph into* option. Technically, you can morph any bean into any other bean.

When you morph a bean, you have the option to delete invalid connections when the bean is morphed. Connections represent some of the high-level logic in your program, so deleting connections can have adverse effects on the program. When the bean is morphed, the new bean type may not have the same bean features (properties, events, and methods). So for any connection that does not have the same bean feature in the new morphed bean, the connection is invalid. It is good that the Visual Composition Editor cleans up the morphed bean by deleting these invalid connections, especially if you plan on doing a lot of redesign with new connections. It is better to inspect the connections and modify the ones that require changes. Usually the morphed bean connections merely need a different source event.

There is a limitation to morphing—you can't morph a parent bean. This means that you cannot use the Morph function for any Containers like Applets, Panels, or JFrames that you defined as a Visual Composition Editor class in the Workbench. The "Morph Into..." menu item displays for the component beans, but not for the parent bean in the Visual Composition Editor. To morph a parent part, you must do it in the code for the class. Go to a view of the source code for the class definition and change the superclass to the desired superclass and save the code. When converting from AWT to JFC, you should first edit the Panels and change them to JPanels. Then you can open a JPanels in the Visual Composition Editor and morph the AWT components into their JFC replacements.

Although the examples for morphing beans usually show morphing GUI beans, it is just as easy to morph nonvisual or logic beans, like the AddCalculatorLogic bean. You can also morph a JavaBean into a variable bean or a serialized bean. Both these types of JavaBeans are described in greater detail in Chapter 9. Morphing is a cool new feature and it can save you time once you are familiar with its capabilities.

Model View Controller

Another key feature in Swing is the move toward better object-oriented design. Swing components apply the Model-View-Controller (MVC) pattern shown in Figure 10.8. The intent of MVC is to separate presentation from the data model. This is accomplished by introducing a controller class that is aware of the presentation object and data object.

MVC is another factor that affects migrating to Swing. Many AWT programs have hard-coded values, or at least initial values, in the GUI beans. Moving

Figure 10.8   MVC pattern.

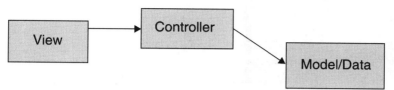

to Swing requires some re-engineering of the software design to use Model beans. There is a lot more information on MVC with Java in technical articles on VisualAge Developer Domain (www.software.ibm.com/vadd).

Objects interested in **Observing/Listening** for state changes in a control implement a listener interface for the control and add themselves to the control's model object. The model object is responsible for broadcasting event objects to listener objects:

```
JTable aTable = new JTable();
aTable.getModel().addListener(aTableModelListener)
```

For example, JTable class allows a model object typed as a TableModel interface to define rows and columns of a Table component. The default **model** class for JTable is **com.sun.java.swing.table.DefaultTableModel**. The default model supports rows and columns as a Vector of Vectors containing String objects. The TableModelInterface implements support for rows and columns:

```
TableModel interface
public void addTableModelListener(TableModelListener);
public Class getColumnClass(int columnIndex);
public int getColumnCount();
public String getColumnName(int columnIndex);
public int getRowCount();
public Object getValueAt(int rowIndex, int
 columnIndex);
public boolean isCellEditable(int rowIndex, int
 columnIndex);
public void
 removeTableModelListener(TableModelListener l);
public void setValueAt(Object aValue, int rowIndex,
 int columnIndex);
```

Swing Model Beans

When using a Swing component, you have three choices for implementing the default model interface. Figure 10.9 shows the three options for implementing the model for a JTable component:

Figure 10.9   Model implementation options.

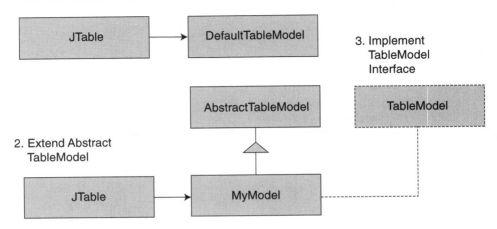

1. Use the DefaultTableModel

2. Extend Abstract TableModel

3. Implement TableModel Interface

- Use the default model.
- Extend an abstract model that implements the default model interface.
- Implement the default model interface directly.

For convenience, VisualAge for Java defines composite Swing controls when necessary. For example, when you select a JTable from the Beans Palette and drop it onto the Visual Composition Editor, VisualAge for Java creates a JScrollPanel and adds a JTable object to it.

As you begin to work with Swing components, you learn the interface for the component default model and connect other beans to the Swing component model properties. By using Swing components, you can separate the view or GUI representation from the domain or model.

Tip

When using Swing components, be aware that the .jar file that contains the Swing components and interfaces is approximately 2MB in size. Also be aware that the Web browser accessing your applet may not be Swing-enabled. For these reasons, it may be better to use Swing components for desktop applications where the .jar file can be placed on each machine in the enterprise.

Using Swing in an Applet

You will build a small Bank Account JApplet in this chapter that will user Java events that you create. The Bank Account applet lets you enter a number for the balance and press a button to add or subtract it from the balance. The Bank Account consists of a visual bean containing a JLabel that displays the current balance, a JLabel to identify the previous JLabel, and two JButtons to add and subtract from the balance. There is also a logic bean that has deposit() and withdraw() methods that contain the Java code to do the appropriate functions.

User-Defined Events

Events generally indicate that a component in a program has reached a certain state, or that a certain externally generated action has taken place. Events usually happen at an unpredictable moment in time. The program does not need to wait for the event to occur, but when it does, the program should be notified and should respond appropriately.

Do not confuse events with exceptions, even though on the surface they appear quite similar. Exceptions have a completely different execution path and occur as the result of an error. Once an exception is thrown, the calling stack of the program is unwound until some component handles the exception in a catch block or the program abnormally terminates. In contrast, if an event is signaled and no component is listening for it, nothing happens.

Types of Events

You have already used a number of events provided in the JDK; they are the source or start of the connections in the Visual Composition Editor. Events are said to be *raised* or *signaled*. Some examples of events that Java classes signal are:

- key
- mouse
- focus
- propertyChanged

If you are struggling to find an existing JDK event, you may need to create your own event. User-defined events improve the usability and durability of your JavaBeans. For example, if you have a bean that represents a disk file, it should raise an end-of-file event to signal that there is no more data to be read. If the bean representing a fuel tank changes state to almost-empty, an event should be fired to turn on a light and warn the driver to get fuel.

The Java event model in Version 1.1 is said to be delegation-based. In the delegation model, there are event sources and event listeners. Listeners are responsible for registering their interest in an event with the source of the event. When the event occurs, the source informs all listeners, which can then act on the event according to their own needs.

Making Your Own Events

Implementing your own events in VisualAge for Java is very simple, because the tool generates all classes necessary to define the event and multicast it to its listeners. Once an event is defined in VisualAge for Java, any class in the Workspace can use it. When connecting an event to a method, VisualAge for Java generates the code necessary to register the target class as a listener and to handle receipt of the notification.

Bank Account Example

The best way to understand how VisualAge for Java makes it simple to create and use your own events is to create an example applet and study the generated code. The example applet is very simple and we concentrate on explaining the creation and use of the event. User-defined events can easily be used in much more complex applications.

The sample applet represents a bank account, which has a balance. You can withdraw from and deposit into the account. When the balance reaches 0, the background color for the balance display changes to red. While the balance is 0 or above, the background is white.

Creating the AccountView

Build this applet under the My Project project, or any appropriate Project in the Workbench.

Start by creating a new package called **userevents** in the VisualAge for Java IDE.

Create the account view bean by following these steps:

Create a new class called **AccountView** subclassing JApplet. Design the bean visually as shown in Figure 10.10.

Open the property editor for the JAppletContentPane that is on the JApplet. Set the LayoutManager of the JAppletContentPane to GridBagLayout.

This program uses JFC beans, so make sure to select the **Swing** category at the left side of the Visual Composition Editor.

From the Swing category on the left side of the Visual Composition Editor, select two JLabel beans and drop them on the applet.

Change the text of the JLabels to **Account balance** and **balance here**. Name the last JLabel bean **lbBalance**.

Figure 10.10 AccountView SmartGuide.

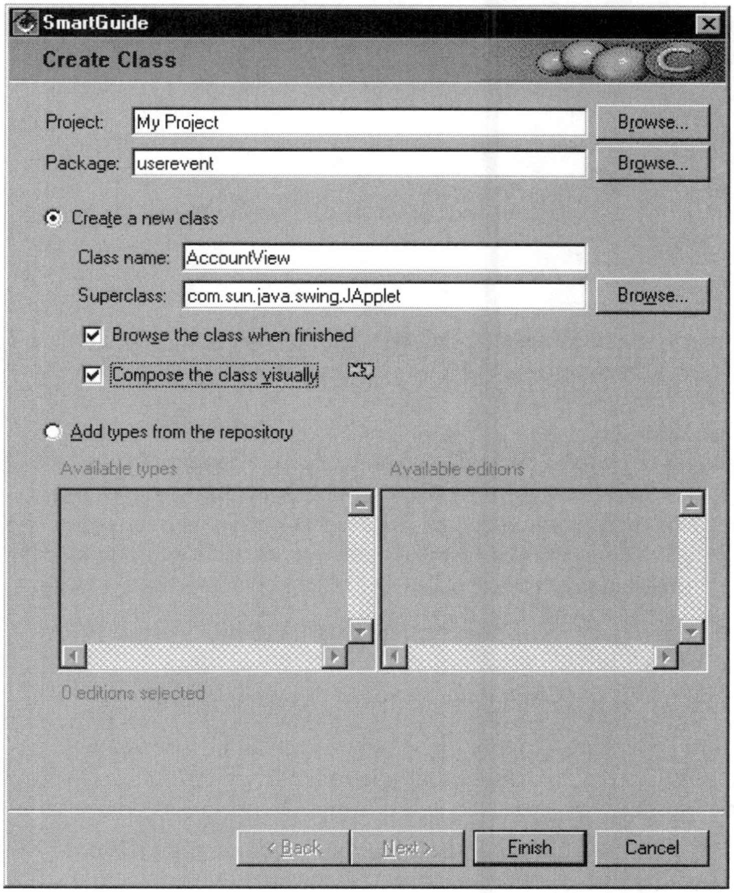

Drop a JPanel on the free-form surface. Set its layout manager property to FlowLayout.

Drop two JButtons onto the JPanel.

Change these JButton bean names to **pbWithdraw** and **pbDeposit,** and change their labels to **Withdraw** and **Deposit,** respectively.

Drag the JPanel that contains the two JButtons to the JApplet and place it below the **balance here** JLabel. The GUI beans in the AccountView should look similar to Figure 10.11.

Edit the **balance here** JLabel and set its Opaque property to True.

Figure 10.11   AccountView bean.

You must set this property in order to change the background color. This is an example of a difference between the AWT classes and the JFC classes.

Creating the AccountModel

The account model consists of two methods, withdraw() and deposit(). They subtract or add $10 from the balance, respectively. You could get fancier and let the user define the amount of the transaction, but the object of this exercise is to build a quick and easy sample to explain user-defined events. Follow these steps to build the account model bean:

In the same userevents package, Create a new class that subclasses java.lang.Object and call it **AccountModel**.

Open the browser for AccountModel and switch to the BeanInfo page.

Add a new int property named **balance**. It should be readable, writeable, bound, and preferred. It is not required that you make it preferred, but it will make the balance property easier to use in the Visual Composition Editor.

Add two methods that return *void* and take no parameters. Call them **withdraw** and **deposit**. The browser for the AccountModel bean should look like Figure 10.12.

You can edit AccountModel fields from many views including the Members page and the Hierarchy page. Switch to either of these browser pages and select the **balance** field. If you cannot see any fields, you need to modify the attribute filters for the browser, which are accessed from a pop-up menu. Set the initial value of the balance property to $100, switch to the Source pane at the bottom, and change the following code:

```
private int fieldBalance = 0; to
private int fieldBalance = 100;
```

Next you add code to the deposit() and withdraw() methods so that they modify the balance property. It's very easy to change this application to

Figure 10.12   AccountModel BeanInfo page.

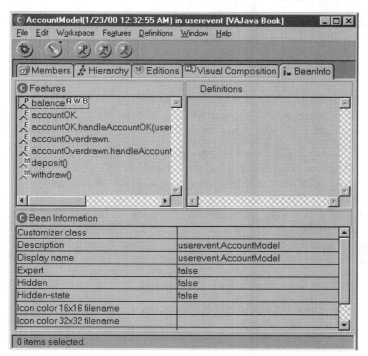

take any amount, but you will hard code a value for simplicity. Select the withdraw() method from the Methods pane and add the following highlighted line to the method:

```
public void withdraw() {
  /* Perform the withdraw method. */
  setBalance(getBalance() - 10);
  return;
}
```

Add code to the deposit() method that increases the balance by 10. Select deposit() from the Methods pane and add the following high-lighted code to the method:

```
public void deposit() {
  /* Perform the deposit method. */
  setBalance(getBalance() + 10);
  return;
}
```

Connect the Beans

Open the VCE for the AccountView bean. Select the Choose Bean button and drop an AccountModel bean on the free-form surface.

Change the bean name to **account**.

Connect the following:

```
account (balance) property → lbBalance (text) property
pbWithdraw (actionPerformed) event → account (withdraw()) method
pbDeposit (actionPerformed) event → account (deposit()) method
```

So far, the AccountView should look like Figure 10.13 as shown in the VCE. Save and test the program. The starting balance should be 100, and you should be able to make deposits and withdrawals to the account. When the account reaches zero and goes negative, nothing happens. Before you can make any more visual connections, you need to define an event and its listener interface. The VisualAge for Java BeanInfo editor has a SmartGuide specifically designed to make this task easy. After you have defined the event, you then visually connect it to the JLabel and set its background color.

Creating a Listener Interface

Next you will add a new event interface to handle the special situation caused when the account balance goes below zero.

With the browser for the AccountModel bean opened, switch to the BeanInfo page.

You might be tempted to press the New Event Set feature button, because you previously used the adjoining buttons to define other JavaBeans features. This button is not for defining Java Events, rather it is used when you want the bean to be the source of an existing event and its event listener. When creating a new event, one that doesn't already exist in the Repository, you need to select **New Listener**

Figure 10.13   Initial connections.

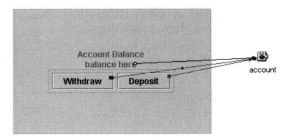

Interface from the Features menu. This option is also available from the pop-up menu in the Features pane. Create a new listener interface by following these steps:

Select **New Listener Interface** from the Features menu. The New Event Listener SmartGuide appears as shown in Figure 10.14.

Event names should indicate what happened, such as the windowClose event. You should be careful and use an event name with a precise tense. It is better to have windowClosing and windowClosed events. This allows you to have code that functions either before or after a window closes.

Enter the name of the event you are creating, in this case, **accountOverdrawn**. By convention, event names start in lowercase. The SmartGuide suggests the names for the following interface and classes:

- Event listener interface
- Event object class
- Event multicaster class

VisualAge for Java assigns these names from the event name. These names usually make sense and you can accept them as assigned. Press the **Next** button.

Figure 10.14   New Event Listener SmartGuide.

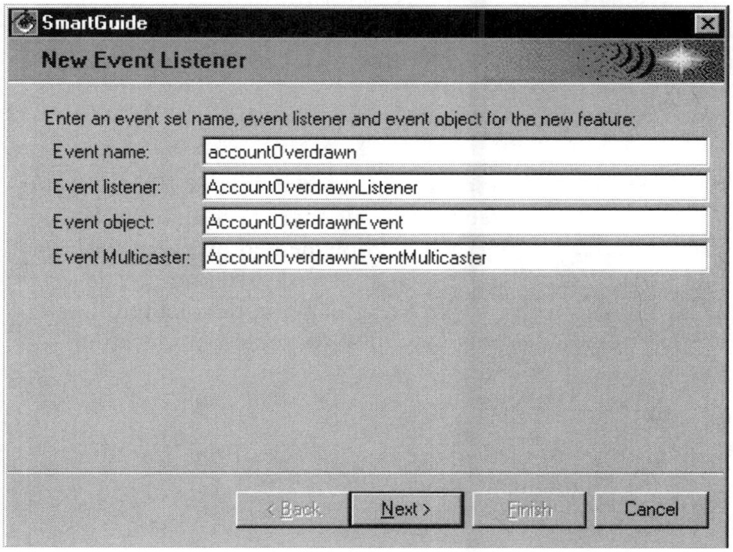

Figure 10.15   Entering a listener method name.

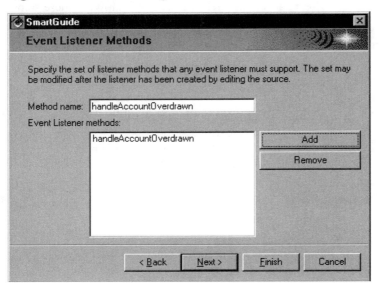

The next page of the SmartGuide appears as shown in Figure 10.15. On this page, enter the name of the listener methods that the multicaster calls when the event occurs. This method is implemented by every class that listens for this event. Enter **handleAccountOverdrawn** and press the **Add** button. It is a convention to use the Event name in the method, but it is not necessary. User-defined events may have more than one method and you can add other methods here.

Press the **Finish** button.

Switch to the Methods page of the browser and note that the BeanInfo SmartGuide created the following methods:

• addAccountOverdrawnListener()

- removeAccountOverdrawnListener()
- fireHandleAccountOverdrawn()

The listener beans use the first two methods to add and remove themselves to the list of interested objects. The bean uses the last method to indicate that the account is overdrawn.

Firing an Event

Switch to the setBalance() method and add the highlighted code to signal the accountOverdrawn event when the balance dips below 0:

```
public void setBalance(int balance) {
    int oldValue = fieldBalance;
    fieldBalance = balance;
    firePropertyChange("balance",
    new Integer(oldValue), new Integer(balance));
  if( fieldBalance < 0)
    fireHandleAccountOverdrawn(
      new AccountOverdrawnEvent(this));
}
```

Now you are ready to use your new event in the AccountView. Open the VCE for the AccountView bean and make the following connection:

```
account (handleAccountOverdrawn) → lbBalance (background)
```

The connection appears dashed because you need to define the color for the background. Double-click the connection line to open the property editor for this connection. Press the **Set parameters** button and set the value to **red**. The completed Applet should look like Figure 10.16.

Save and test the program. Press the **Withdraw** button several times, until the balance becomes less than 0. The balance now appears with a

Figure 10.16 HandleOverdrawnEvent connection.

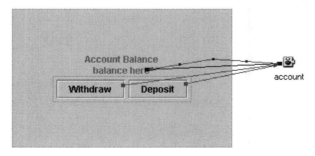

red background. If you want the background to change from red back to clear when the account balance increases, you must create another Event and add the appropriate logic.

How Events Work

Let's examine the code to see how the event works. Select the connection you just made and note its name, which is connEtoM3. Depending on how you built the sample, your connection might have a different name or number. Switch to the Members page of the browser and find the connEtoM3() method. This method is responsible for setting the background color of lbBalance:

```
getlbBalance().setBackground(java.awt.Color.red);
```

You may be wondering when is connEtoM3() called? If you look at the methods for the AccountView class, you see that the handleOverdrawnAccount() method was created when you made the last connection. The multicaster object calls all objects registered as listeners of the accountOverdrawn event. This method determines which object originated the event; if it is the **account** object, it triggers the connEtoM3() as shown in the following code:

```
public void handleAccountOverdrawn(AccountOverdrawnEvent event) {
  // user code begin {1}
  // user code end
  if ((event.getSource() == getaccount()) ) {
    connEtoM3();
  }
  // user code begin {2}
  // user code end
}
```

Event Listener Code

If you look at the declaration for the AccountView bean, you see that it implements the **userEventSample.AccountOverdrawnListener**, as shown in the following code:

```
public class AccountView extends
com.sun.java.swing.JApplet implements
java.awt.event.ActionListener,
java.beans.PropertyChangeListener,
AccountOverdrawnListener
```

In the initConnections() method, the account object registers itself as a listener for the accountOverdrawn event with the addAccountOverDrawnListner(this), as shown in the following code:

```
private void initConnections() {
  // user code begin {1}
  // user code end
  getlbBalance().addPropertyChangeListener(this);
  getaccount().addPropertyChangeListener(this);
  getpbDeposit().addActionListener(this);
  getpbWithdraw().addActionListener(this);
  getaccount().addAccountOverdrawnListener(this);
  connPtoP1SetTarget();
}
```

Summary of Events

As you see, this is a fairly complex mechanism, yet consistent and extensible. The good news is that you do not have to write any of the event supporting classes or implement the listener interface by hand. VisualAge for Java generated a considerable amount of code, and all you had to do was name the event, determine what condition should signal the event, and write one line of code to actually signal the event.

Now that you have created and used user-generated events, you can go back and iterate the AccountModel bean and add a new event interface called **AccountOK**. This event should be signaled when the account balance is no longer negative. Use this event in AccountView to turn the background color of lbBalance to white. There are other ways to design Java applications using events, and you can now create your own user-defined events with confidence.

Summary

This chapter covered two key topics in Java, namely GUI JavaBeans (Swing Components or JFC controls) and user-defined events. You built a Java JFC Applet with a user-defined event using VisualAge for Java. In this chapter, you:

- Learned about the Swing and the JFC components.
- Built a simple JFC program using the JApplet, JLabel, and JButton.
- Learned about morphing JavaBeans.
- Created a user-defined Event and Listener Interface.

Both Swing Components and user-defined events are critical concepts that will help you develop good Java programs. You will learn about additional JFC controls and more complex applications in the following chapters. You should be getting more comfortable with the VisualAge for Java IDE by now. The exercise instructions will continue getting briefer, reflecting your experience.

THE REMINDER APPLICATION

In this chapter, you start a totally new application. Because you are building on the material already covered in this book, the instructions are described in less detail. For example, instead of giving you step-by-step details on how to add a bean to the Visual Composition Editor, the instructions direct you to add or drop a certain bean. By now, you should be able to locate a bean in the beans palette, select it, and drop it in the correct place. You should also be getting used to making connections. The convention used to describe connections consists of the source bean name, the source feature in parenthesis, an arrow, the target bean name, and the target feature in parenthesis. The following connection is an example of this convention:

```
pbClose (actionPerformed) → myWindow (dispose)
```

This connection translates to mean, "connect the **pbClose** Button's **actionPerformed** event to the **myWindow** Frame's **dispose** method." When the bean feature needed for the connection could be ambiguous, the book will clearly specify whether the connection is to a method, property, or event.

Using Embedded Beans

This chapter introduces a key concept in VisualAge for Java called *embedded beans*. This technique uses the power of object-oriented technology to build custom visual and nonvisual components that you can use and reuse in many applications.

Embedded beans can encapsulate complex behavior and present a simplified user interface, exposing only the interface components that are necessary to make the bean perform its function.

Requirements for the Reminder Application

This application provides the functions of a reminder list. It saves and retrieves information related to six categories, as shown in Figure 11.1.

When the user selects a radio button, the information related to that selection appears in the input/output area. The user can edit the text displayed. The input/output area uses a **JTextArea** bean.

The first radio button is pre-selected when the application starts, and the text area displays the information associated with that button. When the user selects a different radio button, the current text in the text area is saved, and the

---

Figure 11.1   Reminder application.

Figure 11.2   Menu bar.

text associated with the newly selected radio button appears in the text area. When the user exits the program, the current text in the text area is saved.

The ReminderHashtable invisible bean provides data persistence. This bean is a subclass of the **Hashtable** class from the JDK 1.1 class library. You will define and complete this bean later in this chapter.

The application has a menu bar with the structure pictured in Figure 11.2.

Clear removes the contents of the text area; you can also access **Clear** using the Ctrl-C key combination.

You can end the program by selecting **Exit** or by pressing the Ctrl-X key combination. At exit, any information displayed on the text area is associated with the currently selected radio button and saved.

Help is displayed in a Web browser, which displays the appropriate .html file. In this manner, help text is contained in a separate file that can eventually be translated to other national languages. Its contents can be changed without affecting the application code.

A toolbar with Cut, Copy, and Paste buttons provides basic editing functions.

An About box displays the current version of the program and other interesting information to the user.

Constructing the Reminder Application

You start building the Reminder application from the bottom up. Below are the beans you construct and later assemble:

- RadioButtonManager
- RadioButtonPanel
- ReminderPanel
- ReminderHashtable
- ReminderApp

You could build the whole application in one layer, starting with a JFrame, laying out the components directly on it, and making connections between beans to complete the project. This is usually not a good design decision. By building finer-grained beans, you can achieve a much higher level of maintainability and reuse. Smaller beans enable you to encapsulate function and present a cleaner public interface to users of those beans.

RadioButtonManager

RadioButtonManager is the bean responsible for handling a group of radio buttons. Its main purpose is to track not only the currently selected radio button, but also the one that was selected previously. This is very important for the Reminder application.

Remember from the spec that when a radio button is selected, the current contents of the text area must be associated with the button that was previously selected and saved. This capability is not readily available with the standard beans; therefore, you will create your own bean with that capability.

The **JRadioButton** class provides the GUI bean to represent a radio button on the panel. Use the **ButtonGroup** invisible bean to associate a group of radio buttons and provide the mutually exclusive selection behavior.

You must associate each radio button in a group to a button. You accomplish this by calling the **add(AbstractButton)** method of the ButtonGroup class for each radio button and passing the **this** attribute of the radio button as the parameter.

The **setSelected()** method of the ButtonGroup class gets called every time a radio button in the group changes state. This presents you with an opportunity to perform some action, like recording the previously selected button, before setting the just-selected button to its new state. This is exactly what the RadioButtmManager class does.

Tip

You use radio buttons when you need to select one and only one option from a group of choices. You always use radio buttons as a group of two or more choices; although each radio button is a separate control, clusters of radio buttons behave as a single control. You should never use a single radio button to give the user a binary choice. Instead, use the **Checkbox** or **JCheckbox** bean for that purpose, and when multiple selections are possible in a group of choices.

Creating the RadioButtonManager Bean

Start creating a new bean, **RadioButtonManager**, by following these steps:

Create a new package in the My Projects project called **reminder**.

Create a new class in the reminder package named **RadioButtonManager**. Make its superclass **com.sun.java.swing.ButtonGroup**. Select the **Browse the class when finished** checkbox and deselect the **Compose the class visually** checkbox.

Press the **Next** button and add the **com.sun.java.swing** package to the **Add import statements** list. Press the **Finish** button to create the class.

Once the class browser opens, select the BeanInfo page.

Add two **java.lang.String** properties. Name them *previousKey* and *currentKey*. Ensure they are **readable, writeable,** and **bound**. These properties will supply the keys necessary to access the Hashtable containing the information related to each radio button. To make these attributes visible in the connections pop-up menu, set the **Preferred** checkbox in the second page of the SmartGuide. If you forget to select the checkbox, you can set to the **Preferred** property to **true** in the **Property Feature Information** pane of the bean info page. You can also use this pane if you change your mind on whether a property should be on the preferred list or not.

Switch to the Members page and add a new method called **setSelected**. This public method should return void, and take two parameters of type **com.sun.java.swing.ButtonGroup** and **boolean**. This method overrides setSelected() in the superclass; it is called by the JVM every time a new radio button is selected. Overriding this method gives you a chance to act upon this event before the superclass does. In our case, we use this opportunity to save the previously and currently selected button's actionCommand, to be used later as keys.

Add the highlighted code below to the generated setSelected() method:

```
/**
 * This method was created in VisualAge.
 * @param m ButtonModel
 * @param b boolean
 */
public void setSelected(ButtonModel m, boolean b) {
  if (m.isPressed()) {
    setPreviousKey(getCurrentKey());
    setCurrentKey(m.getActionCommand());
  }
  super.setSelected(m, b);
}
```

This method is actually called twice each time you select a radio button. The first time is when the currently selected button is deselected and the second time is when the new button is selected. We are only interested in one of these events, when the new button is selected. The ButtonModel parameter contains this information, you use the isPressed() method and set the state of the RadioButtonManager only if the condition is true. Finally, the superclass's setSelected() method is called to complete the operation.

That is all there is to RadioButtonManager. By adding a couple of properties and overriding the setCurrent() method, you have created an invisible bean that not only knows when a radio button is selected, but also remembers the previously selected radio button.

Because the *previousKey* and *currentKey* properties are bound, they will signal property-change events when their values change. Later on, you will use these events in the ReminderPanel bean as triggers to save and restore the contents of the text area.

RadioButtonPanel

RadioButtonPanel will hold a group of six radio buttons and a RadioButtonManager invisible bean. Together, they will give you a composite bean to represent the reminder categories available to the program. Follow these steps to code the new class:

Create a new class in the reminder package. Call this class **RadioButtonPanel**. Make its superclass **com.sun.java.swing.JPanel**. Select the **Compose the class visually** checkbox. Press the **Finish** button to create the class.

The Visual Composition Editor opens with a Swing panel on the freeform surface. Select the panel, and bring up its property sheet, and set:

- the **layout** of the **Panel** to **GridLayout**
- the layout to two columns and three rows

From the Swing palette, drop six **JRadioButton** beans on to the panel. Set the **actionCommand** and the **beanName** of the radio button beans from **rb1** to **rb6**.

Tip

Make sure you set the actionCommand before you set the beanName property. Otherwise, when you set the bean name, the action command appears to be set to the bean name, but a call to **getActionCommand()** returns null. To be sure, save the bean, switch to the Members page and locate the initialize() method. Ensure that the code to add each of the radio buttons to the panel looks like this: `add(getrbX(), getrbX().getName());` if it doesn't, you should delete the radio button and add it again. This time, set the actionCommand first and then the bean name.

Figure 11.3   Adding RadioButtonManager.

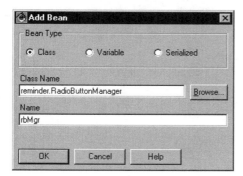

 Drop a **RadioButtonManager** bean onto the free-form surface. Because this bean is not on the beans palette, press the **Choose Bean...** from the beans palette. Name this bean **rbMgr**. Ensure that the **Class** radio button is selected as shown in Figure 11.3.

The next step is to add each of the radio buttons to the button group. You could accomplish this by making the following connections from each of the radio buttons:

```
RadioButtonPanel(initialize) → rbMgr(add)
rbX(this) → connection(button)
```

However, the above approach results in 12 connections and unnecessarily clutters the screen. In this case, a better approach is to write the code directly in the initialize() method of the RadioButtonManager bean. Save your bean and switch to the Members page of the browser. Locate the **initialize()** method and add the following lines of code inside the comments that define the user code 2 section:

```
/**
 * Initialize the class.
 */
/* WARNING: THIS METHOD WILL BE REGENERATED. */
private void initialize() {
  ...
  // user code begin {2}
  getrbMgr().add(getrb1());
  getrbMgr().add(getrb2());
  getrbMgr().add(getrb3());
  getrbMgr().add(getrb4());
  getrbMgr().add(getrb5());
  getrbMgr().add(getrb6());
  // user code end
}
```

Figure 11.4   RadioButtonPanel completed.

rbMgr

Change the text of each of the radio button beans to make up categories of things you want to remember. Figure 11.4 shows the complete bean and a proposed set of labels for the radio buttons.

You can actually run this bean by pressing the Run button. You are able to run this bean, even though it is a panel, because the Visual Composition Editor generated a main() method for this bean, which instantiates the necessary components and then inserts the JPanel in a frame. This helps you test your beans quickly and aids in the iterative development process. Press the Run button now. The running RadioButtonPanel should look like Figure 11.5. Select the radio buttons and notice how you can only select one button at a time.

There is only one more thing to do before you can consider this part is complete. As you remember from the spec, the first radio button in the group must be selected when the Reminder application starts. You can accomplish this in several ways. To ensure that the timing is right and that all components of the application are constructed and initialized before selecting the first radio button, use an event generated by the frame in the ReminderApp. The event is called windowOpened; it triggers the connection to select the button. The connection is (do not attempt this connection yet):

```
reminderFrame(windowOpened)  →  rb1(doClick)
```

Figure 11.5   Running RadioButtonPanel.

The problem is that because the RadioButtonPanel is embedded in another bean, its features are encapsulated and not accessible when this bean is used as a part of composite, more complex bean. You need to make the doClick(int) method of **rb1** visible to the next level of composition. As you learned before, you accomplish this by promoting the required features or, if necessary, the entire bean.

Promote the doClick(int) method of **rb1** by following these steps:

Click on the **rb1** check box to select it and right-click to bring up its pop-up menu. Select **Promote Bean Feature**.

From the Method list, promote the **doClick(int)** method. Accept the proposed name of **rb1DoClick(int)** by pressing the **OK** button. Promoting a bean feature creates a public method, which accesses the particular promoted bean and calls the selected method. In the case of this promotion, the following code is generated:

```
public void rb1DoClick(int pressTime) {
        getrb1().doClick(pressTime);
}
```

The method **rb1DoClick** is also included in the BeanInfo class of the containing bean, so that tools can find out about it. Press **OK** to complete the promotion. Refer to Figure 11.6.

Figure 11.6   Promoting the doClick method.

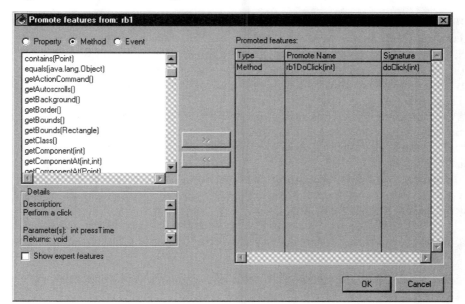

Promote the **previousKey** and **currentKey** properties of rbMgr:

Click on the **rbMgr** bean to select it and right-click on it to bring up its pop-up menu. Select **Promote Bean Feature**.

From the Properties list, select **previousKey**. Accept the proposed name of **rbMgrPreviousKey** by pressing the **OK** button.

Repeat the steps above and promote the **currentKey** property; accept its name as **rbMgrCurrentKey**.

If you want these features to appear on the connection pop-up menu for the RadioButtonPanel bean, switch to the BeanInfo page of the browser and select **Preferred** and **true** on the Property Feature Information pane for each of the features. It is a good idea to do this now.

Save and close the Visual Composition Editor for the RadioButtonPanel bean and proceed to building the next bean.

ReminderPanel

The next step is to create the ReminderPanel bean. This bean encapsulates most of the function needed for the Reminder application to work as specified.

The ReminderPanel contains a RadioButtonPanel, a JScrollPane, a JTextArea, and a **ReminderHashtable** bean. You should be familiar with the first three beans. The ReminderHashtable is a specialization of the **java.util.Hashtable** class, which is part of the standard JDK. Proceed to create the ReminderHashtable.

ReminderHashtable

The **java.util.Hashtable** bean implements a collection class that gives you a way to match a key to a value. You may know a hash table by other names like map, dictionary, or table. The implementation of Hashtable is really not important; but it is what is important to know that it provides a means of storing key/value pairs in a Java program.

A Hashtable has methods such as get() and put() to manipulate its contents. Normally, when a value requested by the get(Object key) is not found in the Hashtable, a null object is returned. For the Reminder application, this is not the required behavior.

Think about it: What is the appropriate action if the user selects a category that currently has no reminders? Clearing the contents of the text area, to indicate no match, is the right thing to do.

The ReminderHashtable extends Hashtable and overrides the get() method to return an empty String if the Hashtable returns null. Setting the text of the text area to an empty string clears it.

Start by creating a new class in the reminder package. Call this class **ReminderHashtable**. Make its superclass **java.util.Hashtable**. Select the

Browse the class when finished checkbox and deselect the **Compose the class visually** checkbox. Press the **Finish** button to create the class.

Ensure that you are in the Members page of the browser and add a new method called **get**. This public method returns **java.lang.Object**, is synchronized, and takes one parameter of type **java.lang.Object** (call the parameter **key**). This method overrides the **get()** method in the superclass. Overriding this method gives you a chance to intercept the call before the superclass executes it. In our case, we use this opportunity to call the superclass's **get()** method and examine the returned object. If it is null, we return an empty string object.

Add the highlighted code below to the generated get method:

```
/**
 * This method was created by a SmartGuide.
 * @return java.lang.Object
 * @param key java.lang.Object
 */
public synchronized Object get( Object key) {
    // call the superclass' get method
    Object result = super.get(key);

    // if value not found for key, return an
    // empty String
    if(result == null)
        return (new String(""));
    // else return the found object representing
    // the found value for the key
    else
        return result;
}
```

The ReminderHashtable bean is now ready for use in the ReminderPanel, which you build next.

Building the ReminderPanel

You build the ReminderPanel as a subclass of **com.sun.java.swing.JPanel**. As mentioned earlier, this panel will combine a RadioButtonPanel, a JScrollPane, a JTextArea, and a ReminderHashtable. Build the ReminderPanel by following these steps:

Create a new class in the reminder package and name it **ReminderPanel**. Make its superclass **com.sun.java.swing.JPanel**. Select the **Browse the class when finished** checkbox and the select the **Compose the class visually** checkbox. Press the **Finish** button to create the class.

The Visual Composition Editor opens with a JPanel object on the free-form surface. Select the panel and bring up its property sheet. Set the layout of the panel to **BorderLayout**.

Add a **RadioButtonPanel** to the north of the border layout on the panel. Call it **rbPanel**.

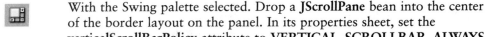

With the Swing palette selected. Drop a **JScrollPane** bean into the center of the border layout on the panel. In its properties sheet, set the **verticalScrollBarPolicy** attribute to **VERTICAL_SCROLLBAR_ALWAYS**.

Drop a **JTextArea** on top of the scroll pane. Call it **reminderText**.

Add a **ReminderHashTable** to the free-form surface. Call it **theTable**. Your Visual Composition Editor should look like Figure 11.7.

Make the following connection:

```
rbPanel(rbMgrPreviousKey)  →  theTable(put)
```

It is important to understand what this connection does and when it executes. As you recall, when you created the *previousKey* property in the RadioButtonManager, you designated it as a bound property. All bound properties fire *propertyChanged* events when their value changes. In our case, the value of *previousKey* changes every time the user selects a new radio button. You coded this behavior in the setSelected() method of the RadioButtonManager bean.

From the spec, you know that every time the user selects a new radio button, the current reminder in the text area must be saved and associated with the previously selected radio button. Using the event generated when *previousKey* changes value is just what you need to put the value of the text area into the reminder Hashtable. The connection above does just that.

The previous connection calls the method:

```
Object put(Object key, Object value)
```

Figure 11.7   All components in place.

theTable

As you can see, it stores two parameters, the key and the value, in the Hashtable. These parameters are readily available. Make the following property-to-parameter connections:

```
rbPanel(rbMgrPreviousKey)  →  connection(key)
reminderText(text)  →  connection(value)
```

The three connections above save the contents of the text area to the Hashtable every time the *previousKey* property changes. This is only half of what you need. Make the following connections to get the contents of the Hashtable every time the *currentKey* property changes and place the result in the text area. The *currentKey* property is used as the key to retrieve the correct value from the Hashtable. Connect:

```
rbPanel(rbMgrCurrentKey)  →  theTable(get)
```

This connection requires one parameter, the key used to retrieve the stored value in the Hashtable. This parameter is readily available. Make the following property-to-parameter connections:

```
rbPanel (rbMgrCurrentKey)  →  connection (key)
connection(normalResult)  →  reminderText(text)
```

The last connection applies the return value of the **Object get(Object key)** method to the contents of the text area. If the key is not found, an empty string is placed into the text area. This produces the effect of clearing its contents. You coded this behavior in the get() method of the ReminderHashtable bean. Once you have completed all the above connections, your Visual Composition Editor should look like Figure 11.8.

Run this panel to test the function you have completed so far. You should be able to do the following:

- Select categories with the radio buttons
- Enter text in the input area

Figure 11.8   Connections completed.

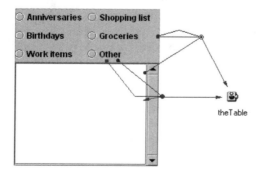

- Switch back and forth between radio buttons
- Display the correct text in the text area for each of the reminder categories

You have made connections to save the contents of the text area to the Hashtable. There is also a requirement to save the text in the text area when the program exits. To accomplish this task, create a new method called **saveCurrentCategory**. This method will be called from the ReminderApp class, which you code next.

Ensure that you are in the BeanInfo page of the browser and add a new method called **saveCurrentCategory**. This public method returns void, is synchronized, and takes no parameters.

Add the following highlighted code to the generated method:

```
public synchronized void saveCurrentCategory()
{
    gettheTable().put(getrbPanel().
      getRbMgrCurrentKey(),
      getreminderText().getText());
    return;
}
```

This method requires a single line of code, which chains a few method calls to other beans in ReminderPanel to perform the put method on the Hashtable. The ReminderApp bean uses this method later.

Double Promotion

The last thing to do, before proceeding to the ReminderApp, is to promote the **rb1DoClick()** method from the RadioButtonPanel bean again. As you remember, you promoted this method when you built that bean. That promotion made the method visible in this bean. If you want it visible at the next level, the ReminderApp, you must promote it again.

Promotions increase the visibility of a feature of a bean only one level at the time. As beans become part of more complex beans, it may or may not be necessary for a particular feature to be visible to these more complex beans. If necessary, you can re-promote features to propagate them to higher level beans.

This is not necessarily a bad thing; it forces you to verify that a feature needs to be visible at the next level of usage, and prevents the public interface of complex beans from becoming cluttered.

Select the rbPanel bean, click the right mouse button, and select **Promote Bean Feature**. From the Method list, select **rb1DoClick(int)**. Change the proposed **Promote Name** from **rbPanelRb1DoClick(int)** to **rb1DoClick(int)**. To change the name, double click the proposed name and overtype the new name in the entry field. This keeps the same name from level to level of promotion.

In the next section, you add the ReminderPanel to a frame so it runs as a stand-alone Java application. You also add function to implement the part of the specification dealing with initialization and persistence.

ReminderApp

Most of the features required for the Reminder Application already exist in the ReminderPanel bean. According to the spec, the features that still need to be implemented include:

- Select the first category when the program starts.
- Provide persistence for reminders between program invocations.
- Ensure that when the program closes, no information is lost.
- Add a main menu bar with File and Help menu items.
- Add a toolbar to provide Cut, Copy, and Paste editing functions.

You have a choice when constructing applications in VisualAge for Java. You can start from scratch by creating a frame (AWT or Swing based), building menus and adding other componets in a form similar to what you have done with the previous beans on this book. However, VisualAge for Java provides you with a SmartGuide to create applications that include menus, toolbars, information areas, and about boxes. You will use the SmartGuide to create the ReminderApp.

Using the Create Application SmartGuide

 From the workbench main toolbar press the **Create Application** button. The Create Application SmartGuide opens. Set the values as shown on Table 11.1 and Figure 11.9.

Press the **Next** button on the SmartGuide. In this page, you decide what GUI features your new application will have. According to the Reminder Application's spec you need:

- Menu bar
- Toolbar
- About dialog

Table 11.1 New Application Settings

Attribute	Value
Project	MyProject
Package	Reminder
Class name	ReminderApp
Create Swing based application	Selected

Figure 11.9   Create Application SmartGuide (1).

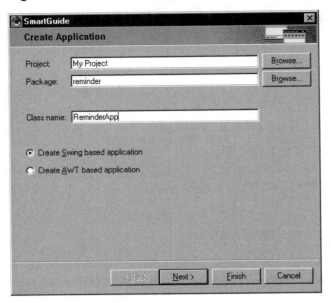

Select those three checkboxes on the SmartGuide. You will have to further
define the menu bar and the toolbar.

Defining the Menu Bar

Press the **Details...** button beside the **Menu bar** checkbox. Delete items from the
Menus pane until you are left with only the **File** and **Help** menu items.

Select the File menu item and remove items. Delete all items from the
Menu Items pane with the exception of the **Exit** menu item. Add a **Clear** and a
-- Separator -- menu item. Use the **Up** and **Down** buttons to order the menu items
as shown in Figure 11.10.

Using the same approach, add a **General Help** and an **About box** menu item
to the **Help** menu. Put a separator between the General Help and About box
menu items.

Defining the Toolbar

Press the **Details...** button beside the **Toolbar** checkbox. Ensure that the **Cut,
Copy,** and **Paste** toolbar buttons are select. Take this opportunity to see what other
buttons are readily available for you to use in your toolbars. See Figure 11.11.

Continue Building the Application

The second page of the SmartGuide should look like Figure 11.12.

Figure 11.10   File menu items.

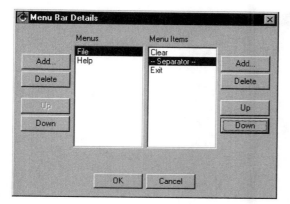

Set Title bar text to: *Reminder Application*. Make sure that the **Center and pack frame on screen** checkbox is not selected. Press the **Finish** button to start the code generation process. Depending on your machine, this may take what appears to be a long time. Considering the amount of code generated, this time is well worth waiting for.

After code generation is complete, the Visual Composition Editor opens to the ReminderApp class. See Figure 11.13.

If you switch to the Workbench, you will see two new classes under the reminder package. They are ReminderApp and ReminderAppAboutBox. Looking

Figure 11.11   Toolbar items.

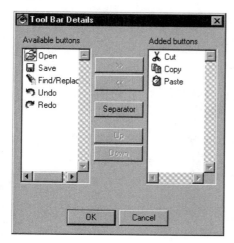

Figure 11.12   Create Application SmartGuide (2).

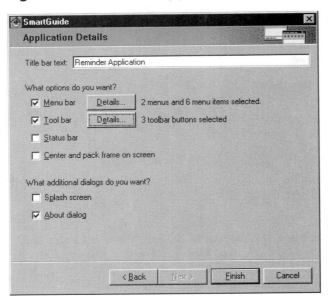

Figure 11.13   ReminderApp in Composition Editor.

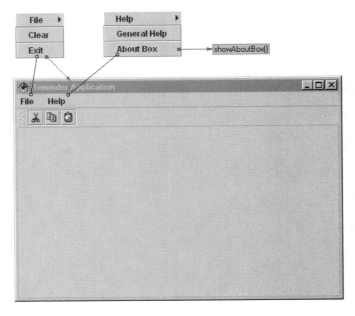

Figure 11.14   ReminderApp up and running.

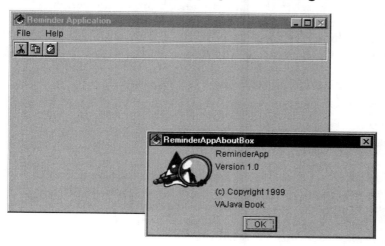

into each of these classes reveals a lot of code—code you didn't have to write. The code in the about box may not be exactly what you want, but it is certainly good enough as a starting point. You can customize the generated code to better suit your needs.

Run the ReminderApp now and see how it behaves, as shown in Figure 11.14. Try out the menu items and the toolbar buttons. Right now they don't do much, but you will change that in the remainder of this chapter. Also, for the time being, ignore the mechanics of constructing menus and menu items, which is covered in "Menus" later in this chapter.

Finishing ReminderApp

The ReminderApp class, as created by the SmartGuide, extends **com.sun.java.swing.JFrame**. The frame will hold a ReminderPanel bean. It also will have the necessary logic to save the Hashtable and start another process, where a Web browser containing the help system will run.

The SmartGuide placed a JPanel bean on top of the JFrame's content pane, which is named **ReminderAppPane**. Select this panel and press the Delete button to remove it from the frame. There is still another JPanel in the frame, called **JFrameContentPane**. This panel is using a border layout, and the toolbar occupies the north cell of the layout. It is on this panel where you will place a ReminderPanel bean.

Add a ReminderPanel bean to the center cell of the border layout on JFrameContentPane. Call it **reminderPanel**.

Placing a bean in the center of a border layout causes that bean to expand in all directions. When there are no other beans on the periphery, the bean in the center touches the borders of the frame. In most cases, this does not look very good. To provide a margin, drop a JLabel bean on the east, south, and west areas of the border layout of the content pane. Replace the text of each of the label beans with a single space. The Visual Composition Editor should look like Figure 11.15.

Make the following connection to select the first category radio button when the window opens:

```
ReminderApp(windowOpened event) → reminderPanel(rb1DoClick)
```

The connection appears dashed because it needs an int parameter to complete the connection. The parameter is the time in milliseconds that the method simulates the button click. Double-click the connection, press the **Set parameters** button, and set the *pressTime* parameter to 60, which is the average time a mouse click lasts. Press **OK** twice to complete the operation.

The *windowOpened* event happens only once in the life of a frame, when it first opens. This makes it a good event to trigger the selection of the first category.

Figure 11.15 Reminder Application.

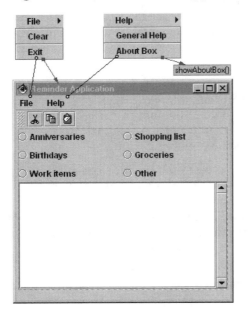

> **NOTE**
>
> ReminderApp, in the connections, refers to the actual JFrame bean on the composition surface.

Tip

Under certain circumstances, you may find it hard to locate a connection on the Visual Composition Editor because it can appear as a very short green line on the screen. If you press the Beans List button, you see a list of all the beans and connections currently in use by the bean. Select the connection and it stands out because of its sizing handles. The Beans List is an excellent tool for finding and connecting beans.

The next connection deals with the application closing. The *windowClosed* event triggers the application closing. This event only happens once in the lifetime of a frame, just before it closes. Connect:

```
ReminderApp(windowClosed event) → reminderPanel(saveCurrentCategory)
```

Run the ReminderApp to see how it behaves so far. When the application starts, the first radio button should be selected. You should be able to select other categories and add text for them. Switching back and forth between categories should properly save and recall the correct text.

Adding Persistence

So far so good. The only problem is that when you close the application and then start it up again, your reminders are gone, because you have not made any provisions for saving the reminders in a nonvolatile persistent type of storage.

To make the reminders persist; you have a variety of choices, some more portable than others. You could:

- Read and write to a flat disk file
- Use the operating system registry
- Use .ini files
- Serialize the Hashtable

Serialization is the Java way of providing persistent storage. It is easy to do because the language was designed with it in mind. Java can serialize a Java bean by storing its type and state. Later on, the serialized data can be used to reconstruct the bean and restore its original state.

Every Java language book that covers JDK 1.1 or later, covers serialization, so we will not spend any time on the internal mechanism that makes serialization possible. Any bean that implements the **java.io.Serializable** interface can be serialized.

Serialized beans are stored as binary files and treated as resources. That means that a Java program using serialized beans must be able to find and access these files. By convention, serialized bean files have an extension of **.ser**. There are no conventions regarding the location of files containing serialized beans. In this project, you will store the serialized ReminderHashtable in the same directory as the class files.

The **java.io.ObjectOutputStream** and **java.io.ObjectInputStream** classes provide the writeObject() and readObject() methods to store and retrieve serialized objects.

This version of VisualAge for Java does not handle serialized beans very gracefully. VisualAge for Java is a consumer of serialized beans, but not a producer. While you will use VisualAge for Java to produce, create, and store serialized beans doing so is not an automated process and there are no SmartGuides to help you create them.

While in the Visual Composition Editor, you cannot use a serialized bean that does not already exist; the tool will not create that very first instance for you. This is a chicken-and-egg situation. You need an existing serialized object before you can use it, but you cannot create it easily inside the tool when you need to use it. We will show you a couple of ways to deal with this problem.

Using Serialized JavaBeans

As mentioned before, you cannot drop a serialized bean on the free-form surface of the Visual Composition Editor unless you already have one to refer to. When you try to use a serialized bean, the Visual Composition Editor asks you for its file name. You cannot just create an empty file with the right name, because the Visual Composition Editor will actually open the file to find out what type of bean it contains. You need a way to create a file containing a legitimate serialized bean.

First Approach

Open the Visual Composition Editor for the **ReminderPanel** bean. You will add a serialized ReminderHashtable bean to replace the one already there. Once it is on the free-form surface, you will move the connections from the existing bean (**theTable**) to the new serialized bean, delete the original bean, and rename the new bean **theTable**.

Press the **Choose Bean...** button from the beans palette.

Press the **Serialized** radio button and notice how the **Class Name** entry field becomes the **File Name** entry field. Pressing the **Browse** button enables you to look for the file containing the bean shown in Figure 11.16. The problem is that the bean doesn't exist yet, so you can't find it. Press the **Cancel** button.

Figure 11.16 Adding a serialized bean.

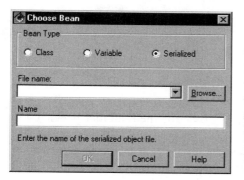

This approach will show you how to create a serialized bean of the type you need (in your case, a ReminderHashtable bean) outside the Visual Composition Editor. This is not as hard as it sounds.

From the main menu, open a Scrapbook window and enter the code shown below. Make sure that you type the first line, where the **outFile** object is created, all in the same line in the Scrapbook. (This line spreads over several lines in the book because of space constraints.) There should be no spaces anywhere between the quotes defining the string with the path and file name.

Make sure you use the drive letter of where VisualAge for Java is installed in your system to make up the correct path to store the bean.

Tip

Make sure that the following directory structure exists on the drive where VisualAge for Java is installed:

`\IBMVJava\IDE\project_resources\My Project\reminder`

If it doesn't, create it before running the code in the Scrapbook or you will get an exception running the code. Select all of the code and press the Run button.

```
java.io.FileOutputStream outFile =
new java.io.FileOutputStream(
    "D:\\IBMVJava\\Ide\\project_resources\\
    My Project\\reminder\\table.ser");
```

```
java.io.ObjectOutputStream outStream = new
    java.io.ObjectOutputStream(outFile);

reminder.ReminderHashtable ht = new
    reminder.ReminderHashtable();

outStream.writeObject(ht);
```

The directory used to create the FileOutputStream is where VisualAge for Java expects the resources and serialized beans to be for the **reminder** package in the **My Project** project.

Now you have an empty ReminderHashtable serialized bean ready for use in the Visual Composition Editor. Return to the Visual Composition Editor and add **table.ser** to the free-form surface by following these steps:

Press the **Choose Bean...** button from the tools palette.

Press the **Serialized** radio button. Press the **Browse** button and find the table.ser file in the directory used in the Scrapbook code above. Name the bean **newTable**. Press the **OK** button as shown in Figure 11.17.

> **NOTE**
>
> Even though you named the bean in the Add Bean dialog, the Visual Composition Editor will not use the name. You need to change the bean name once you add it to the free-form surface.

Now you have two ReminderHashtable beans on the free-form surface, **theTable** and **newTable**. Because these two beans are of the same type,

Figure 11.17   Adding a serialized ReminderTable bean.

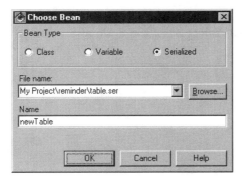

you can move the connections from **theTable** to **newTable**. Select the two connections and drag the ending points from one bean to the other. Move the two connections now.

Since you no longer need the original ReminderHashtable, **theTable**, delete it.

Rename **newTable** to **theTable**. Doing so keeps the references to **theTable** in the other components of the program valid.

Save the bean. From the Bean menu, select **Save Bean**.

There is one other thing to consider. Switch to the Members page and look at the gettheTable() method just created. A new instance of ReminderHashtable is created from the serialized bean file. But what happens if the file is not found at run time? This is a normal and expected condition, especially the first time you run the program. Also, the user might erase this file if he or she wants to start over again.

The generated code does not handle this situation at all. Add the highlighted code below to the gettheTable() method to handle the situation where the file doesn't exist and the bean could not be created. In this case, an exception is thrown and the catch clause creates a new ReminderHashtable.

```
/**
 * Return the theTable property value.
 * @return reminder.ReminderHashtable
 */
/* WARNING: THIS METHOD WILL BE REGENERATED. */
public ReminderHashtable gettheTable() {
   if (ivjtheTable == null) {
      try {
         java.lang.Class iiCls = Class.forName
            ("reminder.ReminderHashtable");
         java.lang.ClassLoader iiClassLoader =
            iiCls.getClassLoader();
         ivjtheTable = (reminder.ReminderHashtable)
            java.beans.Beans.instantiate(
            iiClassLoader,"reminder\\table");
         // user code begin {1}
         // user code end
      } catch (java.lang.Throwable ivjExc) {
         // user code begin {2}
         ivjtheTable = new reminder.ReminderHashtable();
         // user code end
         handleException(ivjExc);
      }
   }
   return ivjtheTable;
}
```

Save the gettheTable() method and test the program. It should still behave as before. That is to say, it will still not save your reminders when you exit. To get the program to do that, you need to write a bit of code in the ReminderApp bean.

Now you have a choice. If you can't wait to get this part of the program completed, go ahead to the next section, "Saving the ReminderHashtable." However, if you continue reading, you will learn a second way to instantiate serialized beans in the Visual Composition Editor, this one without having to create one in the Scrapbook first.

Second Approach

This approach uses a variable; you will learn about variables in detail in a later chapter. For now, suffice it to say that a variable is not a bean in itself; it is a reference to an already existing bean of the same type. For those of you with C++ experience, a variable is very similar to a pointer, but of course Java has no pointers.

To iterate once more on the ReminderPanel bean, follow these steps and replace the serialized ReminderHashtable bean with a variable of the same type:

From the Options menu, select **Add Bean.**

Press the **Variable** radio button. Set the **Interface/Class Name** entry field to **reminder.ReminderHashtable**. Name the bean **newTable**. Press the **OK** button as shown in Figure 11.18.

Now, once again, you have two ReminderHashtable beans on the free-form surface, **theTable** and **newTable**. Notice that the icon representing **newTable** is enclosed in brackets; this signifies that it is variable and not a concrete bean. Because these two beans are of the same type, you can move the connections from **theTable** to **newTable**. Select the two connections and drag the ending points from one bean to the other. Move the two connections now.

Figure 11.18   Adding a ReminderTable variable.

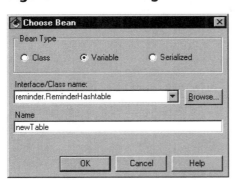

Since you no longer need the serialized ReminderHashtable, **theTable,** delete it.

Rename **newTable** to **theTable.** Doing so keeps references to **theTable** in the other components of the program valid.

Save the bean. From the Bean menu, select **Save Bean.**

Examining the generated code reveals that the gettheTable() method does not do much:

```
/**
 * Return the theTable property value.
 * @return reminder.ReminderHashtable
 */
/* WARNING: THIS METHOD WILL BE REGENERATED. */
public ReminderHashtable gettheTable() {
  // user code begin {1}
  // user code end
  return ivjtheTable;
}
```

This is because a variable needs to be set programmatically. Its initial value is set to null and must be assigned to refer to another object of the same type at the appropriate time in the program. Notice that the code generator assigned the name **ivjtheTable** to the variable.

Add the highlighted code below to the gettheTable() method to attempt to load a serialized ReminderHashtable bean or create a new one if the load fails. The newly created bean is then assigned to the **ivjtheTable** variable.

```
/**
 * Return the theTable property value.
 * @return reminder.ReminderHashtable
 */
/* WARNING: THIS METHOD WILL BE REGENERATED. */
public ReminderHashtable gettheTable() {
  // user code begin {1}
  if(ivjtheTable==null) {
    try{
      String userDir =
        System.getProperty("user.dir");
      String beanLocation = userDir +
        "\\reminder\\table.ser";
      java.io.FileInputStream istream = new
        java.io.FileInputStream(beanLocation);
```

```
      java.io.ObjectInputStream p = new
        java.io.ObjectInputStream(istream);
      ivjtheTable =
        (ReminderHashtable) p.readObject();
        istream.close();
    }
    catch(Exception e){
      ivjtheTable = new
        reminder.ReminderHashtable();
    }
  }
  // user code end
  return ivjtheTable;
}
```

This code is simpler than it appears. The first two lines determine the fully qualified path from which to read the serialized file. The first line gets the **user.dir** property from the System object. This returns the directory from where the program was started, which is usually the root directory of the CLASSPATH. From there, you add the package and file names **\\reminder\\table.ser**. The result is the string, **beanLocation**, which corresponds to the file's location.

Once you have the fully qualified name of the serialized object's file, you open a FileInputStream using the beanLocation string. With the FileInputStream, you create an ObjectInputStream. Finally, you use the readObject() method to read and reconstruct the object, which is cast to a ReminderHashtable and assigned to the ivjtheTable variable.

If, for any reason, any of the steps above throws an exception, we create a new ReminderHashtable so that the program can continue executing.

Saving the ReminderHashtable

The specifications for the Reminder program prescribe that when the program exits, the reminders need to be saved.

Because you already have the code to read a serialized bean, the easiest way to save the reminders is to serialize the ReminderHashtable.

The trigger to save the reminders is the **windowClosed** event. As explained earlier in this chapter, this event only happens once in the lifetime of a frame, just before it closes.

Ensure that you are in the Visual Composition Editor for the **ReminderApp**. Connect:

```
ReminderApp(windowClosed event) →
free-form surface(Event to Code...)
```

As before, ReminderApp in the connection above refers to the actual frame on the free-form surface. Making an event-to-code connection brings up the Event to Code window. In this window, you can connect to any method in the class. You can also create a new method, as shown in Figure 11.19.

You are now in a SmartGuide that facilitates creating a new method in the ReminderApp class. Deselect the **Pass event data ...** checkbox. Overtype the method on the dialog using the code below:

```
/**
 * Comment
 */
private synchronized void saveTable( ) throws
        java.io.IOException {
  String userDir =
    System.getProperty("user.dir");
  String beanLocation = userDir +
    "\\reminder\\table.ser";

  java.io.FileOutputStream outFile = new
    java.io.FileOutputStream(beanLocation);

  java.io.ObjectOutputStream outStream = new
```

Figure 11.19   Event-to-Code window.

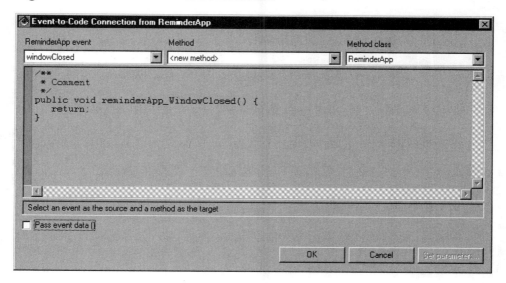

```
   java.io.ObjectOutputStream(outFile);

outStream.writeObject(
   getreminderPanel().gettheTable());

return;
}
```

See Figure 11.20 for the completed method. Press the **OK** button to save the method.

Switch to the Members page of the browser and select the saveTable() method. Verify that the code to serialize and save the bean has been correctly entered as in the code sample above. This code is very similar to that of the second approach to load a serialized bean.

The first line gets the **user.dir** property from the System object. This returns the directory from where the program was started, which is usually the root directory of the CLASSPATH. From there, you add the package and file names: **\\reminder\\table.ser**. The result is the string, **beanLocation**, which corresponds to the file's location.

Once you have the fully qualified name of the serialized object's file, you open a FileOutputStream using the **beanLocation** string. The FileOutputStream is used to create an ObjectOutputStream. Finally, you use the writeObject() method to serialize and store the ReminderHashtable object.

Figure 11.20   Adding the saveTable method.

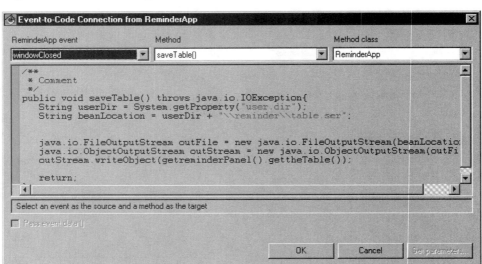

Exiting the Application

If you use the Create Application SmartGuide, the code it generates is enough to exit the program when the window is closed, and you do **not** need to perform the step below. See the generated code in the **main()** method for ReminderApp.

However, if you write your own code for your applications from scratch, make sure that you drop a **System** bean on the free-form surface. You can name it **system**. Then make the following connection:

```
reminderApp(windowClosed event) → system(exit)
```

Once you make the connection, double-click on it to set its properties. Press the **Set Parameters** button and set the *status* parameter to 0. This is the exit code of the program.

Tip

When you set the parameter to the default value, the Visual Composition Editor does not recognize the change and the connection line remains dashed. If you want to turn the dashed green line into a solid line, you must open the property editor for the connection and set the parameter to a non-default value, in this case try 99. Close the property editor to save the change, then reopen the property editor and set it back to the default value.

All connections and coding are now complete. The Visual Composition Editor for the ReminderApp bean should look like Figure 11.21.

If you have been keeping track of the connections from the ReminderApp frame to various methods, you know that there are two actions triggered by the *windowClosed* event. It is very important that these connections execute in the right order, or you might save the table before you put the contents of the current category in the hashtable.

Select the ReminderApp frame, right-click, and from the pop-up menu, select **Reorder Connections From**. This brings up the Reorder Connections window, where you can drag and drop connections to alter the order in which they fire. Make sure that your order is the same as that of the connections in Figure 11.22.

NOTE

Drag and drop connections just like you do any object in the Visual Composition Editor. Point the mouse at the connection you want to move, press and hold down the left mouse button, then drag the connection to the desired position and release it.

Figure 11.21   Connections complete.

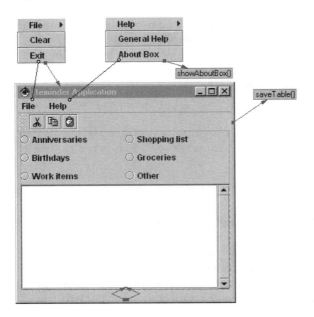

Congratulations! You have finished the first phase of the Reminder application. At this point you should test it and make sure that reminders are saved and restored properly when you exit and restart the program. Once you are happy that it is working fine, you should version the package.

After versioning, and if you have not already done so, you may want to go back to the ReminderPanel bean and try the alternate persistence approach.

Figure 11.22   Verifying the connection order.

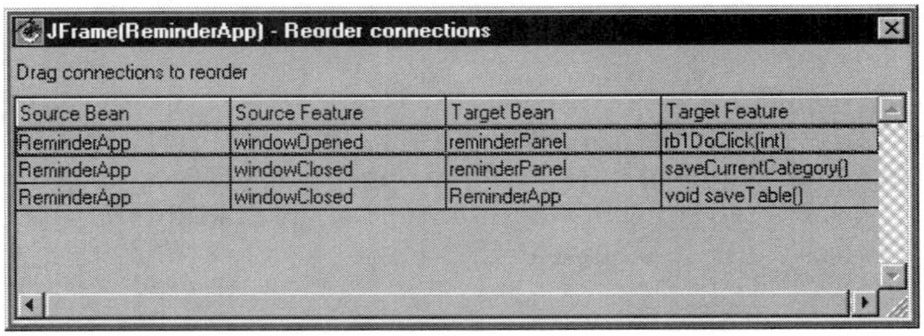

JFrame(ReminderApp) - Reorder connections

Drag connections to reorder

Source Bean	Source Feature	Target Bean	Target Feature
ReminderApp	windowOpened	reminderPanel	rb1DoClick(int)
ReminderApp	windowClosed	reminderPanel	saveCurrentCategory()
ReminderApp	windowClosed	ReminderApp	void saveTable()

Menus

As you have seen, the **Create Application** SmartGuide allows you to create application frames, which contain advanced elements like menus and toolbars. Using the SmartGuide spares you the monotonous chore of creating your own menus. However, it is useful to understand how menus are constructed using Swing components.

 The first component you need is a **JMenuBar**. The menu bar is selected from the tools palette and dropped on the **JFrame**. The best place to drop it is right on top of the title bar. The menu bar gives you the top-level action bar and adds one **JMenu** bean to the bar.

 From then on, you build up your menu bar by dropping additional JMenu beans on the menu bar. To build the drop-down menu items under the menu, drop **JMenuItem** beans on top of the JMenu that you want to drop-down from. Other beans that can be dropped on JMenu beans are:

- JCheckBoxMenuItem
- JRadioButtonMenuItem
- JSeparator

Once your menus are constructed, you usually connect the **actionPerformed** event of the menu item to a method. This is the same as using a button.

The SmartGuide assigns names to the menu items according to their text. See Table 11.2.

You can see the pattern of the naming algorithm. If you don't like the names assigned by the SmartGuide, you can change them in their property sheet in the Composition Editor.

Setting Menu Accelerator Keys

Next, you set up accelerator keys for the menu items. Before you can start entering the accelerator information in the properties sheet for the menu items, you need to add the following import statement to your class declaration. Switch to the Hierarchy page of the class browser for the ReminderApp class, and from the

Table 11.2   Menu Item Bean Names

Menu item text	Bean name
Clear	ClearMenuItem
Exit	ExitMenuItem
General Help	General_HelpMenuItem
About Box	About_BoxMenuItem

Class Hierarchy pane select ReminderApp. Enter the next line of code in the Source pane, right after the comments:

```
import java.awt.event.*;
```

Switch back to the Visual Composition page of the class browser and open the properties sheet for ClearMenuItem. Select the accelerator property. Notice that there is no property editor or customizer for setting accelerators, as indicated by the curly braces { } in the input field. Anything typed between the curly braces is entered as code at the appropriate place by the code generator. Enter the following code inside the curly braces to set the accelerator key for the Clear menu item to Ctrl-C:

```
KeyStroke.getKeyStroke(KeyEvent.VK_C, ActionEvent.CTRL_MASK)
```

The statement KeyEvent.VK_C, defines the virtual key **C**. ActionEvent.CRTL_MASK indicates that the control key is to be used in combination with the virtual key to activate the accelerator action.

The setAccelerator() method of the **JMenuItem** class requires a **KeyStroke** as a parameter. After saving, the generated code looks like this:

```
ivjClearMenuItem.setAccelerator( KeyStroke.getKeyStroke(KeyEvent.VK_C,
ActionEvent.CTRL_MASK) );
```

Proceed to set the other accelerator keys as outlined in Table 11.3.

As you may have noticed, the accelerator keys do not appear beside the menu items in the Visual Composition Editor. This is done to conserve space on the free-form surface. When you run the program, they will be there. Press the Run button to see what the menus look like at run time.

As mentioned before, menu items, like buttons, generate *actionPerformed* events when selected. Therefore, making connections to menu items is very simple. Sometimes, making even very simple connections is not the right design choice.

The **Exit** menu item must perform the same functions as closing the window. As you recall, there were two connections required to properly save and close the application:

- saveCurrentCategory()
- saveTable()

Table 11.3   Accelerator Keys

Menu Item	Accelerator
Exit	Ctrl-X
General Help	Ctrl-H
About Box	Ctrl-A

For the application to exit correctly, those two connections must be duplicated, this time originating from the **ExitMenuItem** menu item. In addition, the frame needs to be disposed. A better design would be to add a method to perform all the necessary clean-up in one place. Connect:

```
ExitMenuItem (actionPerformed event) → free-form surface (Event to Code...)
```

Select the **<new method>** item in the Method drop-down list on the Event to Code window. Create a new private method. Call it **cleanUp**; it should return void and accept no parameters. Press the **OK** button to complete the connection. If you need more details, refer to where you added the **saveTable** method earlier in this chapter.

Switch to the Members page of the browser and add the highlighted code to the cleanUp() method:

```
/**
 * This method was created by a SmartGuide.
 */
private void cleanUp ( )
{
    getreminderPanel().saveCurrentCategory();

    try {
       this.saveTable();
    } catch (java.lang.Throwable ivjExc) {
       handleException(ivjExc);
    }
    dispose();
    return;
}
```

Delete the two connections from the frame's windowClosed event. Their functions are replaced by the `cleanUp()` method. Also, delete the connection from the ExitMenuItem to the frame's dispose() method. The Create Application SmartGuide created this connection.

Make the following connection:

```
ReminderApp (windowClosed event) → free-form surface (Event to code...)
```

Select the cleanUp() method from the middle drop-down list.

As you can see, this is a much cleaner design and a good example of how a little hand coding can replace a lot of connections. In this case, we saved six connections. This code not only performs better, but it also removes some complexity from the Visual Composition Editor display. See Figure 11.23 with no hidden connections.

Figure 11.23 Simplified connections.

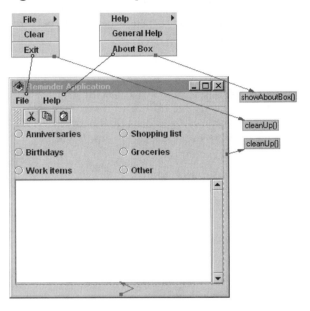

Activating Clear

The next function to implement is the one that clears the text area using the option in the main menu.

Because the JTextArea bean does not have a clear method, you will use the setText(java.lang.String) method, passing as a parameter an empty string. As you remember, the text area is part of the ReminderPanel bean and, as such, encapsulates its features in the bean, making them inaccessible in the ReminderApp.

Open the Visual Composition Editor for the ReminderPanel bean. Select the text area and promote the **this** property. Accept the proposed name of the promoted feature, **reminderText**. Save the bean.

Go back to the Visual Composition Editor for the ReminderApp. Select the reminderPanel bean, right mouse click, and select **Tear-Off Property....** From the list of available properties, select **reminderText**. See Figure 11.24. Drop the property on the free-form surface. This object represents the text area on the reminder panel bean. Name the torn-off property **reminderText**. Now you can connect to its features. Connect:

```
ClearMenuItem(actionPerformed) → reminderText(text)
```

Notice that the connection is dashed, indicating that a parameter is needed. Double-click the connection, and in the property sheet for the connection, press the **Set parameters** button.

Figure 11.24   Selecting a property to tear off.

The next window enables you to pass a constant parameter to the setTextArea(java.lang.String t) method. You want to pass an empty string, so you do not need to enter anything in the **Value** entry field. Do not enter anything; just press **OK** and **OK** again to close the previous window. The connection remains dashed, even though you attempted to enter the required parameter. If you save the bean and look at the generated code, you will see:

```
getreminderText().setText(new java.lang.String());
```

This will do what you want: set the text in the text area to an empty string. However, it is not a good idea to leave a dashed connection in the Visual Composition Editor, as it indicates (falsely, in this case) that something is missing.

To make the connection solid, you must enter something in the Value column of the window and press **OK** to accept it. Press the **Set parameters** button again and delete what you previously typed, effectively leaving an empty string in the Value column. Press **OK** and **OK** again to close the previous window. Now the connection is solid. The generated code in this case looks a little different but still performs the same function:

```
getreminderText().setText("");
```

Test the application again and verify that the text in the input area clears when selecting **Clear** from the File menu. It should also work when you press the Ctrl-C accelerator key.

Enabling the Toolbar Buttons

Now that the reminderText tear-off property is available to you on the free-form surface, it is very easy to implement the functions of the toolbar buttons.

Make the following connections:

```
CutButton(actionPerformed) → reminderText(cut)
CopyButton(actionPerformed) → reminderText(copy)
PasteButton(actionPerformed) → reminderText(paste)
```

The clipboard functions, exploited by the toolbar button through the connections above, are part of the implementation of the **JTextComponent** bean. Since the **JTextArea** extends JTextComponent these functions are available to it as well.

At this point, it is probably a good idea to create a new version of the reminder package.

Activating Help

Adding basic help to an application is not very hard to do. Adding context-sensitive help is another story. One way to implement a simple yet effective help system is to create an .html home page, which is used to browse a local Web site that contains the help for the program. The home page can link to other pages containing the details of the help system.

> **NOTE**
>
> At the time of this writing, JavaHelp is being developed. It is a system and browser independent help system for Java programs. See http://java.sun.com/features/1999/04/javahelp.html for up-to-date developments on this front.

You will implement basic help for the ReminderApp. Selecting **General help** from the Help menu starts a Web browser in another process. The browser starts in the Help's home page for the program.

The most complex part of coding this implementation is determining where the browser is installed. Different operating systems offer different services to find out which is the default browser installed in the system.

Most of these services are used through operating system APIs and must be accessed by native Java methods. First determine which operating system the program is running under using the System.getProperty("os.name") static method. Then choose the appropriate way to determine the default browser for that operating system. This implementation is beyond the scope of this book.

If you are running under an operating system that allows associations between file types and executable programs, you can start the browser automatically by "starting" the actual file or URL. One such system is Windows. If you double-click on an **html** or **htm** type of file and the Web browser opens displaying the selected file, you know that there is an association between that file type and the Web browser. In that case, you might want to use the default browser to display **Help** for your application See "Using the Default Browser," later in this chapter.

In the ReminderApp, the user tells the program which browser to use. The program remembers this information by storing it in the ReminderHashtable, which is already persisted.

Start by dropping another **MenuItem** bean on top of the Help menu, below the General Help menu item already there. Open its property sheet and change the following:

- actionCommand to **Browser**
- beanName to **Browser_setupMenuItem**
- text to **Browser setup...**

 From the **AWT** palette, drop a **FileDialog** bean on the free-form surface somewhere close to Help menu. Name this bean **fileDialog**. Open its property sheet and set:

- file to ***.exe**
- modal to **true**
- title to Select **WEB Browser Executable file**

Make the following connections:

```
Browser_setupMenuItem(actionPerformed) → fileDialog(show)
Browser_setupMenuItem(actionPerformed) → fileDialog(dispose)
Browser_setupMenuItem(actionPerformed) →
free-form surface(Event to code...)
```

In the Event to Code dialog now showing, create and select a new private method called **setBrowser**, which returns void and takes two **java.lang.String** parameters. Name the parameters *directory* and *fileName*. The code in the method makes up a fully qualified path to your Web browser and stores it in the ReminderHashtable.

```
/**
 * This method was created by a SmartGuide.
 * @param fileName java.lang.String
 */
private void setBrowser ( java.lang.String directory,
      java.lang.String fileName)
{
    if(fileName != null)
    {
      getreminderPanel().gettheTable().put("Browser Location",
          directory + fileName);
    }
}
```

```
    return;

}
```

From fileDialog, connect as parameters to the previous connection:

```
fileDialog(directory) → connection(directory)
fileDialog(file) → connection(fileName)
```

Save the bean.

You might be wondering how this sequence of connections works. The first connection between Browser_setupMenuItem and the show() method of the file dialog does just that; it makes the file dialog appear. Because it is modal, the call to show() does not return until the file dialog closes, either by pressing the **Cancel** or the **OK** button. At that point, the call returns and the dispose() method executes, removing the file dialog from the screen. Next, the call to setBrowser() executes, getting its parameters from the file dialog. If the **Cancel** button was pressed, the *file* property of the file dialog is null.

In the setBrowser() method, the *directory* and *fileName* parameters are concatenated and saved in the Hashtable using a key of **Browser Location**. Because the Hashtable is serialized and saved when the program exits, we have a way of remembering this setting.

You could add a number of improvements to this simple implementation. For example, you could disable **General help** until the browser setup completes. Or better still, when the user selects **General help** for the first time, you could invoke the setBrowser routines to do the initial setting. We have chosen the approach you just implemented because it shows all the steps necessary to accomplish the task. We leave these refinements as an exercise to the reader.

Finally, the application is ready to display HTML help. All that remains to do is to make one connection and add a few lines of code. Follow these steps to complete the ReminderApp:

Connect:

```
miGeneralHelp(actionPerformed) → free-form surface(Event to code...)
```

In the Event to Code window now showing, create and select a new private method called **showHelp**, which returns void and takes no parameters.

Save the bean.

The showHelp() method checks to see if a browser location has been set. If the query to the Hashtable does not return an empty string, the fully qualified path to the help home page is constructed and concatenated with the fully qualified path name to the browser. Then the Runtime.exec() method is called to start a new process, invoking the browser and passing as a parameter the starting HTML page.

Switch to the Members page of the browser. Select the
showHelp()method and add the highlighted code:

```
/**
* This method was created by a SmartGuide.
*/
private void showHelp ( ){
  String browser =
    (String)getreminderPanel().
    gettheTable().get("Browser Location");
  if (browser.equals("") == false)
  {
    try
    {
      String userDir =
        System.getProperty("user.dir");
      String helpFile = " " + userDir +
        "\\reminder\\reminderHome.html";
      Runtime.getRuntime().exec( browser +
        helpFile);
    }
    catch (java.io.IOException e) {}
  }
  return;
}
```

Using the Default Browser
If your operating system supports file associations, you may want to try the next
variation of the **showHelp**() method:

```
/**
* This method was created by a SmartGuide.
*/
private void showHelp() {
  String browser = (String) getreminderPanel().
    gettheTable().get("Browser Location");
  String userDir = System.getProperty("user.dir");
  String helpFile = userDir +
    "\\reminder\\reminderHome.html";
  if (browser.equals("") == true) {
    try {
      Runtime.getRuntime().exec("start \"" +
        helpFile + "\"");
```

```
    }
    catch (java.io.IOException e) {}
  }
  else {
    try {
      Runtime.getRuntime().exec(browser + " " +
        helpFile);
    }
    catch (java.io.IOException e) {}
  }
  return;
}
```

In this version of the code, if no entry for the **Browser Location** is found in the hashtable, the default browser is started with the name of the Help .html file.

If you are running inside VisualAge for Java, make sure that you have copied the .html, .gif, and .jpg files from the reminder directory in the CD-ROM to the same directory where you placed the other resources for the project. Usually this directory is: X:\IBMVJava\Ide\project_resources\My Project\reminder where X is the drive where you installed VisualAge for Java. Figure 11.25 shows the completed ReminderApp with all connections.

Figure 11.25 Completed ReminderApp.

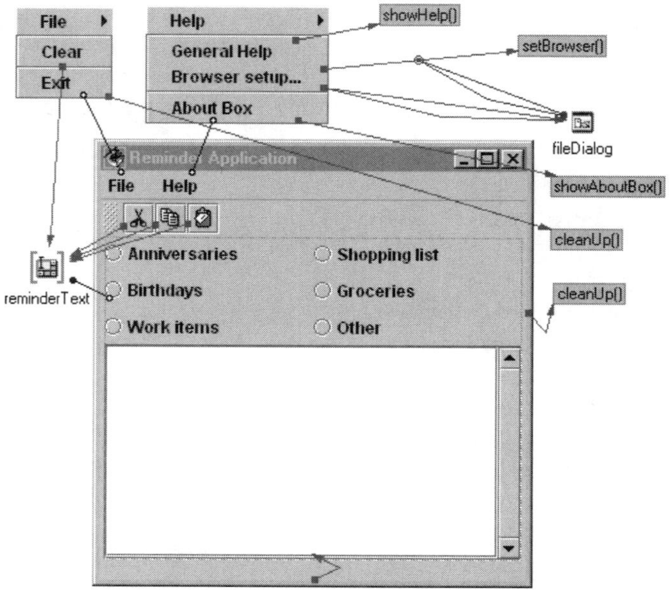

Exporting and Running the Reminder Application

In the Workbench, select the reminder package and export the Java classes and resources to the directory where you want to run the application from. In addition to the exported code, you will have to make available **swingall.jar** in your classpath.

NOTE

Use the swingall.jar file supplied with the CD-ROM. The version of VisualAge for Java included with the CD uses a downlevel version of Swing. A version of VisualAge for Java with the version of Swing in JDK 1.2 is available from IBM at www.ibm.com/software/vadd/Data/Document3793.

Make sure that you have selected the **.java** and the **resource** checkboxes on the Export SmartGuide. You will also have to press the **Details** button beside the resource checkbox and select the **My Project** checkbox. That way, you are assured to export all necessary resources belonging to the project. When asked, choose to overwrite the existing files.

Open a command window and type **java reminder.ReminderApp**. This starts the program running. If you have not yet set the browser information, you should do that now by selecting **Browser setup** from the Help menu. The system's file dialog appears. Find the location of your browser and press **OK** as shown in Figure 11.26.

Figure 11.26   Setting the Web browser.

Figure 11.27 Displaying help in browser.

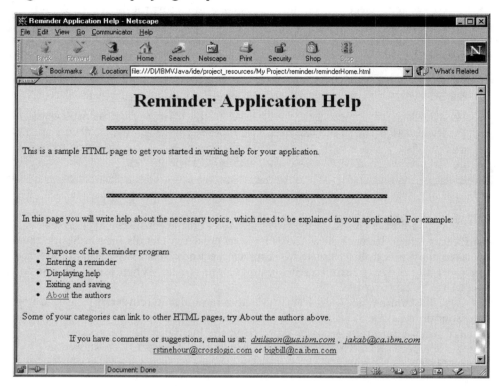

Now that the program knows which Web browser to use, go ahead and select **General help** from the Help menu. The selected browser appears, displaying your help home page, as shown in Figure 11.27.

Summary

We covered a lot of new concepts in this chapter. You built a new application from the ground up. This chapter covered:

- The Create Application SmartGuide
- Menus
- Submenus
- Embedded beans
- JCheckboxGroup

- JRadioButton
- JScrollPane
- JTextArea
- Hashtable
- Event-to-Code connections
- File dialogs
- Displaying .html Help

All of these beans and features give you a broader knowledge of Java programming and prepare you for making your own programs.

What's in Chapter 12

In this chapter, you construct a database application that lets you view and edit database records. You use many new beans included with VisualAge for Java and also beans that come with this book. Some of the beans you use are:

- Select
- SelectTable
- SelectStatus
- NumericField
- UpperCaseField
- JTabbedPane

This chapter combines the above beans to create a complete Java application that you can use as a base for other projects that access databases.

In this chapter, you create a complete application to view, traverse, and edit records in a database. The instructions to build the example in this chapter assume you are running DB2 and have the Sample database installed. The English version of DB2 Personal Edition is on the CD-ROM that accompanies this book. Follow the instructions provided on the CD-ROM and install DB2 and its Sample database. If you have another database manager installed, the exercise will work, but you must substitute the DB2 specific steps with ones for your database.

The application consists of a JTabbedPane with two pages. The first page lets you connect to the database and traverse through its records. You can modify, add, and delete records from the database table, as shown in Figure 12.1.

In addition to the entry panel, this page includes a navigation bar and a status area.

The second page of the application contains a table view of all of the records in the table. See Figure 12.2. In this page, you can select any record and then switch to the Edit entry page and alter the record.

The table view is based on a pre-built Swing component called SelectTable. It is available on the CD-ROM and you must import it into VisualAge for Java before you can use it to build this exercise. The SelectTable bean is one of the

Figure 12.1 Edit view of the Database editor.

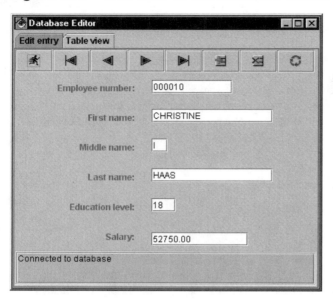

Figure 12.2 Table view of the Database editor.

many components readily available from VisualAge Developer Domain (VADD) at http://www.ibm.com/software/vadd. If you are working with VisualAge for Java, you should become a member of VADD. There is no charge to register for membership, and it offers many benefits, including free beans, code samples, access to support, and program updates. See the links to VADD on the installation section of the CD-ROM.

Introduction to Database Access

There are many ways to access databases from programs created in VisualAge for Java, including:

- Hand coding using the JDBC (Java Database Connectivity) specification
- Data Access Beans
- Data Access Builder (Enterprise edition only)
- VisualAge Persistence Framework (Enterprise edition only)

You can use the first three methods to access databases that don't have complex relationships between tables and object model. They provide a simple mapping between the database tables and Java objects.

Coding using JDBC is easy and involves a few classes with simple methods. JDBC isolates the program logic from the drudgery of accessing the database. It provides a layer that allows you to change database managers and access methods with minimal programming changes.

VisualAge for Java provides the Data Access beans with all editions. These beans are built on JDBC and provide all the benefits of JDBC with improvement on many of its shortfalls. The **Select** and the **DBNavigator** beans encapsulate most of the functionality of the Data Access beans.

The Data Access Builder, in the VisualAge for Java Enterprise Edition, provides a visual way to construct a variety of beans that you can later combine to provide database access to your applications. The beans produced by the Data Access Builder are highly customizable and provide GUI beans to display the table-formatted result set and an input panel. They also produce non-GUI beans that represent the datastore, the database, and a row in the database. These beans can also contain custom methods that are created at build time and they can encapsulate more complex queries in a single method.

To handle complex relationships, you need a framework that you can use to map the object model of your application to the tables in one or more databases. One such framework is the VisualAge Persistence Framework, which is part of VisualAge for Java Enterprise Edition.

For the exercises in this chapter, you use the Data Access beans to access the Employee table of the DB2 Sample database.

Building the Database Editor

This exercise contains many sub-components. You start building the beans for this exercise from the bottom up, in the following sequence:

- EmployeePanel
- EmployeeView
- DBEditor

In the construction of these composite GUI beans, you use other beans that are supplied either on the CD-ROM or with the product. The following list includes some of these beans:

- Select
- SelectTable
- SelectStatus
- UpperCaseField
- NumericField

You also use several other components from the Swing libraries.

Building the EmployeePanel Bean

The EmployeePanel bean is built on a **JPanel**. It contains a number of special text fields used to view and edit the data that corresponds to particular fields of a database record.

It also contains a **Select** bean used to access the database, and connections between the Select bean and the text fields.

Adding the Data Access Beans to the Workspace

Before you begin building the EmployeePanel, you need to add the **IBM Data Access Beans** feature to the VisualAge for Java Workspace.

If you haven't yet added the Data Access Beans feature, perform the following steps: start VisualAge for Java. When the **Workbench** window appears, select File, and then Quick Start, or press **F2**. Select **Features** and **Add Feature** from the **Quick Start** dialog, and press **OK**.

Select **Data Access Beans** from the available features and press **OK**. See Figure 12.3.

Adding this feature not only creates the Data Access Beans project in the workspace, but it also creates a **Database** category on the beans palette of the Visual Composition Editor.

Verify that you now have the IBM Data Access Beans project on the Workbench. If you don't see it, add the feature again before continuing.

Figure 12.3   Adding Data Access Beans feature.

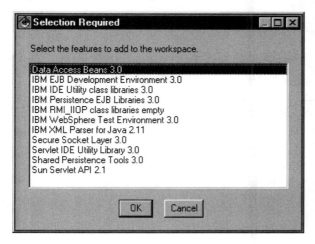

Creating the EmployeePanel Class

Import the **com.ibm.vajbook.textfields** package from the CD-ROM into the My Projects project. This package is part of the **answers.dat** file in the **Answers** directory of the CD-ROM. It contains classes that implement the special text fields:

- NumericField
- UpperCaseField

    Create a new package in the My Projects project called **dataaccess**.

    Start by creating a new class in the **dataaccess** package. Call this class **EmployeePanel**. Make its superclass **JPanel**. Select the **Browse the class when finished** and **Compose the class visually** check boxes. Press the **Finish** button to create the class.

    Set the layout of the panel to GridBag. Drop six JLabel beans onto the panel. Change the text of the labels to:

- Employee number:
- First name:
- Middle initial:
- Last name:
- Education level:
- Salary:

    Set the **horizontalAlignment** and **horizontalTextPosition** properties to **RIGHT**.

Set the **constraints, anchor** property for each of the labels to **EAST**. And the **constraints, fill** property to **NONE**.

Tip

If you want to drop many beans of the same type, you can select the bean from the palette while holding the Ctrl key. This sets sticky selection mode and the cursor remains loaded with the selected bean, allowing you to drop it multiple times. To cancel sticky mode, press the **arrow** icon on the palette, or select another bean.

Opposite to the labels, on a second column of the panel, drop the following special text fields. Name and adjust the properties of the text fields as specified in Table 12.1.

Set the **trimBlanks** property to **true** on all the text fields.

Set the **columns** property of the text fields to two characters larger than the maxLength property.

Set the **constraints, anchor** property for each of the labels to **WEST**. Set the **constraints, fill** property to **NONE**.

Once you finish adding all the beans and modifying their properties, the Visual Composition Editor for the EmployeePanel bean should look like Figure 12.4.

These fields correspond to the columns of the Employee table in the Sample database. For the sake of brevity, you only display and alter the columns that cannot have a NULL value as defined in the database. If you wish, you may add other columns to the panel and later, to the Select bean.

Both the NumericField and the UpperCaseField are extensions of SpecialTextField, which in turn extends JTextField. SpecialTextField adds the abil-

Table 12.1   Text Field Properties

Bean			Accept	
Type	Name	Max Length	Decimal Point	Sign
NumericField	NtfEmpNumber	6	false	false
UpperCaseField	UcfFirstName	12	N/A	N/A
UpperCaseField	UcfMiddleName	1	N/A	N/A
UpperCaseField	ucfLastName	15	N/A	N/A
NumericField	ntfEdLevel	2	false	false
NumericField	ntfSalary	10	true	false

Figure 12.4   Employee panel so far.

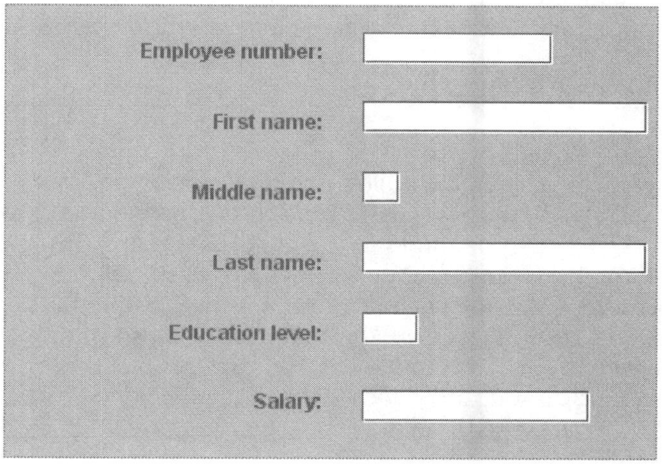

Employee number:

First name:

Middle name:

Last name:

Education level:

Salary:

ity to limit the number of characters entered into the text field as specified by the **maxLength** property.

You can remove blanks from strings used to set the text of these text fields by setting the **trimBlanks** property. Trimming is especially important when you have a limited number of characters in the text field. If you have blanks at the end of the displayed string that extend it to the set maxLength, you cannot enter any more characters. Many database managers pad column entries to the maximum column width. When setting database column text on a text field, it is prudent to remove these extra blanks.

The NumericField bean is based on the JTextField Swing component. It only allows you to enter numbers. Setting the allowDecimalPoint and allowSign properties can further customize the bean. The allowDecimalPoint property will allow one period "." to appear anywhere on the number. The allowSign property will allow a plus "+" or minus "-" sign in the first position of the field.

The UpperCaseField converts any alphabetical character entered to upper case. The conversion also works on strings that you drop into the text field.

The full source for both these special text fields is provided. You can use these examples to create your own special text fields.

Setting the Select Bean

In the next step, you add a **Select** bean to the free-form surface. The Select bean is part of the **com.ibm.ivj.db.uibeans** package.

With the Visual Composition Editor for the EmployeePanel bean open, select the Database category from the beans palette. Drop a **Select** bean to the right of the panel you just built. Name the bean **dbSelect**.

The Select bean is fairly complex and encapsulates the entire behavior necessary to connect and query a database. It requires quite a bit of setting up before you can actually use it in a program. The next few steps guide you through this setup process.

> **NOTE**
>
> Before you can connect to the database while running inside VisualAge for Java, you need to let VisualAge know where to find the database drivers. In the case of DB2, they can be found in the file **db2java.zip**. This file exists in the **\sqllib\java** directory on the drive where DB2 is installed. Select the **Windows, Options** items from the menu bar. On the **Options** dialog, select **Resources** and on the **Workspace class path** entry field enter the fully qualified path to the file. You can also press the **Edit** button, then the **Jar/Zip...** button to locate the file.

Double-click on **dbSelect** to access its property sheet. It looks innocent enough. There are three properties in the non-expert mode that you can set: beanName, query, and readOnly.

Set the readOnly property to **false**. Select the **query** property and press the button on the right- hand column opposite to the property name. See Figure 12.5.

Now you proceed through the **Query** SmartGuide dialogs to define the class, which contains the methods defining your connection to the database and the actual SQL query.

The first step is to define the package, the name of the class that contains the connection specification, and the SQL query that makes access to the Employee table of the Sample database possible. See Figure 12.6.

Figure 12.5   Setting the query property.

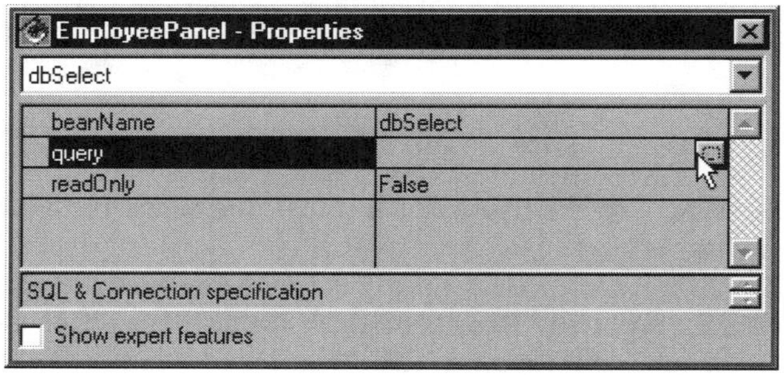

Figure 12.6   Define the Data Access Class.

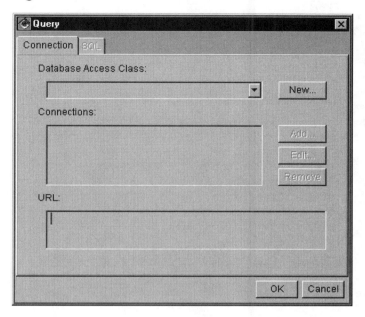

Press the **New...** button on the **Query** dialog. In the **New Database Access Class** dialog that opens, enter **dataaccess** for the Package name and **SelectBeanDefinition** for the Class name. Press **OK**. See Figure 12.7.

Back on the **Query** dialog, press the **Add...** button to define a new Connection Alias. See Figure 12.8. On the **Connection Alias Definition** dialog,

Figure 12.7   Defining the class name.

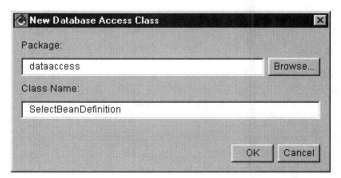

Figure 12.8   Define the Connection Alias.

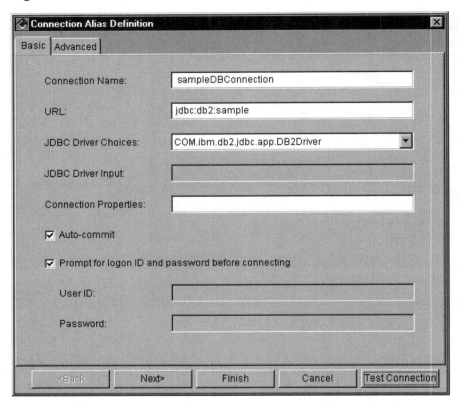

enter **sampleDBConnection** as the Connection Name. Make sure that the **Auto-commit** checkbox is selected.

Setting auto-commit commits each successful transaction without the need to explicitly do so. One disadvantage of setting auto-commit is that you cannot easily roll back changes to the database. However, for this exercise, it reduces the complexity of the user interface. After completing this exercise, you should experiment with this setting to see the results of both the Commit and the Rollback methods of the Select bean.

Set the JDBC driver to **COM.ibm.db2.jdbc.app.DB2Driver**. This driver is used when the database manager is installed on the same machine as the program running the queries. It provides, in this case, the best performance.

The example in this book was built under Windows 98. DB2 does not implement database security when running under Windows 98. Therefore, there is no need to select the **Prompt for logon ID...** checkbox, or to actually provide a **User ID** and **Password** on this dialog. If you are running under an operating system that implements security, for example Windows NT, you must either select the checkbox, or provide the values in this dialog. If you enter a password on the dialog, it is encoded and unreadable in the generated code.

Press the **Test Connection** button to make sure that the parameters you entered are valid and allow a connection to the database. Before you press the button, ensure that your database manager has been started. In the case of DB2, if the default installation parameters were used, the database manager starts automatically when the system starts.

There are a variety of reasons why the database manager may not be running in your system. If you need to start it, issue the **DB2START** command from a Command Prompt window. You should get a confirmation that DB2 has started. Pressing the **Test Connection** button connects you to the database and produces the message shown in Figure 12.9. Press **Finish**.

To continue defining the properties of **dbSelect**, switch to the **SQL** page of the **Query** dialog. Press the **Add...** button to create a new query. The next series of SmartGuides takes you on a step-by-step process to create the exact query you need.

The first step is to name the SQL Specification. You can reuse SQL specs in other instances of Select beans. They appear on a list of available connections and are associated with a particular Data Access Class. See Figure 12.10.

Enter **employeeTable** as the **SQL Name**. Ensure that the **Use SQL Assist SmartGuide** radio button is selected, and press the **OK** button.

A connection to the database is established. This is necessary for the SmartGuide to learn about the database you have selected and customize the next set of dialogs. Figure 12.11 shows the first page of a tabbed dialog where you finish defining the SQL statement. Note that you do not need to know how to write SQL to use the SmartGuide. All you must do is go through a selection process that identifies your needs. The SmartGuide, using this information, then constructs the SQL statement.

First, ensure that the **Select** radio button is selected, then pick which tables you want to access. For this example, locate and select the EMPLOYEE table. The prefix of the table name is the name of the user who was logged on to the

Figure 12.9   Successful connection.

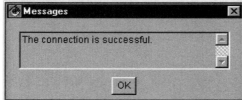

Figure 12.10 New SQL Specification.

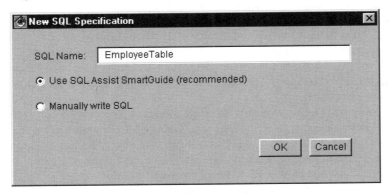

Figure 12.11 Selecting the database table.

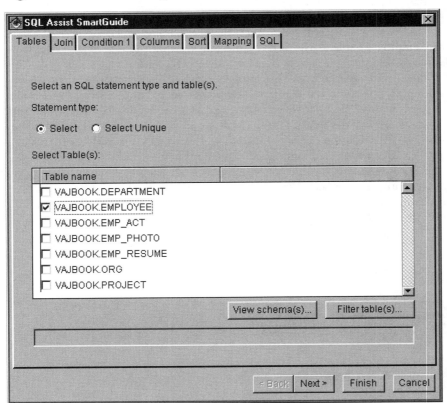

computer when the database was installed, in our case VAJBOOK. In a multiple user system, the prefix, or schema, fully qualifies the table name.

You can select more than one table to perform a **join**. In order to join two or more tables, they must share a column. Since the tables EMPLOYEE and EMP_PHOTO both have an EMPNO column, you can join them. You can use the EMPNO column of the EMPLOYEE table as the foreign key into the EMP_PHOTO table. For this exercise, you do not perform any joins and only need to select the EMPLOYEE table.

Since you are not joining tables, skip the **Join** page of the SmartGuide and move directly to the **Condition** page, as in Figure 12.12. In this page, you give the SmartGuide the selection criteria for this query. For the exercise, select **EMPNO is not blank** to display all employees assigned an employee number.

Notice that under the Columns list near the bottom of the page, an explanation of the query appears.

Figure 12.12   Setting the selection condition.

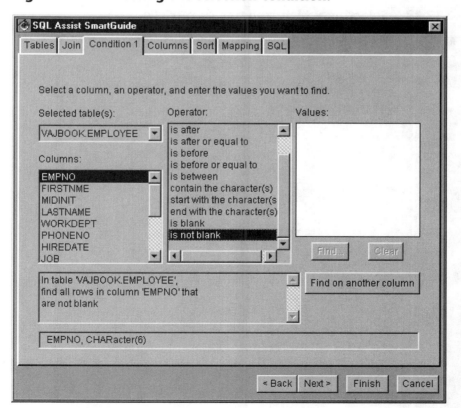

If you want to refine your query by adding another condition, press the **Find on another column** button. Doing so creates another Conditions page where you can further define the selection condition. For this exercise you only enter one condition as mentioned above.

Next, you must decide which columns the query retrieves. For the purpose of simplicity, retrieve only the columns that cannot contain NULL values, as defined in the database. In the **Columns** page of the SmartGuide, select the following columns from the **Columns** list:

- EMPNO
- FIRSTNME
- MIDINIT
- LASTNAME
- EDLEVEL
- SALARY

Figure 12.13   Selecting which columns to retrieve.

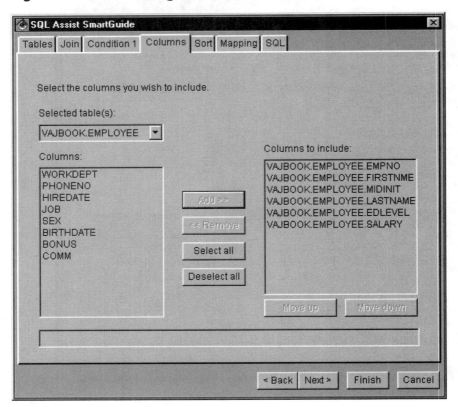

Once you have selected all of the above columns, press the **Add >>** button to move the selected columns to the **Columns to include** list.

If you want to change the order in which you retrieve the columns, reorder them by selecting a column name and using the **Move up** and **Move down** buttons until you achieve the order you desire. See Figure 12.13.

In the next page, you add the sorting order to the SQL statement you are building. For this exercise, select the EMPNO column, press the **Add >>** button, and select **Ascending** for the sort order. You can sort on multiple columns and arrange the various columns according to your needs. Be aware that complex sort patterns seldom produce the expected results. Try to restrict your sort clause to a maximum of two or three columns. See Figure 12.14.

On the **Mapping** page of the SmartGuide, you can modify the default mapping of the selected columns. The **Select** bean performs type conversion between database types (such as VARCHAR, INT, or SMALLINT) to the corresponding Java type (such as String or Integer). By changing the type of a column, you effectively change the corresponding Java type available through the Select bean.

Figure 12.14   Defining the sort column.

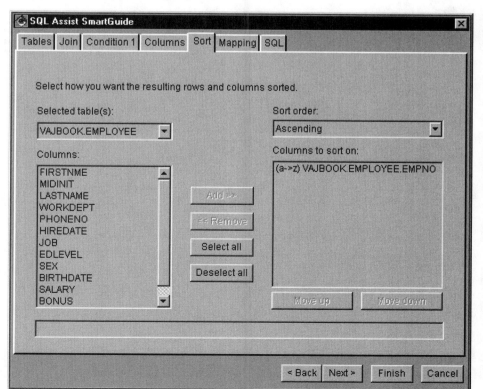

The last page of the SmartGuide displays the complete SQL statement you defined. From this window, you can execute the statement and see if you are retrieving what you need for your application. If the statement is not exactly what you need, go back through the pages of the SmartGuide and refine your query. See Figure 12.15.

Press the **Run SQL...** button and a dialog similar to that in Figure 12.16 appears. You can save the results of the query to a text file. Press the **Close** button to return to the SmartGuide. Press **Finish** on the SmartGuide.

Closing the SmartGuide brings you back to the **Query** dialog. At this point, you have completed defining the connection alias and the SQL query for the **dbSelect** bean. (See Figure 12.17.) Press the **OK** button to complete the generation of the methods in the **SelectBeanDefinition** class you created.

Figure 12.15   Completed SQL statement.

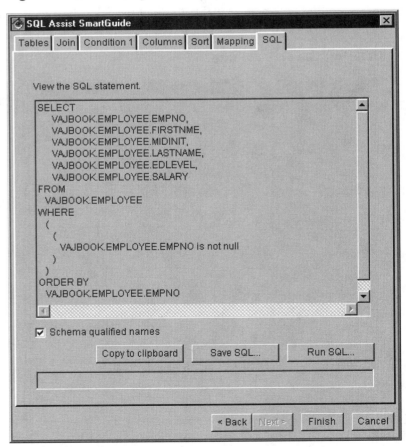

Figure 12.16 SQL result table.

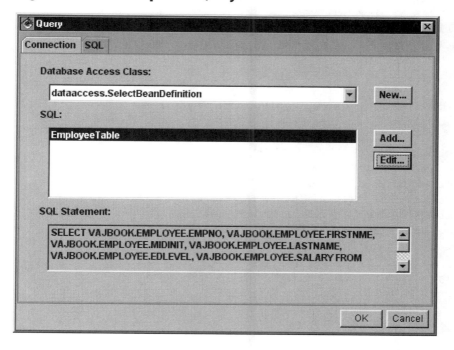

Figure 12.17 Completed Query.

Viewing Generated Methods

Return to the Workbench and find the **SelectBeanDefinition** class under the **dataaccess** package. The two methods that you created with the SmartGuide appear:

- employeeTable()
- sampleDBConnection()

Examining the code reveals nothing unexpected; the first method creates, initializes, and returns a **StatementMetaData** object named **aSpec**.

```
public static StatementMetaData employeeTable()
  throws Throwable
{
 String name = "dataaccess.SelectBeanDefinition.EmployeeTable";

 String statement = "SELECT
   VAJBOOK.EMPLOYEE.EMPNO,
   VAJBOOK.EMPLOYEE.FIRSTNME,
   VAJBOOK.EMPLOYEE.MIDINIT,
   VAJBOOK.EMPLOYEE.LASTNAME,
   VAJBOOK.EMPLOYEE.EDLEVEL,
   VAJBOOK.EMPLOYEE.SALARY FROM VAJBOOK.EMPLOYEE
   WHERE ( ( VAJBOOK.EMPLOYEE.EMPNO is not
     null))
   ORDER BY VAJBOOK.EMPLOYEE.EMPNO";

 StatementMetaData aSpec = null;
 try{
   aSpec = new StatementMetaData();
   aSpec.setName(name);
   aSpec.setSQL(statement);
   aSpec.addTable("VAJBOOK.EMPLOYEE");
   aSpec.addColumn("EMPLOYEE.EMPNO", 1,1);
   aSpec.addColumn("EMPLOYEE.FIRSTNME", 12,12);
   aSpec.addColumn("EMPLOYEE.MIDINIT", 1,1);
   aSpec.addColumn("EMPLOYEE.LASTNAME", 12,12);
   aSpec.addColumn("EMPLOYEE.EDLEVEL", 5,5);
   aSpec.addColumn("EMPLOYEE.SALARY", 3,3);
 }
 catch(java.lang.Throwable e){throw e;}
 return aSpec;
}
```

The first string defines the name of the query. The second string is the actual SQL statement that runs every time the **execute()** method of the **dbSelect** bean is called. The next line of code declares a **StatementMetaData** object. It is then initialized with the query name string, the SQL statement string.

Next, the database table is defined and the desired columns of the EMPLOYEE database table are added to the spec. The numbers after the column names correspond to definitions on the **java.sql.Types** package, and they identify the target and source SQLTypes of the column. In this case, they are the same because you did not change any of the column mappings when you defined the query.

After the last line of "real" code in this method, you find several other lines, which look like a hexadecimal dump:

```
/*V2.0
**start of SQL Assist data**
504b030414g08g08g8e7b9e25gggggggggggggg0cggg6275696
278939785314b5a00805c153d88fb4507a8a344a341fd2944ae9a1f4204591a2652382e
0c9c7b12fe33308e2c177309328
993d7808841fbf ÷
**end of SQL Assist data**/
```

The SQL Assist SmartGuide uses this data to interpret the information you entered the last time you used it to generate this method. You should not delete or change anything in this area of the method. Even though it looks like a multiline comment it is actual data used by the SmartGuide.

The second generated method creates, initializes, and returns a **DatabaseConnection** object named **connection**:

```
public static com.ibm.db.DatabaseConnection
   sampleDBConnection() throws Throwable,
   com.ibm.db.DataException
{
  com.ibm.db.DatabaseConnection
    connection = null;
  try{
    connection = new com.ibm.db.DatabaseConnection();

    connection.setConnectionAlias("
      dataaccess.SelectBeanDefinition.
      SampleDBConnection");

    connection.setDriverName("COM.ibm.db2.jdbc.app.DB2Driver");


    connection.setDataSourceName("jdbc:db2:sample");
```

```
    connection.setUserID("");
    connection.setPassword("", true);
    connection.setPromptUID(false);
    connection.setAutoCommit(true);
  }
  catch(com.ibm.db.DataException e){throw e;}
  catch(java.lang.Throwable e){throw e;}
  return connection;
}
```

To initialize the connection object, you must perform several steps. First, set the connection alias name. This is the name used to make the connection. If a connection already exists for the connection alias, in this or other Select beans, the connection is shared.

The data source name is the URL that defines where the database can be found. The URL contains the database type and name.

The next two lines define the userid and the password used to establish the connection. As explained before, you do not need these, because we built this example on a Windows 98 system. The setPromptUID() method sets the promptUID property to false. This indicates that you do not want a dialog to appear to prompt the user to enter the userid and password.

If you are building this exercise on a system that supports and enforces security, like Windows NT, you have different values here. In that case, you should either set the **promptUID** parameter to **true**, or you should hard code the userid and password properties in the connection object. We recommend the former. Of course, these properties are not set directly on the method, but on the **Connection Alias Definition** dialog. See Figure 12.8.

Connecting the dbSelect Bean

Return to the Visual Composition Editor for the Employee panel bean. So far, you should see the panel with the six labels and the six text fields, and a Select bean.

Next you connect the dbSelect bean to the text fields on the panel. Make property-to-property connections, using the dbSelect beans as the source, to the text fields on the panel:

```
dbSelect(EMPLOYEE.EMPNO_String)    → ntfEmpNo(text)
dbSelect(EMPLOYEE.FIRSTNME_String) → utfFirstName(text)
dbSelect(EMPLOYEE.MIDINIT_String)  → utfMiddleInitial(text)
dbSelect(EMPLOYEE.LASTNAME_String) → utfLastName(text)
dbSelect(EMPLOYEE.EDLEVEL_String)  → ntfEdLvl(text)
dbSelect(EMPLOYEE.SALARY_String)   → ntfSalary(text)
```

You probably noticed that there are three properties for each column in the database: one of type String, one of the equivalent Java types of the native database type. When connecting to text fields, you use the String type property. Your Visual Composition Editor should look like Figure 12.18.

Figure 12.18   Completed connections.

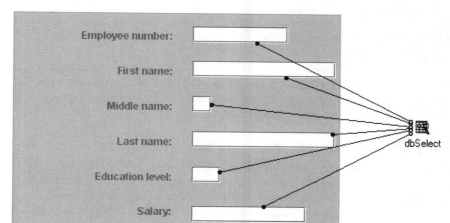

The next step is to adjust the properties of each of the connections to ensure that they are bi-directional. For example, for the first connection, the source and target events are EMPLOYEE.EMPNO_String and keyReleased, respectively. Refer to Figure 12.19. Repeat for each of the connections on this panel.

Figure 12.19   Setting source and target events.

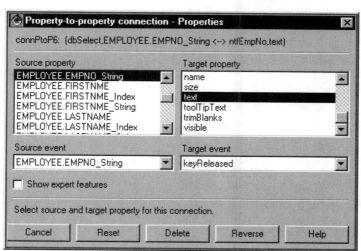

The last thing to do with this bean is to promote the **this** property of the **dbSelect** bean. Select **dbSelect**, click the right mouse button, and from the pop-up menu select **Promote Bean Feature…**. From the Property list, select **this**. Ensure that the **Promoted name** is set to **dbSelect**. Save the EmployeePanel bean and close the Visual Composition Editor.

The EmployeePanel bean is by far the most complex part of this exercise. You are now ready to make the next bean, EmployeeView, which incorporates the EmployeePanel into a fully functional bean to display and update the EMPLOYEE table of the Sample database.

Building the EmployeeView Bean

The EmployeeView bean combines the **EmployeePanel** bean, a **DBNavigator** bean from the **com.ibm.ivj.db.uibeans** package, a **SelectStatus** bean, and an information area to display exceptions and messages implemented as **JTextArea** inside of a **JScrollPane**. See Figure 12.20. You can easily make it all work together with a few connections.

Start by creating a new class in the **dataaccess** package. Call this class **EmployeeView**. Make its superclass **JPanel**. Select the **Browse the class when finished** checkbox and the **Compose the class visually** checkbox. Press the **Finish** button to create the class.

Figure 12.20   Components of EmployeeView.

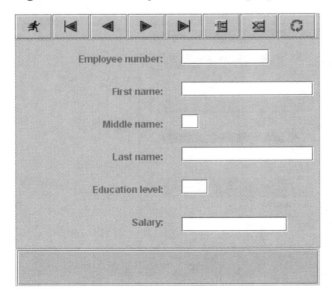

Set the layout of **EmployeeView** to **BorderLayout**. Select the Database category from the beans palette and drop a **DBNavigator** bean on the north cell of **EmployeeView**. Name the bean **dbNavigator**. The DBNavigator bean works together with a Select bean and provides a customizable tool bar. You can use the DBNavigator to traverse the result set in the Select bean. You can also add and delete rows, and commit and rollback transactions. For this exercise, since you are using auto-commit, you do not display the commit and the rollback buttons. Double-click **dbNavigator** to show its property sheet, and set the **showCommit** and **showRollback** properties to false.

Using the **Choose Bean...** icon from the beans palette, add an EmployeePanel bean to the center cell of EmployeeView. Name it **employeePanel**.

From the Swing category of the beans palette, drop a JScrollPane on the south cell of EmployeeView and a JTextArea on top of the scroll pane. Name the text area **infoarea**. Double click on infoarea to open its property sheet. Set the following properties:

- background = System, text color
- lineWrap = true
- rows = 3
- editable = false

Your Visual Composition Editor should look very much like Figure 12.20. In order for dbNavigator to work, you must associate it with a Select bean. In your case, the one that is part of employeePanel. As you remember, you promoted the **this** property of dbSelect in the EmployeePanel bean. Now you need to tear it off from employeePanel so you can use it. Select employeePanel, open the pop-up menu, and select **Tear-Off Property...**. From the Tear-Off Property Dialog box, select dbSelect and press **OK** to finish. See Figure 12.21.

Now you have the dbSelect property of EmployeePanel on the free-form surface. It is connected to the employeePanel bean. To associate dbNavigator to dbSelect, connect:

```
dbSelect(this)  →  dbNavigator(model)
```

The EmployeeView bean actually works right now, with just one connection. Before you try it, you must make provisions to display informational and error messages that might occur when accessing the database.

If you haven't already added the SelectStatus bean to the dataaccess package, do so now. It can be found as part of the answers.dat file on the CD-ROM. Using the **Choose Bean...** icon from the beans palette, add a SelectStatus bean to the free-form surface. Drop it near the dbSelect bean and name it **selectStatus**. Connect:

```
dbSelect(this)  →  selectStatus(theSelectBean)
selectStatus(theMessage)  →  infoarea(text)
dbNavigator(exceptionOccured) →  selectStatus(notifyExceptionOccurred)
```

Figure 12.21 Tearing off dbSelect.

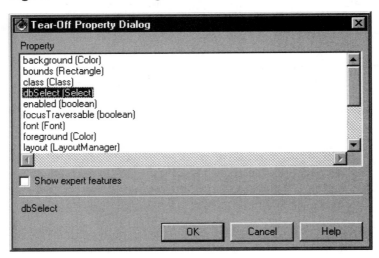

Double-click the last connection and select the **Pass event data** checkbox in the properties dialog for the connection.

The SelectStatus bean simply acts as a focus point for all exceptions and events of the Select and DBNavigator beans. It is a simple controller that monitors the activity of the Select bean and produces the proper messages. Full source is provided for this bean. You can change it to suit your needs.

This completes the EmployeeView bean. Your Visual Composition Editor should look like Figure 12.22.

You can now run the EmployeeView bean by pressing the **Run** button on the Visual Composition Editor. Once it is running, press the **Execute** button of dbNavigator to run your SQL query. If DB2 is not running, you get a message in the **infoarea**. Start DB2 from a command prompt by entering **DB2START** and try again. Notice that dbNavigator is toolTip enabled, it displays help when the mouse pointer is over its buttons.

Before you can consider this bean done, you need to promote the **dbSelect** property again. You need this property in the next bean that you build. Select **dbSelect**, open the pop-up menu, and select **Promote Bean Feature....** From the Property list select **this** and enter **dbSelect** in the **Promoted name** field. Save the bean.

This completes the EmployeeView bean. The next bean you build, **DatabaseEditor**, adds a table view and serves as the main application.

Figure 12.22   Completed EmployeeView bean.

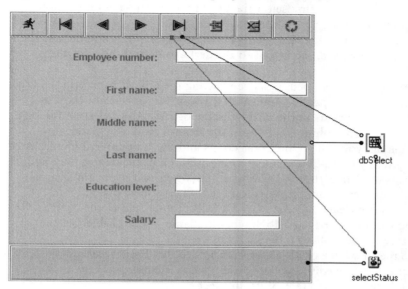

Completing the DatabaseEditor Application

The DatabaseEditor bean is built on a JFrame Swing component. Basically, it contains a JTabbedPane with two pages. The first page contains the EmployeeView bean. The second page is a table view of the complete database table. It is built on a SelectTable bean from the **com.ibm.webrunner.table** package. The SelectTable bean is a specialized JTable bean designed to display the contents of a Select bean's result set. Before continuing, import the **selecttable.jar** file to the My Project project on your workspace.

Start by creating a new class in the **dataaccess** package. Call this class **DBEditor**. Make its superclass **JFrame**. Select the **Browse the class when finished** checkbox and the **Compose the class visually** checkbox. Press the **Finish** button to create the class.

Set the layout property of the JPanel that is inside the frame to **BorderLayout**. Set the title property to **Database Editor**.

From the Swing category of the beans palette, drop a **JTabbedPane** on the center cell of the panel and name it **dbNotebook**. Now you have a tabbed pane, or notebook, with one page. Select the panel inside the page, open its property sheet, and change the **beanName** to **empViewPage**, the **layout** to **BorderLayout**, and the **tabTitle** to **Edit entry**.

Select a JPanel from the Swing category and drop it on the tabbed pane to form the second page of the notebook. The best place to drop it is right on top of the existing page tab. You now have a notebook with two pages.

When changing the properties of the panel that makes up the client area of the notebook page, you must first select the page itself by clicking on the notebook tab and then select the panel.

Select the panel of the second page, open its property sheet, and change the **beanName** to **tableViewPage**, the **layout** to **BorderLayout**, and the **tabTitle** to **Table view**.

With the property sheet open, practice selecting the tabbed pane bean and the pages and panels inside the pages. Confirm that you selected the right bean by observing which bean appears in the properties dialog. At times, selecting the right bean can be difficult. The solution is to open the **Beans List** dialog. See Figure 12.23. In this dialog, you can see the connections and the containment hierarchy of all the beans currently on the Visual Composition Editor. You can also drag and drop components to change their relative position. When you select any bean on the beans list, its properties are displayed on the property sheet dialog.

Press the **Choose Bean...** icon and add a **SelectTable** bean to the center cell of the panel on the second page of **dbNotebook**. Name it **selectTable**. Set the **Editable** property of the table to **false**.

Switch to the first page of dbNotebbok and drop an **EmployeeView** bean onto the center cell of the editViewPage panel. Name it **employeeView**.

Select **employeeView** and tear of its **dbSelect** property. Change the name of the torn-off property to **dbSelect**.

Switch to the **tableViewPage** of the notebook. Connect:

```
dbSelect(this) → selectTable(Select)
```

The tableViewPage of the notebook looks like Figure 12.24. You don't see much in this view at construction time, but at run time, the table contains a column corresponding to each of the database columns in the Select bean.

To test the DBEditor, press the Run button. When the application starts, press the **execute** button on the tool bar. If DB2 is not running, an error occurs

Figure 12.23   The Beans List.

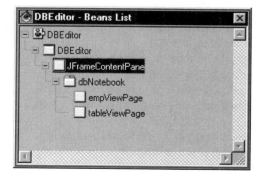

Figure 12.24   Table view page.

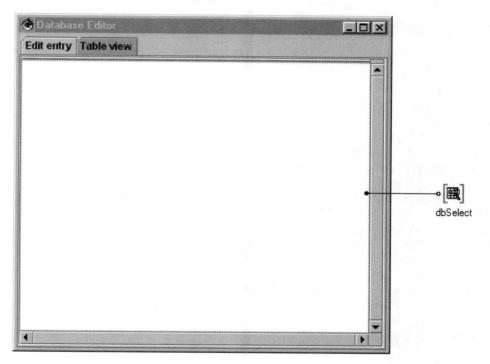

when the DBEditor tries to execute the SQL query. If you get the error, start a
command prompt session and issue a **DB2START** command.

In a production system, you would not expect the users to start DB2 manually. In a finished system, you should handle the exception and start the database
from within your application. To do this on the EmployeeView bean, you would
make an Event-to-Code connection between **exceptionOccurred** from dbNavigator
to a method. You would pass the event information to the method and determine
if the exception was caused by the database not being started. If you want to try it,
use the code excerpt below:

```
public void dbNavigator_ExceptionOccurred
    (com.ibm.ivj.db.uibeans.ExceptionEvent
    exceptionEvent) {
  // check to see if the exception is a database
  // not starteded error
  if(exceptionEvent.toString().
    indexOf("SQL1032N") != -1){
      try{
```

```
        Runtime.getRuntime().exec("DB2START");
    } catch(java.io.IOException e ) {}
    }
    return;
}
```

You could also place this code in the SelectStatus bean in the method that displays the exceptions.

Running the application should produce results similar to those seen in Figures 12.1 and 12.2 at the beginning of this chapter. You can use the dbNavigator buttons to traverse through the database records. While on the **Edit entry** view, you can alter, add, or delete a record. When you move to another record, the application updates any changes you made to a record. There is no update button on the dbNavigator tool bar.

The current record is also the selected record on the Table view. Conversely, the selected record on the table becomes the current record on the Edit entry view. Setting the **Editable** property to **true** on the SelectTable bean enables you to directly edit a record on the Table view. This can be dangerous unless you perform additional programming to improve the bean. There is no easy way to limit the number the characters entered on any particular column of the SelectTable. Some database columns have limited width; for example the middle initial column is limited to 1 character. The column on the table lets you enter as many characters as you want, but when you attempt to save the record to the database, an exception occurs and the record isn't saved. So it's best to leave the table as not editable for the moment.

New Database Access Beans

Several new database access beans were added to VisualAge for Java 3.0. If you look in the Database palette of the Visual Composition Editor, you will see eight beans. Two of them, the **Select** and **DBNavigator** beans, you already used in the preceding exercise. A short description for the other six can be found in Table 12.2. For a full description of these beans, look in the product's online help under the category **Data Access Beans**.

Database access is a complex topic, one that requires an entire book. This chapter gives you a good start at learning how to use databases with VisualAge for Java.

Deploying Applications Using Data Access Beans

If you intend to deploy an application that uses the IBM Data Access Beans, you will have to ship the file **\IBMVJava\eab\runtime30\ivjdab.zip** with your product.

The exercise in this chapter uses the **SelectTable** and supporting JavaBeans from IBM's VisualAge Developer Domain. These beans have already been

Table 12.2   Additional Data Access Beans

Icon	Bean type	Bean Function
Access beans		**Act directly on the database**
	Modify	Similar to the Select bean, but can be used to update, insert, and delete records from the database. Does not return a result set; instead it returns the number of rows affected by the operation.
	ProcedureCall	Use this bean to run a databasestored procedure. You can pass parameters as input, output, or both, and you can access any result set returned by the stored procedure. This is a very well-designed, complex bean. Read the online help to fully grasp its capabilities.
Selector beans		**Act on an existing result set**
	RowSelector	Used to select a row from a result set. You select the number of columns and the starting column. RowSelector implements the JComboBoxModel interface.
	ColumnSelector	Used to select a column from a result set. You select the number of rows and the starting row. ColumnSelector implements the JComboBoxModel interface.
	CellSelector	Allows you to select a single cell from a result set. You specify the column and row number you want to see.
	CellRangeSelector	Allows you to select a range of cells. You specify the starting row and column and the maximum number of rows and columns. The CellRangeSelector implements the JTableModel interface.

included in the **answers.dat** file. The file **selecttable100p.zip**, which contains the classes for these beans, can be found in the **Answers** directory of the CD-ROM.

Both of these zip files need to be defined on the CLASSPATH of the application. Since this is a Swing application, you will also need **swingall.jar** in the CLASSPATH.

Summary

In this chapter, you learned how to access a database from a program built with VisualAge for Java. You used the Data Access Select bean as the main way to communicate to the database. You also learned how to used the following beans:

- SelectTable
- SelectStatus
- NumericField
- UpperCaseField
- JTabbedPane

We encourage you to experiment with these and other beans and builders that come with VisualAge for Java. If you have the Enterprise Edition of the product, try to duplicate this exercise using the Data Access Builder and also the VisualAge Persistence Framework. It is also a good idea to have a basic knowledge of JDBC, since all of these approaches use JDBC to access the database.

TEAM DEVELOPMENT

13

What's in Chapter 13

In this chapter we show you how to use the team development features of VisualAge for Java Enterprise Edition. In this chapter you will learn about:

- The composition of the VisualAge for Java team environment
- The basics of team development
- Developer roles and responsibilities
- Editions
- Program elements
- The development process, including the development cycle, version naming, and development scenarios
- Shared repository on server
- Change control based on ownership
- External SCM support

What's Team Development?

VisualAge for Java Enterprise Edition provides a collaborative team development environment based on a shared repository. Change control starts at the class or interface level and is based on ownership. In the team development environment, all source code is stored in a shared repository on a server. Team members connect from their clients to the shared repository. Once connected, they can:

- Bring other editions of program elements into their workspaces
- Release program element editions they own for other team members to use
- Replace program element editions in their workspace
- Find program elements in the repository
- Add, update, delete, execute, and version program elements

Change Control Based on Ownership

In the VisualAge for Java team development environment, every project, package, and class has an *owner* who is responsible for the quality of that program element. Any number of developers may work on the same class, each in their own open (or timestamped) editions, but it is the owner of the class who merges their work to create a single version that is subsequently released or 'made public' for all to use. Packages and projects can only be versioned by their owners. Owners control the development of program elements acting, in essence, as gatekeepers or controllers.

VisualAge for Java's team features are optimized for prototyping and for iterative, object-oriented, rapid application development. Team development features are flexible and scale to support large enterprise projects.

VisualAge Team Environment

Figure 13.1 shows the client and server components that make up a VisualAge for Java team development environment. Many more users, each with their own workspace, can be added to this environment.

A shared repository must be accessed via a server that runs the repository server program (EMSRV). There may be more than one server in your environment.

Each server has the following components:

Figure 13.1   Client/Server team development environment.

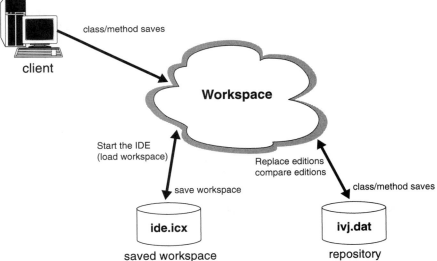

One or more source code repositories (.dat files) shared by the team.

The repository server program (emsrv.exe, emsrv.nlm, or emsrv). This program manages concurrent client access to the shared repositories on the server.

VisualAge for Java clients have the following components:

The Integrated Development Environment or IDE program (ide.exe)

A workspace that contains the developer's current work (ide.icx)

Optionally, a local repository (.dat file) for offline development

The EMADMIN utility (emadmin.exe) is most commonly used by the person responsible for operating the repository server.

Table 13.1 compares and contrasts the workspace with the repository.

Table 13.1   A Comparison of Workspace and Repository

Workspace	Repository
Contains only one copy/edition of any one program element	Contains all editions of all program elements
Load/unload editions from repository only into workspace	Import/export .java, .class, .zip, .jar, .dat files (mini-repositories) from file system into or out of repository
Replace/compare/merge elements with other editions in repository	Editions can be marked for purging or unmarked for purging during next repository compaction
• Each workspace is unique for each user	• One shared repository for a group of developers
• Items are loaded from repository	• Can have other repositories for other groups
	• Developers can, if needed, switch repositories. When switching repositories, all project editions not in target repository must be unloaded from workspace.
May contain scratch editions	Scratch editions aren't tracked
Export open/versioned/released editions of any program elements as .java, .class, .zip, or .jar files	Not possible

(Continues)

Table 13.1   A Comparison of Workspace and Repository (*Continued*)

Workspace	Repository
Export only versioned editions of packages or classes as (mini) .dat repositories	Same
Managed by each developer's instance of the IDE	Managed centrally on a server
Workspace file is c:\IBMVJava\IDE\ program\ide.icx	• Default file name is ivj.dat
	• Although any name can be used, usual extension is .dat
	• Local/offline version of file is c:\IBMVJava\IDE\repository\ivj.dat
	Manages password control when switching workspace owners

The Basics of Team Development

There are many topics around software development with a team. In this section you learn about the different user interface views that VisualAge for Java provides in the team environment. You will learn about different developer roles and their responsibilities. You will learn how to use the different edition types.

The IDE User Interfaces

The team environment provides management tools to support multi-programmer development efforts. The Workbench, for example, has a new **Managing** tab on the notebook, as shown in Figure 13.2, that lets you view the details of program elements or lets owners of program elements to assign or change ownership, add developers to a package group, create open editions, or version and release editions for public use.

The Repository Explorer allows a workspace owner to view, purge, or restore a project or package from the repository, as shown in Figure 13.3.

The workspace owner's unique name is what identifies the developer to the repository server. To add a new user:

From the **File** menu, select the **Quick Start** option.

From the Quick Start window, select the **Team Development** feature and the **Administer Users** option, as shown in Figure 13.4.

Enter the new user information and click the **Save** button shown in Figure 13.5.

Figure 13.2   Managing tab of the Workbench.

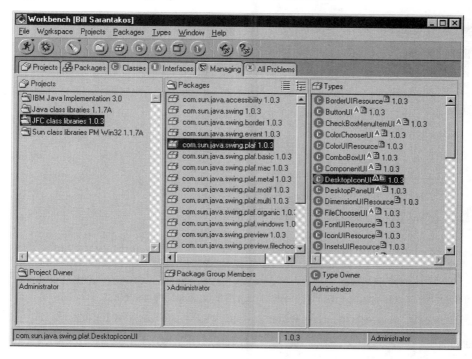

Figure 13.3   Respository Explorer.

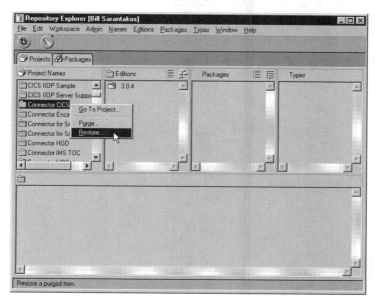

Figure 13.4 Quick Start features.

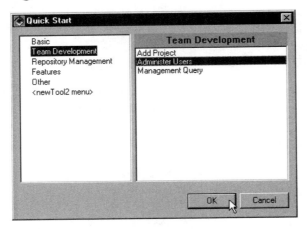

Note that in order to add, change, or delete users, you must first change the workspace owner to **Administrator**. To change the current workspace owner:

From the **Workspace** menu, select **Change Workspace Owner**. A dialog box appears listing all the names from the repository user list.

Select the new workspace owner, and click OK as shown in Figure 13.6.

Figure 13.5 Adding a new user.

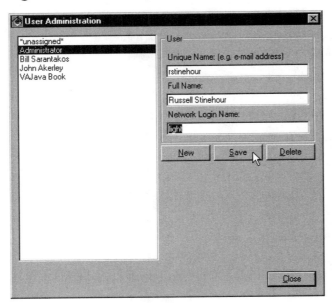

Figure 13.6   Changing the workspace owner.

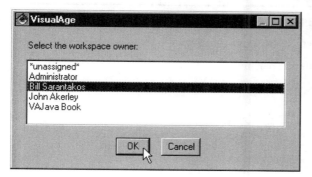

If password validation is enabled on your repository server, you are prompted for the password of the new workspace owner. Type the password and click **OK**.

Developer Roles and Responsibilities

When you work in the team environment, you should work with password protection enabled. You should define a set of roles and responsibilities for team developers on a given project. You should also define a version-naming scheme that helps identify the program element developer, update reason, and relative sequence of the version. In addition, you should manage a project with fixed iterative deliverables, called baselines, that help you and your users manage the development process and meet user expectations. These issues are discussed in more detail in the following sections.

Table 13.2 outlines the roles that a developer can play in the environment and lists the privileges and responsibilities associated with each role. While the privileges of a role can't be changed, it will be up to your development team to

Table 13.2   Roles and Responsibilities

Role	Privileges and Responsibilities
Project owner	• Transfer ownership
	• Create open edition of the project
	• Version the project
	• Create a new package in the project
	• Release a package to the project

(Continues)

Table 13.2   Roles and Responsibilities *(Continued)*

Role	Privileges and Responsibilities
	• Project integrity and consistency
Package owner	• Transfer ownership
	• Create open edition of the package
	• Version the package
	• Add and remove package group members
	• Release a package to its project
	• Package integrity and consistency
Package group member	• Create new classes within package
	• Can be a class owner
	• Can obtain class ownership
Class owner	• Transfer ownership
	• Release class into package
	• Class integrity and consistency
Class developer	• Any defined user
	• Change any type (class or interface)
Administrator	• Install and setup team environment (usually)
	• Add, change, and remove users
	• Assign and change owners initially and as needed thereafter
	• Clean/compress and backup repository

create a development process that enforces or encourages developers to carry out the responsibilities associated with their role to the benefit of the development effort.

Edition Types

Edition is the name given to the collection of program elements that is under source code management. In VisualAge for Java, editions manage types, packages, and projects. You should note that editions are actually nested within each other, with editions of types existing within editions of packages which themselves exist within projects. Table 13.3 identifies the various types of editions that exist within VisualAge for Java and lists their features or properties.

Table 13.3   Types of Editions

Type of Edition	Properties
Open edition	• Read-writeable version • Changeable • Open editions have a timestamp (corresponding to when they were created) for their version name
Versioned edition	• Read-only version • Unchangeable • Frozen • Versioned editions have a user or developer provided name
Released edition	• Part of baseline • Ready for public consumption • An unreleased edition is marked in the workspace with a > symbol ahead of the program element name
Scratch edition	• Like an open edition, but it exists only within a user's workspace, never within the repository • Indicated by <> around the version name • Created from versioned editions (whether or not they are released) • Only for projects and packages • Cannot be released or versioned • For temporary work • Can be converted into an open edition • How they happen: releasing a class or package into containing element that has been versioned recently (since last refresh)

Program Elements

Table 13.4 lists the various program elements that can be created, modified, and deleted within the VisualAge for Java IDE.

Table 13.4   Program Elements

Element	Remarks
Project	• VisualAge for Java only concept
	• Can encapsulate entire development effort, a subsystem, or a significant subset (perhaps based on developers creating it)
	• Used to hold a related set of packages in a common group
	• Can be versioned
Package	• Corresponds to a Java package
	• Can be versioned
Class	• Corresponds to a Java class
	• Can be versioned
Interface	• Corresponds to a Java interface
	• Can be versioned
Methods	• Corresponds to a Java method
	• Cannot be versioned
Resources	• Resources are not versioned or managed in any way
	• Easier access is now provided with a new **Resources** tab in the project browser
	• Anything not a .java source file

The Development Process

There are various elements of a good development process. The sections that follow describe those elements and identify those areas of the process that need to be customized for the particular team or project. The elements discussed will be the ones that are closely related to VisualAge for Java; a complete discussion is beyond the scope of this text.

The Development Cycle

This section describes the usual sequence of activities during a typical development iteration. The length of such cycles should be established by the development team based on the nature of the team or the project requirements. The length of a cycle needs to be varied based on the phase of the project as well.

A typical scenario is for the length of these cycles to start out quite large at the beginning of development and then get shorter and shorter as the project gets closer and closer to completion. By the way, the changes in the length of the cycle do not happen gradually and progressively but rather in steps. To illustrate, a project might start out with iterations of one month while the frameworks and infrastructure of the project are put together. Later, as large features are being added to the system, the iterations may be shortened to two weeks. Close to completion, the iterations could be shortened to a week, a day, or even an hour depending on the resources available to test the more frequent iterations.

Here are the specifics:

Create an open edition of the projects. The project owner creates on open edition of the project. If the project doesn't exist, then the project owner should create it (it will be an open edition initially).

Create open editions of the contained packages and release them. The project owner or the individual package owners create open editions of their packages. Next, these new open editions are released into the new open edition of the project. While this may seem counter intuitive, since the packages actually contain new code, you need to do this because it gives class owners an open edition to release new or changed classes into. Releasing the open editions into the project allows the other developers to load the entire source in one step. Otherwise, after having loaded the new (open) edition of the project, they would have to load each new (open) edition of the packages.

Carry on with normal development. This is where the majority of the time is spent. Developers create code, modify it, test it, version it, and then have it released by the class owner for use by the other developers on the project. The developer may need or want to break up the testing into two steps. The first step is to test their changes with the baseline they started with. The second step is to compare the content of the projects, as loaded in the developer's workspace, with the released content (use the **Compare With => Released Contents** menu), and then load and test with any new code that other class owners have released. This should help ensure that when your code is released for public use, it will not cause regressions or new problems because of incompatibilities introduced while your changes were being made.

Version the packages. Near the end of the iteration, the package owners should declare a cutoff for all changes to their packages. This cutoff may be the same for all packages, or may be based on the time it takes to test a particular package so that all packages are tested by the time the project is supposed to be versioned. Unlike classes, the packages don't need to be released because they've already been released into the project at the beginning of the cycle. They, in effect, acted as collectors for the code while it was under development.

Version the projects. Once the packages have been versioned, the projects can be versioned. Alternatively, the project owner may choose to wait until the code undergoes some testing, whether short and informal, or long and rigorous, before doing so.

As alluded to during the **version the project** step, testing is a standard part of any development project. During testing, switching between one iteration and another needs to be managed carefully. This is the time between the versioning of the packages in the current iteration and the releasing of the new open editions of those packages in the next iteration. During this time period, developers cannot donormal development activities without causing scratch editions to be created in their workspaces. Merging these scratch editions with the open editions created and released later is time consuming and prone to mistakes. If the testing period will be long (more than an hour or two during the work day), you should consider starting the next iteration immediately, and then merging any fixes required for problems discovered during the testing into both the old iteration's code and the new iterations.

Version Naming

Each time you version an open edition (**Manage => Version...**), VisualAge for Java will calculate a new edition name for you. It will display the name along with three choices for you to pick from in the **Versioning Selected Items** dialog. In calculating the new name, the IDE will take the last character in the previous version name, increment it, and then replace the old character with the new character to form the new name. Most of the time, you would expect the last character to be numeric, so the new name seems natural. However, if the last name is a description, like "the first edition," then the new name would be "the first editioo", where the trailing "n" is incremented and becomes an "o". If a previous version does not exist for the item, then VisualAge will use the name 1.0 for the first version by default.

As depicted in Figure 13.7, three options are presented to you while versioning:

Automatic (Recommended). Tells VisualAge for Java to calculate the new edition name for you and proceed immediately to version the edition with that name.

One Name. Lets you give the same name to all the items (program elements) that you have selected in the IDE. If any of the items already has an edition with the same name you've selected, you will be prompted to put in a new name, to skip versioning that particular element, or to stop the versioning process altogether. It will also give you a list of already used names if you like.

Figure 13.7   Versioning Selected Items.

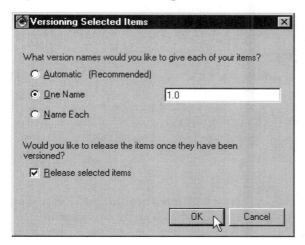

Name Each. Prompts you for a version name for each item selected. It
will calculate a new name for each item, as opposed to the **One Name**
option, which uses the name calculated for the first item.

Versioning Alternative 1

The first alternative naming strategy is really a variation of the standard method
that we're all used to and that VisualAge for Java generates. In addition to specifying a numeric version number, the developer adds their initials to the version
name. The best place to add the initials is at the beginning, so that the IDE can
automatically increment the version numbers on your behalf. Here are some
examples: DN 1.11, DN 1.12, BS 1.13, PJ 3.02, and PJ 3.03. Some teams put the
initials within special characters to separate them from the program element
name. Examples include [BS], (DN), and {RS}.

Versioning Alternative 2

The second alternative is to use version names based on the date. One limitation
of the current repository is that it does not record the date the program element
was versioned, only the date when its open edition was created. This lets a developer know immediately the last time that a particular element was modified.
Examples of this method include: 20001215, 20001003, 20020124, and
2003/02/28.

A further refinement can be made by including a sequence number on the
end. This would allow you to quickly determine a sequence of changes (versions)
made on the same day. A couple of ways of doing this are adding **.0** or **a**. Using

the above examples, here are the modified version names: 19991215.0, 20001003 a, 000124.3, and 99/02/28 e. Of course, as with alternative 1, you can also have developers include their initials.

Development Scenarios

This section describes a number of different ways to tie your team's development process into VisualAge for Java's team development environment. The first method is the way the creators of the team development support envisioned it being used. Next is a way to kludge the environment so that it can be used like a traditional check-in/check-out or serialized development process. Last is a hybrid of the previous two.

Fully Parallel Development

This is the recommended approach. The project manager or team leader is made the owner of the Projects the code will be developed in. The packages are then assigned owners as well. You or your team may decide to assign ownership of all the packages to the person who owns the containing project, or you can assign ownership to lead or senior developers who are responsible for the integrity of the individual packages. Each class's ownership is then assigned to a developer. At the start of a project, the classes may not exist yet—in this case, the developer who creates the class initially is assigned ownership automatically by the IDE. After such a class is versioned and released, the team must decide whether the developer who created the class retains ownership or assigns ownership to another developer in the group.

In this scenario, each developer works more or less independently of the others in their own workspace. The developer can make changes, test, make more changes, and test again. When the developer has completed the changes, the changed classes should be versioned. If the developer owns all the classes that have changed, then the developer can just release them for the entire team to use. By the way, there is no reason why you can't try an experimental change to see if the code can be made more efficient, simpler, more intuitive, or improved in some other way. When making these changes or any other changes , always start out with a versioned piece of code. The version does not have to actually be released. By having the version, if the change does not work out, or if the change will take longer to implement than the current schedule allows, you can roll back the changes to the versioned code you started with.

This development scenario provides an environment that promotes pride in ownership and workmanship. This pride is encouraged because an owner knows that if they release a version that subsequently has a failure or regression, everyone will know exactly who created and who released the code. Some organizations even go so far as to enforce a penalty for such transgressions—usually they are informal and inexpensive, like buying the rest of the team donuts or coffee.

Tip

When you have created open editions that contain work that you want to discard in order to roll back to a previous edition, instead of replacing the current editions with the previously created version, you should first version your current changes. When you version such changes, use a version name like **dead end** or **bad**, perhaps with a comment as to what went wrong. By doing this, your repository is not polluted with a lot of open editions that are not currently under development. Using this method, if someone used the repository explorer, they could actually see how many classes were under active development.

Serialized Development

In this scenario, the Administrator creates a dummy id. Full names typically used for this dummy id include **unassigned, nobody,** or **noone.** Sometimes there are variations that include special symbols as in ***unassigned***. Project and package owners are established just like in the parallel development scenario above.

What differs is that ownership of *all* the classes are initially assigned to the dummy ID. When a developer wants to lock a class, like in a traditional serial check-in/check-out development process, the developer first checks to see that the class is indeed still owned by the dummy ID and if and only if it is, grabs the ownership away from that ID. The developer then makes the changes and tests them as usual. Once satisfied, the developer then versions and releases the class. The class can be released, because the developer is also the class owner. Finally, the developer assigns ownership of the class back to the dummy ID so that the class is available for further development.

Note that VisualAge for Java does not enforce the process here. It is up to each developer to maintain the self-discipline not to grab ownership away from other developers.

In order for this scenario to work, all possible developers need to be added as package group members. If this is not done, then a developer who makes a change must ask a developer who is a package group member to release the code. This exposes the process to having two or more developers making simultaneous changes.

Hybrid Development

In some cases, different parts of a project have different requirements. These requirements can also change over time as portions of the project get closer to completion. There is no reason why you cannot use different scenarios for different portions of the project. Just make sure that you establish a clear communication channel to the entire development team so that each developer knows which process each project and/or package is being developed with.

External SCM Support

Repository management and version control are built into VisualAge for Java Enterprise Edition. The shared repository supports team programming activities. You may want to install external Software Configuration Management (SCM) system support as a complementary feature for one of the following reasons:

You may be more comfortable with a traditional file checkin/checkout approach that enforces serial development of classes.

You already use another SCM tool as the standard in your organization.

The repository in VisualAge for Java manages Java code only. You may want to manage all of your program elements with a single SCM tool.

You have established procedures for archiving program elements on a server for backup/restore purposes.

You may want to integrate multiple programming languages across your enterprise in one SCM.

File-based Versioning

VisualAge for Java provides an interface for checking .java source files into and out of external SCMs. This interface is a feature that you can select when you install VisualAge for Java. It has been tested with the following SCM tools:

ClearCase 3.2 for Windows NT, from Rational Software Corporation

PVCS Version Manager 6.0, from INTERSOLV Inc.

VisualAge TeamConnection Version 3.0, from IBM Corporation

Visual SourceSafe 6.0, from Microsoft (this support is new in VisualAge for Java Version 3)

The interface from VisualAge for Java to external SCM tools uses Microsoft's Source Code Control (SCC) API and is supported for Windows NT, Windows 95, and Windows 98 clients. The VisualAge for Java Workbench window provides the **Tools => External SCM** menu for adding classes to source control, checking classes into and out of the SCM repository, and importing the most recently checked-in version of a class from the SCM tool. Prior to VisualAge for Java Version 2.0, if you wanted to share code with an external SCM, you had to import and export .java source files.

VisualAge for Java does not provide any automatic synchronization of version names between the VisualAge for Java repository and the external SCM tool. VisualAge for Java does not prevent you from changing a program element in your workspace if you neglected to check it out in the external SCM tool. The external SCM menu provides a way for you to use an existing SCM tool without leaving the VisualAge for Java IDE; you are responsible to synchronize the functions of the two systems.

> **NOTE**
>
> The external SCM support provided in VisualAge for Java is *not* intended to be used as a checkin/checkout mechanism for every single change or even for every new version created in the IDE. Rather, the code should be synchronized at specific points during development, like the beginning or end of the day or week, or the beginning or end of an iteration. Each time you perform a **Checkout** or **Get Latest**, it causes a new open edition to be created in the repository and loaded into the workspace. This will pollute your repository with many open editions that are will probably never be versioned, which will cause repository growth and poor performance, and require frequent repository compactions.

Summary

In this chapter, you learned about team development in VisualAge for Java which gives you many tools for managing your Java code development. In order to use these tools, you need to organize your coded development. We discussed some techniques and options that you can employ to fully utilize team development. In this chapter you learned about:

- The composition of the VisualAge for Java team environment
- The basics of team development
- Developer roles and responsibilities
- Editions types
- Program elements
- The development process, including the development cycle, version naming, and development scenarios
- Shared repository on a server
- Change control based on ownership
- External SCM support

SERVLETS

Because it is portable and mobile, Java lends itself well to client-side programming in the form of Applets. An applet lives on a Web server as a set of byte-codes, executed only when a client (Web browser) requests the Applet through an APPLET tag in an HTML document. The byte-codes are then transferred to the client and executed on the client machine. While Java is well suited for client use, it is equally well suited for server use.

Since Java is portable and mobile, server developers can freely move their server applications to different platforms without having to rewrite or even recompile their Java programs. In addition, Java as shipped with the Java Development Kit (JDK), comes with a complete set of communications classes for using TCP/IP sockets and URLs. VisualAge for Java includes all of these classes. Additionally, Java has built-in support for Threads (a mechanism for allowing your Java program to do more than one task at once), serialization of objects (a persistence mechanism for objects), and the ability to call native C/C++ functions.

Sun Microsystems provides the JavaServer Web Development Kit (JSWDK), which contains classes that support servlets as well as a limited Web server for testing servlets, HTML, and JSPs. You can download the JSWDK from www.javasoft .com. Since VisualAge for Java has an open design, you can utilize the JSWDK from within VisualAge for Java to develop and test your sevlets. You can also use IBM WebSphere in VisualAge for Java instead of the JSWDK to develop and test servlets more effectively.

What Is a Servlet?

A servlet is a standard server-side Java program that extends the functionality of a Web server. When the Web server gets a request for a servlet through a URL, it loads the servlet into the server machine's memory (if not already loaded), and executes the servlet. When the servlet completes its task, it sends any generated output back to the Web browser. You can write servlets for administrative purposes, such as managing Web server log files or sending e-mail alerts to administrators. However, what is more interesting and more pervasive is the use of servlets in information systems (IS) applications that run on the Web.

IS servlets typically interface to existing JavaBeans or Enterprise Java Beans (EJBs), which then utilize a database or transactional system to perform the real work. As we have previously discussed, this book breaks down robust applications into layers and follows the Model-View-Controller (MVC) design pattern. Servlets act as the controller layer for applications that run on the Web. Servlets serve as the "glue" between ordinary HTML (the view) and the JavaBeans or EJBs. Servlets can then add additional functionality to the overall Web application by providing session management, user authentication, and user authorization.

Why Use Servlets?

At this point you might be thinking, "I have CGI and Perl—why should I use Java servlets?" CGI (Common Gateway Interface) is a mechanism for integrating programs written in C/C++, Perl, and other languages with a Web server. The simple answer is that servlets offer a better CGI. In most Web applications that use servlets, the client code (HTML) accesses the servlets in the same way that it would access a Perl script through CGI. Therefore, using servlets does not in any way impact how HTML developers do their jobs. Compared to standard CGI, servlets offer better mechanisms in the areas of portability, performance, and security.

Since Java is "write once, run anywhere," your server-side programs are platform-independent. Additionally, servlets can take advantage of pre-packaged component technologies through the use of JavaBeans and EJBs.

Servlets offer better performance than standard CGI. Once the Web server loads a servlet into the server memory, it stays there and listens for requests. When a request arrives, a new Java thread is automatically created and the servlet code is executed in that thread. Java threads are lightweight and their creation is far more efficient than standard CGI, which creates a new operating system process for each request. Since a servlet remains resident in memory, connections to databases can remain open. An intelligent servlet can create pools of database connections and manage them between concurrent users to further improve performance over standard CGI. IBM WebSphere provides a connection manager object to create and manage pools of connections to JDBC databases. Lastly, servlets provide a Session object that you can use to maintain session information across multiple accesses by the same user to the servlets on a Web server. Using the Session object can reduce the need to retrieve the same information over and over again each time a user accesses a server-side application. Sessions can be set up to expire or to persist indefinitely.

Servlets offer better security than standard CGI. Since a servlet runs within the web server context and under the control of the Web server, you can use its authentication and authorization features. Additionally, the JDK includes the java.security and java.security.acl packages, which offer Java Interfaces for creating authentication and authorization functionality. IBM WebSphere provides an implementation of the Java Interfaces in the java.security and java.security.acl packages, as well as administrative screens for maintaining access control lists.

The overall architecture of a servlet appears in Figure 14.1.

Figure 14.1   Servlet architecture.

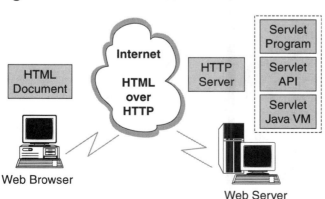

Basic Servlet Concepts

Servlets give a server-side programmer the basic building blocks for creating controllers for Web based applications. To understand servlets, you need to know something about the servlet API, the life cycle, requests, responses, the HttpServlet class, and how to use PrintWriters.

The Servlet API

The Servlet API resides in two packages, javax.servlet and javax.servlet.http. These packages define all of the Java interfaces and classes needed to begin creating servlets. The javax.servlet package defines the basic classes for servlets, including GenericServlet, ServletInputStream, and ServletOutputStream. All servlets must eventually inherit from the class GenericServlet. The javax.servlet package appears in Figure 14.2.

The javax.servlet.http package defines classes that are useful in supporting HTTP functions. Servlets that are intended to act like CGI programs use the classes and interfaces in this package. The most basic class in this package is the HttpServlet class, which provides Java methods for HTTP requests such as POST and GET. Note that HttpServlet is a subclass of GenericServlet. The javax.servlet.http package is shown in Figure 14.3.

The javax.servlet.jsp package defines classes that are useful in supporting JavaServer Pages. JSPs let you create HTML-like documents that are transformed into Java servlets. The javax.servlet.jsp package is shown in Figure 14.4.

Servlet Lifecycle

The servlet life cycle defines the process used to load the servlet into memory, execute it, and then unload it from memory. A Web browser requests a servlet through

Figure 14.2   javax.servlet package.

- GenericServlet A 1.0
- RequestDispatcher 1.0
- Servlet 1.0
- ServletConfig 1.0
- ServletContext 1.0
- ServletException 1.0
- ServletInputStream A 1.0
- ServletOutputStream A 1.0
- ServletRequest 1.0
- ServletResponse 1.0
- SingleThreadModel 1.0
- UnavailableException 1.0

Figure 14.3   javax.servlet.http package.

Cookie 1.0
HttpServlet△ 1.0
HttpServletRequest 1.0
HttpServletResponse 1.0
⚠HttpSession 1.0
HttpSessionBindingEvent 1.0
HttpSessionBindingListener 1.0
HttpSessionContext 1.0
HttpUtils 1.0
NoBodyOutputStream 1.0
⚠NoBodyResponse 1.0

a URL, which can be on the location line of the Web browser or in a link embedded in the HTML document being viewed. A typical servlet URL appears as http://localhost/**servlet**/SimpleServlet. The keyword servlet lets the Web server know that the request is for a servlet and not an HTML page or CGI program. SimpleServlet, in the above example, is the class name or shortname of the desired servlet.

To create a servlet, you must create a subclass of the GenericServlet class or one of its subclasses. When your servlet is first requested, the Web server loads the requested servlet class and all of the associated classes into memory on the web server. Control then passes to the init() method in the servlet. GenericServlet provides an empty init() method. If you wish to perform initialization tasks, such as connecting to a database, you need to provide an init() method in your subclass. The init() method receives only one call, and that is immediately after the Web server loads your servlet into memory.

Each time the servlet is requested (including the first time after the init() method is called) a new thread is created and that thread executes over the service() method. GenericServlet provides an empty service() method. You must override this

Figure 14.4   javax.servlet.jsp package.

HttpJspPage 1.0
JspEngineInfo△ 1.0
JspFactory△ 1.0
JspPage 1.0
JspWriter△ 1.0
PageContext△ 1.0

method if you want to do any real work. Since the service() method is called in its own thread, the Web server is free to take additional requests for the same servlet or for another servlet that it executes in another thread. The service() method is where the work of the servlet is accomplished. You should note that since the service() method is always executed inside a new thread, you must be careful to ensure that everything done in the service() method is thread-safe (re-entrant).

At some later time, when the Web server deems it necessary, the destroy() method of the servlet is called and then the servlet is unloaded from the server's memory. If you provide a destroy() method in your servlet, it is called. Common tasks performed by the destroy() method include disconnecting all database connections and closing all files and other administrative items.

The complete life cycle of a GenericServlet appears in Figure 14.5.

HttpServlets

While GenericServlet provides the basic behavior of a servlet, a mechanism for handling HTTP requests must also be provided. As such, HttpServlet, which is a subclass of GenericServlet, provides Java methods for each of the HTTP request methods. While all of the HTTP methods are supported, the GET and POST methods are the most prevalent. HttpServlet provides the doGet() and doPost() Java methods to handle the HTTP GET and POST methods.

When an HttpServlet is requested via a URL, the service() method reads the HTTP header and determines which HTTP method to call. That method is then invoked.

Request and Response Parameters

When the service(), doGet(), doPost(), or other doXXX() methods are called, two parameters are always passed. These parameters represent the request information from the Web browser and the response information provided by the servlet.

- ServletRequest—enables the servlet to access the requested information such as parameters, session information, and HttpServletRequest information on the HTTP header and Cookies.

Figure 14.5   Servlet life cycle.

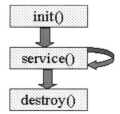

- ServletResponse—gives the servlet facilities to create a response document for the Web browser. You can set the content type and write data in the form of the specified content type to an encapsulated PrintWriter object. The PrintWriter is the channel by which the servlet communicates with the Web browser.

JavaServer Web Development Kit

The JSWDK contains all of the classes you need to develop and test servlets. You can obtain the JSWDK from Sun Microsystems Javasoft web site at no charge. Point your web browser to http://java.sun.com/products/servlet/index.html and follow the links to download the JSWDK. Once you have obtained the zipped file, install it by simply unzipping it to the C: drive. The default installation directory is C:\JSWDK1.0.1. The rest of this discussion assumes that you have used the default installation directory.

In order to use the JSWDK in VisualAge for Java, you need to import the classes contained in several .jar files shipped with the JSWDK. From the VisualAge for Java workbench, import the classes contained in the following .jar files into the My Project project (you may prefer to create a new project entitled JSWDK):

C:\JSWDK-1.0.1\webserver.jar

C:\JSWDK-1.0.1\lib\jspengine.jar

C:\JSWDK-1.0.1\lib\servlet.jar

C:\JSWDK-1.0.1\lib\xml.jar

In order to view the source for selected classes, you need to additionally import the files contained in the **C:\JSWDK-1.0.1\src** directory. Lastly, to test your installation, you need to import the examples found in the **C:\JSWDK-1.0.1\examples** directory.

To start the server, run the **StartUp** class in the **com.sun.web.shell package**. However, you must properly set the classpath for StartUp prior to running it. Be sure to include any projects that you want StartUp to be able to load for you and also include the various directories for finding HTML and JSP pages as documented in the C:\JSWDK-1.0.1\StartServer.bat file.

IBM WebSphere

The IBM WebSphere Test Environment is included in the Enterprise Edition of VisualAge for Java. We will use this environment to test our servlet examples. While the JSWDK provides all of the necessary classes to develop servlets as well as a Web server, IBM WebSphere Application Server provides much more. The following is a short list of features for the IBM WebSphere product.

- All of the function found in the JSWDK
- IBM Connection Manager for managing database connections
- IBM Data Access Beans for accessing data from JDBC databases
- The ability to mark servlets to be preloaded when the Web server starts, instead of waiting for the first request for them
- Dynamic reloading of modified servlets without rebooting the Web server machine
- An implementation of the JSP 1.0 and 0.91 specifications
- A servlet runner much like the **StartUp** class that also has a plug-in facility for handling standard HTML pages and JSP files (this class is called **SERunner** and allows for complete testing of servlets)
- A JSP monitor for debugging JSP-generated servlets

VisualAge for Java Enterprise Edition lets you run the WebSphere Application Server inside VisualAge for Java during development. You can test servlets as you build them and you can even set break points in servlets to help you debug them.

In order to utilize the IBM WebSphere Test Environment inside of VisualAge for Java, you must add it as a feature. Add the "IBM WebSphere Test Environment" feature to your workspace. Once it is loaded, you will use the SERunner class to start IBM WebSphere. To use SERunner, you must first change its classpath to include the **My Project** project, which we will use for our servlets and JavaBeans. Go to the com.ibm.servlet package and select the SERunner class. Next, open the Properties dialog and add My Project to the list of projects to include in the classpath. Run SERunner and the Console displays seen in Figure 14.6.

The SERunner program listens on port 8080 instead of the default HTTP port 80. Once SERunner starts, open your Web browser on http://127.0.0.1:8080/servlet/HelloWorldServlet. After a few seconds, the Web browser displays the output of the HelloWorldServlet, as shown in Figure 14.7.

If you do not get the following output in your Web browser, check to see if any error messages appear in the VisualAge for Java console. Also, check to see if the VisualAge for Java Debugger window is open.

Writing Your First Servlet

For your first servlet, you will write a simple servlet that subclasses from HttpServlet and implements the doPost() method to support POST requests. The servlet merely echoes all of the fields contained in the HTML form. The simple servlet takes demographic information from an HTML document in a Web browser and then echoes that information back to the browser in the form of an HTML document. This servlet uses the HTTP POST method for communication between the Web browser and Web server.

Figure 14.6   SERunner output.

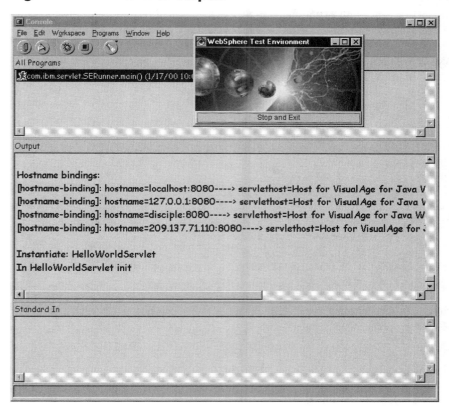

Figure 14.7   HelloWorldServlet output.

Building the HTML Form

Since our servlet echoes all of the fields in any HTML form, we can put anything on the form. Our form contains 3 fields—First Name, Last Name, and Phone Number. Use Notepad or some other editor to create a file named PostExample.html. If you have IBM WebSphere Studio, use PageDesigner to build the page without writing HTML. Enter the HTML code as shown in the following code sample.

```
<HTML>
<HEAD>
<TITLE>Post Servlet Example</TITLE>
</HEAD>
<BODY>
<FORM NAME="PostExampleServlet"
ACTION= "http://127.0.0.1:8080/servlet/example.PostServlet"
METHOD="post"
ENCODE="application/x-www-form-urlencoded">
Test the PostExampleServlet with a few input fields
<BR>
First Name <INPUT TYPE="text" SIZE=20
MAXLENGTH=30 NAME="firstName" VALUE="enterFirstName">
<BR>
Last Name <INPUT TYPE="text" SIZE=30
MAXLENGTH=40 NAME="lastName" VALUE="
enter last name">
<BR>
Phone Number <INPUT TYPE="text" SIZE=30
MAXLENGTH=40 NAME="phonenum"
VALUE="enter phone number">
<BR>
Press submit to invoke the servlet. If all goes well,
 you get a response page containing the above information.
<BR>
<INPUT TYPE="submit" NAME="Submit" VALUE="Submit">
<BR>
</FORM>
</BODY>
</HTML>
```

Create the PostServlet

Create the PostServlet with the following steps:

From the VisualAge for Java workbench, select the My Project project. Create two new packages named **example.domain** and **example.servlet**.

Next, create a new class with the attributes in Table 14.1.

Table 14.1   New Class Attributes

Package Name	example.servlet
Class Name	PostServlet
Super Class	HttpServlet
Import the following packages	javax.servlet.* javax.servlet.http.* java.io.* java.net.* java.util.*

Next, create the doPost() method and then a private supporting method named getFormInput().

From the workbench, open the PostServlet class to the hierarchy page of the class browser. Press the "M" button to create a new method. Give the new method the attributes in Table 14.2.

Enter the following code between the {} that define the beginning and end of the method.

```
// Get the input form contents
Properties formInput = getFormInput(req);

// Obtain output stream from response object
PrintWriter out = new
PrintWriter(res.getOutputStream());

// Set content type on the response header
res.setContentType("text/html");
```

Table 14.2   New Method Attributes

Method name	doPost()
Method return type	Void
Parameters	HttpServletRequest—req HttpServletResponse—res
Exceptions to list in throws clause	ServletException IOException

```
    // Begin writing the output HTML to the
output writer
    out.println("<html>");
    out.println("<head><title>PostServlet" +
"Complete</title></head>");
    out.println("<body>");
    out.println("<h2><br><br>PostServlet: " +
"Listing of your Input Form  </h2>");

    // Dump the properties and values to the output writer
    formInput.list(out);

    // Finish writing the output HTML to the
output writer
    out.println("<br>Listing Complete.");
    out.println("<br>");
    out.println("<h2>Post Servlet.</h2>");
    out.println("</body></html>");
    out.flush();
    return;
```

The doPost() method invokes every time a client requests the servlet. Our implementation of doPost() calls getFormInput() and then writes the results along with additional HTML to the PrintWriter.

Create the getFormInput() method. From the workbench, open the PostServlet class to the hierarchy page of the class browser. Press the "M" button to create a new method. Give the new method the attributes in Table 14.3.

Enter the following code between the {} that define the beginning and end of the method.

```
Properties formInput = new Properties();

Enumeration fieldNames =  req.getParameterNames();
while (fieldNames.hasMoreElements())
```

Table 14.3 New Method Attributes

Method name	getFormInput()
Method return type	Properties
Parameters	HttpServletRequest—req
Access	Private

```
    {
        String paramName =
          (String)fieldNames.nextElement();
        String paramValue = (String)
          req.getParameterValues(paramName)[0];

        formInput.put(paramName, paramValue);
    }
    return formInput;
```

The getFormInput() method uses the Properties class to hold the field names and values from the HTML form. Our sample simply lists the contents of the Properties object as part of the HTML output from the doPost() method.

In order to test your servlet, ensure that SERunner is started. Next, start a Web browser and open the PostExample.html file that you created. The HTML document should appear in the Web browser as shown in Figure 14.8.

Enter a first name, last name, and phone number. Press the Submit button. Output from the PostServlet is shown in Figure 14.9.

There are many ways to use servlets, and this chapter only shows some of the basic uses. Server-side Java is a fast-growing area of intense Java development. There are a lot of design issues related to servlets.

Figure 14.8   PostExample HTML form.

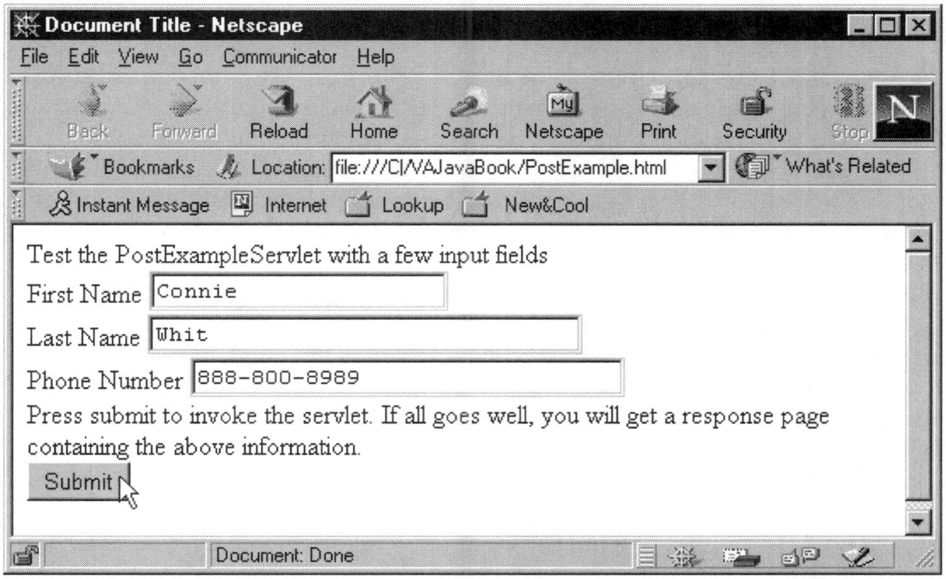

Figure 14.9   PostServlet output.

Servlet Sessions and State Information

Although the PostServlet shown above illustrates how to write a servlet, it is not very interesting or useful. Most real world applications use domain or business objects to hold application state information and provide application behavior. In a real world example, you would want to allow the end user to access the servlet from different HTML pages. The application may require that information be maintained across different pages. You can maintain state information via an HTTPSession object, which lives on the server and is associated with a particular Web browser through a "sessionid" stored in a "cookie." Cookies are objects managed by the client's Web browser. The servlet API supports access of client state information stored in an HTTPSession object. The HTTPSession object is obtained from the request, HTTPRequest, given to the servlet when called. Let's update our PostServlet example to allow the end user to register themselves with the servlet; taking the appropriate action based on the end user's input. We will use the IBM WebSphere Test Environment in VisualAge for Java to help test our updated servlet.

Creating the Domain Class

Create the Person class using the information in Table 14.4.

Table 14.4   New Class Attributes

Package Name	example.domain
Class Name	Person
Super Class	Objdect
Import the following packages	none*

Using the Bean Info tab of the Person class browser, add the JavaBean properties listed in Table 14.5 to the Person class:

Table 14.5   Person Class Properties

Property	Type
FirstName	String
LastName	String
PhoneNumber	String*

Next, add a toString() method to the Person class to display the properties of the Person object.

```
public String toString() {
   return getLastName() + ", " + getFirstName() + " <" +
getPhoneNumber() + ">";
}
```

Updating the PostServlet Class

Now you can update the PostServlet class to take action based upon which button the end user selects. Begin by providing a doGet() method, which will replace the PostExample.html file and write the initial form to the client browser. Note that the doGet() method uses a private method named writeInputUpdateHtml() to perform the print to the client browser. This will let you change the application later in this chapter.

```
public void doGet(HttpServletRequest req, HttpServletResponse res)
throws javax.servlet.ServletException, java.io.IOException {
  // Write out the registration input page
  writeInputUpdateHtml(req, res);
  return;
}
```

The writeInputUpdateHtml() method obtains a PrintWriter object from the response object and then prints HTML to the client browser. Additionally, you set the content type for the response, obtain the session from the request, and then print the input form to the Web browser. If the session exists, the method obtains the person object from the session. If the session does not exist, it is created and a Person object is created and placed in the session.

```
private void writeInputUpdateHtml(HttpServletRequest req,
HttpServletResponse res) throws java.io.IOException {
  PrintWriter out = res.getWriter();
  res.setContentType("text/html");

  // Declare a Person
  Person person = null;

  // Get a session.  If one is present, use it otherwise create
  HttpSession session = req.getSession(true);
  if (session.isNew()) {
    // New session? Create new person, place in session
    person = new Person();
    session.putValue("person", person);
  } else {
    // If an existing session, get the person object out
    person = (Person) session.getValue("person");
  }
  out.println("<HTML>");
  out.println("<HEAD>");
  out.println("<TITLE>Input page for PostServlet</TITLE>");
  out.println("</HEAD>");

  out.println("<BODY>");
  out.println("<H1>Test the PostServlet with a few input" +
              "fields</H1>");
  out.println("Press <B>Register</B> to invoke the servlet. If" +
              "all goes");
  out.println("well, you get a response");
  out.println("page containing the above information.");
  out.println(" <BR>");
  out.println("<FORM NAME=\"PostServlet\"");
  out.println("\taction=\"http://127.0.0.1/servlet/" +
              "example.servlet.PostServlet\"");
  out.println("\tmethod=\"POST\" >");
  out.println("<TABLE>");
  out.println("<TR>");
```

```
out.println("<TD>First Name</TD>");
out.println("<TD> <INPUT TYPE=\"text\" SIZE=20 MAXLENGTH=30" +
   " NAME=\"firstname\" VALUE=\"" + person.getFirstName() +
   "\"></TD>");
out.println("</TR> <TR>");
out.println("<TD>Last Name</TD>");
out.println("<TD><INPUT TYPE=\"text\" SIZE=20 MAXLENGTH=30" +
            " NAME=\"lastname\" VALUE=\"" + person.getLastName() +
            "\"></TD>");
out.println("</TR> <TR>");
out.println("<TD>Phone Number</TD>");
out.println("<TD><INPUT TYPE=\"text\" SIZE=20 MAXLENGTH=30" +
            " NAME=\"phonenum\" VALUE=\"" + person.getPhoneNumber()
+
            "\"></TD>");
out.println("</TR> <TR>");
out.println("<TD><INPUT TYPE=\"submit\" NAME=\"action\"" +
            "VALUE=\"Register\"></TD>");
out.println("</TR>");
out.println("</TABLE>");
out.println("</FORM>");
out.println("</BODY>");
out.println("</HTML>");
}
```

The doPost() method needs to be enhanced to get the input form contents, obtain a new or existing session, create a Person object, and, based on the input request, do the right thing. The doPost() method needs Java code for the actions listed in Table 14.6.

Table 14.6   doPost() Method Actions

Action	DoPost() response
Register	Put the Person object in the form into the session and send the writeConfirmOutputHtml() message.
Confirm	Get a Person object from the session and send the doRegistration() message to register the Person. Then send the writeCompleteOutputHtml() message to thank the person for registering.
Return	Call the writeInputUpdateHtml() message to redisplay the input page to allow the user to re-enter the Person.

```
public void doPost(HttpServletRequest req, HttpServletResponse res)
throws javax.servlet.ServletException, java.io.IOException {

  // Get the input form contents
  Properties formInput = getFormInput(req);

  // Obtain an new or existing session
  HttpSession session = req.getSession(true);
  if (session == null) {
    req.setAttribute("msg",
"Could not find or create a session.");
    writeErrorHtml(req, res);
    return;
  }

  // Declare a Person
  Person person = null;

  // Based on the action parm, do the right thing.
  if (formInput.getProperty("action").equals("Register")) {
    // Create a Person object from the variables in the Form
    person = parsePerson(formInput);
    if (person == null) {
      req.setAttribute("msg",
          "The Input form did not contain any data!" );
      writeErrorHtml(req, res);
      return;
    } else {
      session.putValue("person", person);
      writeConfirmOutputHtml(req, res);
    }
  } else
    if (formInput.getProperty("action").equals("Confirm")) {
      person = (Person) session.getValue("person");
      doRegistration(person);
      writeCompleteOutputHtml(req, res);
    } else
      if(formInput.getProperty("action").equals("Return")) {
        // Return - populate with values from session
        writeInputUpdateHtml(req, res);
      } else {
        req.setAttribute("msg",
                         "Form used does not contain valid " +
                         "action. Valid actions include:" +
                         " Register, Confirm, or Return.");
```

```
        writeErrorHtml(req, res);
    }
  return;
}
```

The first bold lines in the doPost() method demonstrate how error messages are handled. The first line sets the Attribute "msg" in the HttpServletRequest object. The third line sends the request in the private method writeErrorHtml(). The writeErrorHtml() method creates a PrintWriter object, gets the error message out of the HttpServletRequest, and writes out the error message to the client browser.

```
private void writeErrorHtml(HttpServletRequest req, HttpServletResponse
res) throws javax.servlet.ServletException, java.io.IOException {
  PrintWriter out = res.getWriter();
  res.setContentType("text/html");
  String msg = (String) req.getAttribute("msg");

  // Begin writing the output HTML to the output writer
  out.println("<HTML>");
  out.println("<HEAD><TITLE>PostServlet" +
              " Complete</TITLE></HEAD>");
  out.println("<BODY>");
  out.println("<H1>PostServlet: An Error Has Occured! </H1>");
  out.println(msg);
  out.println("</BODY>");
  out.println("</HTML>");
  return;
}
```

The getAttribute() message sent to the HttpServletRequest object gets the error message string to be printed. The doRegistration() method is an empty method for this example.

```
private void doRegistration(Person aPerson) {
  // Do database operations here to save person to a datasource
  }
```

The parsePerson() method sent by the doPost() method pulls the input form Person properties out of the form input.

```
private Person parsePerson(Properties props) {
  Person aPerson = new Person();
  boolean containsData = false;

  String fname = props.getProperty("firstname");
  if ((fname != null) && (fname.length() > 0)) {
    aPerson.setFirstName(fname);
```

```
      containsData = true;
   }

   String lname = props.getProperty("lastname");
   if ((lname != null) && (lname.length() > 0)) {
      aPerson.setLastName(lname);
      containsData = true;
   }

   String phnnum = props.getProperty("phonenum");
   if ((phnnum != null) && (phnnum.length() > 0)) {
      aPerson.setPhoneNumber(phnnum);
      containsData = true;
   }

   if (!containsData) {
      aPerson = null;
   }

   return aPerson;
   }
```

The writeConfirmOutputHtml() method gets the session and then the Person out of the session. If there is no session or if the Person is null, then an error has occurred. Once the Person object has been retrieved from the session, the confirmation output page is printed and the user must then confirm or return to re-enter the Person information.

```
/**
* @param req javax.servlet.http.HttpServletRequest
 * @param res javax.serv let.http.HttpServletResponse
 * @exception javax.servlet.ServletException The exception description.
 * @exception java.io.IOException The exception description.
 */

private void writeConfirmOutputHtml(HttpServletRequest req,
HttpServletResponse res) throws javax.servlet.ServletException,
java.io.IOException {

   PrintWriter out = res.getWriter();
   res.setContentType("text/html");

   // Declare a Person
   Person person = null;

   // Get a session.  If present, use it otherwise return an error
```

```
    HttpSession session = req.getSession(false);
    if (session == null) {
      // No session exists.  This is an error.
      req.setAttribute("msg",
              "You cannot call the output page " +
              " writting method unless a valid session exists." );
      writeErrorHtml(req, res);
      return;
    } else {
      // If an existing session, get the person object out
      person = (Person) session.getValue("person");
      if (person == null) {
        req.setAttribute("msg",
                          "A person does not exist in a session.");
        writeErrorHtml(req, res);
        return;
      }
    }

    // Begin writing the output HTML to the output writer
    out.println("<HTML>");
    out.println("<HEAD><TITLE>PostServlet"
      " Complete</TITLE></HEAD>");
    out.println("<BODY>");
    out.println("<H1>Is the below information correct?  </H1>");

    out.println(" <BR>");
    out.println("<FORM NAME=\"PostServlet\"");
    out.println("\taction=\"http://127.0.0.1/servlet/" +
                " example.servlet.PostServlet\"");
    out.println(   "\tmethod=\"POST\" >");
    out.println("<TABLE>");
    out.println("<TR>");
    out.println("<TD>First Name</TD>");
    out.println("<TD>" +  person.getFirstName() + "</TD>");
    out.println("</TR> <TR>");
    out.println("<TD>Last Name</TD>");
    out.println("<TD>" + person.getLastName() + "</TD>");
    out.println("</TR> <TR>");
    out.println("<TD>Phone Number</TD>");
    out.println("<TD>" + person.getPhoneNumber() + "</TD>");
    out.println("</TR> <TR>");
    out.println("<TD><INPUT TYPE=\"submit\" NAME=\"action\"" +
                "VALUE=\"Confirm\"></TD>");
    out.println("<TD><INPUT TYPE=\"submit\" NAME=\"action\"" +
```

```
                "VALUE=\"Return\"></TD>");
  out.println("</TR>");
  out.println("</TABLE>");
  out.println("</FORM>");
  out.println("</BODY>");
  out.println("</HTML>");
  return;
}
```

The writeCompleteOutput() method gets the session and then the Person out of the session. If there is no session or if the Person is null, an error has occurred. Once the Person object has been retrieved from the session, the completion output page is printed and the user is thanked for registering.

```
private void writeCompleteOutputHtml(HttpServletRequest req,
HttpServletResponse res) throws javax.servlet.ServletException,
java.io.IOException {
  PrintWriter out = res.getWriter();
  res.setContentType("text/html");

  // Declare a Person
  Person person = null;

  // Get a session.  If present, use it otherwise return an error
  HttpSession session = req.getSession(false);
  if (session == null) {
    // No session exists.  This is an error.
    req.setAttribute("msg",
                     "You cannot call the output page writting" +
                     " method unless a valid session exists." );
    writeErrorHtml(req, res);
    return;
  } else {
    // If an existing session, get the person object out
    person = (Person) session.getValue("person");
    if (person == null) {
      req.setAttribute("msg",
                       "A person does not exist in a session." );
      writeErrorHtml(req, res);
      return;
    }
  }

  // Begin writing the output HTML to the output writer
  out.println("<HTML>");
out.println("<HEAD><TITLE>PostServlet" +
```

```
         " Complete</TITLE></HEAD>");
    out.println("<BODY>");
    out.println("<H1>Registration Complete!</H1>");
    out.println("Thanks <B><U>" + person.getFirstName() + " " +
        person.getLastName() + "</U></B> for registering. " +
        "Please come an visit again soon.");
    out.println("</BODY>");
    out.println("</HTML>");
    return;
}
```

Running the New PostServlet

To execute the PostServlet using the WebSphere Test Environment from within
VisualAge for Java, you need to first check the classpath of the SERunner class
and make sure it includes the **My Project** project. Next run the **SERunner** class.
Verify that the WebSphere Application Server is running by viewing the console.
Then from the pop-up menu, launch the **PostServlet** servlet. Figures 14.10
through 14.14 show the PostServlet output pages.

Figure 14.10   Blank Input page.

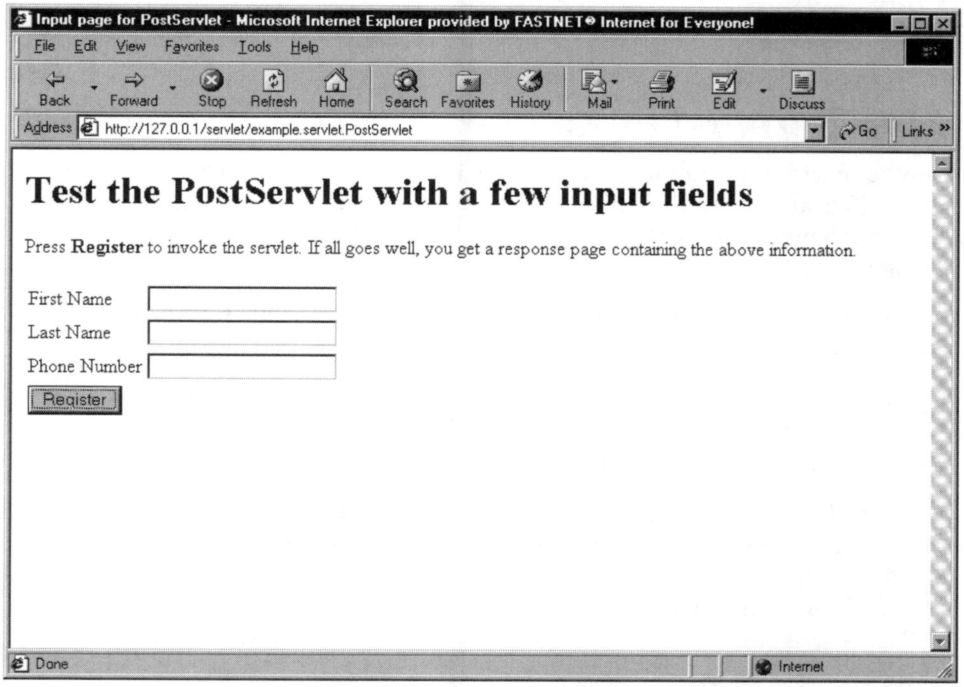

Figure 14.11   Error page.

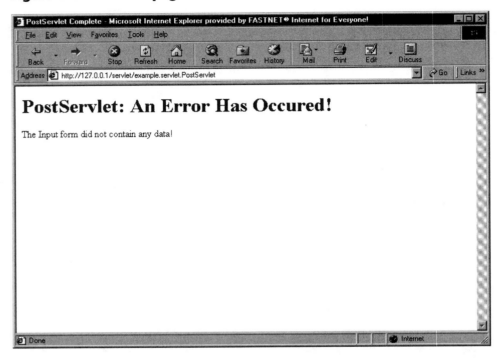

Java Server Pages

Another exciting feature in VisualAge for Java is support for Java Server Pages (JSPs). JSPs are one of the newest additions to the servlet world and offer a very clean mechanism for creating dynamic Web pages. Some of the goals of JSPs include:

- Encourage separation of the view from the domain and controller logic
- Provide a way for non-Java programmers to create dynamic Web pages
- Provide a way for the Web server to create dynamic Web pages by the web server
- Provide a way to utilize JavaBeans from within a JSP

The JSP language is a superset of the familiar HTML language. JSP adds tags such as the **<jsp:useBean>** tag that lets you add Java code to an otherwise static HTML page.

The following code sample shows some very simple JSP.

Figure 14.12   Input page.

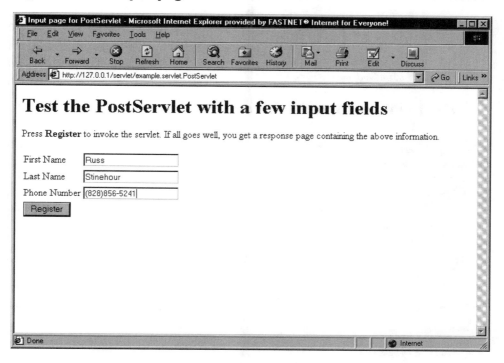

```
<html>
<head>
<title>Sample JSP Example </title>
</head>
<body>

Todays Date is
<%= new java.util.Date() %>.
<br>
</body>
```

The bold line, **<%= new java.util.Date() %>**, is JSP-specific syntax in *Scriptlet* form. When the WebSphere Application Server is requested to serve this JSP for the first time, WebSphere compiles the page into a servlet and then executes the servlet. The generated servlet simply echoes all of the HTML tags. However, the JSP-specific tags are converted to valid Java code and placed in the appropriate place within the servlet. *Scriptlets* end up in the service() method of the servlet. You can place any valid Java code in a *Scriptlet*.

Figure 14.13   Confirmation page.

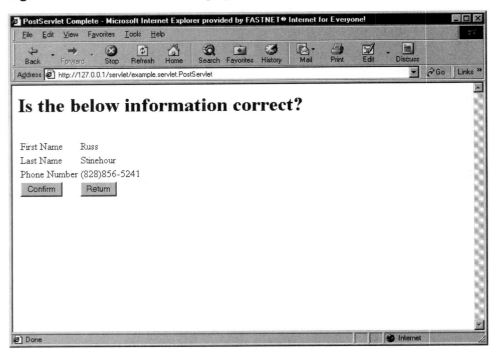

The net result is a generated HTML page with the *Scriptlet* code resolved. The resulting HTML appears as the following:

```
<html>
<head>
<title>Sample JSP Example </title>
</head>
<body>

Todays Date is
Wed Jan 6 09:30:00 PDT 1999.
<br>
</body>
```

In addition to *Scriptlets*, JSPs also support a <jsp:useBean> tag that allows access to JavaBeans and their associated behavior. The JavaBeans used may be as simple as a calculator or as complex as a business domain object with data stored in a DB2 database. An example code segment that uses the <jsp:useBean> tag follows:

Figure 14.14   Completion page.

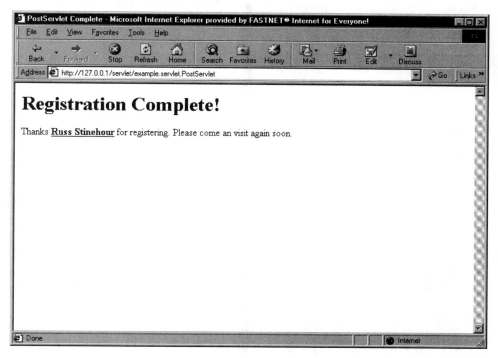

```
<HTML><HEAD>
<TITLE>Output page for servlet Bean</TITLE>
</HEAD>

<jsp:useBean id="SalesBean" Class="marketing.SalesBean"
 SCOPE=REQUEST></jsp:useBean>

<TABLE BORDER=3 FRAME=box
RULES=rows ALIGN="CENTER"
  WIDTH="100%" CELLPADDING="1"
CELLSPACING="1">
<CAPTION>Sales Forcast Results</CAPTION>
<TR>
  <TH ALIGN="CENTER" WIDTH="33%">QTR</TH>
  <TH ALIGN="CENTER" WIDTH="33%">REGION</TH>
  <TH ALIGN="CENTER" WIDTH="33%">TARGET</TH>
</TR>
```

```
<% for (int I=0; I < SalesBean.getUSERID_FORCST_QTR().length;
I++) { %>
<TR>
  <TD ALIGN="CENTER">
  <jsp:getProperty name="SalesBean"
  property="USERID_FORCST_QTR"/></TD>
  <TD ALIGN="CENTER">
  <jsp:getProperty name="SalesBean"
  property="USERID_FORCST_REGION"/></TD>
  <TD ALIGN="CENTER">
<jsp:getProperty name="SalesBean"
property="USERID_FORCST_TARGET"/></TD>
</TR>
<% } %>

</TABLE>
</BODY></HTML>
```

This example identifies a JavaBean using the <jsp:useBean> tag, then uses a Scriptlet with a for loop in it to build a loop. Inside the loop, the <jsp:getProperty/> tag accesses the properties within the JavaBean, thus providing data for the generated HTML table.

VisualAge for Java includes the IBM WebSphere Test Environment, which lets you test JSPs in the VisualAge for Java IDE. When using WebSphere within VisualAge for Java, there are some special facilities to test and debug servlets and JSPs. The Servlet Runner allows VisualAge for Java to act as a Web server that serves up HTML documents, JSPs, and servlets.

Another tool is the JSP monitor, which lets you view the execution of a JSP. The monitor shows the JSP on one side of the screen and the generated Java Servlet on the other side, which lets you debug and trace JSP pages. You need to add the IBM JSP Execution Monitor feature to get this function. Remember to add features by selecting File, Quick Start, Features, and Add Feature.

After you add the feature, you need to enable it. You can select Workspace, Tools, and JSP Execution Monitor. This displays a simple dialog that lets you start and stop the monitor. This does not display the Execution Monitor. The JSP Execution Monitor displays only when a JSP runs, as shown in Figure 14.15.

There are a few things to remember about JSPs. Running inside the IDE is slower because VisualAge for Java is parsing and compiling the JSP and running in the JRE (Java Run-time Environment) internally in VisualAge for Java. Although the JSP is converted to a servlet, you cannot debug the servlet because of its dependency on the JSP file. But the Monitor is very helpful for viewing the Java tags to the generated servlet code.

Figure 14.15   JSP Monitor.

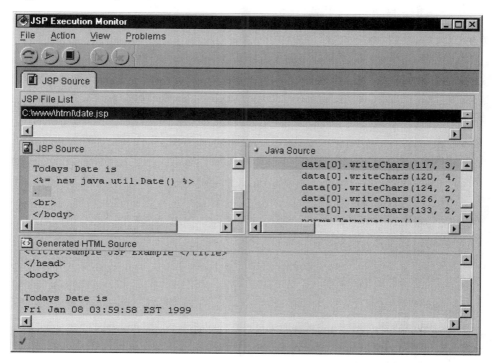

Converting the PostServlet to Use JSPs

JSPs can be used to simplify the Java programmer's task and place the HTML in a JSP file where it can be more easily maintained. The PostServlet methods used to print HTML to the client browser can be easily modified to forward control to a JSP. The ServletContext is sent the message to get the RequestDispatcher and the RequestDispatcher is sent the forward message. Control is then passed to the JSP. Following are the code changes to the various write methods.

```
/**
*/
private void writeInputUpdateHtml(HttpServletRequest req,
HttpServletResponse res) throws java.io.IOException,
ServletException {
   getServletContext().getRequestDispatcher(
"registration.jsp").forward(req, res);
}
```

```
private void writeErrorHtml(HttpServletRequest req, HttpServletResponse
res) throws javax.servlet.ServletException, java.io.IOException {
  getServletContext().getRequestDispatcher(
"error.jsp").forward(req, res);
  return;
}

private void writeConfirmOutputHtml(HttpServletRequest req,
HttpServletResponse res) throws javax.servlet.ServletException,
java.io.IOException {
  getServletContext().getRequestDispatcher(
"registrationconfirm.jsp").forward(req, res);
  return;
}

private void writeCompleteOutputHtml(HttpServletRequest req,
HttpServletResponse res) throws javax.servlet.ServletException,
java.io.IOException {
  getServletContext().getRequestDispatcher("
registrationcomplete.jsp").forward(req, res);
  return;
}
```

The JSP files follow. It is important to note that these JSP files were created in the IBM WebSphere Studio Page Designer using drag and drop facilities.

The registration.jsp file is listed below. This JSP file provides an identical solution to the preceding PostServlet example. **The bold lines show the Java code embedded in the file.**

```
<!DOCTYPE HTML PUBLIC "-//W3C//DTD HTML 4.0//EN">
<HTML>
<HEAD>
<META name="GENERATOR" content="IBM WebSphere Page Designer V3.0.1 for
Windows">
<META http-equiv="Content-Style-Type" content="text/css"><TITLE>Input
page for PostServlet</TITLE>
</HEAD>
<BODY>
<jsp:useBean class="example.domain.Person" id="person" scope="ses-
sion" />
<FORM NAME="PostExampleServlet"
action="http://127.0.0.1/servlet/example.servlet.PostServlet"
method="POST" ENCODE="application/x-www-form-urlencoded">
<H1>Test the PostExampleServlet with a few input
fields</H1>
```

```
         <BR>
         <BR>
         <TABLE border="1">
           <TBODY>
             <TR>
               <TD width="111">First Name</TD>
               <TD><!--METADATA type="DynamicData" startspan
<INPUT type="text" size="20" maxlength="30" name="firstname"
  valueproperty="person.firstName" dynamicelement>
  --><INPUT maxlength="30" name="firstname" size="20" type="text"
  value="<%= person.getFirstName() %>"><!--METADATA
  type="DynamicData" endspan--></TD>
             </TR>
             <TR>
               <TD>Last Name</TD>
               <TD width="64"><!--METADATA type="DynamicData" startspan
<INPUT type="text" size="30" maxlength="40" name="lastname"
  valueproperty="person.lastName" dynamicelement>
  --><INPUT maxlength="40" name="lastname" size="30" type="text"
  value="<%= person.getLastName() %>"><!--METADATA
  type="DynamicData"    endspan--></TD>
             </TR>
             <TR>
               <TD>Phone Number</TD>
               <TD><!--METADATA type="DynamicData" startspan
<INPUT type="text" size="30" maxlength="40" name="phonenum"
  valueproperty="person.phoneNumber" dynamicelement>
  --><INPUT maxlength="40" name="phonenum" size="30" type="text"
  value="<%= person.getPhoneNumber() %>"><!--METADATA
  type="DynamicData" endspan--></TD>
             </TR>
             <TR>
               <TD></TD>
               <TD></TD>
             </TR>
             <TR>
               <TD></TD>
               <TD><INPUT type="submit" name="action" value="Register"></TD>
             </TR>
           </TBODY>
         </TABLE>
         <BR>
         <BR>
         Press <B><U>Register</U></B> to invoke the servlet. If all goes
```

well, you get a response page containing the above
information.

</FORM>
</BODY>
 </HTML>

The registrationconfirm.jsp file displays the confirmation information and
prompts the end user to confirm or return to re-enter the information.

```
<!DOCTYPE HTML PUBLIC "-//W3C//DTD HTML 4.0//EN"><!-- Sample JSP file
-->
<HTML>
<HEAD>
<META name="GENERATOR" content="IBM WebSphere Page Designer V3.0.1 for
Windows">
<META http-equiv="Content-Style-Type" content="text/css">
<TITLE>PostServlet Complete</TITLE>
</HEAD>
<BODY BGCOLOR="#FFFFFF">
<jsp:useBean class="example.domain.Person" id="person" scope="ses-
sion" />
<FORM NAME="PostExampleServlet"
action="http://127.0.0.1/servlet/example.servlet.PostServlet"
method="POST" ENCODE="application/x-www-form-urlencoded">
<H1>Is the below information correct?  </H1>
<BR>
<BR>
<TABLE border="1">
  <TBODY>
    <TR>
      <TD width="111">First Name</TD>
      <TD><!--METADATA type="DynamicData" startspan
<WSPX:PROPERTY property="person.firstName">
  --><%= person.getFirstName() %><!--METADATA type="DynamicData"
endspan--></TD>
    </TR>
    <TR>
      <TD>Last Name</TD>
      <TD width="64"><!--METADATA type="DynamicData" startspan
<WSPX:PROPERTY property="person.lastName">
  --><%= person.getLastName() %><!--METADATA type="DynamicData"
  endspan--></TD>
    </TR>
```

```
      <TR>
        <TD>Phone Number</TD>
        <TD><!--METADATA type="DynamicData" startspan
   <WSPX:PROPERTY property="person.phoneNumber">
      --><%= person.getPhoneNumber() %><!--METADATA type="DynamicData"
      endspan--></TD>
      </TR>
      <TR>
        <TD></TD>
        <TD></TD>
      </TR>
      <TR>
        <TD><INPUT type="submit" name="action" value="Confirm"></TD>
        <TD><INPUT type="submit" name="action" value="Return"></TD>
      </TR>
    </TBODY>
  </TABLE>
  <BR>
  <BR>
  Press <U>Confirm</U> to continue.  Press
    <U>Return</U> to go back to the update screen. <BR>
  <BR>
  </FORM>
  </BODY>
  </HTML>
```

The registrationcomplete.jsp displays an HTML page to thank the user for registering.

```
<HTML>
<HEAD>
<META name="GENERATOR" content="IBM WebSphere Page Designer V3.0.1
   for Windows">
<META http-equiv="Content-Style-Type" content="text/css"><TITLE>
Registration Complete!
</TITLE>
</HEAD>
<BODY BGCOLOR="#FFFFFF">
<jsp:useBean class="example.domain.Person" id="person"
   scope="session" />
<H1>Registration Complete!</H1>
<P><BR>
Thanks <B><U><!--METADATA type="DynamicData" startspan
```

```
<WSPX:PROPERTY property="person.firstName">
  --><%= person.getFirstName() %><!--METADATA type="DynamicData"
  endspan--> <!--METADATA type="DynamicData" startspan
<WSPX:PROPERTY property="person.lastName">
  --><%= person.getLastName() %><!--METADATA type="DynamicData"
  endspan--></U></B> for registering. Please come an visit again
soon.</P>
</BODY>
</HTML>
```

The error.jsp displays an error message. The actual message is obtained from the Request instead of the session. The Request is used because the error may be that a session cannot be obtained.

```
<!DOCTYPE HTML PUBLIC "-//W3C//DTD HTML 4.0//EN"><!-- Sample JSP
  file -->
<HTML>
<HEAD>
<META name="GENERATOR" content="IBM WebSphere Page Designer V3.0.1
  for Windows">
<META http-equiv="Content-Style-Type" content="text/css"><TITLE>
Put Your Title Here
</TITLE>
</HEAD>
<BODY BGCOLOR="#FFFFFF">
<jsp:useBean id="msg" class="java.lang.String" scope="request" />
<TABLE border="1">
  <TBODY>
    <TR>
      <TD></TD>
      <TD>
      <H1>PostServlet: An Error Has Occured!</H1>
      </TD>
    </TR>
    <TR>
      <TD></TD>
      <TD><!--METADATA type="DynamicData" startspan
<WSPX:PROPERTY property="msg">
--><%= msg %><!--METADATA type="DynamicData" endspan--></TD>
    </TR>
  </TBODY>
</TABLE>
</BODY>
</HTML>
```

Table 14.7 Directory Locations of Application Deliverables

Application Deliverable	Directory Location
Java Servlets	X:\WebSphere\AppServer\hosts\default_host\default_app\servlets
HTML files	X:\WebSphere\AppServer\hosts\default_host\default_app\web
JSP files	X:\WebSphere\AppServer\hosts\default_host\default_app\web

Deploying Server-Side Java

Deploying servlets and JSPs depends on which Web application server you have selected. If you have selected IBM WebSphere Application Server to support your server-side Java, then you can use the directory locations in Table 14.7 to place your application deliverables.

Summary

Well, that was a very quick tour through a number of more advanced topics focused on server-side Java. In this chapter you:

- Learned the basics of server-side programming with Java servlets.
- Installed the JSWDK.
- Installed the JSWDK in VisualAge for Java.
- Wrote an example HttpServlet that used the POST HTTP method.
- Learned how to use the JSP Execution Monitor.
- Learned how to extend the servlet by using JSP files.

Server-side programming is a very powerful technology and there are entire books dedicated to showing you its many features. The next chapter covers Enterprise JavaBeans, which extend the function of server-side Java.

What's in Chapter 15

In the beginning... Java was used primarily in client-side GUI applications. With the maturity and acceptance of the language and the tools, many organizations are starting to use Java for their server-side programming.

The JavaBeans specification allows the interoperability of objects in various different development environments. Similarly, the Enterprise JavaBeans (EJB) specification enables developers to create server-side, distributed objects in a consistent fashion. The specification also defines a deployment strategy so that you can deploy EJBs without regard to any specific platform or EJB server.

In this chapter, you will gain a basic knowledge of EJBs and learn how to:

- Create an EJB Group
- Create an Entity EJB with Container Managed Persistence (CMP)
- Map container-managed EJB fields to columns of a database table
- Generate the EJB support code needed to run in an EJB Server
- Programmatically locate and use an EJB
- Configure and start the EJB servers supplied with VisualAge for Java
- Create a session EJB to control the transfer between two bank accounts
- Modify a servlet to use the EJBs to perform the transfer and display a results JSP indicating success or failure of the transaction

VisualAge for Java Enterprise Edition Version 3 allows the creation, testing, and deployment of Enterprise JavaBeans that conform to the Sun EJB specification.

If you are not familiar with Enterprise JavaBeans, read the mini EJB tutorial to get an idea of what EJBs are about.

For the exercise in this chapter, you first develop the Account EJB using the features in VisualAge for Java. This EJB is suitable for an enterprise, like a bank, to maintain information about a client's account. In this case, you use it in a Web Banking Application.

Next, you develop a session EJB to control the transfer of money between two bank accounts. This is done under transaction control to ensure that if either of the transactions (withdraw and deposit) fails, the whole transaction is rolled back.

The session EJB is used by a servlet, which is called from an HTML form to perform the transfer transaction. Then a JSP is displayed to inform the user whether the transaction succeeded or failed.

You also create, in DB2, the database tables necessary to support the Account EJB, using the instructions and code provided.

Throughout the development process of the EJB, you generate, deploy, and test your EJBs using the VisualAge for Java EJB Test Environment.

EJB Prerequisites

First you need to ensure that you have installed VisualAge for Java Enterprise Edition Version 3 on your computer.

Once you have installed VisualAge for Java, you need to ensure that the **IBM EJB Development Environment 3.0** feature is loaded. This feature loads several projects into your workspace:

- IBM EJB Samples
- IBM EJB Tools
- IBM Persistence EJB Library
- IBM RMI_IIOP class libraries

The feature also has co-requisite features that load automatically if not already available in the Workspace. The projects loaded are:

- IBM WebSphere Test Environment
- IBM Servlet IDE Utility class libraries
- Servlet API Classes
- Secure Socket Layer
- IBM XML Parser for Java
- VisualAge Persistence
- VisualAge Persistence Common Runtime

Once the VisualAge for Java EJB Development Environment feature is loaded, a new page named **EJB** appears in the Workbench between the **Interfaces** and **Managing** pages, as shown in Figure 15.1 for how this should look.

EJB Tutorial

The purpose of this book is not to explain every feature of the Java language or all the published Java APIs and specs. It is rather to teach you how to use the tools and features in VisualAge for Java to make use of these exciting new technologies.

The Enterprise JavaBean specification is quite complex and a separate subject on its own right. If you are reading this chapter, you probably have a good

Figure 15.1   The EJB development environment.

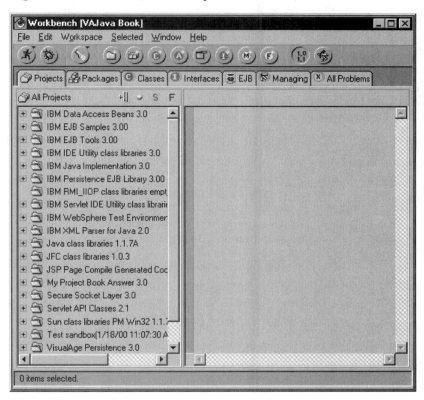

idea of what EJBs are about and you are looking for a tool that will help you implement this technology in your Enterprise Java applications.

As an introduction, a short EJB tutorial follows. If you are truly interested in EJBs, you should read a more specialized book on EJBs and then come back to this book for implementation details using VisualAge for Java.

What Are EJBs?

Enterprise JavaBeans are the implementation of artifacts that follow the EJB specification. These artifacts are, of course, written using the Java language. The EJB specification lays down the base for an Enterprise Java component architecture. This concept is similar to the JavaBean specification. JavaBeans are also Java components, but that is where the similarity ends.

The majority of this book is dedicated to the design of JavaBeans components. You have worked with both GUI and logic JavaBeans. One of the features of JavaBeans is that you can compose other, more complex beans from basic beans. For example, you can combine a complex user interface component made up of many GUI widgets with logic beans that provide the business logic. JavaBeans technology lets you combine these beans using tools and, in the case of VisualAge, connect beans together to perform the various functions necessary to meet the requirements of your program. Connections are implemented using the event model of the JavaBean specification.

In contrast, Enterprise JavaBeans are not visual and are rarely, if ever, directly combined with other beans in a Visual Composition Editor. Connections are usually not made to other components, as there is no predefined event notification mechanism to make connections possible.

EJBs are distributed objects and, in many cases, do not run in the same tier as other components of the application, like the GUI. EJBs run inside an EJB container, which in turn runs and is managed by an Enterprise JavaBean Server (EJS). The EJS is frequently an integral part of an application server, such as the IBM WebSphere Application Server. Application servers provide additional services to the EJS and EJB containers, such as optimized high-performance database access, connection pooling, and access to legacy systems.

The intent of the EJB spec is to isolate the developer from the drudgery and complexity of writing the underlying infrastructure code to communicate to and from clients, access databases, deal with security and provide transaction support. Those tasks are handled by the code generated by the EJB container as the result of deploying the EJB. There will be more on deployment later in this chapter. Being isolated from the infrastructure lets the developer focus on solving the business problem at hand.

The EJB container will handle issues related to:

- Distribution
- Multithreading
- Transaction management
- Resource management
- Persistent state management
- Security services

Thus, the EJB specification defines a component model for developing and deploying object-oriented, multi-tiered, enterprise Java applications.

In an application implementing a logical three-tier architecture, EJBs typically run in the middle tier, where the application server is king. EJBs communicate with other middle-tier components such as servlets and with third-tier services such as databases. EJBs can also be accessed from Java Applets or Applications.

Types of EJBs

The next two sections describe the two major types of EJBs, session beans and entity beans.

Session Beans

Session beans are associated with a particular client at run time. There is a one-to-one relationship between the client and the EJB. Session beans are created and destroyed by a client and are therefore considered transient, and do not survive system shutdown.

Within the session bean category there are two distinct types:

Stateless session beans. Stateless beans, as their name implies, have no internal state; therefore no instance variables should be coded in these types of beans. Because there is no state kept between the invocation of methods, stateless beans can be pooled by the container to provide a level of caching, thus improving server performance. A session EJB client is not guaranteed to access the same instance of the EJB on each method call. Because these beans do not hold any state, they do not need to be passivated.

> **Definition:**
>
> *Passivation* is the act of removing an EJB from active service. This can be because of resource constraints or because the particular bean has not been used for a long period of time. The container manages passivation. It involves storing the state of the EJB so that it can be later brought back into service by *activation*. One strategy for passivation is the serialization of the EJB; therefore EJBs implement the Serializable interface.
>
> The EJB spec defines the ejbPassivate() and ejbActivate() methods, which are called by the container at the appropriate times.

Stateful session beans. Stateful session beans do possess internal state and therefore need to handle passivation and activation. Because these types of beans can have instance variables, each client uses its own instance of the EJB. There is no sharing or pooling, and the client uses the same instance of the EJB throughout the session.

Session beans are mainly used as providers of services, ranging from the simple to the complex. One such complex service could be the coordination of actions that involve multiple entity beans as they participate in a transaction involving many databases and tables. Session beans are often used as controllers. Stateful session beans can also be used to store intermediate results of a long-lived session or computation.

Entity Beans

In contrast to session beans, multiple clients can share entity beans. Entity beans persist across multiple invocations and across multiple clients. Because they are persistent, they survive system shutdown and even system crashes.

Entity beans usually represent persistent data on the third tier, such as a row in a database table. Entity beans can also create and remove rows from a database table. In addition, they know how to find existing rows based on criteria and create new entity beans that represent those rows.

Entity beans can be classified into two categories:

Container managed (CMP). Like its name implies, this type of entity bean isolates the developer from writing code to handle persistence. The container is responsible for saving state and for persisting the data. The developer need not be concerned with details of how to access the database or even which database the EJB is related to at run time.

Bean managed (BMP). As opposed to CMP beans, BMP beans are responsible for saving their own state to handle the persistence issue. The container will call the EJB to perform functions such as **load** and **store** at the appropriate times. It is up to the EJB to implement the logic to perform these operations. This makes the EJB less adaptable, as well as harder to code and maintain.

You may be wondering why use BMP entity beans at all. The truth is that many containers cannot implement complex relationships between the object and data models in CMP beans. When the container cannot do what you need done, you must resort to BMP beans, where through a lot of hard work, you can code anything that is required without being constrained by the container.

In VisualAge for Java, complex relationships are handled by using the VisualAge Persistence tool (VAP). VAP provides you with a very rich framework to handle multiple table relationships and object associations. When you use VAP in VisualAge for Java, you must always export a **Deployed JAR** file to the WebSphere Application Server, so that the container does not need to generate any of the support classes for the EJB.

How Do EJBs Work?

By now, you can see that EJBs are not just simple classes you code, export, and make available to your programs to use, like you did with JavaBeans.

We mentioned that the EJB model was one of distributed objects. In this model, middle-tier EJBs are accessed by means of a proxy on the client. There have been many implementations of this architecture in the past. **RMI** is the Java implementation of calling methods on remote objects. For accessing non-Java objects, **CORBA** provides its own implementation using the **IIOP** protocol for communication between clients and remote objects. EJBs use a combination of these two strategies by using the RMI protocol over an IIOP transport. This combination gives us the RMI/IIOP protocol.

You, as an EJB developer, concern yourself with the creation of the actual **Bean** class. This class contains the business logic necessary for the EJB to perform its function. You also work on the **Home** and **Remote** interfaces of your EJB, and sometimes with a file designated as the **Deployment Descriptor**.

The Home interface provides EJB clients with the lifecycle services of the EJB. These methods are defined in the interface and implemented in the bean class. Lifecycle methods are those used to create, remove, or find EJBs. Typically, the classes that make up the home interface implement the **Factory** design pattern. This is a pattern that defines a factory as an "object maker". The home interface is used to obtain an instance of an EJB. For more information on design patterns, please refer to the book *Design Patterns, Elements of Reusable Object-Oriented Software,* by Erich Gamma, et al. (ISBN 020163361-2).

The Remote interface exposes to the client the business methods of the EJB. Only methods defined in the remote interface are accessible to the client. The actual implementation of business logic is on the bean class. See Figure 15.2.

VisualAge for Java automatically creates the Deployment Descriptor file. If you use another tool, you may have to create it manually. This file contains information about the bean and it is included in the JAR file, which is deployed on the server. The Deployment Descriptor is the file in the JAR file manifest marked as *the* EJB.

The Deployment Descriptor contains information about the EJB's quality of service attributes, such as Transactional Attributes, Levels of Isolation, and EJB Identity. It also contains the Java Naming and Directory Interface (JNDI) name for the bean. The client uses the JNDI name to find a bean within a JNDI namespace. Environment variables, which may be required by the bean, can also be defined in this file. EJB quality of service attributes can be set globally for the whole EJB or on a method-by-method basis. The EJB container uses the Deployment Descriptor when generating the supporting classes for the EJB.

In VisualAge for Java, most of your work is done in the bean class itself. There are facilities to add lifecycle and business methods to the proper interfaces using pull-down menus on the user interface of the tool. You will experience these when you do the exercise.

EJB Clients

When we talk about EJB clients, we don't necessarily mean the code that your client, or user of the software, sees through a GUI. EJB clients are the programming elements that use the EJBs. Clients can be Applets, Java Applications, servlets, JavaBeans, or other EJBs. Clients are responsible for locating or creating the EJB and invoking the business methods of the EJB. Clients talk to EJBs using the Home and EJBObject Stubs. See Figure 15.2.

Figure 15.2 shows some of the classes involved in the EJB implementation of the **Proxy** design pattern. For all intents and purposes, the client assumes it's talk-

Figure 15.2   EJB Proxy pattern implementation.

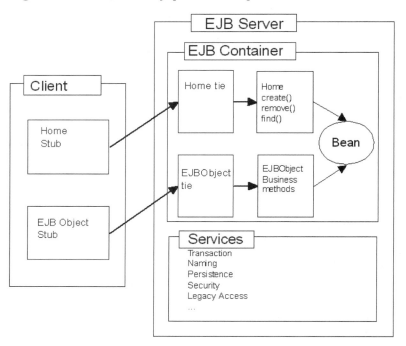

ing to a real object, but in reality the client code talks to the **stubs,** which in turn talk to **skeletons,** or **ties** in EJB lingo, on the server. Between the stub and the tie is the network—the communication protocol and transport layer. The marshaling and unmarshaling of data is handled by the code in the stubs and ties and is transparent to the developer.

Clients never communicate directly to the actual EJB bean; the EJBObject object always acts as in intermediary. The EJBObject implements the remote interface of the bean. The container provides the implementation of the EJBObject class.

Depending on the type of bean you are working with, there will be at least 12 classes involved with each EJB, more if you are working with entity beans. As mentioned before, the developer does the bulk of the work in the actual Bean class and the Home and Remote interfaces. The Container is responsible for generating the remainder of the classes. While developing inside VisualAge for Java, the tool plays the role of the EJB Container and generates the supporting code.

Deploying EJBs

Regardless of the type of EJB client, you must perform several steps before the EJB can be used. Remember that the actual EJB Bean class, the class that contains the logic to be executed, does not exist within the client code. The client has access to the stub in the Proxy pattern implementation. The process of interpreting the Bean class, Home interface, Remote interface and Deployment Descriptor is the job of the EJB Container.

The EJB Container will gather information from the components mentioned above and generate all the supporting classes to make the EJB accessible and available from your client code. As mentioned before, the Container relies on the information in the Deployment Descriptor to generate the supporting classes for the EJB, which conform to the quality of service specified by the bean developer in a way consistent with the capability of the deployment environment. The container also generates concrete implementations of the classes needed on the server side.

During deployment, several key questions are asked of the EJB deployer to satisfy the needs of the EJB. These are things like database names, JDBC drivers, user IDs, and passwords. This is done to "explain" to the Container operating and environmental deployment considerations.

While developing inside VisualAge for Java, you have the advantage of testing your EJBs in a totally integrated environment. During the exercise that follows, you will learn to set many of the deployment types of parameter within VisualAge for Java; equivalent settings must be performed at the time of deployment to an external EJB server.

Building EJBs Exercise

What follows is an exercise using EJBs. It assumes that you have read and completed the exercises in the Servlet and JSP chapters. If you haven't done so, and are not familiar with the topics in those chapters, please go back and take the time to complete them before you continue. This exercise builds and depends on those skills.

The goal of this exercise is to perform a transfer between two bank accounts using a Web-based application. You are given the HTML page to provide input for the servlet. You are also given the servlet that will service the request to transfer the money and the JSPs that will display the resulting new balances in case of success or a JSP that will display a message in case the operation fails.

> **NOTE**
> See the readme file on the CD-ROM for instruction on how to install these startup files.

Application Scenario

Transferring money between two accounts appears, on the surface, to be a simple operation. However, there are a number of considerations to be aware of. The most important one is that both the withdrawal and the deposit must complete successfully before the transfer operation can be considered complete.

Both the deposit and withdrawal operations will be conducted under the transactional control of the Container. In this mode, all operations involved in the transaction must succeed, or else all completed transactions will be rolled back. This is one of the benefits of using EJBs for this kind of work. Transaction control is inherent in EJBs. You as the developer need not be concerned with its implementation, only with the definition of the transactional attributes through the Deployment Descriptor.

The end user will access the server through an HTML form. This form has some JavaScript to provide a level of validation on the client side. It checks to ensure that:

- The To and From accounts are different

- The transfer amount is not blank

- The transfer amount contains only a valid character string representing a number

If the above requirements are not met, the form is not dispatched. If the values are correct, pressing the **submit** button of the form will cause the **doPost**() method of the **FundsTransferServlet** to be called.

After retrieving the values of the form from the request object, the servlet invokes its **dotTansfer**() method. This method creates an **AccountTransfer** session EJB, and invokes the EJB's **transfer**() method. The session bean creates two **Account** entity EJBs and performs the withdrawal and deposit operations. Depending on the result of the transfer operation, an appropriate JSP is used to display the status.

In the next section, you will build the two EJBs and complete the servlet. You will then test the completed application inside VisualAge for Java using its EJB Development Environment.

Building the Account EJB

Ensure VisualAge for Java is started and properly configured as explained above. From the Workbench, switch to the **EJBs** page. Figure 15.3 is how the EJBs page should look initially.

Creating the VAJBookEJBChapter EJB Group

An EJB group is a VisualAge for Java concept that enables you to develop related EJBs together. These related EJBs are usually deployed together on the same EJB Server. This is precisely the way EJBs are tested within VisualAge for Java. Only the entire EJB group can be loaded into and tested within the VisualAge for Java EJB Development Environment.

Figure 15.3   The EJBs page.

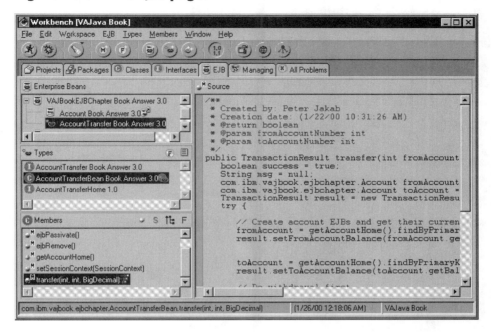

Create an **EJB Group**. As usual within VisualAge for Java, there are at least two ways of doing this:

- Select the Add **EJB Group** icon from the tool bar menu, or,
- From the **Enterprise Beans** pane (top-left window) pop-up menu, select Add, **EJB Group...** The **Add EJB** Group SmartGuide appears.

As you have done in other SmartGuides, enter **My Project** for the project name.

Enter **VAJBookEJBChapter** in the TextField under the **Create a new EJB group named:** radio button and leave that radio button selected as shown in Figure 15.4. The EJB group name must be a valid Java identifier, since the EJB generator uses the name as part of a package where it stores metadata.

Finally, press the **Finish** button to create the VAJBookEJBChapter EJB group, as shown in Figure 15.4.

Creating the Account EJB

Now, switch back to the Projects page of the Workbench. A newly created package named **VAJBookEJBChapterEJBReserved** now exists in your project. As you

Figure 15.4   Adding an EJB Group.

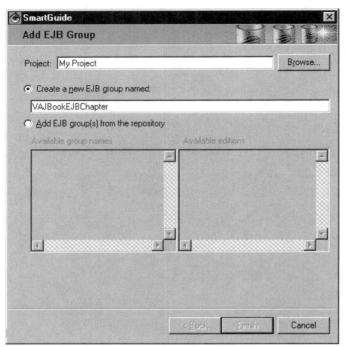

can see by the name, this is a package reserved by the EJB development environment to contain information related to the EJB group you created. Do not touch *anything* in this package.

In your project, create a package named **com.vajbook.ejb** to contain the EJBs for this exercise. Once you have created the package, switch back to the EJB page.

Create the Account EJB by selecting the **Add EJB** icon or selecting **Add, Enterprise Bean…** from the VAJBookEJBChapter pop-up menu. This opens the **Create EJB** SmartGuide.

Leave the default radio buttons selected (Create a new EJB and Create a new Bean class) as shown in Figure 15.5.

Enter **Account** in the **Bean name:** field.

For the **Bean type:** select **Entity bean with container-managed persistence fields (CMP).**

Make sure that **com.vajbook.ejb** is specified in the *Package* entry field. This is very important because the Create EJB Smartguide will be generating a lot of code and it needs to go in the correct package.

Select the **Next** button. Do not change any of the default settings on this page. However, note the default names generated by the SmartGuide. Ensure that the **Create finder helper interface...** checkbox is selected.

Create the following **CMP fields** for the EJB by pressing the first **Add** button and completing the **Create CMP Field** dialog with the values in Table 15.1.

Finally, select the **Finish** button and the code for the EJB is generated.

After the SmartGuide finishes generating code, you may see a red "X", indicating an error, beside the Account EJB. This could be caused because you have not yet mapped the EJB to the database table, which contains the real accounts. This is normal and will be corrected later in the exercise.

In the Projects page, the **VAJBookEJBChapterEJBReserved** package contains a new class named **Account**. The **com.vajbook.ejb** package has five new classes and interfaces with names that begin with **Account**. The EJBs page should resemble Figure 15.6.

Implementing the Methods on Account EJB

The next steps help you create the **deposit()** and **withdraw()** methods for the Account EJB. These methods constitute the business logic of the bean. Remember that the developer writes the business logic for the EJB on the bean class.

From the EJB page, select the **AccountBean** class and click the **Create Method or Constructor** icon (or use the class's pop-up menu) to open the **Create Method** SmartGuide.

In the entry field, replace **public void newMethod()** with **public void deposit(java.math.BigDecimal howMuch)**.

Select **Finish** to generate the method, as shown in Figure 15.7.

Repeat the previous steps to add the **void withdraw(java.math.BigDecimal howMuch)**.

Table 15.1   Container Managed Fields

Field Name	Type	Key Field	Getter & Setter	Promote Getter & Setter
accountNumber	Int	Yes	No	Yes
customerId	Int	No	Yes	Yes
balance	java.math.BigDecimal	No	Yes	Yes

Figure 15.5   Creating an EJB.

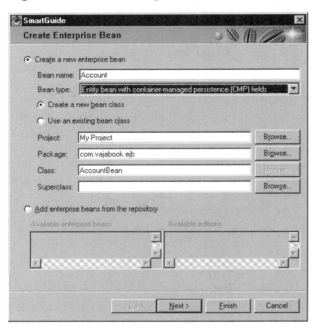

Figure 15.6   The Account EJB.

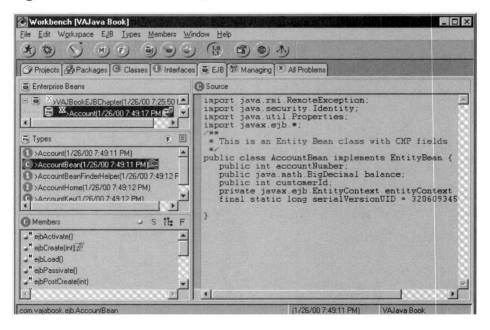

Figure 15.7 Adding a method.

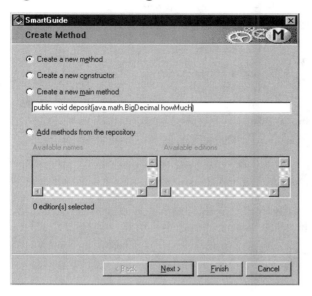

Select the **deposit**() method, and in the source pane enter the highlighted code below to complete coding the deposit business logic:

```
public void deposit(java.math.BigDecimal howMuch) {
    setBalance(getBalance().add(howMuch));
}
```

Select the **withdraw**() method and in the source pane enter the highlighted code below to complete coding the deposit business logic:

```
public void withdraw(java.math.BigDecimal howMuch) {
    // Check to see if there is enough money
    // Assume no negative balaces are allowed
    java.math.BigDecimal balance = getBalance();
    if (balance.compareTo(howMuch) < 0) {
        // Indicate not enough money
        try {
            javax.ejb.EntityContext context = getEntityContext();
            context.setRollbackOnly();
        }
        catch (Exception e) {
            System.out.println("Error setting rollback " + e);
        }
    }
}
```

```
  else {
    // Go ahead and withdraw the money
    setBalance(balance.subtract(howMuch));
  }
}
```

As you can see, there is quite a bit more work in doing a withdrawal operation than in making a deposit. The first line of code gets the current balance of the account, which is then compared with the amount of the withdrawal. If there is enough money, the withdrawal amount is subtracted from the balance. If there is not enough money in the account, we must somehow signal that this operation did not and cannot take place.

Since this operation will be called in the context of a transaction, and we have chosen by default to let the container handle transactions, we must let the context know that this part of the transaction did not take place.

The mechanism for doing this is to obtain the Entity Context of the EJB and set a flag called roll back. The lines below accomplish that task:

```
javax.ejb.EntityContext context = getEntityContext();
context.setRollbackOnly();
```

You will see how this interacts in the transfer operation in the **AccountTransfer** session bean, which you write later in this chapter.

If you get errors in VisualAge for Java after entering this code, you may have skipped one of the previous steps.

Adding to the Remote Interface

Now that you have written the internals of the EJB, you must identify those methods that form the interface available to clients. This involves adding the methods to the EJB remote interface. The Account EJB remote interface is a class named **com.vajbook.ejb.Account**. Add the required methods to the remote interface as follows:

With the AccountBean still selected, select the **deposit**() method from the **Methods** pane.

From the deposit pop-up menu, select **Add To** and **EJB Remote Interface**. Note the icon that appears after the method name. This is the visual cue that you've added the class to the remote interface. Also note that the icon is actually different from the one on the **ejbCreate** method that is part of the home interface.

Similarly, add the **withdraw**() method to the remote interface. Now the two business methods are available to the client.

The Account interface is the EJBObject for the Account EJB. If you select it, you see the methods that are available to the EJB clients.

Selecting any of these methods and examining their signature reveals that they all have a `throws java.rmi.RemoteException` clause as part of their signature. This is required of all methods, which are part of the remote interface.

Creating the Account Database

In order to test your work, you need to create the database table that the Account EJB uses to store its instances, and load the table with some fictitious data. While you can use any database that can be accessed using a JDBC driver, these instructions use the IBM DB2 Universal Database (UDB).

Database Authorization

A valid Windows NT userid named **userid** must exist with a password of **password**. It does not matter whether **userid** is uppercase or lowercase. The **password** is case sensitive and to change it you must edit the .ddl file. Make sure that the password in the .ddl file and the password used to set up the **userid** user match. The id must have sufficient authority to create database tables. See the relevant DB2 documentation for details. If you want to use a different ID to connect to the database and create the tables, change line three in the .ddl file and substitute the alternate id and password in the appropriate places. If you are using Windows 95 or 98, you must logon as **userid** with **password**.

Here's what you need to do:

Start by opening a DB2 Command Window. To accomplish this, select **Start** from the Windows TaskBar, **Programs, DB2 for Windows NT,** and finally **Command Window.** A window titled **DB2 CLP** (command line processor) opens.

If DB2 isn't already running, enter **db2start**. If you are uncertain whether it is running, entering the command reports its status.

Locate the supplied **ais.DDL** file. To create the required table and load it with data, enter the following command in the window opened during the last step:

```
db2 -tf ais.ddl
```

If you have any problems creating the database, or want to recreate it at some point, run the following commands in the command window to delete the existing database:

```
db2 connect reset
db2 drop database ais
```

Note that the name of the database is **AIS**.

> **NOTE**
>
> In order to run EJBs and servlets on your machine, TCP/IP must be set up correctly. From a DOS prompt, enter **hostname** to obtain the name of your machine. Use the returned name with the **ping** command to see if your machine responds. Suppose that the hostname command returned **goldie**. At a DOS prompt, enter **ping goldie**. Your machine should reply without errors or timeouts. Now try **ping localhost**. Again, you should get a good response with no errors or timeouts. A valid response will look similar to:
>
> **C:> ping localhost**
>
> **Pinging localhost [127.0.0.1] with 32 bytes of data:**
> **Reply from 127.0.0.1: bytes=32 time<10ms TTL=128**
> **...**

Mapping an EJB to a Database

Mapping is the process by which you identify, associate, or match the persistent fields of an EJB with the columns of the database tables where the corresponding data is stored. There are three approaches to mapping an EJB and a database. The first approach, referred to as **top-down,** involves creating the database table directly from an existing EJB. The second approach, referred to as **bottom-up,** involves creating the EJB based on an existing database table. The third approach, and the one used here, is a **meet-in-the-middle** approach where an EJB is mapped to an existing table. This third approach is usually the most common, as organizations taking advantage of object technology start mapping their newly created object models to existing databases that they have been using to run their enterprises.

Creating a Database Schema

In order to complete the following section, the JDBC drivers must be accessible to the VisualAge for Java Workspace. From the Workbench select **Window =>** **Options...,=> Resources.** Under **Workspace class path,** press the **Edit** button. On the next dialog, press the **Add JAR/Zip** button. Find your way on the file system until you reach the x:\sqllib\java\db2java.zip file, where x: is the drive where you installed DB2. Accept all dialogs to work your way back to the Workbench. You have just added the zip file containing the DB2 drivers to the Workspace classpath.

The first mapping step is to create a representation of the database schema within VisualAge for Java. Import the schema as follows:

 From the EJB page, open the schema browser by selecting the **Open Database Schemas Browser** icon.

From the **Schemas** menu item, select **Import/Export Schema** and **Import Schema from Database....**

When prompted, enter **VAJBook** for the name of the schema. Once entered, the **Database Connection Info** window appears.

Enter the database connection information in the window as indicated in Figure 15.8. The userid and password are case sensitive. Press the **Test** button to ensure that you can actually connect to the database. It will be easier to fix any problems now, on this dialog, rather than later, after the code is generated. Select **OK** when done.

When the **Select Tables** window appears, select the **USERID** entry from the **Qualifiers** list. Press the **Build Table List** button to display the list of tables with a **USERID** qualifier or schema, as shown in Figure 15.9.

From the **Tables** list, select the table with the name **ACCOUNT** and then select **OK** to close the window. This updates the contents of the **Schema Browser**, as shown in Figure 15.10.

From the **Schemas** menu item, select **Save Schema...** to open the **Save Schema** SmartGuide.

Enter **My Project** for the project name and **com.vajbook.ejb.metadata** for the package name as shown in Figure 15.11. Since this is a new package, be sure to type in the package name instead of using the Browse button to find the package. Select **Finish** when done.

Figure 15.8   Database Connection Info window.

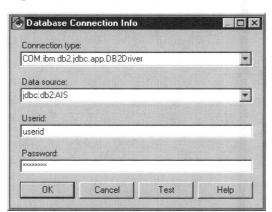

Figure 15.9   Select Tables window.

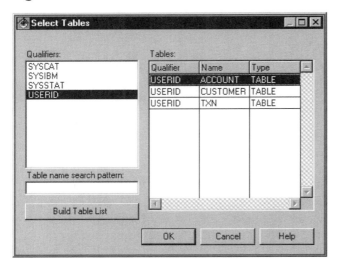

Schemas are saved as metadata and are interpreted by VAP. If you switch over to the Projects view, you will see the **com.vajbook.ejb.metadata** package. In the package a class named VAJBookSchema now exists. Like the classes in the reserved package, these classes are not meant to be touched by human hands.

Figure 15.10   Updated Schema Browser.

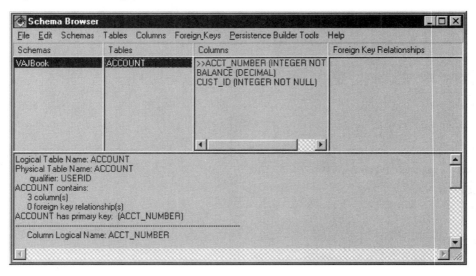

Figure 15.11   Save Schema SmartGuide.

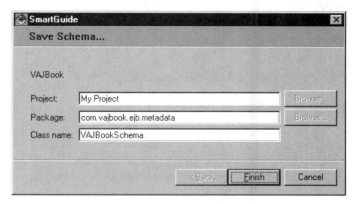

Creating a Schema Mapping

The next step is to create a mapping from the EJB to the database. Mapping is the process of associating database table columns with a persistent object's, a CMP EJB, container managed fields. Create the mapping as follows:

From the EJB page, open the map browser by selecting the **Open Schema Maps Browser** icon. Answer "Yes" to any prompts that appear.

From the **Datastore_Maps** menu item, select **New EJB Group Map....**

Enter the map information in the **New Datastore Map** window, as indicated in Figure 15.12 Select **OK** and the Map Browser updates to show the new mapping.

Select the **VAJBook** Datastore map and select the **Account** Persistent class. From the **Table_Maps** menu, select **New Table Map** and **Add Table Map with No Inheritance....**

Figure 15.12   New Datastore Map window.

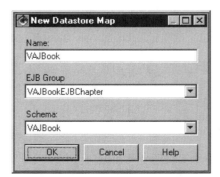

When the **Table Map With No Inheritance** window opens, select
ACCOUNT from the choice list and then press the **OK** button.

From the **Table Maps** pane of the Map Browser, select the **ACCOUNT
(primary)** entry (you may need to select **Account** from the Persistent
Classes pane first).

Again in the **Table Maps** pane, select **Edit Property Maps...** from the
pop-up menu of the **ACCOUNT** table. This opens the **Property Map
Editor** dialog, as shown in Figure 15.13.

For each of the entries in the **Class Attribute** column, select a **Simple**
mapping from the **Map Type** choice list. A simple map indicates to the
tool that an attribute of the EJB will directly map to a column on the
table. A complex map allows you to define a method that can combine
multiple columns into a single attribute of the EJB. For example, if the
table had columns for **street, city, state, and zip code,** they could be
combined into a single attribute on the EJB called **address**.

Now you map the actual column names to the fields, or attributes, on
the EJB. For each of the entries in the **Table Column** column, select the
column name that matches the name listed in the **Class Attribute** column
of the same entry.

Figure 15.13   Property Map Editor.

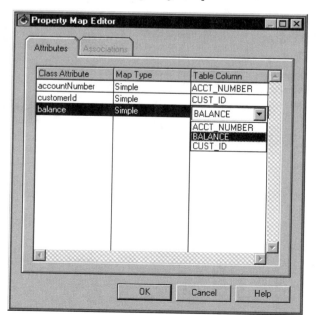

Figure 15.14   Update Map Browser.

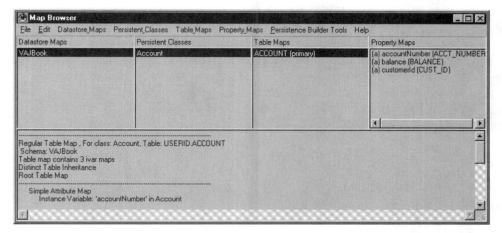

Select **OK** to close the Property Map Editor. The **Map Browser** updates to display the new mapping, as shown in Figure 15.14.

From the **Datastore_Maps** menu item, select **Save Datastore Map** to open the **Save Datastore Map** SmartGuide.

Enter **My Project** for the project name and **com.vajbook.ejb.metadata** for the package name.

If you previously had errors of the **Account** EJB, they should now be corrected. There should be no red "x" beside the Account EJB anywhere. If you still have errors showing you will have to back track and fix them before you can proceed.

Generating the EJB Code

Now that you have written the Account EJB and mapped it to the database, use VisualAge for Java to generate the supporting classes for the EJB. VisualAge for Java generates the code when you select the **Account** EJB from the Enterprise Beans pane and, from its pop-up menu, select **Generate Deployed Code**. Figure 15.15 shows the complete list of types created and generated for the Account EJB.

Generating the deployed code within VisualAge for Java creates all the classes you see in Figure 15.15. When running in a production environment, generating these classes is the job of the EJB container in the EJS of your choice. You only need to supply a JAR file with the Home and Remote interfaces, the Bean class, and a Deployment Descriptor. This JAR file can be produced in VisualAge for Java.

Figure 15.15   Account EJB types.

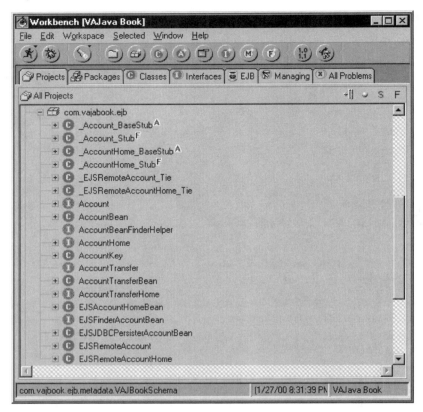

Testing the Account EJB

Your new EJB is ready to be tested. Using VisualAge for Java to develop EJBs gives you the advantage of testing and debugging them without having to deploy them to a real EJS. The VisualAge for Java EJB Development Environment provides all the facilities you need. In fact, you will be running the WebSphere Application Server Advanced Edition code inside of VisualAge for Java. You might not realize it now, but this combination is very powerful.

Starting the EJB Servers

In order to run EJBs in VisualAge for Java, you must configure and start three servers. These servers represent your EJS. They are:

- Location Daemon service
- Persistent name server
- EJB Server

Figure 15.16   EJB Server Configuration window.

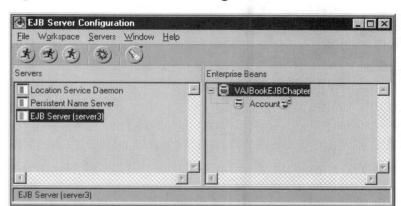

The first two servers are used to locate the EJBs in the Java Naming and Directory Interface (JNDI) name space. The EJB server is the one that provides the run-time environment for the EJBs.

Before you can start the servers, the EJB group must be added to the **Server Configuration**. From the Workbench, switch to the EJB page and from the Enterprise Beans pane select the **VAJBookEJBChapter** EJB group.

Using the VAJBookEJBChapter's pop-up menu, select **Add To…, Server Configuration** menu item to bring up the **EJB Server Configuration** window, as shown in Figure 15.16.

Open the EJB Server's properties and modify them as indicated in Figure 15.17. In case you don't remember, the password used in the protected Password field is **password**. These properties tell the EJB server how to connect to the database server and are mandatory for CMP EJBs.

 You must start the servers in a particular order. First start the Location Service Daemon (LSD) by selecting it and then pressing the **Start Server** icon , or from its pop-up selecting **Start Server**. Once started, the runner icon will appear next to the Service in the Server Configuration window. Nothing will be sent to the Console window.

Next, in the exact same way, start the Persistent Name Server (PNS). Once started, the runner icon will appear next to the Service in the Server Configuration window. Additionally, lots of messages will be written to the Console window.

Finally, start the **EJB Server**. Once started, the runner icon will appear next to the Service in the Server Configuration window. Additionally, lots of messages will be written to the Console window.

Figure 15.17 EJB Server properties.

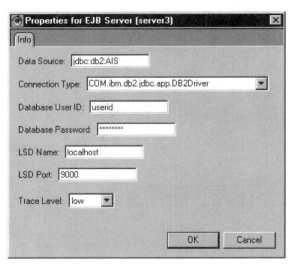

As you start each server, you see the runner icon appear at the end of the entry. You also see each server produce output in the **Console** window. The first server produces no output. The **Persistent name Server** and EJB Server produce many lines of output. If something goes wrong, start at the end of the output and work your way back to diagnose the problem. Sometimes the problem is as simple as not having started the database server (DB2).

When you see the "**E Server open for business**" messages on the console for each of the servers, you know they are ready. Be careful when looking for this message on the Persistent Name Server output, because after the EJB Server starts, the message will scroll up on the console message area. This is due to messages sent to the console when the EJB Server registers the EJBs with the name server.

Testing the Account EJB

Now that the three servers are up, you can test the EJB. But how will you test it without a client? The VisualAge for Java EJB Development Environment creates a test client for you.

Creating the Test Client

On the EJB Server Configuration window, select the EJB Server from the Servers pane. Now you see the EJB Group on the Enterprise Beans pane. If necessary, expand the VAJBookEJBChapter EJB group. Select the **Account** EJB, and from its pop-up menu select **Generate..., Test Client**. The test client can also be generated, in a similar manner, directly from the EJB page of the Workbench.

Figure 15.18   Account EJB Test Client.

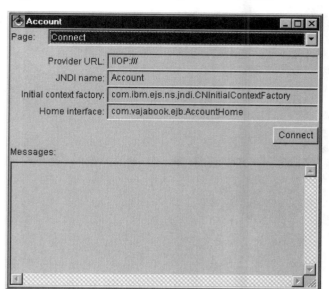

To start the test client, select **Run Test Client** from the EJB's pop-up menu. You may also start it by pressing the Run test client icon on the toolbar of the EJB Server Configuration window. Start the test client for the Account EJB now. When the test client comes up, it should look like Figure 15.18.

Normally, you do not need to change the values of the four entry fields on the test client Connect page. After you press the Connect button, the test client connects to the naming service using the URL provided. The current URL of IIOP:/// is what you need to connect to the Persistent Name Server inside VisualAge for Java. If you wanted to use another server you would enter its URL here.

The JNDI name is the EJB name that is registered on the name server. Using this name, the test client performs a search on the name server, which returns a reference to the Home interface of the EJB.

Press the **Connect** button. If the connection is successful and the JNDI name is found, the test client switches to the Home Interface page of the window. See Figure 15.19.

On the Methods pane of this page, you see the lifecycle methods of the EJB. Since this is an CMP EJB you see a **create(int)** method, which will create a new row on the ACCOUNT table of the AIS database. There is also a **findByPrimaryKey(AccountKey)** method, which will attempt to find a row in the ACCOUNT table where the AccountKey matches that of the table. The

Figure 15.19   Account EJB Test Client, Home interface.

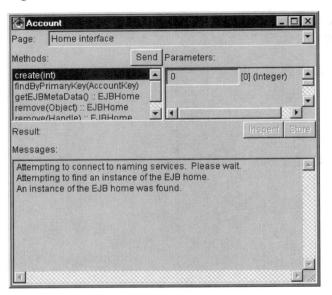

AccountKey class was created by VisualAge for Java for you. The **remove()** methods should be used with extreme care. Remember that entity EJBs represent rows in a database table. Guess what the remove() method does? It deletes the row from the table.

You can invoke any of the methods on the Methods pane. The mechanism is simple. Select the method you are interested in, set up the parameters with the proper values, and press the **Send** button. It gets a bit more complex when the parameters to a method are objects. You must create the object before you can include it as a parameter.

You will now use the Home interface of the EJB to find an Account EJB whose account number is 3. Select the **findByPrimaryKey(AccountKey)** method. Before you can send the method to the EJB, you must supply the key. In order to construct an instance the **AccountKey** object, press the **New** button on the **Parameters** pane. A new window opens. In this window you see all the public constructors for the class you are trying to instantiate. In our case the **AccountKey** class has two constructors, the default constructor, which is of no use for creating an unique key, and a constructor which takes an integer. Select the **AccountKey(int)** constructor and enter the number 3 in the entry field. Press the **Send** button to instantiate the account key object, press the **Done** button to close the window. Now you can press the **Send** button on the test client to send the findByPrimaryKey() method to the home interface. See Figure 15.20.

Figure 15.20   Finding account number 3.

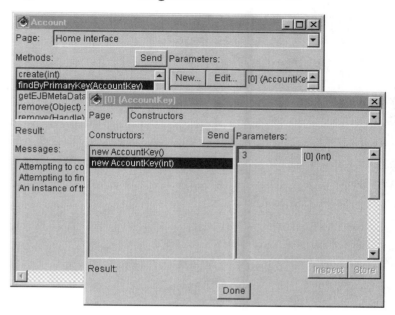

Your machine will churn for few moments while the database manager finds the account in the table. If the acocunt is not found, you will see a javax.ejb.FinderException was thrown in the **Messages** area of the test client. Because Account number "3" does exist in the database, the test client will now switch to the **Remote interface** page. You can switch between the pages of the test client by Selecting from the **Page** drop-down list.

On the **Remote interface**, find the business methods of the EJB. Look through the methods and notice that both the **deposit()** and **withdraw()** methods you created are available. You also see other methods that were created by the SmartGuide, which you used to create the EJB.

Select the **getBalance()** method and press the **Send** button. In the result area you will see how much money is in the account. Experiment with the other methods and see how they affect the balance. Note that both the **deposit()** and **withdraw()** methods take java.math.BigDecimal parameters to indicate how much money is involved in the transaction. You must instantiate objects of this type before invoking the method. This is done using an approach similar to what you used to create the **AccountKey** in the previous step. See Figure 15.21.

By now you start to see some of the power of EJBs. You are actually querying and updating the database without having written any database or SQL code

Figure 15.21   Getting the account balance.

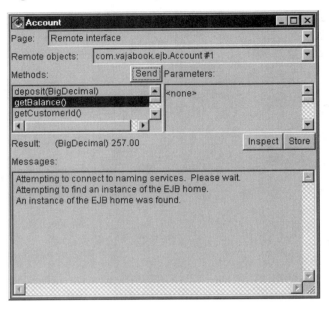

at all. You are also performing these operations under transaction control. You will see how that works in the next section.

When you are finished testing your EJB, stop the servers and close the Server Configuration window. If need be, you can debug your EJB code just like you debug anything else in VisualAge for Java. Find the source in any of the Source Browsers, set breakpoints, run the operation, and debug to your heart's content. If you need to generate the deployed code for an EJB that is currently running on the EJB server, you will have to stop the server before VisualAge for Java will generate the code.

Creating the AccountTransfer Session EJB

Now that you are an expert at creating and testing EJBs within the VisualAge for Java EJB Development Environment, it is time to create another EJB. This time the instructions will be shorter. Creating a session EJB takes fewer steps than creating an entity CMP bean.

The AccountTransfer EJB will be responsible for coordinating two Account beans, which will move an amount of money from one to the other. The withdrawal and deposit operations built into the Account beans are used for this purpose.

Make sure that the VAJBookEJBChapter EJB group is selected. Create a new session EJB and name it **AccountTransfer**. Ensure that the bean's package is **com.vajbook.ejb**. This is important. Accept all other default values and press the **Finish** button to create the EJB.

Adding the Transfer Method to the EJB

Soon you will write a method to perform the transfer operation between two accounts. This method will need to find the two accounts that participate in the transaction. The accounts are modeled as Account EJBs.

As you remember from the mini-tutorial, before you can use an EJB, you need to find its Home interface, and from the Home interface you can find an EJB by using its primary key. This is what you did using the test client in the previous section. The difference is that in this case, the EJB client for the Account EJBs is the AccountTransfer EJB. That means that the AccountTransfer EJB is responsible for finding the Home of the account EJBs and then using the Home interface to find the particular Account EJB representing that account in the database.

The getAccountHome() Method

Select the AccountTransferBean class and add a new **protected** method called **getAccountHome()**. The method takes no parameters, and returns an object of type com.vajbook.ejb.AccountHome.

Before you can write the body of the method you need to declare a protected instance variable of type **com.vajbook.ejb.AccountHome**. Name it **accountHome** and initialize it to a value of **null**.

```
public class AccountTransferBean implements SessionBean {
   private javax.ejb.SessionContext mySessionCtx = null;
   final static long serialVersionUID = 3206093459760846163L;
   protected com.vajbook.ejb.AccountHome accountHome = null;
}
```

Save the class definition.

Select the **getAccountHome()** method just created and fill in its body with the code below:

```
protected AccountHome getAccountHome()
   throws javax.naming.NamingException
{
   if (accountHome == null) {
     try {
       java.util.Hashtable namingProps = new java.util.Hashtable();
         namingProps.put(javax.naming.Context.PROVIDER_URL,
           "iiop:///");
         namingProps.put(
           javax.naming.Context.INITIAL_CONTEXT_FACTORY,
           "com.ibm.ejs.ns.jndi.CNInitialContextFactory");
         javax.naming.InitialContext initContext = new
         javax.naming.InitialContext(namingProps);
         java.lang.Object o = initContext.lookup("Account");
         accountHome = (AccountHome)
```

```
          javax.rmi.PortableRemoteObject.narrow(
          o, AccountHome.class);
      }
   catch (ClassCastException e) {
      throw new javax.naming.NamingException(e.getMessage());
   }
 }
 return accountHome;
}
```

This method implements the **singleton** design pattern. The accountHome object is only located once per instance of the object. The first time the method is called, accountHome will be null and the code to locate the Home interface executes.

The first step is to find the initial context of the JNDI name space. The initial context represents the starting point of the tree where the names are stored. The initial context constructor takes a **Hashtable** object as a parameter. In the hashtable, you store the URL of the provider of the naming service, in this case **iiop:///**, and the name of the class that implements the factory that creates the initial context, in this case **com.ibm.ejs.ns.jndi.CNInitialContextFactory**. These values are keyed in the hashtable by constants defined in the **java.naming.Context** interface.

Once you have an **InitialContext** object, you can ask it to look for a particular name. The name must be bound, or registered, with the naming service. Doing so is the job of the EJS. The **lookup()** method returns an **Object**. Before you can use the object, you need to perform a special "cast" operation to convert it to the actual AccountObject you need. This is performed by calling the static method **narrow** of the class **javax.rmi.PortableRemoteObject**. This method takes the object returned by the lookup() method and the class of the object you want to convert to.

As you can see, finding the Home object and converting it to a usable form looks a bit strange, especially if you are not used to finding and instantiating objects that potentially do not reside on your own machine. Remember that EJBs are remote objects.

Once you have the Home object, which is really a Home object stub, you can use it to invoke lifecycle methods for the EJB.

The transfer() Method

Select the AccountTransferBean class and add a new method called **transfer()**. The method takes three parameters—the account number to withdraw money from, the account number to deposit money into, and the amount of money involved in the transaction—and returns a **TransactionResult** object.

```
public com.vajbook.ejbchapter.TransactionResult transfer(
   int fromAccountNumber,
   int toAccountNumber,
   java.math.BigDecimal amount)
   throws javax.ejb.CreateException, java.rmi.RemoteException
```

Define the method so it can throw both a **javax.ejb.CreateException** and a **java.rmi.RemoteException.** Note that this method might have problems because the TransactionResult class may not yet exist. If you did not load the My Project project from the CD, then these errors are expected.

The TransactionResult Class

The transfer() method returns an object of type **com.vajbook.ejbchapter .TransactionResult**. This class is included on the CD-ROM with this book. It is a very simple class used to encapsulate the results of a transaction. Ensure that you have loaded the **My Project** project into VisualAge for Java before continuing.

> **NOTE**
>
> There are two versions of the **com.vajbook.ejbchapter** package in the .dat file supplied on the CD-ROM. One is the **completed** version, and the other is the **startup** version. Make sure you load the startup version, so you can use it to complete the coding in the classes it contains. The completed version can be used for reference or if you want to save some time typing the code in.

This is a typical usage of a JavaBean, designed to display the results of a transaction by a JSP. Take a minute to examine this class. Switch to the Projects page of the workbench and find the class under the com.vajbook.ejbchapter.TransactionResult package. All attributes are strings and they represent the following attributes:

- fromAccountNumber
- toAccountNumber
- fromAccountBalance
- toAccountBalance
- transactionSuccess
- message

Because objects of this type will travel across the network and because the class is a JavaBean, it must implement the java.io.Serializable interface.

Completing the transfer() Method

Switch back to the EJB page of the workbench. Find the transfer() method you just created and fill in its body with the code shown below:

```
public com.vajbook.ejbchapter.TransactionResult transfer(
   int fromAccountNumber,
```

```
      int toAccountNumber,
      java.math.BigDecimal amount)
      throws javax.ejb.CreateException, java.rmi.RemoteException
{
  com.vajbook.ejb.Account fromAccount = null;
  com.vajbook.ejb.Account toAccount = null;
  com.vajbook.ejbchapter.TransactionResult result = new
    com.vajbook.ejbchapter.TransactionResult();
  try {
    // Create account EJBs and get their current balances
    fromAccount = getAccountHome().
      findByPrimaryKey(new AccountKey(fromAccountNumber));
    result.setFromAccountBalance(fromAccount.getBalance().
      toString());

    toAccount = getAccountHome().
      findByPrimaryKey(new AccountKey(toAccountNumber));
    result.setToAccountBalance(
      toAccount.getBalance().toString());

    // Do withdrawal first
    fromAccount.withdraw(amount);

    // Now do the deposit
    toAccount.deposit(amount);
  }
  catch (javax.transaction.TransactionRolledbackException trbe) {
    result.setMessage(
      "Could not complete transaction,Ó +
      Ò perhaps you are out of money?");
    result.setTransactionSuccess(false);
  }
  catch (javax.ejb.FinderException e) {
    result.setMessage("Account number not found on database");
    result.setTransactionSuccess(false);
  }
  catch (Exception e) {
    result.setMessage("Problem... -> " + e);
    result.setTransactionSuccess(false);
  }

  if (result.getTransactionSuccess() == true) {
    result.setFromAccountBalance(
      fromAccount.getBalance().toString());
    result.setToAccountBalance(toAccount.getBalance().toString());
```

```
      result.setMessage("Transaction completed successfully");
   }
   return result;
}
```

This method is long, but not overly complex. The first three lines after the declaration of the method define the two Account EJBs and the TransferResult object, which will be used to communicate the result to the calling servlet.

Inside the **try** block, the **fromAccount** is found using the corresponding method parameter. The AccountHome is obtained first by calling the **getAccountHome()** method. Then the **findByPrimaryKey** of the Home interface is invoked to look in the database and find that particular account. Since the account number passed in cannot be used directly because it is an **int**, you create a new **AccountKey** object using the int parameter.

```
fromAccount = getAccountHome().
   findByPrimaryKey(new AccountKey(fromAccountNumber));
```

If the Account EJB is found, processing continues, otherwise a **FinderException** is thrown and caught. The appropriate message and status are recorded in the TransactionResult object and processing of the method ends. The calling servlet examines the TransactionResult's **transactionSuccess** attribute and displays the appropriate success or failure JSP. If the EJB is found, its current balance is recorded in the TransactionResult object. The same processing is done for the **toAccount**.

Once you have both Account EJBs, you first process the **withdraw()** operation. If there is not enough money in the account, the method sets the rollback flag of the current transaction.

```
// Snipped from withdraw() method in AccountBean class
javax.ejb.EntityContext context = getEntityContext();
context.setRollbackOnly();
```

Calling setRollbackOnly() on the Entity context causes a RolledbackException to be thrown by the container. Remember, we are executing all these methods under the transactional control of the EJB Container. If the exception is thrown, it is caught. The appropriate message and status are recorded in the TransactionResult object and processing of the method ends. Just like before, and for all exceptions thrown, the calling servlet examines the TransactionResult's **transactionSuccess** attribute and displays the appropriate success or failure JSP.

If the withdraw operation executes without failure, then the next step is to deposit the same amount of money into the toAccount EJB. No failures are expected from the EJB when depositing the money.

Near the end of the transfer operation, you check the **transactionSuccess** attribute of the TransactionResult object. It was set to **true** initially and changed to false if some failure occurred while transferring the money. If it still true, that means no failures occurred and you can exit the method, but not before you set the new balances and a new message into the TransactionResult object. Because all the attributes of this bean are Strings, some type conversions are necessary.

After you are able to save this method successfully, it must be promoted to the Remote Interface, otherwise the EJB client will not able to see or use it. From the **Members** pane of the **AccountTransferBean** class, right mouse click and from the pop-up menu select **Add to...**, **EJB Remote Interface**.

Testing the AccountTransfer EJB

From the **Enterprise Beans** pane, select the AcountTransfer EJB, right mouse click and from the pop-up menu select **Generate, Deployed Code**, and **Generate, Test Client**.

From the EJB menu item, select **Open To, Server Configuration**. Start all three servers. On the test client, select the EJB Server and from the right pane select the AccountTransfer bean. Using its pop-up menu start the test client.

Test your EJB by first connecting to the naming service. After connecting, the test client switches to its Home interface page. Since this is a session EJB, there are no finder methods. You must create a session EJB before you can use it. From the Home interface page of the test client, select **create()** and press the **Send** button. After creating a new instance of the EJB, the test client switches to its Remote interface page. Select the **transfer(int, int, BigDecimal)** method, fill in the parameters, and press the **Send** button. Try a toAccount of 3 and a fromAccount of 4. Use a value such as 200.00 for the amount.

Try this scenario with different amounts and different account numbers. Set breakpoints in the transfer(), withdraw(), and deposit() methods. Single step through the operations to understand what is happening. Try to withdraw an amount larger than the balance available on the **fromAccount**. What happens if you enter an invalid account number?

You can verify what is happening in the database by using the DB2 Control Center and opening the ACCOUNT table on the AIS database.

Completing the Exercise

You are getting close to testing your EJBs in a more lifelike environment. But before you do that, you need to understand some of the methods in the **FundsTransferServlet**.

The **FundsTransferServlet** servlet has been provided for you in the CD-ROM and is part of the My Project project. This servlet is called from the AccountTransfer.html Web page. This page, along with two JSPs, can also be found on the CD-ROM. See Table 15.2 for a list of external files and the location you should copy them to for them to work properly in the VisualAge for Java EJB Development Environment.

Table 15.2   Location of External Files

File Name	Location in file system
AccountTransfer.html	X:\IBMVJava\IDE\project_resources\IBM WebSphere Test Environment\hosts\default_host\default_app\web
TransferOK.jsp	X:\IBMVJava\IDE\project_resources\IBM WebSphere Test Environment\hosts\default_host\default_app\web
TransferFailed.jsp	X:\IBMVJava\IDE\project_resources\IBM WebSphere Test Environment\hosts\default_host\default_app\web

Switch to the Projects page of the Workbench. Find the **FundsTransferServlet** servlet in the **com.vajbook.ejbchapter** package of the **My Project** project. This is the same package that contains the **TransactionResult** class discussed earlier.

The **FundsTransferServlet** servlet is an HttpServlet. Only the **doPost()** method is overridden from its superclass. This is because it is only legal to call this servlet from an HTML form with a METHOD=POST clause in its FORM definition.

The **doPost()** method gets dispatched when the user presses the **Submit** button on the form.

```
public void doPost(HttpServletRequest req, HttpServletResponse res)
throws ServletException, java.io.IOException {
  // Get the input form contents
  Properties formInfo = null;
  try {
    formInfo = getFormInfo(req);
    TransactionResult result = doTransfer(formInfo);
    req.setAttribute(TX_RESULT, result);
    if (result.getTransactionSuccess() == true) {
      getServletConfig().getServletContext().
        getRequestDispatcher("/TransferOK.jsp").forward(req, res);
    }
    else {
      getServletConfig().getServletContext().
        getRequestDispatcher("/TransferFailed.jsp").
        forward(req, res);
    }
  }
  catch (InvalidParameterException e) {
    // Send then back to where they came from
    res.sendRedirect(req.getHeader(REFERER));
  }
```

```
    return;
}
```

The first line of code inside the **try** block calls the getFormInfo() method to retrieve the information entered on the form of the HTML page. This method returns a Properties object called formInfo. If you look at this method, you will see that it extracts the two account numbers and the amount to be transferred between them. If any of the parameters is not found, an InvalidParameterException is thrown.

The actual HTML form does a lot of the checking to ensure that only valid parameters are entered. Of course, this is not a form you would use in a live application. The account numbers are pre-filled with only the accounts existing in the database. Also, there is no security applied to the application. Consider this only a test bed for the servlet, EJBs, and JSPs, using a more realistic environment.

The next line of code calls the **doTransfer()** method and passes the formInfo as a parameter. This method returns a TransactionResult object. This object is placed in the HttpServletRequest object as an attribute called **TX_RESULT**. Doing so makes it available to the JSPs.

Next you check whether the transaction failed or not. Depending on the outcome, either the TransferFailed or the TranferOK JSP is called.

If an invalid parameter was entered on the form, the user is sent back to the originating page to correct the error.

Lastly, take a few minutes to investigate and understand the **doTransfer()** method of the servlet:

```
private TransactionResult doTransfer(Properties formInfo) {
  // create the AccountTransfer Session EJB
  TransactionResult result = null;
  try {
    // Get account numbers from formInfo
    int fromAccount =
      Integer.parseInt(formInfo.getProperty(FROM_ACCOUNT));
    int toAccount =
      Integer.parseInt(formInfo.getProperty(TO_ACCOUNT));

    // Get amount from form
    String amountAsString = formInfo.getProperty(TRANSFER_AMOUNT);
    //Convert amount to BigDecimal
    java.math.BigDecimal amount = new
      java.math.BigDecimal(amountAsString);

    // Create account transfer EJB and start transfer transaction
    com.vajbook.ejb.AccountTransfer accountTransferEJB =
      getAccountTransferHome().create();
    result = accountTransferEJB.transfer(
```

```
        fromAccount, toAccount, amount);

    // Remove transfer EJB
    accountTransferEJB.remove();

    // Save amount of transfer for use in JSP
    result.setTransactionAmount(amountAsString);
    result.setFromAccountNumber(
      formInfo.getProperty(FROM_ACCOUNT));
    result.setToAccountNumber(formInfo.getProperty(TO_ACCOUNT));
  }
  catch (javax.naming.NamingException e) {
    result.setMessage("Something wrong with EJB name" + e);
    result.setTransactionSuccess(false);
  }
  catch (javax.ejb.CreateException ce) {
    result.setMessage("Could not create AccountTransfer EJB" + ce);
    result.setTransactionSuccess(false);
  }
  catch (java.rmi.RemoteException re) {
    result.setMessage("Remote Exception" + re);
    result.setTransactionSuccess(false);
  }
  catch (javax.ejb.RemoveException rve) {
    result.setMessage("Error removing EJB" + rve);
    result.setTransactionSuccess(false);
  }
  return result;
}
```

Aside from a lot of type conversions in the beginning of the method and a lot of catch blocks at the end to handle any possible errors, the work in this method is done in the lines in bold.

The first line creates a new AccountTransfer EJB. It uses a helper method **getAccountTransferHome()**. This method is very similar to the **getAccountHome()** method in the AccountTransfer EJB. Once you have the Home interface for the EJB, you can ask it to create a new instance of the EJB, you actually get an instance of the Remote interface.

From then on, it is just a matter of calling the **transfer()** method of the AccountTransfer EJB. As you remember, this method returns a TransactionResult object. Since you are finished using the EJB, you remove it. Lastly, you update the information in the TransactionResult object to reflect the results and values used in the transaction.

Testing the Completed Exercise

That's it—you have finished coding. To test the completed exercise, start the **WebSphere Test Environment**. Select the **Workspace, Tools, Launch WebSphere Test Environment** menu item. This will start a Web server for HTML pages and a servlet server for both servlets and JSPs. In addition, make sure that all three EJB-related servers are up and running. The test clients should be closed at this time.

Once you have established that all servers are up, start your Web browser. At the URL line, enter: **http://localhost:8080/AccountTransfer.html**. After a few moments, depending on your machine's speed, you will see the HTML page shown in Figure 15.22.

Try entering a variety of values and see how the form responds. There is some JavaScript code in the form to handle most common errors. For example, the **from** and **to** accounts must be different numbers, and the amount entered

Figure 15.22   Account transfer HTML form.

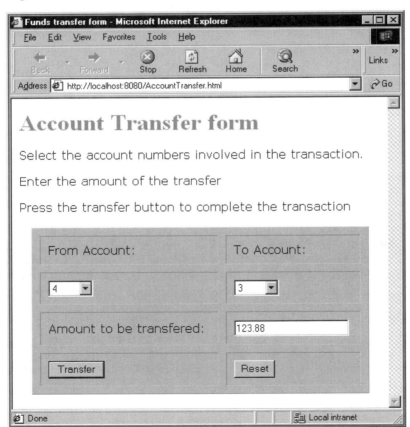

Figure 15.23   Transfer successful.

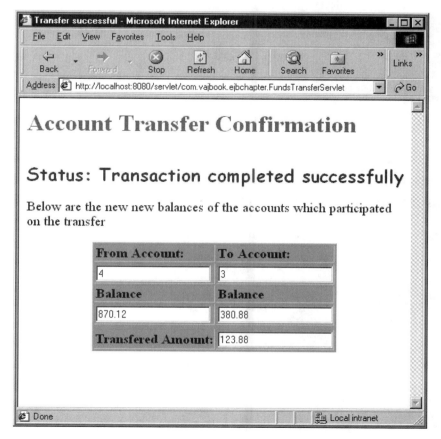

must be a valid number. You can examine this code by viewing the HTML source from your browser.

Now, enter two distinct account numbers and transfer a small amount of money, so that you can be sure that the transaction will not fail because of lack of funds. After the operation completes, you see a screen similar to Figure 15.23. Note that the first time the transaction completes successfully, it may take a little time to display the results because the JSP needs to be compiled.

Now try to enter a very large amount to make the transaction fail. This time the resulting page looks like Figure 15.24.

If you don't get similar results, you will have to debug the program. This is just like debugging any Java program in VisualAge for Java. That is the beauty of developing in this environment.

Figure 15.24   Transfer failed.

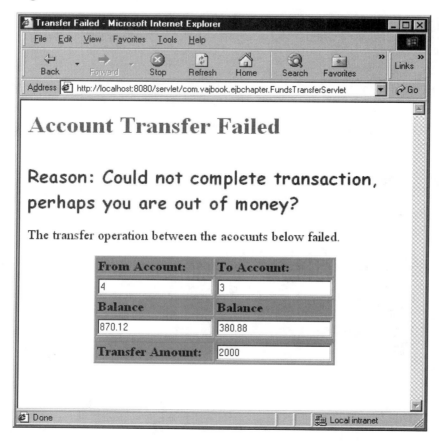

This completes the exercise. Good job!

Summary

In this chapter, you learned about the principles of Enterprise JavaBeans. You built, tested, debugged, and deployed a small Web-based application to transfer money between two bank accounts. To develop this exercise you:

- Created an EJB Group.
- Created an entity EJB.
- Created a session bean.
- Mapped an entity EJB to an existing database.

- Tested and debugged the EJBs using the VisualAge for Java EJB Development Environment.

- Learned how to manage the EJB Servers.

- Learned how to generate deployed code and test clients.

- Used a servlet to create the session EJB.

- Used the session EJB as a controller to transfer the money under Container Managed Transaction control.

Enterprise JavaBeans are a powerful way to develop Java code that runs on servers and can easily be distributed across an enterprise. With this power comes some complexity; it takes a while to fully understand the power of EJBs. As the technology develops, better containers and enterprise application servers will come to market, and with them better and easier-to-use tools will also be developed.

There is a lot more that you can do with EJBs and also a lot more function within VisualAge for Java to support EJBs. This chapter has introduced you to the basic concepts. Practice and real life opportunities will help you hone your EJB skills.

What's in Chapter 16

At this point, you should have a good working knowledge of the VisualAge for Java IDE. While we couldn't show you all of its rich features, you should be ready for a more rapid and enjoyable development experience. While using the IDE, you may realize that it does not do all the tasks you need it to do, or you would like it to do something in a slightly different way. That is actually no problem at all. The developers of the tool have created interfaces that allow you to plug in externally written tools. In this chapter you will learn how to write such tools by:

- Installing a supplied tool into the environment
- Learning the various places where an external tool can be launched
- Learning about the parameters that are passed to external tools by the IDE
- Loading, accessing, and learning about the Tool API
- Learning about the requirements placed on an external tool
- Learning how to test within the IDE
- Learning where to install a new tool
- Learning what is needed to install a tool
- Looking at, reading about, installing, and using the supplied samples

Using the VisualAge for Java API

In order to install the supplied Demo Tool, unpack the **tooldemo.zip** file into the root directory of your VisualAge for Java Version 3 installation (C:\IBMVJAVA by default). If VisualAge for Java is currently running, you need to shut it down and restart it in order for the IDE to detect the new tool and install it (in other words, make it available to the user within the IDE).

Let's take a look at the components of the .zip file:

- **IDE\TOOLS\newTool1\default.ini**
  This file is used by the IDE to install the tool into the IDE environment. It tells the IDE where and how to install the tool. More information on the format of this file is provided later.

- **IDE\TOOLS\newTool1\newTool directory and content**
  This directory contains the Java code that implements the classes of the newTool package. If you would like to review the source code within the IDE, load the **newTool** package from the supplied repository into your repository and then into your workspace.

- **IDE\TOOLS\newTool1\help\newTool.htm**
  This file contains the HTML help displayed when help is requested for the tool.

- **IDE\TOOLS\newTool2**
  This subdirectory is almost an exact mirror of the **newTool1** directory. While it also contains a default.ini, the content of the file is different, in order to show a second method of installing tools. The newTool subdirectory is exactly the same. This tool does not actually have its own help file—it reuses the help from the newTool1 directory. This reference is made in the default.ini file.

Understanding How External Tools Are Invoked

To understand how to build an external tool, you must first understand how tools interface and interact with the IDE. The tool being invoked in each of the figures is the *Demo Tool* that is implemented by the *newTool.Demo* class provided with this text. The Demo tool is provided as a resource to help you understand how the IDE interfaces or calls external tools. The Demo tool is very simple—it lists the items selected in the IDE (if any) in the main listbox (JList) and also displays the parameters passed to the tool (if any) in a read-only entry field (JTextField).

When a registered tool is selected from the Tools menu of the IDE, the tool's main entry point (as registered) is invoked and it is passed parameters that describe the elements or resources that the tool was invoked against, (if any). Table 16.1 describes each different way a tool may be invoked from the IDE and the corresponding figure that illustrates such a tool being invoked.

The first three figures give you a sample of where in the IDE the external tools install their menu items and therefore where a user would invoke them.

Figure 16.1 illustrates how external tools are invoked against types (classes or interfaces) in the IDE. For packages or projects, the procedure is extremely similar except that you use the pop-up menu on those program elements instead.

VisualAge for Java Version 3 has introduced a way to access project resources from within the IDE. If you open a Project browser on any project, you should see a new tab named **Resources**. External tools may now be invoked against the four different categories of resources: resources of a particular extension, resources with no extension, resources in a particular directory, and finally, any resource (including the previous three). See Figure 16.2.

Figure 16.3 shows how general or generic external tools are invoked. Such tools may also be invoked from the **Workspace => Tools menu**. These are tools

Table 16.1   Tool Invocation and Their Corresponding Figures

Element or Resource Selected in IDE	Corresponding Figure or Explanation
Types (Interfaces or Classes)	Figure 16.1
Packages	Similar to Figure 16.1
Projects	Similar to Figure 16.1
Workspace	Use **Workspace >> Tools** menu
Resources—any and all (see **Resources** tab of Project browser)	Similar to Figure 16.1
Resources—for a particular extension (.properties in this case)	Similar to Figure 16.1
Resources—for a resource file without an extension	Similar to Figure 16.1
Resources—for a resource directory	Similar to Figure 16.1
Quick Start—Other category	Figure 16.2
Quick Start—New category	Similar to Figure 16.2
Help for Tools	Figure 16.3
Open... action on a resource	No visible difference in the IDE

that do not act against a specific IDE element or resource. A typical use for this type of tool is to set global properties for tools that are invoked against specific elements or resources.

Figures 16.4 through 16.8 illustrate the output produced by the sample Demo Tool provided with this text. (See Table 16.2.) What follows is a more detailed explanation of the output.

Figure 16.4 shows the output when the Demo Tool is invoked against one or more classes and/or interfaces (types). The tool shows, in the list box, the particular types that were selected in the IDE and passed as arguments to the tool. The tool adds a line for each and every argument except the first one. The first argument passed to the tool tells it what type of IDE element the tool was invoked for. In this case, a –c is passed. The complete argument list is shown in the read-only entry field that appears at the bottom of the tool's output window. In this case, the tool was invoked with four arguments:

```
-c
newTool.Demo
newTool.ShowParms
newTool.ShowParmsBeanInfo
```

Figure 16.1 Tool Invocation for Types.

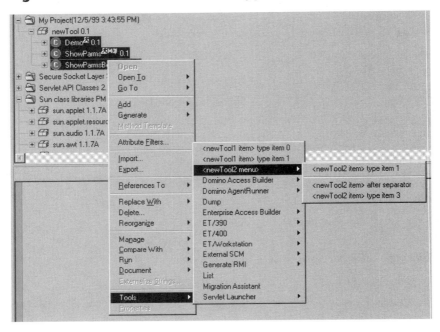

Figure 16.2 Tool Invocation from the Other Category of the Quick Start Dialog.

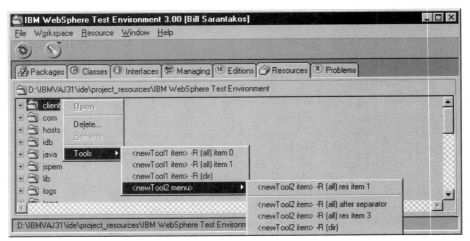

Figure 16.3 Browser Invocation from the Tool Help Menu.

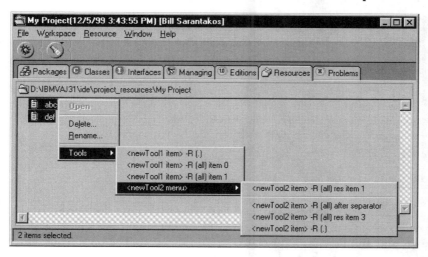

Table 16.2 Demo Tool Output and Their Corresponding Figures

Element or Resource Selected in IDE	Corresponding Figure
Types (Interfaces or Classes)	Figure 16.4
Packages	Figure 16.5
Projects	Figure 16.6
Workspace	Figure 16.7
Resources—any and all	Figure 16.8
Resources—for a particular extension (.properties in this case)	Figure 16.8
Resources—for a resource file Figure 16.8 without an extension	Figure 16.8
Resources—for a resource directory	Figure 16.8
Quick Start—Other category	Figure 16.7
Quick Start—New category	Figure 16.7
Help for Tools	Not shown (HTML file within a browser)

Figure 16.4   Output of Class Demo Tool.

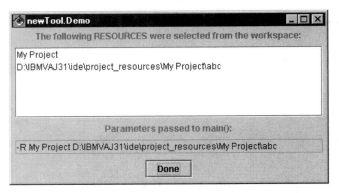

Each argument is shown on a separate line. This is because with projects, arguments will contain embedded spaces, and the line breaks show where one argument ends and another starts for clarity within this text. The output shown in this figure is the result of the tool invocation shown in Figure 16.1.

Figure 16.5 shows the output when the Demo Tool is invoked against one or more packages. In this case, the list box shows a line for each package selected. To let the tool know that packages are being passed as parameters, a **–p** is passed as the first argument. Here are the arguments in this case:

```
-p
sun.applet
sun.applet.resources
sun.audio
sun.awt
sun.awt.im
sun.awt.image
```

Figure 16.5   Output of Package Demo Tool.

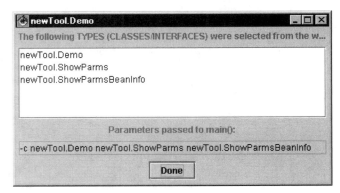

Figure 16.6   Output of Project Demo Tool.

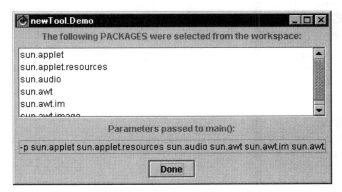

Figure 16.6 shows the output when the Demo Tool is invoked against one or more projects. In this case, the list box shows a line for each project selected. To let the tool know that projects are being passed as parameters, a –P is passed as the first argument. Here are the arguments in this case:

```
-P
IBM WebSphere Test Environment
IBM XML Parser for Java
Java class libraries
JFC class libraries
My Project
```

Figure 16.7 shows the output when the Demo Tool is invoked as a generic/workspace tool. In this case, the list box shows nothing. No arguments at all are passed to the tool.

Figure 16.7   Output of Workspace Demo Tool.

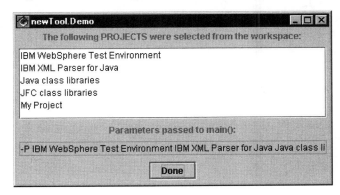

Figure 16.8   Output of Resource Demo Tool.

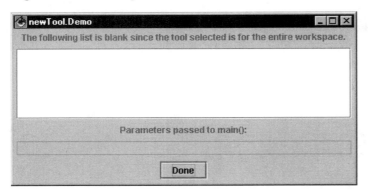

Figure 16.8 shows the output when the Demo Tool is invoked against one or more resources. In this case, the list box shows two lines for each resource selected. The first line corresponds to the project that the resource is found in, while the second line corresponds to the fully qualified filename of the resource. To let the tool know that resources are being passed as parameters, a **–R** is passed as the first argument. Here are the arguments in this case:

```
-R
My Project
D:\IBMVAJ31\ide\project_resources\My Project\abc
```

Using the Demo Tool

Invoke the tool by using the **Tools** menu item and selecting one of the sub-items. All the sub-items provided with the tool start with the text **<newTool1 item>** or **<newTool2 item>**. As you can probably tell, the items that start with <newTool1 item> were configured and installed by the files found in the **IDE\TOOLS\newTool1** directory. Similarly, for **newTool2**.

See Figures 16.1 through 16.3 for examples on how to invoke the tools. For whichever Demo tool menu item you invoke for a particular resource, the tool will display the same results for the same selected items.

Writing External Tools

These are the steps involved in writing you own tools:

- Add the Tool API code to your workspace by loading the **IBM IDE Utility class libraries** (with version labeled **3.0**) project.
- If you haven't already done so, create a project that you will create your code in.

- Write your code using the Tool API and whatever other classes you need to implement the function you are providing.
- Test your code within the IDE.
- Deploy/install the tool within the IDE and test using the menu items you have configured for it.

More information on the above is provided in the subsequent sections.

The Tool API Packages

The Tool Integration API is composed of two packages:

- com.ibm.ivj.util.base—contains workspace and repository access classes
- com.ibm.ivj.util.builders—contains code builder classes

The Base Package

The types found in the com.ibm.ivj.util.base package let you query and manipulate both the user's workspace and the repository. Most of the types used by the programmer are actually interfaces. The **Model** interface is the base class of a hierarchy of nine types (including Model itself). The immediate subtypes of Model are **RepositoryModel** and **WorkspaceModel**.

The types derived from WorkspaceModel are **Project, Package**, and **Type**. These Workspace types are used to associate workspace-related data with the corresponding IDE element. You also use these types to version, release, create open editions, delete, navigate program elements (and their hierarchy), and open a browser against a particular element.

The types derived from RepositoryModel are **ProjectEdition, PackageEdition**, and **TypeEditon**. These repository or edition types are used to retrieve information about an edition, and to load a particular edition into the workspace.

Each workspace type has a link or reference to its corresponding repository type. These links are shown as dotted lines in Figure 16.9.

Since the IDE does let you manipulate methods under version control, there are not corresponding interfaces for methods in the Model hierarchy. The types in the **builders** package does let you manipulate the source of individual methods. Also, you can use standard Java introspection to find out more about a class and its methods.

Other classes and interfaces in the package include:

ToolEnv. This is the class you start things off with. Using this class' **connectToWorkspace**() method, one obtains a reference to a **Workspace** object. If you haven't loaded the prerequisite projects or set up the classpath correctly, then this method returns null.

Workspace. This interface provides methods to manipulate the IDE workspace including finding elements currently loaded in the workspace,

Figure 16.9   Model hierarchy in com.ibm.ivj.util.base.

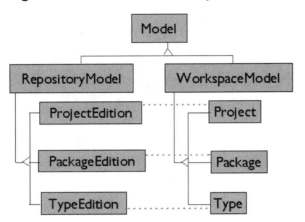

importing or exporting code into or out of workspace, and launching (opening) SmartGuides and browsers.

Repository. This interface provides methods to query which projects and packages are in the repository, among other things.

ImportCodeSpec/ExportCodeSpec. Encapsulates the information needed to import and export Java code from the workspace.

ImportInterchangeSpec/ExportInterchangeSpec. Encapsulates the information needed to import and export mini-repositories from or to the workspace or main repository.

ToolData. Stores a name/value pair. This pair can be associated with either a workspace element or a repository edition.

WorkspaceLog. This class lets you write messages to the IDE Log window. You can even force the Log window to the top so that the user will be sure to see the message.

The Builders Package
The interfaces provided in the com.ibm.ivj.util.builders package let you manipulate source code programmatically. You can either create new code from scratch or manipulate existing code.

The interfaces located in the com.ibm.util package are:

BuilderFactory. Returns builders to manipulate methods and types.

MethodBuilder. Creates new methods or works with existing method source.

TypeBuilder. Manipulates existing types or creates new types.

External Tool Requirements

The tool code that you write must be written as an application, that is, the class that is registered to be invoked by the IDE, must have a standard **main**() method coded within it.

When the IDE executes the tool through the Tools menu, only the following projects are made available on the tool's classpath:

- IBM IDE Utility class libraries
- c:\ibmvjava\ide\project_resources\ibm ide utility local implementation\
- c:\ibmvjava\ide\program\lib
- c:\ibmvjava\ide\program\lib\classes.zip

Testing Tools in the IDE

In order to test your newly developed code within the IDE, you need to make a couple of modifications to your class' **Class Path** property. Here is what you need to do:

- Open the class' Properties dialog and switch to the Class Path tab.
- Add the **IBM IDE Utility class libraries** project to the **Project path** by using the **Edit...** button.
- Add C:\IBMVJAVA\IDE\project_resources\IBM IDE Utility local implementation\; to the Extra directories path within the same properties dialog.

You also need to specify command line parameters when calling your class to simulate what the IDE passes to your program when it is invoked from the Tools menu. In the same **Properties** dialog in which you just modified the classpath, switch to the **Program** tab and enter those parameters. As an example, if the demo tool was invoked against the class that implements the tool, the parameters would be '-c newTool.Demo'.

Installing External Tools

When installing a tool, you must create a subdirectory for it in the **C:\IBMJAVA\IDE\TOOLS** directory. If you have installed the Demo Tool as documented earlier, you should see the **newTool1** and **newTool2** subdirectories, among many others, in that directory. These directories are known as the **base** directories for each tool. If you have not installed any other tools, you'll note that the other directories all have a name starting with **com-ibm-**. All such directories are for IBM supplied tools. IBM suggests you name your tool directories in a similar way that you name your Java packages, except that you replace the '.' in the names with '-'. This will help avoid conflicts between two or more tool vendors when installing their tools into the VisualAge for Java IDE.

Requirements for Installing Tools

Here is a list of the potential items that need to be installed into the base directory for your tool.

- **default.ini** file (required). This file describes to the tool exactly which class to invoke for a particular tool, which type of element it is allowed to be invoked on, or when it can be invoked. The exact format of the file will be explained below. It is also referred to as the control file.

- Java code (required). These are the Java .class, .jar, .zip or other files that implement the tool. The base directory of the tool becomes part of the classpath when the tool is invoked, so the Java files should be installed in their proper directories relative to that base directory.

- HTML files (optional). If the tool is supplying and configuring help information, it must be supplied as HTML. While these files can actually be installed anywhere on the file system (as long as the default.ini file is configured to point to them properly), you should keep them in the same directory tree as the tool (or perhaps shared with a prerequisite tool).

- resource files (optional). These are any files needed by the Java code that are not code themselves. These include, but are not limited to, files with extensions like .properties, .ini, and .gif.

Once these files are installed, the IDE will not install or update itself until it is started the next time.

default.ini File Format

The default.ini file describes to the IDE how the tool is to be integrated into the environment. There is a very specific syntax to be followed within the file. The file allows you to specify any new menu items that will appear in various places in the IDE, and the class to be called when a particular menu item is selected. There are five ways in which a tool may be registered:

Selection-oriented. These tools are listed under the **Selected => Tools** menu item when classes, interfaces, packages, or projects are selected within the IDE. The tools are also listed under the **Tools** menu item for the selected items' pop-up menu.

Workspace-oriented. These tools are listed under the **Workspace =>** **Tools** menu item.

Quick Start-oriented. These tools are listed either in the **Other** category of the **Quick Start** window or in a new category set up by the tool during installation.

Help-oriented. This allows the tool to register a help file for itself.

Action-oriented. This allows a tool to be invoked instead of the default action when **Open** is selected for a resource.

Here is a brief summary of the syntax in a default.ini file. Take a look at the default.ini files provided with the Demo Tool to see real examples of how these directives are coded.

- Name=<description>
  where <description> is the name of the tool; This name appears in a couple of places within the IDE.

- Version=<vernum>
  where <vernum> is the version number of the tool.

- Help-Item=<desc>,<html file>
  where <desc> is what will appear as the menu item under **Help => Tools** and <html file> is the HTML file to be displayed in the default browser. The file name specified for <html file> should be relative to the base directory or should be fully qualified.

- Menu-Group=<group name>
  where <group name> is the text that will appear as a menu item under the **Tools** menu item. The items specified by the Menu-Items directive will appear as sub-items of this menu.

- Menu-Items=<tool entry>[;<tool entry>]*
  where <tool entry> can be either '<menu desc>,<class>,<indicator>' or '-,-,<indicator>' where <menu desc> is the menu item text, <class> is the fully qualified name of the class to be invoked, and <indicator> is one of –P, -p, -c, or -R and indicates for which type of IDE element the tool is to be invoked against. '-P' indicates the tools may be invoked for a project, '-p' for a package, '-c' for a class or an interface, and '-R' for a resource file. The –R indicator also has three other variations: '-R.ext' indicates the tool can only be run against resource files with a .ext extension, '-R.' indicates the tool can only be run against resource files without an extension, and '-R/' indicates the tool can be run against a resource directory.

  The form that starts with '-,-,' actually causes a separator line to be inserted between the proceeding item and the next item.

  Since these lines can get very long, a line may be continued on the next line by specifying a '\' as the last character on the line. The convention seems to be to add a '\' after the ';' between tool entries.

  If a Menu-Group directive is not specified, all the tool entries show up as entries directly under the **Tools** menu.

- Quick-Start-Group=<category name>
  where <category name> is the category name the tool will show up under in the Quick Start window.

- Quick-Start-Items=<tool entry>[;<tool entry>]*
  where <tool entry> is <menu desc>,<class> and <menu desc> is the menu
  text and <class> is the class to be invoked.

  If a Quick-Start-Group is not specified, the tools will be listed under the
  Other category.

- Action-Items=<tool entry>[;<tool entry>]*
  where <tool entry> is 'OPEN,<class>,-R.[<ext>]', <class> is the class to be
  invoked, and <ext> is an optional extension file name. If <ext> is not specified, the tool can only be invoked on a resource file without an extension.

Updating a Tool

If you need to update the code for a particular tool, all you need to do is update
the necessary files in the base directory of the tool. The next time the tool is
invoked, the updated code will be called.

If you would like to change the way a tool is registered or to add, update or
delete menu items for a particular tool, you need to modify the default.ini file and
then restart the IDE. The default.ini file is only read during startup.

External Tool Examples

The Baseline Tool

This tool allows you to version all program elements within a selected project
with the exact same name. This is the type of thing you may want to do when
shipping a level of code externally, for example either for independent testing or
verification or for deployment to production. By doing this, you will be able to
quickly identify fixes or changes to the "base line" code.

Instead of presenting all the code here and having you go through the trouble
of entering it all, the code has been provided in a repository file and an explanation of the particularly important code fragments will be discussed here.

From the main() method, the following code fragment obtains a workspace
reference using the ToolEnv class. If a reference is not obtained, then either the set
up is wrong or the tool is not being run within VisualAge for Java.

```
workspace = ToolEnv.connectToWorkspace();
if (workspace == null) {
   System.out.println("Error, workspace is null—check classpath or
that code is being run inside VAJ");
   System.exit(99);
}
```

The tool expects only one project to be selected with its name being passed
in as args[1]. The following line obtains a reference to a Project object representing the project selected in the workspace.

```
project = workspace.loadedProjectNamed(args[1]);
```

In checkVersion(), the line:

```
ProjectEdition[] projectEditions = project.getAllEditions();
```

obtains references to all the editions of that project that are found in the repository. There are similar lines to obtain all editions of packages within a project and all editions of types within a package.

In makeVersion(), the createNewEdition() method is called on any of the references to the Project, Package, or Type classes to create a new edition of the element. Similarly, createVersion() is used against exactly the same classes to convert an open edition of an element to a version. Finally, the release() method is called to make the versioned element 'public'.

When running the tool, you need to enter the version name to be used—you do this by entering the information in the **Standard In** pane of the **Console** window and then pressing the **Submit** button in its toolbar.

The baseline tool can be installed by unpacking the baseline.zip file into the VisualAge Java install directory.

Ownership Query Tool

This tool allows you to query the selected program elements and determine which developer owns it. This tool is very useful when working with other developers in a team environment. This is a good example that shows that a tool does not have to involve a lot of code to be useful. The following is a typical scenario you may follow when using the tool:

Change or create any program elements as necessary.

Use the **Workspace>>Management Query** tool to display program elements that you have either not versioned or not released.

Remove any elements from the list that you are not ready to version and/or release at the time.

Select all the elements remaining in the Management Query dialog (you can do this quite easily by 'swiping' all the elements with the mouse pointer).

Run the Ownership Query tool by selecting the **Tools>>query>>owner** menu item.

If needed, version any type that is an open edition.

Using the output of the query tool, either obtain the ownership of elements, using **Manage>>Change Owner...** if that is the local team development process, or notify the owner(s) that you have a new version that needs to be released/integrated.

Release any elements that are owned by you if you haven't already released them.

Close the Management Query dialog.

From the processTypes() method, the following two lines of code are note-worthy:

```
Type tgtType = ws.loadedTypeNamed(typeName);
String ownerName = tgtType.getOwnerName();
```

The loadedTypeNamed() method is used to obtain a reference to a Type object. There are similar methods for the other program elements as well (see the other process*() methods for details).

The getOwnerName() method is used to obtain the owner of a program element. The getOwnerName() method is actually defined in the **Model** interface, so the method is available from any of the repository or workspace interfaces that implement/extend Model.

The ownership query tool can be installed by unpacking the ownership.zip file into the VisualAge Java install directory.

Package Rename Tool

This tool allows you to change all references within a package, say A, from one package, say B, to another package, say C. You would need a tool like this when you reorganize your code in situations like splitting up packages that have grown to include an unruly number of classes. Another example would be the renaming of packages because they have evolved to be either more general or more specialized and their original name is no longer appropriate.

Using this tool to deal with code generated by the Visual Composition Editor is not recommended. While it will probably appear to work initially, the VCE stores information about the class in the repository and that information, being in a private or internal format, cannot be manipulated. Subsequently, when the class is opened in the visual composition editor, the code in the class will not match what the tool believes it had generated previously.

The class that is actually registered with the IDE for this tool is **RenamePkgRefsFrame** although the **RenamePkgRefs** class does the real work. RenamePkgRefs is actually reusable by any number of visual and invisible beans.

In the constructor for RenamePkgRefs, the **isDesignTime()** method is called to check if the class is being constructed within a builder tool. In this case, the code needs to distinguish between whether or not it is being constructed in the VCE and is not being constructed for the purposes of doing real work. If it is in the VCE, it does not bother trying to obtain a reference to the workspace.

In the doit() method, the following code:

```
BuilderFactory factory = workspace.createBuilderFactory();
```

obtains a **BuilderFactory** object from the workspace. A BuilderFactory is used to create references to type and method builders, **createTypeBuilder()** and **createMethodBuilder()** respectively.

Using a builder object, you can get and set the source of a type (the class header as seen in the IDE) or a method. Once changes have been made to the code, the **save()** method can be called to save the source into the repository and compile the new code.

The package rename tool can be installed by unpacking the rename.zip file into the VisualAge Java install directory.

Summary

In this chapter, you learned how VisualAge for Java allows developers to extend the power of the IDE by writing and plugging in their own tools. This chapter showed you:

- How external tools are invoked
- How external tools are registered
- How to use the Tools API to access elements of the workspace and the repository
- How to test a tool being written within the IDE
- What is required to install a new tool
- How and where to install a new tool

With a little imagination, and the knowledge you have gained here, you can extend the power of the VisualAge for Java IDE to make it an even better tool in helping you develop the applications of the future.

Advanced Enterprise Development Topics

> **What's in Chapter 17**
>
> This chapter covers a few remaining topics related to building enterprise applications using VisualAge for Java. There are no exercises in this chapter, but there is a lot of information on relevant development topics. In this chapter you will:
>
> - Learn how to develop in VisualAge for Java using JDK 1.2
> - Learn about the other Java tools in VisualAge for Java
> - Understand the common visual design patterns and learn how to improve your designs

Developing with JDK 1.2

Sun promotes JDK 1.2 as the version for Java development. Java developers are in different stages of developing and deploying Java over the different JDK versions. Most developers will move to JDK 1.2 as it becomes more reliable and when enough development tools support it. VisualAge for Java Version 3 includes three different copies of the product that support:

1. JDK 1.1.7. Includes the IDE, Debugger, VCE, WebSphere Test Environment, complete toolset, and team versioning.

2. JDK 1.2. Includes the IDE, Debugger, VCE, and team versioning. As the other tools support JDK 1.2, they will be added to this version of VisualAge for Java.

3. Linux operating system. Includes the IDE, Debugger, VCE, and versioning. This version of the product demonstrates IBM's support for Linux.

When you are designing Java applications, you need to decide which JDK you will use, because that affects how you implement the applications. Specific JDK support is a key reason why developers select and use Java tools. For example, if you choose to develop based on JDK 1.2, your Java tools need to support JDK 1.2. When you buy VisualAge for Java, it comes with two different CD-ROMs; one for JDK 1.1.7 and one for JDK 1.2. You need to install the appropriate VisualAge for Java product for the JDK you intend to use.

JDK 1.2 Features

There are many new features in JDK 1.2 that developers want to use, including collection classes and security classes. IBM recognizes the requirement to use these new classes, so IBM back-ported the classes for JDK 1.7 and they are available from IBM. You can get more information about IBM's JDKs at www.ibm.com/java/jdk.

JDK 1.2 Packages

When Sun developed JDK 1.2, they made a number of changes to parts that came from JDK 1.1. Some of these changes include deprecated methods and placing classes in different package names. These changes affect JDK 1.1 code and the code generators in VisualAge for Java.

When you install VisualAge for Java Version 3 for JDK 1.2, you will see hundreds of errors in the All Problems Page. Most of these errors come from the many deprecated methods in JDK 1.2.

If you are converting a program form JDK 1.1 to JDK 1.2, you will need to use the new package names in your Java code. This affects import statements and any fully qualified class names that include package names. Depending on the amount of code, these updates could be very time consuming. The many tools and SmartGuides in VisualAge for Java also use the new JDK 1.2 package names.

Additional Tools

There are many more tools in VisualAge for Java that focus on specific Java interfaces. All these tools are included in VisualAge for Java Enterprise Edition and need to be added as new features so that you can use them. The following sections describe some of these additional tools and how you can use them.

Persistence Builder

The Persistence Builder is a very powerful tool designed to help you create persistent beans. You used the Persistence Builder in Chapter 15, "Using Enterprise JavaBeans," when you mapped objects to a relational database. The Persistence Builder is well suited for complex object-to-data mapping. If you are merely accessing a single table or running a simple query, you should use the Select bean that is part of the Data Access Beans feature in VisualAge for Java.

The Persistence Builder is somewhat complex and has a number of advanced features in the tool. The .pdf file included with VisualAge for Java provides more information on how to use its many features. There is an IBM Redbook with a complete example dedicated to using the Persistence Builder. You can find it on the Web at www.redbooks.ibm.com/pubs/pdfs/redbooks/sg24542601.pdf. There are also a number of articles in the VADD Technical Journal that are another good source of information of the Persistence Builder (see www7.software.ibm.com/vad.nsf/ webgroup1nlarchive?openview&Count=7&TargetFrame=webgroup1nlarchive).

Servlet Builder

The Servlet Builder is an interesting tool that adds function to the Visual Composition Editor so you can create servlets. It adds a set of HTML components to the beans palette so that you can design an HTML form with HTML components as the user interface. You can use the same logic beans that you have used throughout this book in the Servlet Builder.

The Servlet Builder is great for creating prototypes, because it uses the same visual connections that you have learned in this book. However, the generated servlets are not as fast as hand-coded servlets that you learned about in Chapter 14. When you deploy the generated servlets, you must include the Servlet Builder run-time file. Additionally, it is far more efficient to run HTML forms than Servlet Builder classes, which in turn generate HTML. You can use the Servlet Builder to experiment and prototype servlets, and when you are ready to implement the real servlet, you can recode the HTML form needed for the servlet.

SAP Access Builder

SAP is a large software company that sells software to automate business processes, and many customers throughout the world use this software. The SAP system runs on most of the popular relational databases, and it uses a proprietary programming language to access its business objects. SAP recognizes that Java programmer need to access these systems, so they added the BAPI (Business Application Program Interface).

The SAP Access Builder provides an easy way for programmers to use BAPIs and another SAP interface called RFC (Remote Function Call) in Java programs. The SAP Access Builder generates JavaBeans and EJBs that map to the business objects in the SAP system, such as Customer, Invoice, and Inventory. You can use the generated JavaBeans like any other JavaBeans in the VCE, Servlets, JSPs, and other VisualAge for Java tools.

The SAP access builder automates the coding of JavaBeans to access a SAP system. Java programs generated with the SAP Access Builder require a run-time DLL. You should refer to the documentation and the VisualAge for Java Web site at www-4.ibm.com/software/ad/vajava/ for the operating systems currently supported by the run-time DLL.

RMI Access Builder

RMI stands for Remote Method Invocation and this API was introduced in JDK 1.1. It allows JavaBeans to remotely call methods in JavaBeans on another computer. It is very common to design an Applet or JFrame that communicates with a server using RMI. To use RMI, you need to create additional classes for a stub, skeleton, client proxy, and server proxy. The RMI Access Builder is very easy to use and automates the task of creating the required supporting classes for RMI.

You can test the remote bean using the RMI Registry in VisualAge for Java. First start the RMI Registry by selecting **Window => Options => RMI Registry**, and the Registry opens as shown in Figure 17.1. From the Options window you can start the RMI Registry, which is a service that lets you instantiate server classes in VisualAge for Java. Once the Registry is started, you can instantiate a server class in Workbench. Select the Sever class, then from the pop-up menu select **Instantiate in Server**.

Enterprise Data Access Builder

The Enterprise Data Access Builder is one of the three tools in VisualAge for Java for accessing relational databases using JDBC. It has been part of VisualAge for Java since Version 1 and it generates JavaBeans that map to relational database tables.

IBM is not enhancing the Enterprise Data Access Builder, because the Persistence Builder has the same mapping function with many more features. Additionally, the Enterprise Access Builder generates JavaBeans that support the AWT controls, but they do not support JFC controls or some helpful features in WebSphere like connection pooling.

Figure 17.1   RMI Registry.

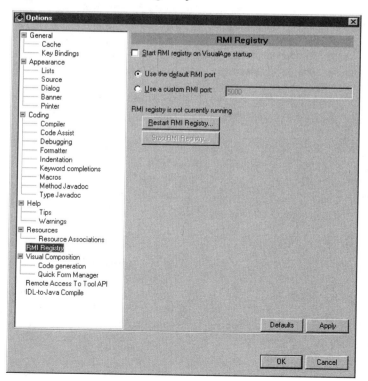

Visual Design Patterns

The Visual Composition Editor in VisualAge for Java utilizes the unique *construction from beans* paradigm. Most developers find the Visual Composition Editor easy to use, especially because it generates a lot of the code needed for your program. However, you still must write some of your code in your programs, as you have seen throughout this book. When developing programs with the Visual Composition Editor, keep a healthy balance between drawing connections and writing code.

Just as with writing code, there are many ways to use connections. When you combine connections, the result is a visual design pattern. This section covers some of the many visual design patterns you see when you use the Visual Composition Editor. With each pattern example, a small sample is provided to illustrate each pattern. Many of the patterns have performance considerations, so alternative patterns or suggestions are provided.

After many years of working with VisualAge for Java customers has shown that most, initially developers seem to use too many visual connections. Connections are easier to create and maintain, but they do not generate the simplest, most efficient code. So ironically it is best to minimize the number of visual connections. Also, the VCE is not well suited for server-side programming, which is becoming increasingly important in Java applications.

GUI Connection Pattern

This pattern shows a common misuse of connections, as shown in Figure 17.2. These connections set GUI beans and function properly. However, they are very inefficient and create visual clutter. You should use connections for high-level functions.

You can easily simplify this GUI connection pattern by writing code. You can create and call a class method, as shown in Figure 17.3. You can name the method clearAll() and give it the function of calling the setter methods for each field. This reduces visual clutter, reduces code size, and improves performance.

Figure 17.2   GUI connection pattern.

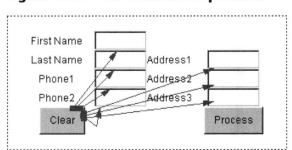

Figure 17.3   Simplifying the GUI connection pattern.

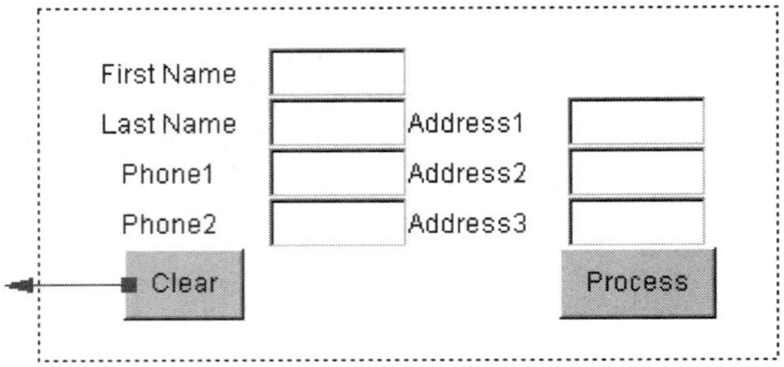

First Name
Last Name   Address1
Phone1   Address2
Phone2   Address3
Clear   Process

Aggregation Pattern

Sometimes you see a collection of logic beans that have only one connection to another bean. Figure 17.4 shows this group of beans highlighted. This pattern happens as programs evolve through the iterative development process.

The best way to solve this problem is to aggregate the logic beans as shown in Figure 17.5. You need to create a new bean, move the components to the new bean, recreate the connections, and substitute the new aggregate bean for the discrete components previously used. You have created a composite logic bean that provides the function under the covers and simplifies the connections.

Circular Pattern

This pattern frequently occurs through iterative development, as shown in Figure 17.6. This sample is over-simplified. Some developers string many beans together. If the beans use a lot of property-to-property connections, the program slows down as all the connection methods are called. There are a number of ways to fix this pattern,

Figure 17.4   Aggregation pattern.

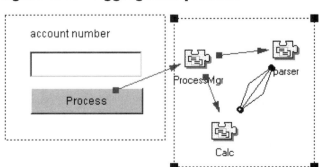

account number

Process

ProcessMgr

parser

Calc

Figure 17.5   Simplifying the aggregation pattern.

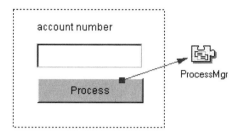

all of which require some redesign and re-implementation. Be careful using property-to-property connections, because they usually signal events in both directions.

Monolithic Pattern

Some developers are accustomed to writing procedural applications. When they start developing object-oriented applications using the Visual Composition Editor, they put the logic in the bean and call it from the user interface with connections similar to Figure 17.7. This pattern is difficult to maintain, impractical for reuse, and a good example of weak object-oriented programming. The solution for this design pattern is better use of logic beans. Substitute Event-to-Code connections with logic JavaBeans when you can reuse the function provided in the code.

Tight Coupling Pattern

Some visual programs have a large number of property-to-property connections, as shown in Figure 17.8. This is not inherently bad, but it creates a very tight coupling of the beans. Also, depending on what is in the target bean, the pattern might cause performance problems. One solution for this is to pass an object,

Figure 17.6   Circular pattern.

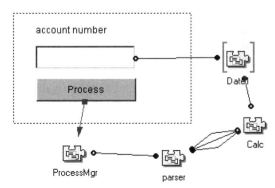

Figure 17.7 Monolithic pattern.

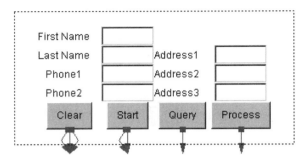

array, or vector to the target bean. This solution is similar to the solution for the diamond pattern and it is a much more flexible design.

Diamond Pattern

An easily identified pattern is the diamond, shown in Figure 17.9. This effect happens when you promote a large number of individual features in an embedded bean. When you connect a lot of these promoted features to another bean, the connection lines form a diamond shape.

You can improve the diamond pattern as shown in Figure 17.10. You can redefine the method to accept a parameter. You should also promote an aggregation of the properties, and then you can pass an object, array, or vector to the target bean.

Figure 17.8 Tight coupling pattern.

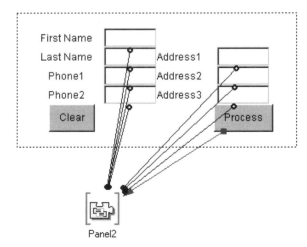

Figure 17.9   Diamond pattern.

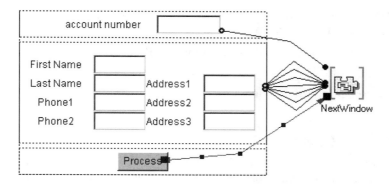

Visual Patterns Summary

The patterns discussed in this section frequently occur in visual programming, and it is good to be able to identify them and improve them as needed. With any fairly complex program, there are many different ways to implement the design. As mentioned in this section, the iterative development process causes programs to evolve. You should review each iteration so that you can alter the design patterns that adversely affect the performance, maintenance, or extensibility of the program.

Figure 17.10   Simplifying the diamond pattern.

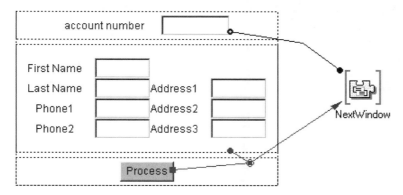

Summary

This chapter was a quick tour through a number of more advanced enterprise Java development topics. In this chapter you:

- Learned how to use VisualAge for Java that supports JDK 1.2.
- Learned about some of other tools in VisualAge for Java.
- Reviewed some common visual design patterns.

Wrapping Up the Book

After completing this book, you have learned many of the basic concepts used to implement good object-oriented Java applications. You have developed a number of well-designed and functional sample programs that cover a broad range of AWT and JFC JavaBeans and business logic. You have learned how to use the many functions in VisualAge for Java to develop JavaBeans. You have also learned about server-side Java programming, including servlets, JSPs, and EJBs. Now you have more confidence that you can produce good Java software using VisualAge for Java.

Programming is both a science and an art, and a good software professional should develop the best application possible under the constraints of the project. This means that experience and planning are key components to good software development. You need to budget time for iterating the design, testing, incorporating user feedback, adding error detection and correction, and creating online help and documentation. There is a lot more to Java application development than painting screens and making connections.

We hope this book helped you learn how to effectively use VisualAge for Java. There are a lot of exercises in this book, and some are fairly complex, so if you have made it here, you should be proud. We hope you enjoyed this book as much as we enjoyed writing it.

RELATED PUBLICATIONS

Akerley, John, Li, Nina, Parlavecchia, Antonello. *Programming with VisualAge for Java Version 2.0*. Prentice Hall, 1999.

Chang, Daniel and Dan Harkey. *Client/Server Data Access with Java*. John Wiley & Sons, 1998.

Daconta, Michael C. *Java for C/C++ Programmers*. John Wiley & Sons, 1996.

Flanagan, David. *Java in a Nutshell*. O'Reilly, 1999.

Horstmann, Cay S. *Core Java 2*. John Wiley & Sons, 1998.

McGraw, Gary and Edward Felten. *Java Security*. John Wiley & Sons, 1996.

Roman, Ed. *Mastering Enterprise JavaBeans*. John Wiley & Sons, 1999.

Vanhelsuwe, Laurence. *Mastering JavaBeans*. Sybex, 1997.

INDEX

International License Agreement for Evaluation of Programs

Part 1—General Terms

PLEASE READ THIS AGREEMENT CAREFULLY BEFORE USING THE PROGRAM. IBM WILL LICENSE THE PROGRAM TO YOU ONLY IF YOU FIRST ACCEPT THE TERMS OF THIS AGREEMENT. BY USING THE PROGRAM YOU AGREE TO THESE TERMS. IF YOU DO NOT AGREE TO THE TERMS OF THIS AGREEMENT, PROMPTLY RETURN THE UNUSED PROGRAM TO IBM.

The Program is owned by International Business Machines Corporation or one of its subsidiaries (IBM) or an IBM supplier, and is copyrighted and licensed, not sold.

The term "Program" means the original program and all whole or partial copies of it. A Program consists of machine-readable instructions, its components, data, audio-visual content (such as images, text, recordings, or pictures), and related licensed materials.

This Agreement includes Part 1 - General Terms and Part 2 - Country-unique Terms and is the complete agreement regarding the use of this Program, and replaces any prior oral or written communications between you and IBM. The terms of Part 2 may replace or modify those of Part 1.

1. License

Use of the Program

IBM grants you a nonexclusive, nontransferable license to use the Program.

You may 1) use the Program only for internal evaluation, testing or demonstration purposes, on a trial or "try-and-buy" basis and 2) make and install a reasonable number of copies of the Program in support of such use, unless IBM identifies a specific number of copies in the documentation accompanying the Program. The terms of this license apply to each copy you make. You will reproduce the copyright notice and any other legends of ownership on each copy, or partial copy, of the Program.

THE PROGRAM MAY CONTAIN A DISABLING DEVICE THAT WILL PREVENT IT FROM BEING USED UPON EXPIRATION OF THIS LICENSE. YOU WILL NOT TAMPER WITH THIS DISABLING DEVICE OR THE PROGRAM. YOU SHOULD TAKE PRECAUTIONS TO AVOID ANY LOSS OF DATA THAT MIGHT RESULT WHEN THE PROGRAM CAN NO LONGER BE USED.

You will 1) maintain a record of all copies of the Program and 2) ensure that anyone who uses the Program does so only for your authorized use and in compliance with the terms of this Agreement.

You may not 1) use, copy, modify or distribute the Program except as provided in this Agreement; 2) reverse assemble, reverse compile, or otherwise translate the Program except as specifically permitted by law without the possibility of contractual waiver; or 3) sublicense, rent, or lease the Program.

This license begins with your first use of the Program and ends on the earlier of 1) termination of this license in accordance with the terms of this Agreement or 2) when the Program automatically disables itself. You will destroy the Program and all copies made of it within ten days of when this license ends.

2. No Warranty

SUBJECT TO ANY STATUTORY WARRANTIES WHICH CANNOT BE EXCLUDED, IBM MAKES NO WARRANTIES OR CONDITIONS EITHER EXPRESS OR IMPLIED, INCLUDING WITHOUT LIMITATION, THE WARRANTY OF NON-INFRINGEMENT AND THE IMPLIED WARRANTIES OF MERCHANTABILITY AND FITNESS FOR A PARTICULAR PURPOSE, REGARDING THE PROGRAM OR TECHNICAL SUPPORT, IF ANY. IBM MAKES NO WARRANTY REGARDING THE CAPABILITY OF THE PROGRAM TO CORRECTLY PROCESS, PROVIDE AND/OR RECEIVE DATE DATA WITHIN AND BETWEEN THE 20TH AND 21ST CENTURIES.

This exclusion also applies to any of IBM's subcontractors, suppliers or program developers (collectively called "Suppliers").

Manufacturers, suppliers, or publishers of non-IBM Programs may provide their own warranties.

3. Limitation of Liability

NEITHER IBM NOR ITS SUPPLIERS ARE LIABLE FOR ANY DIRECT OR INDIRECT DAMAGES, INCLUDING WITHOUT LIMITATION, LOST PROFITS, LOST SAVINGS, OR ANY INCIDENTAL, SPECIAL, OR OTHER ECONOMIC CONSEQUENTIAL DAMAGES, EVEN IF IBM IS INFORMED OF THEIR POSSIBILITY. SOME JURISDICTIONS DO NOT ALLOW THE EXCLUSION OR LIMITATION OF INCIDENTAL OR CONSEQUENTIAL DAMAGES, SO THE ABOVE EXCLUSION OR LIMITATION MAY NOT APPLY TO YOU.

4. General

Nothing in this Agreement affects any statutory rights of consumers that cannot be waived or limited by contract.

IBM may terminate your license if you fail to comply with the terms of this Agreement. If IBM does so, you must immediately destroy the Program and all copies you made of it.

You may not export the Program.

Neither you nor IBM will bring a legal action under this Agreement more than two years after the cause of action arose unless otherwise provided by local law without the possibility of contractual waiver or limitation.

Neither you nor IBM is responsible for failure to fulfill any obligations due to causes beyond its control.

There is no additional charge for use of the Program for the duration of this license.

IBM does not provide program services or technical support, unless IBM specifies otherwise.

The laws of the country in which you acquire the Program govern this Agreement, except 1) in Australia, the laws of the State or Territory in which the transaction is performed govern this Agreement; 2) in Albania, Armenia, Belarus, Bosnia/Herzegovina, Bulgaria, Croatia, Czech Republic, Georgia, Hungary, Kazakhstan, Kirghizia, Former Yugoslav Republic of Macedonia (FYROM), Moldova, Poland, Romania, Russia, Slovak Republic, Slovenia, Ukraine, and Federal Republic of Yugoslavia, the laws of Austria govern this Agreement; 3) in the United Kingdom, all disputes relating to this Agreement will be governed by English Law and will be submitted to the exclusive jurisdiction of the English courts; 4) in Canada, the laws in the Province of Ontario govern this Agreement; and 5) in the United States and

Puerto Rico, and People's Republic of China, the laws of the State of New York govern this Agreement.

Part 2 - Country-unique Terms

AUSTRALIA:

No Warranty (Section 2): The following paragraph is added to this Section: Although IBM specifies that there are no warranties, you may have certain rights under the Trade Practices Act 1974 or other legislation and are only limited to the extent permitted by the applicable legislation.

Limitation of Liability (Section 3): The following paragraph is added to this Section: Where IBM is in breach of a condition or warranty implied by the Trade Practices Act 1974, IBM's liability is limited to the repair or replacement of the goods, or the supply of equivalent goods. Where that condition or warranty relates to right to sell, quiet possession or clear title, or the goods are of a kind ordinarily acquired for personal, domestic or household use or consumption, then none of the limitations in this paragraph apply.

GERMANY:

No Warranty (Section 2): The following paragraphs are added to this Section: The minimum warranty period for Programs is six months.

In case a Program is delivered without Specifications, we will only warrant that the Program information correctly describes the Program and that the Program can be used according to the Program information. You have to check the usability according to the Program information within the "money-back guaranty" period. **Limitation of Liability (Section 3):** The following paragraph is added to this Section: The limitations and exclusions specified in the Agreement will not apply to damages caused by IBM with fraud or gross negligence, and for express warranty.

INDIA:

General (Section 4): The following replaces the fourth paragraph of this Section: If no suit or other legal action is brought, within two years after the cause of action arose, in respect of any claim that either party may have against the other, the rights of the concerned party in respect of such claim will be forfeited and the other party will stand released from its obligations in respect of such claim.

IRELAND:

No Warranty (Section 2): The following paragraph is added to this Section: Except as expressly provided in these terms and conditions, all statutory conditions, including all warranties implied, but without prejudice to the generality of the foregoing, all warranties implied by the Sale of Goods Act 1893 or the Sale of Goods and Supply of Services Act 1980 are hereby excluded.

ITALY:

Limitation of Liability (Section 3): This Section is replaced by the following: Unless otherwise provided by mandatory law, IBM is not liable for any damages which might arise.

NEW ZEALAND:

No Warranty (Section 2): The following paragraph is added to this Section: Although IBM specifies that there are no warranties, you may have certain rights under the Consumer Guarantees Act 1993 or other legislation which cannot be excluded or limited. The

Consumer Guarantees Act 1993 will not apply in respect of any goods or services which IBM provides, if you require the goods and services for the purposes of a business as defined in that Act. **Limitation of Liability (Section 3):** The following paragraph is added to this Section: Where Programs are not acquired for the purposes of a business as defined in the Consumer Guarantees Act 1993, the limitations in this Section are subject to the limitations in that Act.

UNITED KINGDOM:

Limitation of Liability (Section 3): The following paragraph is added to this Section at the end of the first paragraph: The limitation of liability will not apply to any breach of IBM's obligations implied by Section 12 of the Sales of Goods Act 1979 or Section 2 of the Supply of Goods and Services Act 1982.

To use this CD-ROM, your system must meet the following requirements:

Platform/Processor/Operating System. Windows 95, Windows 98, Windows NT® 4.0 with Service Pack 3 or Service Pack 4 or Windows 2000. Pentium® processor or higher recommended (minimum processor speed 90 Mhz). For customers who wish to use the Euro currency symbol on Windows, a free update is available from Microsoft from the following web address: http://microsoft.com/windows/euro.asp. This patch is not required if you are using Windows NT 4.0 with SP4 applied.

RAM. 64 MB RAM minimum (96 MB RAM recommended).

Hard Drive Space. 250 MB required for full install. If you are migrating from Version 2.0 of VisualAge for Java, your migrated repository will increase in size to include the repository shipped with Version 3.02. You can expect an increase in the size of the repository of at least 35 MB for a basic installation. In addition, you must have at least 2 MB free on your Windows system drive, and your environment variable TEMP or TMP must point to a valid temporary directory with at least 6 MB free.

Peripherals. TCP/IP installed and configured. A mouse or pointing device. SVGA (800x600) display or higher. Java Development Kit (JDK) (TM) 1.1.7 for deploying all applications. Frames-capable Web browser such as Netscape Navigator 4.04 or higher, or Microsoft (R) Internet Explorer 4.01 or higher. Recommended browser is Netscape Navigator 4.7 or Internet Explorer 5.0.